Richard Edgcumbe
Byron: the last phase

seVerus

Edgcumbe, Richard: Byron: the last phase
Hamburg, SEVERUS Verlag 2012
Nachdruck der Originalausgabe von 1910

ISBN: 978-3-86347-296-2
Druck: SEVERUS Verlag, Hamburg, 2012

Der SEVERUS Verlag ist ein Imprint der Diplomica Verlag GmbH.

Bibliografische Information der Deutschen Nationalbibliothek:
Die Deutsche Nationalbibliothek verzeichnet diese Publikation in der
Deutschen Nationalbibliografie; detaillierte bibliografische Daten sind
im Internet über http://dnb.d-nb.de abrufbar.

© **SEVERUS Verlag**
http://www.severus-verlag.de, Hamburg 2012
Printed in Germany
Alle Rechte vorbehalten.

Der SEVERUS Verlag übernimmt keine juristische Verantwortung oder
irgendeine Haftung für evtl. fehlerhafte Angaben und deren Folgen.

SEVERUS

BYRON:
THE LAST PHASE

BY RICHARD EDGCUMBE

TO

MRS. CHARLES CALL,

DAUGHTER OF EDWARD TRELAWNY, BYRON'S
COMPANION IN GREECE,

I DEDICATE THIS WORK AS A MARK OF AFFECTION

AND ESTEEM

PREFACE

THIS book has no pretensions; it is merely a record of events and impressions which nearly forty years of close study have accumulated. There seems to be a general agreement that the closing scenes of Byron's short life have not been adequately depicted by his biographers. From the time of Byron's departure from Ravenna, in the autumn of 1821, his disposition and conduct underwent a transformation so complete that it would have been difficult to recognize, in the genial, unselfish personality who played so effective a rôle at Missolonghi, the gloomy misanthrope of 1811, or the reckless libertine of the following decade.

The conduct of Byron in Greece seems to have come as a revelation to his contemporaries, and his direction of complex affairs, in peculiarly trying circumstances, certainly deserves more attention than it has received. Records made on the spot by men whose works are now, for the most part, out of print have greatly simplified my task, and I hope that the following pages may be acceptable to those who have not had an opportunity of studying that picturesque phase of Byron's career. I should have much preferred to preserve silence on the subject of his separation from his wife. Unfortunately, the late Lord Lovelace, in giving his sanction to the baseless and

PREFACE

forgotten slanders of a bygone age, has recently assailed the memory of Byron's half-sister, and has set a mark of infamy upon her which cannot be erased without referring to matters which ought never to have been mentioned.

In order to traverse statements made in 'Astarte,' it was necessary to reveal an incident which, during Byron's lifetime, was known only by those who were pledged to silence. With fuller knowledge of things hidden from Byron's contemporaries, we may realize the cruelty of those futile persecutions to which Mrs. Leigh was subjected by Lady Byron and her advisers, under the impression that they could extract the confession of a crime which existed only in their prurient imaginations. Mrs. Leigh, in one of her letters to Hobhouse, says, 'I have made it a rule to be silent—that is to say, As Long As I Can.' Although the strain must have been almost insupportable she died with her secret unrevealed, and the mystery which Byron declared 'too simple to be easily found out' has hitherto remained unsolved. I regret being unable more precisely to indicate the source of information embodied in the concluding portions of this work. The reader may test the value of my statements by the light of citations which seem amply to confirm them. At all events, I claim to have shown by analogy that Lord Lovelace's accusation against Mrs. Leigh is groundless, and therefore his contention, that Byron's memoirs were destroyed *because they implicated Mrs. Leigh*, is absolutely untenable. Those memoirs were destroyed, as we now know, because both Hobhouse and Mrs. Leigh feared possible revelations concerning another person, whose feelings and interests formed the paramount consideration of those who were parties to the deed. Lord John Russell, who had read the memoirs, stated in 1869 that Mrs. Leigh was *not* implicated in them, a fact which proves that they were not burned for the purpose of shielding *her*.

Lord Lovelace tells us that Sir Walter Scott, who had heard full particulars from Thomas Moore, remarked, 'It is a pity, but there *was* a reason—*premat nox alta.*' Facts which they hoped deep oblivion would hide have come to the surface at last, and I deeply regret that circumstances should have imposed upon me a duty which is repugnant both to my inclination and instincts. After all is said, the blame rightly belongs to Lady Byron's grandson, who, heedless of consequences, stirred the depths of a muddy pool. He tells us, in 'Astarte,' (1) that the papers concerning Byron's marriage have been carefully preserved; (2) that they form *a complete record of all the causes of separation;* and (3) that they contain *full information on every part of the subject.*

In those circumstances it is strange that, with the whole of Lady Byron's papers before him, Lord Lovelace should have published only documents of secondary importance which do not prove his case. After saying, 'It should be distinctly understood that no misfortunes, blunders, or malpractices, have swept away Lady Byron's papers, or those belonging to the executors of Lord Byron,' he leaves the essential records to the imagination of his readers, and feeds us on hints and suggestions which are not borne out by extracts provided as samples of the rest. It is impossible not to suspect that Lord Lovelace, in arranging the papers committed to his charge, discarded some that would have told in favour of

Mrs. Leigh, and selected others which colourably supported his peculiar views.

In matters of this kind everything depends upon the qualifications of the accuser and the reliability of the witness. Lord Lovelace in a dual capacity certainly evinced an active imagination.

As an example, 'Astarte,' which was designed to blast the fair fame of Mrs. Leigh, was used by him to insult the memory of the late Mr. Murray (who he admits showed him many acts of kindness), and to repudiate promises which he undoubtedly made, to edit his grandfather's works. Rambling statements are made with design to discredit both Mr. Gifford, the editor of the *Quarterly*, and Mr. Murray, the friend of Lord Byron. Even personal defects are dragged in to prejudice the reader and embitter the venom of irrelevant abuse. It was as if Plutarch, in order to enhance the glory of Antony, had named 'the Last of the Romans' Cassius the Short-sighted. Fortunately, written proofs are in existence to controvert Lord Lovelace's assertions — proofs which were used with crushing effect — otherwise Mr. Murray might have found himself in a position quite as helpless as that of poor Mrs. Leigh herself. So unscrupulous a use of documents in that case suggests the possibility that a similar process may have been adopted in reference to Mrs. Leigh. It is indeed unfortunate that Lady Byron's papers cannot be inspected by some unprejudiced person, for we have nothing at present beyond Lord Lovelace's vague assertions. Were those papers thoroughly sifted they would surely acquit Mrs. Leigh of the crime that has been so cruelly laid to her charge. Meanwhile I venture to think that the following pages help to clear the air of much of that mystery which surrounds the lives of Lord Byron and his sister.

In conclusion, I desire to record my personal obligation to the latest edition of the 'Poems,' edited by Mr. Ernest Hartley Coleridge; and of the 'Letters and Journals,' edited by Mr. Rowland Prothero, volumes which together form the most comprehensive and scholarly record of Byron's life and poetry that has ever been issued.

R. E.

August, 1909.

BYRON: THE LAST PHASE

PART I

'... Le cose ti fien conte,
Quando noi fermerem li nostri passi
Sulla trista riviera d' Acheronte.'
Inferno, Canto III., 76-78.

CHAPTER I

'A LARGE disagreeable city, almost without inhabitants'—such was the poet Shelley's description of Pisa in 1821. The Arno was yellow and muddy, the streets were empty, and there was altogether an air of poverty and wretchedness in the town. The convicts, who were very numerous, worked in the streets in gangs, cleaning and sweeping them. They were dressed in red, and were chained together by the leg in pairs. All day long one heard the slow clanking of their chains, and the rumbling of the carts they were forced to drag from place to place like so many beasts of burden. A spectator could not but be struck by the appearance of helpless misery stamped on their yellow cheeks and emaciated forms.

On the Lung' Arno Mediceo, east of the Ponte di Mezzo, stands the Palazzo Lanfranchi, which is supposed to have been built by Michael Angelo. Here, on November 2, 1821, Lord Byron arrived, with his servants, his horses, his monkey, bulldog, mastiff, cats, peafowl, hens, and other live stock, which he had brought with him from Ravenna. In another quarter of the city resided Count Rugiero Gamba, his son Pietro, and his daughter Countess Teresa

Guiccioli. On the other side of the Arno, nearly opposite to Byron's residence, lived the poet Shelley, with his wife and their friends Edward and Jane Williams.

In the middle of November, Captain Thomas Medwin, a relative of Shelley's, arrived at Pisa; and on January 14, 1822, came Edward John Trelawny, who was destined to play so important a part in the last scenes of the lives of both Shelley and Byron.

Byron was at this time in his thirty-third year. Medwin thus describes his personal appearance:

'I saw a man of about five feet seven or eight, apparently forty years of age. As was said of Milton, Lord Byron barely escaped being short and thick. His face was fine, and the lower part symmetrically moulded; for the lips and chin had that curved and definite outline that distinguishes Grecian beauty. His forehead was high, and his temples broad; and he had a paleness in his complexion almost to wanness. His hair, thin and fine, had almost become grey, and waved in natural and graceful curls over his head, that was assimilating itself fast to the "bald first Cæsar's." He allowed it to grow longer behind than it is accustomed to be worn, and at that time had mustachios which were not sufficiently dark to be becoming. In criticizing his features, it might, perhaps, be said that his eyes were placed too near his nose, and that one was rather smaller than the other. They were of a greyish-brown, but of a peculiar clearness, and when animated possessed a fire which seemed to look through and penetrate the thoughts of others, while they marked the inspirations of his own. His teeth were small, regular, and white. I expected to discover that he had a club-foot; but it would have been difficult to have distinguished one from the other, either in size or in form. On the whole, his figure was manly, and his countenance handsome and prepossessing, and very expressive. The familiar ease of his conversation soon made me perfectly at home in his society.'

BYRON'S PERSONAL APPEARANCE

Trelawny's description is as follows:

'In external appearance Byron realized that ideal standard with which imagination adorns genius. He was in the prime of life, thirty-four; of middle height, five feet eight and a half inches; regular features, without a stain or furrow on his pallid skin; his shoulders broad, chest open, body and limbs finely proportioned. His small highly-finished head and curly hair had an airy and graceful appearance from the massiveness and length of his throat; you saw his genius in his eyes and lips.'

Trelawny could find no peculiarity in his dress, which was adapted to the climate. Byron wore:

'a tartan jacket braided—he said it was the Gordon pattern, and that his mother was of that race—a blue velvet cap with a gold band, and very loose nankin trousers, strapped down so as to cover his feet. His throat was not bare, as represented in drawings.'

Lady Blessington, who first saw Byron in April of the following year, thus describes him:

'The impression of the first few minutes disappointed me, as I had, both from the portraits and descriptions given, conceived a different idea of him. I had fancied him taller, with a more dignified and commanding air; and I looked in vain for the hero-looking sort of person, with whom I had so long identified him in imagination. His appearance is, however, highly prepossessing. His head is finely shaped, and his forehead open, high, and noble; his eyes are grey and full of expression, but one is visibly larger than the other. The nose is large and well shaped, but, from being a little *too thick*, it looks better in profile than in front-face; his mouth is the most remarkable feature in his face, the upper lip of Grecian shortness, and the corners descending; the lips full, and finely cut.

'In speaking, he shows his teeth very much, and they are white and even; but I observed that even in his smile—and he smiles frequently—there is something of a scornful expression in his mouth, that is evidently natural, and not, as many suppose, affected. This particularly struck me. His chin is large and well shaped, and finishes well the oval of his face. He is extremely thin—indeed, so much so that his figure has almost a boyish air. His face is peculiarly pale, but not the paleness of ill-health, as its character is that of fairness, the fairness of a dark-haired person ; and his hair (which is getting rapidly grey) is of a very dark brown, and curls naturally : he uses a good deal of oil in it, which makes it look still darker. His countenance is full of expression, and changes with the subject of conversation ; it gains on the beholder the more it is seen, and leaves an agreeable impression. . . . His whole appearance is remarkably gentlemanlike, and he owes nothing of this to his toilet, as his coat appears to have been many years made, is much too large—and all his garments convey the idea of having been purchased ready-made, so ill do they fit him. There is a *gaucherie* in his movements, which evidently proceeds from the perpetual consciousness of his lameness, that appears to haunt him ; for he tries to conceal his foot when seated, and when walking has a nervous rapidity in his manner. He is very slightly lame, and the deformity of his foot is so little remarkable, that I am not now aware which foot it is.

' His voice and accent are peculiarly agreeable, but effeminate—clear, harmonious, and so distinct, that though his general tone in speaking is rather low than high, not a word is lost. His manners are as unlike my preconceived notions of them as is his appearance. I had expected to find him a dignified, cold, reserved, and haughty person, but nothing can be more different; for were I to point out the prominent defect of Lord Byron, I should say it was flippancy, and a total want of that natural self-possession and dignity, which ought to characterize a man of birth and education.'

Medwin tells us, in his ' Journal of the Conversations of Lord Byron,' that Byron's voice had a flexibility, a variety in its tones, a power and pathos, beyond any he ever heard ; and his countenance was capable of expressing the tenderest as well as the strongest emotions, which would perhaps have made him the finest actor in the world.

The Countess Guiccioli, who had a longer acquaintance with Byron than any of those who have attempted to portray him, says :

'Lord Byron's eyes, though of a light grey, were capable of all extremes of expression, from the most joyous hilarity to the deepest sadness, from the very sunshine of benevolence to the most concentrated scorn or rage. But it was in the mouth and chin that the great beauty as well as expression of his fine countenance lay. His head was remarkably small, so much so as to be rather out of proportion to his face. The forehead, though a little too narrow, was high, and appeared more so from his having his hair (to preserve it, as he said) shaved over the temples. Still, the glossy dark brown curls, clustering over his head, gave the finish to its beauty. When to this is added that his nose, though handsomely, was rather thickly shaped, that his teeth were white and regular, and his complexion colourless, as good an idea, perhaps, as it is in the power of mere words to convey may be conceived of his features. In height he was five feet eight inches and a half. His hands were very white, and, according to his own notions of the size of hands as indicating birth, aristocratically small. . . . No defect existed in the formation of his limbs ; his slight infirmity was nothing but the result of weakness of one of his ankles. His habit of ever being on horseback had brought on the emaciation of his legs, as evinced by the post-mortem examination; the best proof of this is the testimony of William Swift, bootmaker at Southwell, who had the honour of working for Lord Byron from 1805 to 1807.'

It appears that Mrs. Wildman (the widow of the Colonel who had bought Newstead from Byron) not long before her death presented to the Naturalist Society of Nottingham several objects which had belonged to Lord Byron, and amongst others his boot and shoe trees. These trees are about nine inches long, narrow, and generally of a symmetrical form. They were accompanied by the following statement:

'William Swift, bootmaker at Southwell, Nottinghamshire, having had the honour of working for Lord Byron when residing at Southwell from 1805 to 1807, asserts that these were the trees upon which his lordship's boots and shoes were made, and that the last pair delivered was on the 10th May, 1807. He moreover affirms that his lordship had not a club foot, as has been said, but that both his feet were equally well formed, one, however, being an inch and a half shorter than the other.* The defect was not in the foot, but in the ankle, which, being weak, caused the foot to turn out too much. To remedy this, his lordship wore a very light and thin boot, which was tightly laced just under the sole, and, when a boy, he was made to wear a piece of iron with a joint at the ankle, which passed behind the leg and was tied behind the shoe. The calf of this leg was weaker than the other, and it was the left leg.

'(Signed) WILLIAM SWIFT.'

'This, then,' says Countess Guiccioli, 'is the extent of the defect of which so much has been said, and which has been called a deformity. As to its being visible, all those who knew him assert that it was so little evident, that it was even impossible to discover in which of the legs or feet the fault existed.'

Byron's alleged sensitiveness on the subject of his lameness seems to have been exaggerated.

'When he did show it,' continues Countess Guiccioli, 'which was never but to a very modest extent, it was only because, physically speaking, he suffered from it. Under the sole of the weak foot he at times experienced a painful sensation, especially

* Medwin, in his book 'The Angler in Wales,' vol. ii., p. 211, says: The *right* foot, as everyone knows, being twisted inwards, so as to amount to what is generally known as a club-foot.'

after long walks. Once, at Genoa, Byron walked down the hill from Albaro to the seashore with me by a rugged and rough path. When we had reached the shore he was very well and lively. But it was an exceedingly hot day, and the return home fatigued him greatly. When home, I told him that I thought he looked ill. "Yes," said he, "I suffer greatly from my foot; it can hardly be conceived how much I suffer at times from that pain;" and he continued to speak to me about this defect with great simplicity and indifference.'

We have been particular to set before the reader the impression which Byron's personal appearance made upon those who saw him at this time, because none of the busts or portraits seem to convey anything like an accurate semblance of this extraordinary personality. Had the reader seen Byron in his various moods, he would doubtless have exclaimed, with Sir Walter Scott, that 'no picture is like him.'

The portrait by Saunders represents Byron with thick lips, whereas 'his lips were harmoniously perfect,' says Countess Guiccioli. Holmes almost gives him a large instead of his well-proportioned head. In Phillips's picture the expression is one of haughtiness and affected dignity, which Countess Guiccioli assures us was never visible to those who saw him in life. The worst portrait of Lord Byron, according to Countess Guiccioli, and which surpasses all others in ugliness, was done by Mr. West, an American, 'an excellent man, but a very bad painter.' This portrait, which some of Byron's American admirers requested to have taken, and which Byron consented to sit for, was begun at Montenero, near Leghorn. Byron seems only to have sat two or three times for it, and it was finished from memory. Countess Guiccioli describes it as 'a frightful caricature, which his family or friends ought to destroy.' As regards busts, she says:

'Thorwaldsen alone has, in his marble bust of Byron, been able to blend the regular beauty of his features with the sublime expression of his countenance.'*

On January 22, 1822, Byron's mother-in-law, Lady Noel, died at the age of seventy.

'I am distressed for poor Lady Byron,' said the poet to Medwin: 'she must be in great affliction, for she adored her mother! The world will think that I am pleased at this event, but they are much mistaken. I never wished for an accession of fortune; I have enough without the Wentworth property. I have written a letter of condolence to Lady Byron—you may suppose in the kindest terms. If we are not reconciled, it is not my fault.'

There is no trace of this letter, and it is ignored by Lord Lovelace in 'Astarte.' It may be well here to point out how erroneous was the belief that Miss Milbanke was an heiress. Byron on his marriage settled £60,000 on his wife, and Miss Milbanke was to have brought £20,000 into settlement; but the money was not paid. Sir Ralph Milbanke's property was at that time heavily encumbered. Miss Milbanke had some expectations through her mother and her uncle, Lord Wentworth; but those prospects were not mentioned in the settlements. Both Lord Wentworth and Sir Ralph Milbanke were free to leave their money as they chose. When Lord Wentworth died, in April 1815, he left his property to Lady Milbanke for her life, and at her death to her daughter, Lady Byron. Therefore, at Lady Noel's death Byron inherited the whole property by right of his wife. But one of the terms of the separation provided that this property

* 'Trelawny held a like opinion.'

should be divided by arbitrators. Lord Dacre was arbitrator for Lady Byron, and Sir F. Burdett for Byron. Under this arrangement half the income was allotted to the wife and half to the husband. In the *London Gazette* dated 'Whitehall, March 2, 1822,' royal licence is given to Lord Byron and his wife that they may 'take and use the surname of Noel only, and also bear the arms of Noel only; and that the said George Gordon, Baron Byron, may subscribe the said surname of Noel before all titles of honour.' Henceforward the poet signed all his letters either with the initials N. B. or with 'Noel Byron' in full.

Byron was at this time in excellent health and spirits, and the society of the Shelleys made life unusually pleasant to him. Ravenna, with its gloomy forebodings, its limited social intercourse, to say nothing of its proscriptions—for nearly all Byron's friends had been exiled—was a thing of the past. The last phase had dawned, and Byron was about to show another side of his character. Medwin tells us that Byron's disposition was eminently sociable, however great the pains which he took to hide it from the world. On Wednesdays there was always a dinner at the Palazzo Lanfranchi, to which the *convives* were cordially welcomed. When alone Byron's table was frugal, not to say abstemious. But on these occasions every sort of wine, every luxury of the season, and every English delicacy, were displayed. Medwin says he never knew any man do the honours of his house with greater kindness and hospitality. On one occasion, after dinner, the conversation turned on the lyrical poetry of the day, and a question arose as to which was the most perfect ode that had been produced. Shelley contended for Coleridge's on Switzerland, beginning, 'Ye clouds,' etc.; others named some of Moore's 'Irish Melodies' and Campbell's 'Hohenlinden'; and, had Lord Byron not been present, his own Invocation to Manfred, or Ode to Napoleon, or on Prometheus, might have been cited. 'Like Gray,' said Byron, 'Campbell smells too much of the oil: he is never satisfied with what he does; his finest things have been spoiled by over-polish—the sharpness of the outline is worn off. Like paintings, poems may be too highly finished. The great art is effect, no matter how produced.'

And then, rising from the table, he left the room, and presently returned with a magazine, from which he read 'The Burial of Sir John Moore' with the deepest feeling. It was at that time generally believed that Byron was the author of these admirable stanzas; and Medwin says: 'I am corroborated in this opinion lately (1824) by a lady, whose brother received them many years ago from Lord Byron, in his lordship's own handwriting.'

These festive gatherings were not pleasing to Shelley, who, with his abstemious tastes and modest, retiring disposition, disliked the glare and surfeit of it all. But Shelley's unselfish nature overcame his antipathy, and for the sake of others he sacrificed himself. In writing to his friend Horace Smith, he marks his repugnance for these dinners, 'when my nerves are generally shaken to pieces by sitting up, contemplating the rest of the company making themselves vats of claret, etc., till three o'clock in the morning.' Nevertheless, companionship with Byron seemed for a time, to Shelley and Mary, to be like 'companionship with a demiurge who could create rolling worlds at pleasure in the void of space.'

SHELLEY NO INFLUENCE OVER BYRON

Shelley's admiration for the poetic achievements of Byron is well known:

> 'Space wondered less at the swift and fair creations of God when he grew weary of vacancy, than I at the late works of this spirit of an angel in the mortal paradise of a decaying body. So I think—let the world envy, while it admires as it may.'[*]

And again: 'What think you of Lord Byron's last volume? In my opinion it contains finer poetry than has appeared in England since the publication of "Paradise Regained." "Cain" is apocalyptic; it is a revelation not before communicated to man.'

Byron recognized Shelley's frankness, courage, and hardihood of opinion, but was not influenced by him so much as was at that time supposed by his friends in England. In writing to Horace Smith (April 11, 1822), Shelley begs him to assure Moore that he had not the smallest influence over Byron's religious opinions.

> 'If I had, I certainly should employ it to eradicate from his great mind the delusions of Christianity, which, in spite of his reason, seem perpetually to recur, and to lay in ambush for the hours of sickness and distress. "Cain" was *conceived* many years ago, and begun before I saw him last year at Ravenna. How happy should I not be to attribute to myself, however indirectly, any participation in that immortal work!'

'Byron,' says Professor Dowden in his 'Life of Shelley,' 'on his own part protested that his *dramatis personæ* uttered their own opinions and sentiments, not his.'

Byron undoubtedly had a deep-seated reverence for religion, and had a strong leaning towards the Roman

---

[*] Letter to Mr. Gisborne, January 12, 1822. Professor Dowden's 'Life of Shelley,' vol. ii., p. 447.

Catholic doctrines. Writing to Moore (March 4, 1822), he says:

'I am no enemy to religion, but the contrary. As a proof, I am educating my natural daughter a strict Catholic in a convent of Romagna; for I think people can never have *enough* of religion, if they are to have any. . . . As to poor Shelley, who is another bugbear to you and the world, he is, to my knowledge, the *least* selfish and the mildest of men—a man who has made more sacrifices of his fortune and feelings for others than any I ever heard of. With his speculative opinions I have nothing in common, nor desire to have.'

Countess Guiccioli, a woman of no ordinary intuitive perceptions, with ample opportunities for judging the characters of both Shelley and Byron, makes a clear statement on this point:

'In Shelley's heart the dominant wish was to see society entirely reorganized. The sight of human miseries and infirmities distressed him to the greatest degree; but, too modest himself to believe that he was called upon to take the initiative, and inaugurate a new era of good government and fresh laws for the benefit of humanity, he would have been pleased to see such a genius as Byron take the initiative in this undertaking. Shelley therefore did his best to influence Byron. But the latter hated discussions. He could not bear entering into philosophical speculation at times when his soul craved the consolations of friendship, and his mind a little rest. He was quite insensible to reasonings, which often appear sublime because they are clothed in words incomprehensible to those who have not sought to understand their meaning. But he made an exception in favour of Shelley. He knew that he could not shake his faith in a doctrine founded upon illusions, by his incredulity; but he listened to him with pleasure, not only on account of Shelley's good faith and sincerity, but also because he argued upon false data, with such talent and originality, that he was both interested and amused. Lord Byron had examined every form of philosophy by the light of common sense, and by the instinct of his genius. Pantheism in particular was odious to him. He drew no distinction between absolute Pantheism which mixes up that which is infinite with that which is finite, and that form of Pantheism which struggles in vain to keep clear of Atheism. Shelley's views, clothed in a veil of spiritualism, were the most likely to interest Byron, but they did not fix him. Byron could never consent to lose his individuality, deny his own freedom of will, or abandon the hope of a future existence. As a matter of fact, Byron attributed all Shelley's views to the aberrations of a mind which is happier when it dreams than when it denies.'

'Shelley appears to me to be mad with his metaphysics,' said Byron on one occasion to Count Gamba. 'What trash in all these systems! say what they will, mystery for mystery, I still find that of the Creation the most reasonable of any.'

Thus it will be seen that the opinions of Lord Byron on matters of religion were far more catholic than those of his friend Shelley, who could not have influenced Byron in the manner generally supposed. That a change came over the spirit of Byron's poetry after meeting Shelley on the Lake of Geneva is unquestionable; but the surface of the waters may be roughened by a breeze without disturbing the depths below. Like all true poets, Byron was highly susceptible to passing influences, and there can be no doubt that Shelley impressed him deeply.

The evident sincerity in the life and doctrines of Shelley—his unworldliness; the manner in which he had been treated by the world, and even by his own family, aroused the sympathy of Byron, at a time when he himself was for a different cause smarting under somewhat similar treatment. Although

Byron and Shelley differed fundamentally on some subjects they concurred in the principles of others. Byron had no fixed religious opinions—that was the string upon which Shelley played—but there is a wide difference between doubt and denial. Gamba, after Byron's death, wrote thus to Dr. Kennedy:

'My belief is that Byron's religious opinions were not fixed. I mean that he was not more inclined towards one than towards another of the Christian sects; but that his feelings were thoroughly religious, and that he entertained the highest respect for the doctrines of Christ, which he considered to be the source of virtue and of goodness. As for the incomprehensible mysteries of religion, his mind floated in doubts which he wished most earnestly to dispel, as they oppressed him, and that is why he never avoided a conversation on the subject, as you are well aware. I have often had an opportunity of observing him at times when the soul involuntarily expresses its most sincere convictions; in the midst of dangers, both at sea and on land; in the quiet contemplation of a calm and beautiful night, in the deepest solitude. On these occasions I remarked that Lord Byron's thoughts were always imbued with a religious sentiment. The first time I ever had a conversation with him on that subject was at Ravenna, my native place, a little more than four years ago. We were riding together in the Pineta on a beautiful spring day. "How," said Byron, "when we raise our eyes to heaven, or direct them to the earth, can we doubt of the existence of God? or how, turning them inwards, can we doubt that there is something within us, more noble and more durable than the clay of which we are formed? Those who do not hear, or are unwilling to listen to these feelings, must necessarily be of a vile nature." I answered him with all those reasons which the superficial philosophy of Helvetius, his disciples and his masters, have taught. Byron replied with very strong arguments and profound eloquence, and I perceived that obstinate contradiction on this subject, which forced him to reason upon it, gave him pain. This incident made a deep impression upon me. . . . Last year, at Genoa, when we were preparing for our journey to Greece, Byron used to converse with me alone for two or three hours every evening, seated on the terrace of his residence at Albaro in the fine evenings of spring, whence there opened a magnificent view of the superb city and the adjoining sea. Our conversation turned almost always on Greece, for which we were so soon to depart, or on religious subjects. In various ways I heard him confirm the sentiments which I have already mentioned to you. "Why, then," said I to him, "have you earned for yourself the name of impious, and enemy of all religious belief, from your writings?" He answered, "They are not understood, and are wrongly interpreted by the malevolent. My object is only to combat hypocrisy, which I abhor in everything, and particularly in religion, and which now unfortunately appears to me to be prevalent, and for this alone do those to whom you allude wish to render me odious, and make me out worse than I am."'

We have quoted only a portion of Pietro Gamba's letter, but sufficient to show that Byron has been, like his friend Shelley, 'brutally misunderstood.' There was no one better qualified than Count Gamba to express an opinion on the subject, for he was in the closest intimacy with Byron up to the time of the latter's death. There was no attempt on Byron's part to mystify his young friend, who had no epistolary intercourse with those credulous people in England whom Byron so loved to 'gull.' The desire to blacken his own character was reserved for those occasions when, as he well knew, there would be most publicity. Trelawny says:

'Byron's intimates smiled at his vaunting of his vices, but comparative strangers stared, and noted his sayings to retail to their friends, and that is the way many scandals got abroad.'

According to the same authority, George IV. made

the sport known as 'equivocation' the fashion; the men about town were ashamed of being thought virtuous, and bragged of their profligacy. 'In company,' says Trelawny, 'Byron talked in Don Juan's vein; with a companion with whom he was familiar, he thought aloud.'

Among the accusations made against Byron by those who knew him least was that of intemperance—intemperance not in meat and drink only, but in everything. It must be admitted that Byron was to blame for this; he vaunted his propensity for the bottle, and even attributed his poetic inspirations to its aid. Trelawny, who had observed him closely, says:

'Of all his vauntings, it was, luckily for him, the emptiest. From all that I heard or witnessed of his habits abroad, he was and had been exceedingly abstemious in eating and drinking. When alone, he drank a glass or two of small claret or hock, and when utterly exhausted at night, a single glass of grog; which, when I mixed it for him, I lowered to what sailors call "water bewitched," and he never made any remark. I once, to try him, omitted the alcohol; he then said, "Tre, have you not forgotten the creature comfort?" I then put in two spoonfuls, and he was satisfied. This does not look like an habitual toper. Byron had not damaged his body by strong drinks, but his terror of getting fat was so great that he reduced his diet to the point of absolute starvation. He was the only human being I ever met with who had sufficient self-restraint and resolution to resist this proneness to fatten. He did so; and at Genoa, where he was last weighed, he was ten stone and nine pounds, and looked much less. This was not from vanity of his personal appearance, but from a better motive, and, as he was always hungry, his merit was the greater. Whenever he relaxed his vigilance he swelled apace. He would exist on biscuits and soda-water for days together; then, to allay the eternal hunger gnawing at his vitals, he would make up a horrid mess of cold potatoes, rice, fish, or greens, deluged in vinegar and swallow it like a famished dog. Either of these unsavoury dishes, with a biscuit and a glass or two of Rhine wine, he cared not how sour, he called feasting sumptuously. Byron was of that soft, lymphatic temperament which it is almost impossible to keep within a moderate compass, particularly as in his case his lameness prevented his taking exercise. When he added to his weight, even standing was painful, so he resolved to keep down to eleven stone.'

While on this subject, it is not uninteresting to contrast the effects of Byron's regimen of abstinence by the light of a record kept by the celebrated wine-merchants, Messrs. Berry, of St. James's Street. This register of weights has been kept on their premises for the convenience of their customers since 1765, and contains over twenty thousand names. The following extract was made by the present writer on November 2, 1897:*

Date.	Stone.	lbs.	Age.
January 4, 1806 (boots, no hat)	13	12	18
July 8, 1807 (shoes)	10	13	19
July 23, 1807 (shoes, no hat)	11	0	19
August 13, 1807 (shoes, no hat)	10	11½	19
January 13, 1808 (see Moore's 'Life')	10	7	20
May 27, 1808 (Messrs. Berry)	11	1	—
June 10, 1809 (Messrs. Berry)	11	5¾	21
July 15, 1811 (Messrs. Berry)	9	11½	23
(*Circa*) June, 1823 (see Trelawny)	10	9	35

It will be seen at a glance that between the ages of eighteen and thirty-five Byron had reduced his weight by three stone and three pounds. The fluctuations between the ages of nineteen and thirty-five are not remarkable. This record marks the consistency of a heroic self-denial under what must often have been a strong temptation to appease the pangs of hunger.

* 'Lord Byron.'

CHAPTER II

Byron's life at Pisa, as afterwards at Genoa, was what most people would call a humdrum, dull existence. He rose late.

'Billiards, conversation, or reading, filled up the intervals,' says Medwin, 'till it was time to take our evening drive, ride, and pistol-practice. On our return, which was always in the same direction, we frequently met the Countess Guiccioli, with whom he stopped to converse a few minutes. He dined at half an hour after sunset, then drove to Count Gamba's, the Countess Guiccioli's father, passed several hours in their society, returned to his palace, and either read or wrote till two or three in the morning; occasionally drinking spirits diluted with water as a medicine, from a dread of a nephritic complaint, to which he was, or fancied himself, subject.'

On Sunday, March 24, 1822, while Byron, Shelley, Trelawny, Captain Hay, Count Pietro Gamba, and an Irish gentleman named Taaffe, were returning from their evening ride, and had nearly reached the Porta alle Piagge at the eastern end of the Lung' Arno, Sergeant-Major Masi, belonging to a dragoon regiment, being apparently in a great hurry to get back to barracks, pushed his way unceremoniously through the group of riders in front of him, and somewhat severely jostled Mr. Taaffe. This gentleman appealed

THE AFFRAY AT PISA

to Byron, and the latter demanded an apology from the sergeant, whom he at first mistook for an officer. The sergeant lost his temper, and called out the guard at the gateway. Byron and Gamba dashed through, however, and before the others could follow there was some 'dom'd cutting and slashing'; Shelley was knocked off his horse, and Captain Hay received a wound in his face. Masi in alarm fled, and on the Lung' Arno met Byron returning to the scene of the fray: an altercation took place, and one of Byron's servants, who thought that Masi had wounded his master, struck at him with a pitchfork, and tumbled the poor fellow off his horse. There was a tremendous hubbub about this, and the legal proceedings which followed occupied two months, with much bluster, false swearing, and injustice, as a natural consequence. The court eventually came to the conclusion that there was no evidence for criminal proceedings against any of Byron's domestics, but, in consideration of Giovanni Battista Falcieri—one of Byron's servants—having a black beard, he was condemned to be escorted by the police to the frontier and banished from the grand-duchy of Tuscany.

At the same time the Gambas (who had nothing whatever to do with the affair) were told that their presence at Pisa was disagreeable to the Government. In consequence of the hint, Byron and the Gambas hired the Villa Dupuy, at Montenero, near Leghorn. Here, on June 28, 1822, a scuffle took place in the gardens of the villa between the servants of Count Gamba and of Byron, in which Byron's coachman and his cook took part. Knives were drawn as usual. Byron appeared on the balcony with his pistols, and threatened to shoot the whole party if they did not drop their knives, and the police had to be called in to quell the disturbance. The Government, who were anxious to be rid of Byron, took advantage of this riot at the Villa Dupuy. Byron's courier and Gamba's valet were sent over the frontier of the grand-duchy under police escort, and the Gambas were warned that, unless they left the country within three days, formal sentence of banishment would be passed upon them. As soon as Byron heard the news, he wrote a letter to the Governor of Leghorn, and asked for a respite for his friends. A few days grace were granted to the Gambas, and on July 8 they took passports for Genoa, intending to go first to the Baths of Lucca, where they hoped to obtain permission to return to Pisa. While negotiations were proceeding Byron returned to the Palazzo Lanfranchi.*

On April 20, 1822, there died at Bagnacavallo, not far from Ravenna, Byron's natural daughter Allegra, whose mother, Claire Clairmont, had joined the Shelleys at Pisa five days previously. The whole story is a sad one, and shall be impartially given in these pages.

When Shelley left Ravenna in August, 1821, he understood that Byron had determined that Allegra should not be left behind, alone and friendless, in the Convent of Bagnacavallo, and Shelley hoped that an arrangement would be made by which Claire might have the happiness of seeing her child once more. When Byron arrived at Pisa in November, and Allegra was not with him, Claire Clairmont's anxiety was so great that she wrote twice to Byron, protesting against leaving her child in so unhealthy a place,

* 'Letters and Journals of Lord Byron,' edited by Rowland Prothero, vol. vi., appendix iii.

and entreated him to place Allegra with some respectable family in Pisa, or Florance, or Lucca. She promised not to go near the child, if such was his wish, nor should Mary or Shelley do so without Byron's consent. Byron, it appears, took no notice of these letters. The Shelleys, while strongly of opinion that Allegra should in some way be taken out of Byron's hands, thought it prudent to temporize and watch for a favourable opportunity. Claire held wild schemes for carrying off the child, schemes which were under the circumstances impolitic, even if practicable. Both Mary and Shelley did their utmost to dissuade Claire from any violent attempts, and Mary, in a letter written at this time, assures Claire that her anxiety for Allegra's health was to a great degree unfounded. After carefully considering the affair she had come to the conclusion that Allegra was well taken care of by the nuns in the convent, that she was in good health, and would in all probability continue so.

On April 15 Claire Clairmont arrived at Pisa on a visit to the Shelleys, and a few days later started with the Williamses for Spezzia, to search for houses on the bay. Professor Dowden says :*

'They cannot have been many hours on their journey, when Shelley and Mary received tidings of sorrowful import, which Mary chronicles in her journal with the words " Evil news." Allegra was dead. Typhus fever had raged in the Romagna, but no one wrote to inform her parents with the fact.'

Lord Byron felt the loss bitterly at first.

'His conduct towards this child,' says Countess Guiccioli, 'was always that of a fond father. He was dreadfully agitated by the first intelligence of her

* 'Life of Shelley,' vol. ii., p. 494.

illness; and when afterwards that of her death arrived, I was obliged to fulfil the melancholy task of communicating it to him. The memory of that frightful moment is stamped indelibly on my mind. A mortal paleness spread itself over his face, his strength failed him, and he sank into a seat. His look was fixed, and the expression such that I began to fear for his reason; he did not shed a tear; and his countenance manifested so hopeless, so profound, so sublime a sorrow, that at the moment he appeared a being of a nature superior to humanity. He remained immovable in the same attitude for an hour, and no consolation which I endeavoured to afford him seemed to reach his ears, far less his heart.'

Writing to Shelley on April 23, 1822, Byron says:

'I do not know that I have anything to reproach in my conduct, and certainly nothing in my feelings and intentions towards the dead. But it is a moment when we are apt to think that, if this or that had been done, such events might have been prevented, though every day and hour shows us that they are the most natural and inevitable. I suppose that Time will do his usual work. Death has done his.'

Whatever may be thought of Byron's conduct in the matter of Miss Claire Clairmont—conduct which Allegra's mother invariably painted in the darkest colours—the fact remains as clear as day, that Byron always behaved well and kindly towards the poor little child whose death gave him such intense pain. The evidence of the Hoppners at Venice, of Countess Guiccioli at Ravenna, and of the Shelleys, all point in the same direction; and if any doubt existed, a close study of the wild and wayward character of Claire Clairmont would show where the truth in the matter lay. Byron was pestered by appeals from Allegra's mother, indirectly on her own behalf, and directly on behalf of the child. Claire never understood that, by reason of Byron's antipathy to her, the surest way of not getting what she wanted was to ask for it; and, with appalling persistency, she even persuaded Shelley to risk his undoubted influence over Byron by intercessions on her behalf, until Byron's opinion of Shelley's judgment was shaken. After making full allowance for the maternal feeling, so strong in all women, it was exceedingly foolish of Claire not to perceive that Byron, by taking upon himself the adoption of the child, had shielded her from scandal; and that, having surrendered Allegra to his care, Claire could not pretend to any claim or responsibility in the matter. It should also be pointed out that, in sending Allegra to the convent at Bagnacavallo, Byron had no intention of leaving her there for any length of time. It was merely a provisional step, and, at Hoppner's suggestion, Byron thought of sending the child to a good institution in Switzerland. In his will he had bequeathed to the child the sum of £5,000, which was to be paid to her either on her marriage or on her attaining the age of twenty-one years (according as the one or the other should happen first), with the proviso that she should not marry with a native of Great Britain. Byron was anxious to keep her out of England, because he thought that his natural daughter would be under great disadvantage in that country, and would have a far better chance abroad.

CHAPTER III

ON April 26, 1822, the Shelleys left Pisa for Lerici, and on May 1 they took up their abode in the Casa Magni, situated near the fishing-village of San Terenzo. Towards the close of May, Byron moved to his new residence at Montenero, near Leghorn.

Leigh Hunt's arrival, at the end of June, added considerably to Byron's perplexities. The poet had not seen Hunt since they parted in England six years before, and many things had happened to both of them since then. Byron, never satisfied that his promise to contribute poetry to a joint stock literary periodical was wise, disliked the idea more and more as time went on, and Shelley foresaw considerable difficulties in the way of keeping Byron up to the mark in this respect. Hunt had brought over by sea a sick wife and several children, and opened the ball by asking Byron for a loan of money to meet current expenses. Byron now discovered that Leigh Hunt had ceased to be editor of the *Examiner*, and, being absolutely without any source of income, had no prospect save the money he hoped to get from a journal not yet in existence. He ought, of course, to have told both Byron and Shelley that in coming to Italy with his family—a wife and six children—he would naturally expect one or both of his friends to provide the necessary funds. This information Hunt withheld, and although both Byron and Shelley knew him to be in pecuniary embarrassment, and had every wish to assist him, they were both under the impression that Hunt had some small income from the *Examiner*. Byron was astonished to hear that his proposed coadjutor in a literary venture had not enough money in his pockets even for one month's current expenses. He was not inclined to submit tamely to Hunt's arrangements for sucking money out of him.

Beginning as he meant to go on, Byron from the first showed Hunt that he had no intention of being imposed upon, and the social intercourse between them was, to say the least of it, somewhat strained. Byron and Shelley between them had furnished the ground-floor of the Palazzo Lanfranchi for the Hunt family, and had Shelley lived he would, presumably, have impoverished himself by disbursements in their favour; but his death placed the Hunts in a false position. Had Shelley lived, his influence over Byron would have diminished the friction between Byron and his tactless guest. The amount of money spent by Byron on the Hunt family was not great, but, considering the comparative cheapness of living in Italy at that time, and the difference in the value of money, Byron's contribution was not niggardly. After paying for the furniture of their rooms in his palace, and sending £200 for the cost of their voyage to Italy, Byron gave Leigh Hunt £70 while he was at Pisa, defrayed the cost of their journey from Pisa to Genoa, and supplied them with another £30 to enable them to travel to Florence. There was really no occasion for Byron to make Hunt a present of £500, which he seems to have done, except Hunt's absolute incapacity to make both ends meet, which was his perpetual weakness. From the manner in which Hunt treats his pecuniary transactions with the wide-awake Byron, it is evident that the sum would have risen to thousands if Byron had not turned a deaf ear to the 'insatiable applicant' at his elbow.

On the first visit which Trelawny paid to Byron at the Palazzo Lanfranchi after Hunt's arrival, he found Mrs. Hunt was confined to her room, as she generally was, from bad health. Trelawny says:

'Hunt, too, was in delicate health—a hypochondriac; and the seven children, untamed, the eldest a little more than ten, and the youngest a yearling, were scattered about playing on the large marble staircase and in the hall. Hunt's theory and practice were that children should be unrestrained until they were of an age to be reasoned with. If they kept out of his way he was satisfied. On my entering the poet's study, I said to him, "The Hunts have effected a lodgment in your palace;" and I was thinking how different must have been his emotion on the arrival of the Hunts from that triumphant morning after the publication of "Childe Harold" when he "awoke and found himself famous."'

Truth told, the Hunts' lodgment in his palace must have been a terrible infliction to the sensitive Byron. His letters to friends in England at this time are full of allusions to the prevailing discomfort. Trelawny tells us that

'Byron could not realize, till the actual experiment was tried, the nuisance of having a man with a sick wife and seven disorderly children interrupting his solitude and his ordinary customs—especially as Hunt did not conceal that his estimate of Byron's poetry was not exalted. At that time Hunt thought highly of his own poetry and underestimated all other. Leigh Hunt thought that Shelley would have made a great poet if he had written on intelligible subjects. Shelley soared too high for him, and Byron flew too near the ground. There was not a single subject on which Byron and Hunt could agree.'

After Shelley and his friend Williams had established the Hunts in Lord Byron's palace at Pisa, they returned to Leghorn, Shelley 'in a mournful mood, depressed by a recent interview with Byron,' says Trelawny.

It was evident to all who knew Byron that he bitterly repented having pledged himself to embark on the literary venture which, unfortunately, he himself had initiated. At their last interview Shelley found Byron irritable whilst talking with him on the fulfilment of his promises with regard to Leigh Hunt. Byron, like a lion caught in a trap, could only grind his teeth and bear it. Unfortunately, it was not in Byron's nature to bear things becomingly; he could not restrain the exhibition of his inner mind. On these occasions he was not at his best, and forgot the courtesy due even to the most unwelcome guest. Williams appears to have been much impressed by Byron's reception of Mrs. Hunt, and, writing to his wife from Leghorn, says:

'Lord Byron's reception of Mrs. Hunt was most shameful. She came into his house sick and exhausted, and he scarcely deigned to notice her; was silent, and scarcely bowed. This conduct cut Hunt to the soul. But the way in which he received our friend Roberts, at Dunn's door,* shall be described when we meet: it must be acted.'

Shelley and Edward Williams, two days after that letter had been written—on Monday, July 8, 1822, at

---

* Henry Dunn kept a British shop at Leghorn.

three o'clock in the afternoon—set sail on the *Ariel* for their home on the Gulf of Spezzia. The story is well known, thanks to the graphic pen of Edward Trelawny, and we need only allude to the deaths of Shelley and Williams, and the sailor lad Charles Vivian, in so far as it comes into our picture of Byron at this period.

Byron attended the cremation of the bodies of Shelley and Williams, and showed his deep sympathy with Mary Shelley and Jane Williams in various ways.

Writing to John Murray from Pisa on August 3, 1822, he says:

'I presume you have heard that Mr. Shelley and Captain Williams were lost on the 7th ultimo in their passage from Leghorn to Spezzia, in their own open boat. You may imagine the state of their families: I never saw such a scene, nor wish to see another. You were all brutally mistaken about Shelley, who was, without exception, the *best* and least selfish man I ever knew. I never knew one who was not a beast in comparison.'*

Writing August 8, 1822, to Thomas Moore, Byron says in allusion to Shelley's death:

'There is thus another man gone, about whom the world was ill-naturedly, and ignorantly, and brutally mistaken. It will, perhaps, do him justice *now*, when he can be no better for it.'

In another letter, written December 25, 1822, Byron says:

'You are all mistaken about Shelley. You do not know how mild, how tolerant, how good he was in society; and as perfect a gentleman as ever crossed a drawing-room, when he liked, and where he liked.'

* For Byron's opinion of Shelley's poetry, see appendix to 'The Two Foscari': 'I highly admire the poetry of "Queen Mab" and Shelley's other publications.'

THE 'LIBERAL A BAD BUSINESS

Byron's opinion of Leigh Hunt, and his own connection with that ill-fated venture known as *The Liberal*, is concisely given by Byron himself in a letter to Murray. *The Liberal*, published October 15, 1822, was fiercely attacked in the *Literary Gazette* and other periodicals. The *Courier* for October 26, 1822, calls it a 'scoundrel-like publication.' Byron writes:

' I am afraid the journal *is* a *bad* business, and won't do ; but in it I am sacrificing *myself* for others—I can have no advantage in it. I believe the brothers Hunt to be honest men ; I am sure they are poor ones. They have not a rap : they pressed me to engage in this work, and in an evil hour I consented ; still, I shall not repent, if I can do them the least service. I have done all I can for Leigh Hunt since he came here ; but it is almost useless. His wife is ill, his six children not very tractable, and in the affairs of the world he himself is a child. The death of Shelley left them totally aground ; and I could not see them in such a state without using the common feelings of humanity, and what means were in my power to set them afloat again.'

In another letter to Murray (December 25, 1822) Byron says :

' Had their [the Hunts'] journal gone on well, and I could have aided to make it better for them, I should then have left them, after my safe pilotage off a lee-shore, to make a prosperous voyage by themselves. As it is, I can't, and would not if I could, leave them amidst the breakers. As to any community of feeling, thought, or opinion between Leigh Hunt and me, there is little or none. We meet rarely, hardly ever ; but I think him a good-principled and able man, and must do as I would be done by. I do not know what world he has lived in, but I have lived in three or four ; and none of them like his Keats and Kangaroo *terra incognita*. Alas ! poor Shelley ! how he would have laughed had he lived, and how we used to laugh now and then, at various things, which are grave in the Suburbs !'

It is perhaps not generally known that Shelley bequeathed a legacy of £2,000 to Byron. Byron's renunciation of this token of friendship is ignored by Professor Dowden in his life of Shelley. Writing to Leigh Hunt on June 28, 1823, Byron says:

'There was something about a legacy of two thousand pounds which he [Shelley] has left me. This, of course, I declined, and the more so that I hear that his will is admitted valid; and I state this distinctly that, in case of anything happening to me, my heirs may be instructed not to claim it.'

Towards the end of September, 1822, Byron and the Countess Guiccioli left the Palazzo Lanfranchi, and moved from Pisa to Albaro, a suburb of Genoa. At the Villa Saluzzo, where the poet resided until his departure for Greece, dwelt also Count Gamba and his son Pietro, who occupied one part of that large house, while Byron occupied another part, and their establishments were quite separate. The first number of *The Liberal* which had been printed in London, reached Byron's hands at this time. The birth of that unlucky publication was soon followed by its death, as anyone knowing the circumstances attending its conception might have foreseen. Shelley's death may be said to have destroyed the enterprise and energy of the survivors of that small coterie, who, in the absence of that vital force, the fine spirit that had animated and held them together, 'degenerated apace,' as Trelawny tells us. Byron 'exhausted himself in planning, projecting, beginning, wishing, intending, postponing, regretting, and doing nothing. The unready are fertile in excuses, and his were inexhaustible.'

In December, 1822, Trelawny laid up Byron's yacht *The Bolivar*, paid off the crew, and started on horseback for Rome. *The Bolivar* was eventually sold by Byron to Lord Blessington for 400 guineas. Four or five years after Byron's death this excellent little sea-boat, with Captain Roberts (who planned her for Byron) on board, struck on the iron-bound coast of the Adriatic and foundered. Not a plank of her was saved.

'Never,' said Captain Roberts in narrating the circumstance many years afterwards, 'was there a better sea-boat, or one that made less lee-way than the dear little *Bolivar*, but she could not walk in the wind's eye. I dared not venture to put her about in that gale for fear of getting into the trough of the sea and being swamped. To take in sail was impossible, so all we had left for it was to luff her up in the lulls, and trust to Providence for the rest. Night came on dark and cold, for it was November, and as the sea boiled and foamed in her wake, it shone through the pitchy darkness with a phosphoric efflorescence. The last thing I heard was my companion's exclamation, "Breakers ahead!" and almost at the same instant *The Bolivar* struck: the crash was awful; a watery column fell upon her bodily like an avalanche, and all that I remember was, that I was struggling with the waves. I am a strong swimmer, and have often contested with Byron in his own element, so after battling long with the billows, covered with bruises, and more dead than alive, I succeeded in scrambling up the rocks, and found myself in the evergreen pine-forest of Ravenna, some miles from any house. But at last I sheltered myself in a forester's hut. Death and I had a hard struggle that bout.'*

On April 1, 1823, Lord and Lady Blessington called on Byron at the Casa Saluzzo. Lady Blessington assures us that, in speaking of his wife, Byron declared that he was totally unconscious of the cause of her leaving him. He said that he left no means

---

* 'The Angler in Wales,' by Thomas Medwin, vol. ii., pp. 144-146.

untried to effect a reconciliation, and added with bitterness: 'A day will arrive when I shall be avenged. I feel that I shall not live long, and when the grave has closed over me, what must she feel!'

In speaking of his sister, Byron always spoke with strong affection, and said that she was the most faultless person he had ever known, and that she was his only source of consolation in his troubles during the separation business.

'Byron,' says Lady Blessington, 'has remarkable penetration in discovering the characters of those around him, and piques himself on it. He also thinks that he has fathomed the recesses of his own mind; but he is mistaken. With much that is *little* (which he suspects) in his character, there is much that is *great* that he does not give himself credit for. His first impulses are always good, but his temper, which is impatient, prevents his acting on the cool dictates of reason. He mistakes temper for character, and takes the ebullitions of the first for the indications of the nature of the second.'

Lady Blessington seems to have made a most searching examination of Byron's character, and very little escaped her vigilance during the two months of their intimate intercourse. She tells us that Byron talked for effect, and liked to excite astonishment. It was difficult to know when he was serious, or when he was merely 'bamming' his aquaintances. He admitted that he liked to *hoax* people, in order that they might give contradictory accounts of him and of his opinions. He spoke very highly of Countess Guiccioli, whom he had passionately loved and deeply respected. Lady Blessington says: 'In his praises of Madame Guiccioli it is quite evident that he is sincere.'

Byron confessed that he was not happy, but admitted that it was his own fault, as the Countess Guiccioli, the only object of his love, had all the qualities to render a reasonable being happy. In speaking of Allegra, Byron said that while she lived her existence never seemed necessary to his happiness; but no sooner did he lose her than it appeared to him as though he could not exist without her. It is noteworthy that, one evening, while Byron was speaking to Lady Blessington at her hotel at Genoa, he pointed out to her a boat at anchor in the harbour, and said: 'That is the boat in which my friend Shelley went down—the sight of it makes me ill. You should have known Shelley to feel how much I must regret him. He was the most gentle, most amiable, and *least* worldly-minded person I ever met; full of delicacy, disinterested beyond all other men, and possessing a degree of genius, joined to a simplicity, as rare as it is admirable. He had formed to himself a *beau-idéal* of all that is fine, high-minded, and noble, and he acted up to this ideal even to the very letter. He had a most brilliant imagination, but a total want of worldly wisdom. I have seen nothing like him, and never shall again, I am certain.'

We may, upon the evidence before us, take it for certain that Byron only admired two of his contemporaries—Sir Walter Scott and Shelley. He liked Hobhouse, and they had travelled together without a serious quarrel, which is a proof of friendship; but he felt that Hobhouse undervalued him, and, as Byron had a good deal of the spoiled child about him, he resented the friendly admonitions which, it seems, Hobhouse unsparingly administered whenever they were together. Tom Moore was a 'croney'—a man to laugh and sit through the night with—but there was nothing, either in his genius or his conduct, which Byron could fall down and worship, as he seemed capable of doing in the case of Shelley and Scott.

It is evident that Lady Byron occupied his thoughts continually; he constantly mentioned her in conversation, and often spoke of the brief period during which they lived together. He told Lady Blessington that, though not regularly handsome, he liked her looks. He said that when he reflected on the whole tenor of her conduct—the refusing any explanation, never answering his letters, or holding out any hopes that in future years their child might form a bond of union between them—he felt exasperated against her, and vented this feeling in his writings. The mystery of Lady Byron's silence piqued him and kept alive his interest in her. It was evident to those who knew Byron during the last year of his life that he anxiously desired a reconciliation with her. He seemed to think that, had his pecuniary affairs been in a less ruinous state, his temper would not have been excited as it constantly was, during the brief period of their union, by demands of insolent creditors whom he was unable to satisfy, and who drove him nearly out of his senses, until he lost all command of himself, and so forfeited his wife's affection. Byron felt himself to blame for such conduct, and bitterly repented of it. But he never could divest himself of the idea that his wife still took a deep interest in him, and said that Ada must always be a bond of union between them, though perchance they were parted for ever.

'I am sure,' said Lady Blessington, 'that if ten individuals undertook the task of describing Byron,

RELATIONS WITH COUNTESS GUICCIOLI

no two of the ten would agree in their verdict respecting him, or convey any portrait that resembled the other, and yet the description of each might be correct, according to individual opinion. The truth is, that the chameleon-like character or manner of Byron renders it difficult to portray him; and the pleasure he seems to take in misleading his associates in their estimation of him increases the difficulty of the task.'

On one occasion Byron lifted the veil, and showed his inmost thoughts by words which were carefully noted at the time. He spoke on this occasion from the depth of his heart as follows:

'Can I reflect on my present position without bitter feelings? Exiled from my country by a species of ostracism—the most humiliating to a proud mind, when *daggers* and not shells were used to ballot, inflicting mental wounds more deadly and difficult to be healed than all that the body could suffer. Then the notoriety that follows me precludes the privacy I desire, and renders me an object of curiosity, which is a continual source of irritation to my feelings. I am bound by the indissoluble ties of marriage to *one* who will *not* live with me, and live with one to whom I cannot give a legal right to be my companion, and who, wanting that right, is placed in a position humiliating to her and most painful to me. Were the Countess Guiccioli and I married, we should, I am sure, be cited as an example of conjugal happiness, and the domestic and retired life we lead would entitle us to respect. But our union, wanting the legal and religious part of the ceremony of marriage, draws on us both censure and blame. She is formed to make a good wife to any man to whom she attaches herself. She is fond of retirement, is of a most affectionate disposition, and noble-minded and disinterested to the highest degree. Judge then how mortifying it must be to me to be the cause of placing her in a false position. All this is not thought of when people are blinded by passion, but when passion is replaced by better feelings—those of affection, friendship, and confidence—when, in short, the *liaison* has all of marriage but its forms, then it is that we wish to give it the respectability of wedlock. I feel this keenly, reckless as I appear, though there are few to whom I would avow it, and certainly not to a man.'

There is much in this statement which it is necessary for those who wish to understand Byron's position at the close of his life to bear in mind. We may accept it unreservedly, for it coincides in every particular with conclusions independently arrived at by the present writer, after a long and patient study of all circumstances relating to the life of this extraordinary man. At the period of which we write—the last phase in Byron's brief career—the poet was, morally, ascending.

His character, through the fire of suffering, had been purified. Even his pride—so assertive in public—had been humbled, and he was gradually and insensibly preparing himself for a higher destiny, unconcious of the fact that the hand of Death was upon him. 'Wait,' he said, 'and you will see me one day become all that I ought to be. I have reflected seriously on all my faults, and that is the first step towards amendment.'

CHAPTER IV

CERTAIN it is, that in proportion to the admiration which Byron's poetic genius excited, was the severity of the censure which his fellow-countrymen bestowed on his defects as a man. The humour of the situation no doubt appealed to Byron's acute sense of proportion, and induced him to feed the calumnies against himself, by painting his own portrait in the darkest colours. Unfortunately, the effects of such conduct long survived him; for the world is prone to take a man at his own valuation, and 'hypocrisy reversed' does not enter into human calculations. It is unfortunate for the fame of Byron that his whole conduct after the separation was a glaring blunder, for which no subsequent act of his, no proof of his genius, could by any possibility atone.

Truth told, the obloquy which Byron had to endure, after Lady Byron left him, was such as might well have changed his whole nature. It must indeed have been galling to that proud spirit, after having been humbly asked everywhere, to be ostentatiously asked nowhere. The injustice he suffered at the hands of those who were fed on baseless calumnies raised in his breast a feeling of profound contempt for his fellow-creatures—a contempt which led him into many follies; thus, instead of standing up against the storm and meeting his detractors face to face, as he was both capable of and justified in doing, he chose to leave England under a cloud, and, by a system of mystification, to encourage the belief that he thoroughly deserved the humiliation which had been cast upon him. As a consequence, to employ the words of Macaulay,

'all those creeping things that riot in the decay of nobler natures hastened to their repast; and they were right; they did after their kind. It is not every day that the savage envy of aspiring dunces is gratified by the agonies of such a spirit, and the degradation of such a name.'

Lady Blessington tells us that Byron had an excellent heart, but that it was running to waste for want of being allowed to expend itself on his fellow-creatures. His heart teemed with affection, but his past experiences had checked its course, and left it to prey on the aching void in his breast. He could never forget his sorrows, which in a certain sense had unhinged his mind, and caused him to deny to others the justice that had been denied to himself. He affected to disbelieve in either love or friendship, and yet was capable of making great sacrifices for both.

'He has an unaccountable passion for misrepresenting his own feelings and motives, and exaggerates his defects more than an enemy could do; and is often angry because we do not believe all he says against himself. If Byron were not a great poet, the charlatanism of affecting to be a Satanic character, in this our matter-of-fact nineteenth century, would be very amusing: but when the genius of the man is taken into account, it appears too ridiculous, and one feels mortified that he should attempt to pass for something that all who know him rejoice that he is not. If

Byron knew his own power, he would disdain such unworthy means of attracting attention, and trust to his merit for commanding it.'

As Lady Blessington remarks in her 'Conversations of Lord Byron,' from which we have largely quoted, Byron's pre-eminence as a poet gives an interest to details which otherwise would not be worth mentioning. She tells us, for instance, that one of the strongest anomalies in Byron was the exquisite taste displayed in his descriptive poetry, and the total want of it that was so apparent in his modes of life.

'Fine scenery seemed to have no effect upon him, though his descriptions are so glowing, and the elegancies and comforts of refined life Byron appeared to as little understand as value.'

Byron appeared to be wholly ignorant of what in his class of life constituted its ordinary luxuries.

'I have seen him,' says Lady Blessington, 'apparently delighted with the luxurious inventions in furniture, equipages, plate, etc., common to all persons of a certain station or fortune, and yet after an inquiry as to their prices—an inquiry so seldom made by persons of his rank—shrink back alarmed at the thought of the expense, though there was nothing alarming in it, and congratulate himself that he had no such luxuries, or did not require them. I should say that a bad and vulgar taste predominated in all Byron's equipments, whether in dress or in furniture. I saw his bed at Genoa, when I passed through in 1826, and it certainly was the most vulgarly gaudy thing I ever saw; the curtains in the worst taste, and the cornice having his family motto of " Crede Byron" surmounted by baronial coronets. His carriages and his liveries were in the same bad taste, having an affectation of finery, but *mesquin* in the details, and tawdry in the *ensemble*. It was evident that he piqued himself on them, by the complacency with which they were referred to.'

In one of Byron's expansive moods—and these were rare with men, though frequent in the society of Lady Blessington—Byron, speaking of his wife, said:

'I am certain that Lady Byron's first idea is, what is due to herself; I mean that it is the undeviating rule of her conduct. I wish she had thought a little more of what is due to others. Now, my besetting sin is a want of that self-respect which she has in *excess;* and that want has produced much unhappiness to us both. But though I accuse Lady Byron of an excess of self-respect, I must in candour admit, that if any person ever had an excuse for an extraordinary portion of it, she has; as in all her thoughts, words, and deeds, she is the most decorous woman that ever existed, and must appear a perfect and refined gentlewoman even to her *femme-de-chambre.* This extraordinary degree of self-command in Lady Byron produced an opposite effect on me. When I have broken out, on slight provocations, into one of my ungovernable fits of rage, her calmness piqued, and seemed to reproach me; it gave her an air of superiority, that vexed and increased my wrath. I am now older and wiser, and should know how to appreciate her conduct as it deserved, as I look on self-command as a positive virtue, though it is one I have not the courage to adopt.'

In speaking of his sister, shortly before his departure for Greece, Byron maintained that he owed the little good which he could boast, to her influence over his wayward nature. He regretted that he had not known her earlier, as it might have influenced his destiny.

'To me she was, in the hour of need, as a tower of strength. Her affection was my last rallying point, and is now the only bright spot that the horizon of England offers to my view.' 'Augusta,' said Byron, 'knew all my weaknesses, but she had love enough to bear with them. She has given me such good advice, and yet, finding me incapable of following it, loved and pitied me the more, because I was erring. This is true affection, and, above all, true Christian feeling.'

But we should not be writing about Byron and his foibles eighty-four years after his death, if he had not been wholly different to other men in his views of life. Shortly after his marriage, for no sufficient, or at least for no apparent reason, Byron chose to immolate himself, and took a sort of Tarpeian leap, passing the remainder of his existence in bemoaning his bruises, and reviling the spectators who were not responsible for his fall. One of the main results of this conduct was his separation from his child, for whom he seems to have felt the deepest affection. We find him, at the close of his life, constantly speaking of Ada, 'sole daughter of his heart and house,' and prophesying the advent of a love whose consolations he could never feel.

'I often, in imagination, pass over a long lapse of years,' said Byron, 'and console myself for present privations, in anticipating the time when my daughter will know me by reading my works; for, though the hand of prejudice may conceal my portrait from her eyes,[*] it cannot hereafter conceal my thoughts and feelings, which will talk to her when he to whom they belonged has ceased to exist. The triumph will then be mine; and the tears that my child will drop over expressions wrung from me by mental agony—the certainty that she will enter into the sentiments which dictated the various allusions to her and to myself in my works—consoles me in many a gloomy hour.'

This prophecy was amply fulfilled. It appears that, after Ada's marriage to Lord King, Colonel Wildman

[*] Lady Noel left by her will to the trustees a portrait of Byron, with directions that it was not to be shown to his daughter Ada till she attained the age of twenty-one; but that if her mother were still living, it was not to be so delivered without Lady Byron's consent.

met her in London, and invited her to pay him a visit at Newstead Abbey. One morning, while Ada was in the library, Colonel Wildman took down a book of poems. Ada asked the name of the author of these poems, and when shown the portrait of her father—Phillips's well-known portrait—which hung upon the wall, Ada remained for a moment spell-bound, and then remarked ingenuously: 'Please do not think that it is affectation on my part when I declare to you that I have been brought up in complete ignorance of all that concerns my father.' Never until that moment had Ada seen the handwriting of her father, and, as we know, even his portrait had been hidden from her. When Byron's genius was revealed to his daughter, an enthusiasm for his memory filled her soul. She shut herself up for hours in the rooms which Byron had used, absorbed in all the glory of one whose tenderness for her had been so sedulously concealed by her mother. On her death-bed she dictated a letter to Colonel Wildman, begging that she might be buried at Hucknall-Torkard, in the same vault as her illustrious father. And there they sleep the long sleep side by side—separated during life, united in death—the prophecy of 1816 fulfilled in 1852:

> 'Yet, though dull Hate as duty should be taught,
> I know that thou wilt love me; though my name
> Should be shut from thee, as a spell still fraught
> With desolation, and a broken claim:
> Though the grave closed between us,—'twere the same,
> I know that thou wilt love me; though to drain
> *My* blood from out thy being were an aim
> And an attainment,—all would be in vain,—
> Still thou wouldst love me, still that more than life retain.'

CHAPTER V

THERE is no doubt that Byron had a craving for celebrity in one form or another. In the last year of his life his thoughts turned with something like apathy from the fame which his pen had brought him* towards that wider and nobler fame which might be attained by the sword. In the spirit of an exalted poet who has lately passed from us, if such prescience were possible, Byron might have applied these stirring lines to himself:

> 'Up, then, and act! Rise up and undertake
> The duties of to-day.   Thy courage wake!
> Spend not life's strength in idleness, for life
> Should not be wasted in Care's useless strife.
> No slothful doubt let work's place occupy,
> But labour!   Labour for posterity!

> 'Up, then, and sing! Rise up and bare the sword
> With which to combat suffering and wrong.
> Console all those that suffer with thy word,
> Defend Man's heritage with sword and song!
> Combat intrigue, injustice, tyranny,
> And in thine efforts God will be with thee.'

'I have made as many sacrifices to liberty,' said Byron, 'as most people of my age; and the one I am about to undertake is not the least, though probably

---

* It was at this time that Byron endeavoured to suppress the fact that he had written 'The Age of Bronze.'

it will be the last; for with my broken health, and the chances of war, Greece will most likely terminate my career. I like Italy, its climate, its customs, and, above all, its freedom from cant of every kind; therefore it is no slight sacrifice of comfort to give up the tranquil life I lead here, and break through the ties I have formed, to engage in a cause, for the successful result of which I have no very sanguine hopes. I have a presentiment that I shall die in Greece. I hope it may be in action, for that would be a good finish to a very *triste* existence, and I have a horror of death-bed scenes; but as I have not been famous for my luck in life, most probably I shall not have more in the manner of my death.'

It was towards the close of May, 1823, that Byron received a letter telling him that he had been elected a member of the Committee which sat in London to further the Greek cause. Byron willingly accepted the appointment, and from that moment turned his thoughts towards Greece, without exactly knowing in what manner he could best serve her cause. He experienced alternations of confidence and despondency certainly, but he never abandoned the notion that he might be of use, if only he could see his way clearly through the conflicting opinions and advice which reached him from all sides.

The presentiment that he would end his days in Greece, weighed so heavily on his mind, that he felt a most intense desire to revisit his native country before finally throwing in his lot with the Greeks. He seems to have vaguely felt that all chances of reconciliation with Lady Byron were not dead. He would have liked to say farewell to her without bitterness, and he longed to embrace his child. But the objections to a return to England were so formidable that he was compelled to abandon the idea.

His proud nature could not face the chance of a cold reception, and a revival of that roar of calumny which had driven him from our shores. He told Lady Blessington that he could laugh at those attacks with the sea between him and his traducers; but that on the spot, and feeling the effect which each libel produced upon the minds of his too sensitive friends, he could not stand the strain. Byron felt sure that his enemies would misinterpret his motives, and that no good would come of it.

After Byron had made up his mind to visit Greece in person, he does not appear ever to have seriously thought of drawing back. On June 15, 1823, he informed Trelawny, who was at Rome, that he was determined to go to Greece, and asked him to join the expedition. Seven days later Byron had hired a vessel to transport himself, his companions, his servants, and his horses, to Cephalonia.

On July 13, Byron, with Edward Trelawny, Count Pietro Gamba, and a young medical student,* with eight servants, embarked at Genoa on the English brig *Hercules*, commanded by Captain Scott. At the last moment a passage was offered to a Greek named Schilitzy, and to Mr. Hamilton Browne. Gamba tells us that five horses were shipped, besides arms, ammunition, and two one-pounder guns which had belonged to *The Bolivar*. Byron carried with him 10,000 Spanish dollars in ready-money, with bills of exchange for 40,000 more.

Passing within sight of Elba, Corsica, the Lipari Islands (including Stromboli,) Sicily, Italy, etc., on August 2, the *Hercules* lay between Zante and Cephalonia; and the next day she cast anchor in Argostoli

* Dr. Bruno.

the principal port of Cephalonia. The Resident, Colonel Napier, was at that time absent from the island. Shortly after Byron's arrival, Captain Kennedy, Colonel Napier's secretary, came on board, and informed him that little was known of the internal affairs of Greece. The Turks appeared to have been in force at sea, while the Greeks remained inactive at Hydra, Spezia, and Ipsara. It was supposed that Mr. Blaquière had gone to Corfu, while the famous Marco Botzari, to whom Byron had been especially recommended, was at Missolonghi. Before taking any definite step, Byron judged it best to send messengers to Corfu and Missolonghi, to collect information as to the state of affairs in the Morea. To pass the time, Byron and some of his companions made an excursion to Ithaca. The first opportunity of showing his sympathy towards the victims of barbarism and tyranny occurred at this period. Many poor families had taken refuge at Ithaca, from Scio, Patras, and other parts of Greece. Byron handed 3,000 piastres to the Commandant for their relief, and transported a family, in absolute poverty, to Cephalonia, where he provided them with a house and gave them a monthly allowance.

The following narrative, written by a gentleman who was travelling in Ithaca at that time, seems to be worthy of reproduction in these pages:

'It was in the island of Ithaca, in the month of August, 1823, that I was shown into the dining-room of the Resident Governor, where Lord Byron, Count Gamba, Dr. Bruno, Mr. Trelawny, and Mr. Hamilton Browne, were seated after dinner, with some of the English officers and principal inhabitants of the place. I had been informed of Lord Byron's presence, but had no means of finding him out, except by recollection of his portraits; and I am not ashamed to confess that I was puzzled, in my examination of the various countenances before me, where to fix upon "the man." I at one time almost settled upon Trelawny, from the interest which he seemed to take in the schooner in which I had just arrived; but on ascending to the drawing-room I was most agreeably undeceived by finding myself close to the side of the great object of my curiosity, and engaged in easy conversation with him, without presentation or introduction of any kind.

'He was handling and remarking upon the books in some small open shelves, and fairly spoke to me in such a manner that not to have replied would have been boorish. "'Pope's Homer's Odyssey'—hum!—that is well placed here, undoubtedly; 'Hume's Essays,'—'Tales of my Landlord;' there you are, Watty! Are you recently from England, sir?" I answered that I had not been there for two years. "Then you can bring us no news of the Greek Committee? Here we are all waiting orders, and no orders seem likely to come. Ha! ha!" "I have not changed my opinion of the Greeks," he said. "I know them as well as most people" (a favourite phrase), "but we must not look always too closely at the men who are to benefit by our exertions in a good cause, or God knows we shall seldom do much good in this world. There is Trelawny thinks he has fallen in with an angel in Prince Mavrocordato, and little Bruno would willingly sacrifice his life for the *cause*, as he calls it. I must say he has shown some sincerity in his devotion, in consenting to join it for the little matter he makes of me." I ventured to say that, in all probability, the being joined with him in any cause was inducement enough for any man of moderate pretensions. He noticed the compliment only by an indifferent smile. "I find but one opinion," he continued, "among all people whom I have met since I came here, that no good is to be done for these rascally Greeks; that I am sure to be deceived, disgusted, and all the rest of it. It may be so; but it is chiefly to satisfy myself upon these very points that I am going. I go prepared for anything, expecting a deal of roguery and imposition, but hoping to do some good."

'"Have you read any of the late publications on Greece?" I asked.

'"I never read any accounts of a country to which I can myself go," said he. "The Committee have sent me some of their 'Crown and Anchor' reports, but I can make nothing of them."

'The conversation continued in the same familiar flow. To my increased amazement, he led it to his works, to Lady Byron, and to his daughter. The former was suggested by a volume of "Childe Harold" which was on the table; it was the ugly square little German edition, and I made free to characterize it as execrable. He turned over the leaves, and said:

'Yes, it was very bad; but it was better than one that he had seen in French prose in Switzerland. "I know not what my friend Mr. Murray will say to it all. Kinnaird writes to me that he is wroth about many things; let them do what they like with the book—they have been abusive enough of the author. The *Quarterly* is trying to make amends, however, and *Blackwood's* people will suffer none to attack me but themselves. Milman was, I believe, at the bottom of the personalities, but they all sink before an American reviewer, who describes me as a kind of fiend, and says that the deformities of my mind are only to be equalled by those of my body; it is well that anyone can see them, at least." Our hostess, Mrs. Knox, advanced to us about this moment, and his lordship continued, smiling: "Does not your Gordon blood rise at such abuse of a clansman? The gallant Gordons 'bruik nae slight.' Are you true to your name, Mrs. Knox?" The lady was loud in her reprobation of the atrocious abuse that had recently been heaped upon the noble lord, and joined in his assumed clannish regard for their mutual name. "Lady Byron and you would agree," he said, laughing, "though I could not, you are thinking; you may *say* so, I assure you. I dare say it will turn out that I have been terribly in the wrong, *but I always want to know what I did.*" I had not courage to touch upon this delicate topic, and Mrs. Knox seemed to wish it passed over till a less public occasion. He spoke of Ada exactly as any parent might have done of a beloved absent child, and betrayed not the slightest confusion, or conscious-

THE FOUNTAIN OF ARETHUSA

ness of a sore subject, throughout the whole conversation.

'I now learnt from him that he had arrived in the island from Cephalonia only that morning, and that it was his purpose (as it was mine) to visit its antiquities and localities. A ride to the Fountain of Arethusa had been planned for the next day, and I had the happiness of being invited to join it. Pope's "Homer" was taken up for a description of the place, and it led to the following remarks:

"Yes, the very best translation that ever was, or ever will be; there is nothing like it in the world, be assured. It is quite delightful to find Pope's character coming round again; I forgive Gifford everything for that. Puritan as he is, he has too much good sense not to know that, even if all the lies about Pope were truths, his character is one of the best among literary men. There is nobody now like him, except Watty,* and he is as nearly faultless as ever human being was."

'The remainder of the evening was passed in arranging the plan of proceeding on the morrow's excursion, in the course of which his lordship occasionally interjected a facetious remark of some general nature; but in such fascinating tones, and with such a degree of amiability and familiarity, that, of all the libels of which I well knew the public press to be guilty, that of describing Lord Byron as inaccessible, morose, and repulsive in manner and language, seemed to me the most false and atrocious. I found I was to be accommodated for the night under the same roof with his lordship, and I retired, satisfied in my own mind that favouring chance had that day made me the intimate (almost confidential) friend of the greatest literary man of modern times.

'The next morning, about nine o'clock, the party for the Fountain of Arethusa assembled in the parlour of Captain Knox; but Lord Byron was missing. Trelawny, who had slept in the room adjoining his lordship's, told us that he feared he had been ill during the night, but that he had gone out in a boat very early in the morning. At this moment I happened to be standing at the window, and saw the object of our anxiety in

* Byron's sobriquet for Walter Scott.

the act of landing on the beach, about ten or a dozen yards from the house, to which he walked slowly up. I never saw and could not conceive the possibility of such a change in the appearance of a human being as had taken place since the previous night. He looked like a man under sentence of death, or returning from the funeral of all that he held dear on earth. His person seemed shrunk, his face was pale, and his eyes languid and fixed on the ground. He was leaning upon a stick, and had changed his dark camlet-caped surtout of the preceding evening for a nankeen jacket embroidered like a hussar's—an attempt at dandyism, or dash, to which the look and demeanour of the wearer formed a sad contrast. On entering the room, his lordship made the usual salutations; and, after some preliminary arrangements, the party moved off, on horses and mules, to the place of destination for the day.

'I was so struck with the difference of appearance in Lord Byron that the determination to which I had come, to try to monopolize him, if possible, to myself, without regard to appearances or *bienséance*, almost entirely gave way under the terror of a freezing repulse. I advanced to him under the influence of this feeling, but I had scarcely received his answer when all uneasiness about my reception vanished, and I stuck as close to him as the road permitted our animals to go. His voice sounded timidly and quiveringly at first; but as the conversation proceeded, it became steady and firm. The beautiful country in which we were travelling naturally formed a prominent topic, as well as the character of the people and of the Government. Of the latter, I found him (to my amazement) an admirer. "There is a deal of fine stuff about that old Maitland," he said; "he knows the Greeks well. Do you know if it be true that he ordered one of their brigs to be blown out of the water if she stayed ten minutes longer in Corfu Roads?" I happened to know, and told him that it was true. "Well, of all follies, that of daring to say what one cannot dare to do is the least to be pitied. Do you think Sir Tom would have really executed his threat?" I told his lordship that I believed he certainly would, and that this knowledge of his being in earnest in everything he said was the cause, not only of the quiet termination of that affair, but of the order and subordination in the whole of the countries under his government.

'The conversation again insensibly reverted to Sir Walter Scott, and Lord Byron repeated to me the anecdote of the interview in Murray's shop, as conclusive evidence of his being the author of the "Waverley Novels." He was a little but not durably staggered by the equally well-known anecdote of Sir Walter having, with some solemnity, denied the authorship to Mr. Wilson Croker, in the presence of George IV., the Duke of York, and the late Lord Canterbury. He agreed that an author wishing to conceal his authorship had a right to give *any answer whatever* that succeeded in convincing an inquirer that he was wrong in his suppositions.

'When we came within sight of the object of our excursion, there happened to be an old shepherd in the act of coming down from the fountain. His lordship at once fixed upon him for Eumæus, and invited him back with us to "fill up the picture." Having drunk of the fountain, and eaten of our less classical repast of cold fowls, etc., his lordship again became lively, and full of pleasant conceits. To detail the conversation (which was general and varied as the individuals that partook of it) is now impossible, and certainly not desirable if it were possible. I wish to observe, however, that on this and one very similar occasion, it was very unlike the kind of conversation which Lord Byron is described as holding with various individuals who have written about him. Still more unlike was it to what one would have *supposed* his conversation to be; it was exactly that of nine-tenths of the cultivated class of English gentlemen, careless and unconscious of everything but the present moment. Lord Byron ceased to be more than one of the party, and stood some sharp jokes, practical and verbal, with more good nature than would have done many of the ciphers whom one is doomed to tolerate in society.

'We returned as we went, but no opportunity presented itself of introducing any subject of interest beyond that of the place and time. His lordship seemed quite restored by the excursion, and in the evening came to the Resident's, bearing himself towards everybody in the same easy, gentlemanly way that rendered him the delight and ornament of every society in which he chose to unbend himself.

'The Resident was as absolute a monarch as Ulysses, and I dare say much more hospitable and obliging. He found quarters for the whole Anglo-Italian party, in the best houses of the town, and received them on the following morning at the most luxurious of breakfasts, consisting, among other native productions, of fresh-gathered grapes, just ripened, but which were pronounced of some danger to be eaten, as not having had the " first rain." This is worthy of note, as having been apparently a ground of their being taken by Lord Byron in preference to the riper and safer figs and nectarines; but he deemed it a fair reason for an apology to the worthy doctor of the 8th Regiment (Dr. Scott), who had cautioned the company against the fruit.

'" I take them, doctor," said his lordship, "as I take other prohibited things—in order to accustom myself to any and all things that a man may be compelled to take where I am going—in the same way that I abstain from all superfluities, even salt to my eggs or butter to my bread; and I take tea, Mrs. Knox, without sugar or cream. But tea itself is, really, the most superfluous of superfluities, though I am never without it."

'I heard these observations as they were made to Dr. Scott, next to whom I was sitting, towards the end of the table; but I could not hear the animated conversation that was going on between his lordship and Mrs. Knox, beyond the occasional mention of " Penelope," and, when one of her children came in to her, " Telemachus "—names too obviously *à propos* of the place and persons to be omitted in any incidental conversation in Ithaca.

'The excursion to the " School of Homer " (why so called nobody seemed to know) was to be made by water; and the party of the preceding day, except the lady, embarked in an elegant country boat with four rowers, and sundry packages and jars of eatables and drinkables. As soon as we were seated under the awning—Lord Byron in the centre seat, with his face to the stern—Trelawny took charge of the tiller. The other passengers being seated on the side, the usual small flying general conversation began. Lord Byron seemed in a mood calculated to make the company think he meant something more formal than ordinary talk. Of course there could not be anything said in the nature of a dialogue, which, to be honest, was the kind of conversation that I had at heart. He began by informing us that he had just been reading, with renewed pleasure, David Hume's Essays. He considered Hume to be by far the most profound thinker and clearest reasoner of the many philosophers and metaphysicians of the last century. "There is," said he, "no refuting him, and for simplicity and clearness of style he is unmatched, and is utterly unanswerable." He referred particularly to the Essay on Miracles. It was remarked to him, that it had nevertheless been specifically answered, and, some people thought, refuted, by a Presbyterian divine, Dr. Campbell of Aberdeen. I could not hear whether his lordship knew of the author, but the remark did not affect his opinion; it merely turned the conversation to Aberdeen and "poor John Scott," the most promising and most unfortunate literary man of the day, whom he knew well, and who, said he, knew him (Lord Byron) as a schoolboy. Scotland, Walter Scott (or, as his lordship always called him, "Watty"), the "Waverley Novels," the "Rejected Addresses," and the English aristocracy (which he reviled most bitterly), were the prominent objects of nearly an hour's conversation. It was varied, towards the end of the voyage, in this original fashion: "But come, gentlemen, we must have some inspiration. Here, Tita, l'Hippocrena!"

'This brought from the bows of the boat a huge Venetian gondolier, with a musket slung diagonally across his back, a stone jar of two gallons of what turned out to be English gin, another porous one of water, and a quart pitcher, into which the gondolier poured the spirit, and laid the whole, with two or three large tumblers, at the feet of his expectant lord, who quickly uncorked the jar, and began to pour its contents into the smaller vessel.

'"Now, gentlemen, drink deep, or taste not the Pierian spring; it is the true poetic source. I'm a rogue if I have drunk to-day. Come" (handing tumblers round to us), "this is the way;" and he nearly half filled a tumbler, and then poured from the height of his arm out of the water-jar, till the tumbler sparkled in the sun like soda-water, and drunk it off while effervescing, glorious gin-swizzle, a most tempting beverage, of which everyone on board took his share, munching after it a biscuit out of a huge tin case of them. This certainly exhilarated us, till we landed within some fifty or sixty yards of the house to which we were directed.

'On our way we learned that the Regent of the island—that is, the native Governor, as Captain Knox was the protecting Power's Governor (Viceroy over the King!)—had forwarded the materials of a substantial feast to the occupant (his brother); for the *nobili Inglesi*, who were to honour his premises. In mentioning this act of the Regent to Lord Byron, his remark was a repetition of the satirical line in the imitation address of the poet Fitzgerald, "God bless the Regent!" and as I mentioned the relationship to our approaching host, he added, with a laugh, "and the Duke of York!"

'On entering the mansion, we were received by the whole family, commencing with the mother of the Princes—a venerable lady of at least seventy, dressed in pure Greek costume, to whom Lord Byron went up with some formality, and, with a slight bend of the knee, took her hand, and kissed it reverently. We then moved into the adjoining *sala*, or saloon, where there was a profusion of English comestibles, in the shape of cold sirloin of beef, fowls, ham, etc., to which we did such honour as a sea appetite generally produces. It was rather distressing that not one of the entertainers touched any of these luxuries, it being the Greek Second or Panagia Lent, but fed entirely on some cold fish fried in oil, and green salad, of which last Lord Byron, in adherence to his rule of accustoming himself to eat anything eatable, partook, though with an obvious effort—as well as of the various wines that were on the table, particularly Ithaca, which is exactly port as made and drunk in the country of its growth.

'I was not antiquary enough to know to what object

of antiquity our visit was made, but I saw Lord Byron in earnest conversation with a very antique old Greek monk in full clerical habit. He was a Bishop, sitting on a stone of the ruined wall close by, and he turned out to be the *Esprit fort* mentioned in a note at the end of the second canto of "Childe Harold"—a freethinker, at least a freespeaker, when he called the sacrifice of the Maso *una Coglioneria*.

'When we embarked on our return to Vathi, Lord Byron seemed moody and sullen, but brightened up as he saw a ripple on the water, a mast and sail raised in the cutter, and Trelawny seated in the stern with the tiller in hand. In a few minutes we were scudding, gunwale under, in a position infinitely more beautiful than agreeable to landsmen, and Lord Byron obviously enjoying the not improbable idea of a swim for life. His motions, as he sat, tended to increase the impulse of the breeze, and tended also to sway the boat to leeward. "I don't know," he said, "if you all swim, gentlemen; but if you do, you will have fifty fathoms of blue water to support you; and if you do not, you will have it over you. But as you may not all be prepared, starboard, Trelawny—bring her up. There! she is trim; and now let us have a glass of grog after the gale. *Tita, i fiaschi!*" This was followed by a reproduction of the gin-and-water jars, and a round of the immortal swizzle. To my very great surprise, it was new to the company that the liquor which they were enjoying was the product of Scotland, in the shape of what is called "low-wines," or semi-distilled whisky —chiefly from the distillery of mine ancient friend, James Haig of Lochrin; but the communication seemed to gratify the noble drinker, and led to the recitation by one of the company, in pure lowland Scotch, of Burns's Petition to the House of Commons in behalf of the national liquor. The last stanza, beginning

'" Scotland, my auld respeckit mither,"

very much pleased Lord Byron, who said that he too was more than half a Scotchman.

'The conversation again turned on the "Waverley Novels," and on this occasion Lord Byron spoke of "The Bride of Lammermoor," and cited the passage where the mother of the cooper's wife tells her husband (the cooper) that she "kent naething aboot what he might do to his wife; but the deil a finger shall ye lay on my dochter, and *that ye may foond upon.*" Shortly afterwards, the conversation having turned upon poetry, his lordship mentioned the famous ode on the death of Sir John Moore as the finest piece of poetry in any language. He recited some lines of it. One of the company, with more presumption than wisdom, took him up, as his memory seemed to lag, by filling in the line :

'"And he looked like a warrior taking his rest,
With his martial cloak around him."

'Lord Byron, with a look at the interloper that spoke as if death were in it, and no death was sufficiently cruel for him, shouted, "He *lay*—he *lay* like a warrior, not he *looked.*" The pretender was struck dumb, but, with reference to his lordship's laudation of the piece, he ventured half to whisper that the "Gladiator" was superior to it, as it is to any poetical picture ever painted in words. The reply was a benign look, and a flattering recognition, by a little applausive tapping of his tobacco-box on the board on which he sat.

'On arriving at Vathi, we repaired to our several rooms in the worthy citizens' houses where we were billeted, to read and meditate, and write and converse, as we might meet, indoors or out; and much profound lucubration took place among us, on the characteristics and disposition of the very eminent personage with whom we were for the time associated. Dr. Scott, the assistant-surgeon of the 8th Foot, who had heard of, though he may not have witnessed, any of the peculiarities of the great poet, accounted for them, and even for the sublimities of his poetry, by an abnormal construction or chronic derangement of the digestive organs—a theory which experience and observation of other people than poets afford many reasons to support :

'" Is it not strange now—ten times strange—to think,
And is it not enough one's faith to shatter,
That right or wrong direction of a drink,
A *plus* or *minus* of a yellow matter,

> One half the world should elevate or sink
> To bliss or woe (most commonly the latter)—
> That human happiness is well-formed chyle,
> And human misery redundant bile!"

'The next morning the accounts we heard of Lord Byron were contradictory: Trelawny, who slept in the next room to him, stating that he had been writing the greater part of the night, and he alleged it was the sixteenth canto of "Don Juan"; and Dr. Bruno, who visited him at intervals, and was many hours in personal attendance at his bedside, asserting that he had been seriously ill, and had been saved only by those *benedette pillule* which so often had had that effect. His lordship again appeared rowing in from his bath at the Lazzaretto, a course of proceeding (bathing and boating) which caused Dr. Bruno to wring his hands and tear his hair with alarm and vexation.

'It was, however, the day fixed for our return to Cephalonia, and, having gladly assented to the proposition to join the suite, we all mounted ponies to cross the island to a small harbour on the south side, where a boat was waiting to bear us to Santa Eufemia, a Custom-house station on the coast of Cephalonia, about half an hour's passage from Ithaca, which we accordingly passed, and arrived at the collector's mansion about two o'clock.

'During the journey across the smaller island, I made a bold push, and succeeded in securing, with my small pony, the side-berth of Lord Byron's large brown steed, and held by him in the narrow path, to the exclusion of companions better entitled to the post. His conversation was not merely free—it was familiar and intimate, as if we were schoolboys meeting after a long separation. I happened to be "up" in the "Waverley Novels," had seen several letters of Sir Walter Scott's about his pedigree for his baronetage, could repeat almost every one of the "Rejected Addresses," and knew something of the *London Magazine* contributors, who were then in the zenith of their reputation—Hazlitt, Charles Lamb, Talfourd, Browning, Allan Cunningham, Reynolds, Darley, etc. But his lordship pointed at the higher game of

Southey, Gifford (whom he all but worshipped), Jeffrey of the *Edinburgh Review*, John Wilson, and other Blackwoodites. He said they were all infidels, as every man has a right to be; that Edinburgh was understood to be the seat of all infidelity, and he mentioned names (Dr. Chalmers and Andrew Thomson, for examples) among the clergy as being of the category. This I never could admit. He was particularly bitter against Southey, sneered at Wordsworth, admired Thomas Campbell, classing his " Battle of the Baltic" with the very highest of lyric productions. "Nothing finer," he said, "was ever written than—

'" There was silence deep as death,
And the boldest held his breath
For a time."

'We arrived at one of the beautiful bays that encircle the island, like a wavy wreath of silver sand studded with gold and emerald in a field of liquid pearl, and embarked in the collector's boat for the opposite shore of Santa Eufemia, where, on arrival, we were received by its courteous chief, Mr. Toole, in a sort of state—with his whole establishment, French and English, uncovered and bowing. He had had notice of the illustrious poet's expected arrival, and had prepared one of the usual luxurious feasts in his honour—feasts which Lord Byron said "played the devil" with him, for he could not abstain when good eating was within his reach. The apartment assigned to us was small, and the table could not accommodate the whole party. There were, accordingly, small side or "children's tables," for such guests as might choose to be willing to take seats at them. "Ha!" said Lord Byron, "England all over—places for Tommy and Billy, and Lizzie and Molly, if there were any. Mr. —— " (addressing me), "will you be my Tommy?"—pointing to the two vacant seats at a small side-table, close to the chair of our host. Down I sat, delighted, opposite to my companion, and had a *tête-à-tête* dinner apart from the head-table, from which, as usual, we were profusely helped to the most recherché portions. "Verily," said his lordship, " I cannot abstain." His conversation, however, was directed chiefly to his

MONASTERY ON THE HILL OF SAMOS

host, from whom he received much local information, and had his admiration of Sir Thomas Maitland increased by some particulars of his system of government. There were no vacant apartments within the station, but we learned that quarters had been provided for us at a monastery on the hill of Samos, across the bay. Thither we were all transported at twilight, and ascended to the large venerable abode of some dozen of friars, who were prepared for our arrival and accommodation. Outside the walls of the building there were some open sarcophagi and some pieces of carved frieze and fragments of pottery.

'I walked with his lordship and Count Gamba to examine them, speculating philosophically on their quondam contents. Something to our surprise, Lord Byron clambered over into the deepest, and lay in the bottom at full length on his back, muttering some English lines. I may have been wrong, or idly and unjustifiably curious, but I leaned over to hear what the lines might be. I found they were unconnected fragments of the scene in " Hamlet," where he moralizes with Horatio on the skull :

> '" Imperious Cæsar, dead and turned to clay,
> Might stop a hole to keep the wind away ;
> O, that that earth, which held the world in awe,
> Should patch a wall to expel the winter's flaw !"

'As he sprang out and rejoined us, he said: "Hamlet, as a whole, is original; but I do not admire him to the extent of the common opinion. More than all, he requires the very best acting. Kean did not understand the part, and one could not look at him after having seen John Kemble, whose squeaking voice was lost in his noble carriage and thorough right conception of the character. Rogers told me that Kemble used to be almost always hissed in the beginning of his career. 'The best actor on the stage,' he said, 'is Charles Young. His Pierre was never equalled, and never will be.'" Amid such flying desultory conversation we entered the monastery, and took coffee for lack of anything else, while our servants were preparing our beds. Lord Byron retired almost immediately from the *sala*. Shortly afterwards we were astonished and alarmed by the entry of Dr. Bruno, wringing his hands and tearing his hair—a practice much too frequent with him—and ejaculating: "*O Maria, santissima Maria, se non è già morto—cielo, perchè non son morto io!*" It appeared that Lord Byron was seized with violent spasms in the stomach and liver, and his brain was excited to dangerous excess, so that he would not tolerate the presence of any person in his room. He refused all medicine, and stamped and tore all his clothes and bedding like a maniac. We could hear him rattling and ejaculating. Poor Dr. Bruno stood lamenting in agony of mind, in anticipation of the most dire results if immediate relief were not obtained by powerful cathartics, but Lord Byron had expelled him from the room by main force. He now implored one or more of the company to go to his lordship and induce him, if possible, to save his life by taking the necessary medicine. Trelawny at once proceeded to the room, but soon returned, saying that it would require ten such as he to hold his lordship for a minute, adding that Lord Byron would not leave an unbroken article in the room. The doctor again essayed an entrance, but without success. The monks were becoming alarmed, and so, in truth, were all present. The doctor asked me to try to bring his lordship to reason; "he will thank you when he is well," he said, "but get him to take this one pill, and he will be safe." It seemed a very easy undertaking, and I went. There being no lock on the door, entry was obtained in spite of a barricade of chairs and a table within. His lordship was half undressed, standing in a far corner like a hunted animal at bay. As I looked determined to advance in spite of his imprecations of "Back! out, out of my sight! fiends, can I have no peace, no relief from this hell! Leave me, I say!" and he lifted the chair nearest to him, and hurled it direct at my head; I escaped as I best could, and returned to the *sala*. The matter was obviously serious, and we all counselled force and such coercive measures as might be necessary to make him swallow the curative medicine. Mr. Hamilton Browne, one of our party, now volunteered an attempt, and the silence that succeeded his entrance augured well for his success. He returned much sooner than expected, telling the doctor that he might go to sleep; Lord Byron had taken both the pills, and had lain down on my mattress and bedding, prepared for him by my servant, the only regular bed in the company, the others being trunks and portable tressels, with such softening as might be procured for the occasion. Lord Byron's beautiful and most commodious patent portmanteau bed, with every appliance that profusion of money could provide, was mine for the night.

'On the following morning Lord Byron was all dejection and penitence, not expressed in words, but amply in looks and movements, till something tending to the jocular occurred to enliven him and us. Wandering from room to room, from porch to balcony, it so happened that Lord Byron stumbled upon their occupants in the act of writing accounts, journals, private letters, or memoranda. He thus came upon me on an outer roof of a part of the building, while writing, as far as I recollect, these very notes of his conversation and conduct. What occurred, however, was not of much consequence—or none—and turned upon the fact that so many people were writing, when he, the great voluminous writer, so supposed, was not writing at all. The journey of the day was to be over the Black Mountain to Argostoli, the capital of Cephalonia. We set out about noon, struggling as we best could over moor, marsh ground, and watery wastes. Lord Byron revived; and, lively on horseback, sang, at the pitch of his voice, many of Moore's melodies and stray snatches of popular songs of the time in the common style of the streets. There was nothing remarkable in the conversation. On arrival at Argostoli, the party separated—Lord Byron and Trelawny to the brig of the former, lying in the offing, the rest to their several quarters in the town.'

CHAPTER VI

AFTER an absence of eight days the party returned to Argostoli, and went on board the *Hercules*. The messenger whom Byron had sent to Corfu brought the unwelcome intelligence that Mr. Blaquière had sailed for England, without leaving any letters for Byron's guidance. News also reached him that the Greeks were split up into factions, and more intent on persecuting and calumniating each other than on securing the independence of their country. This was depressing news for a man who had sacrificed so much, and would have damped the enthusiasm of most people in Byron's position; but it neither deceived nor disheartened him. He was, and had always been, prepared for the worst. He made up his mind not to enter personally into the arena of contending factions, but to await further developments at Cephalonia, hoping to acquire an influence which might eventually be employed in settling their internal discords. As he himself remarked, 'I came not here to join a faction, but a nation. I must be circumspect.' Trelawny, in his valuable record of events at this time, is hard on Byron. He mistook Byron's motives, and thought that he was 'shilly-shallying and doing nothing.' But Trelawny, though mistaken, was sincere. He was in every sense of the word a man of

BYRON MOVES TO METAXATA

action, and full of a wild enthusiasm for the Greek cause. It was not in his nature to await events, but rather to create them, and Byron's wise decision made him restive. He determined to proceed to the Morea, and induced Hamilton Browne to go with him. Byron gave them letters to the Greek Government, if they could find any such authority, expressing his readiness to serve them when they had satisfied him how he could do so.

Gamba takes a calmer view of Byron's hesitation. He says that Byron well knew that prudence had never been in the catalogue of his virtues; that he knew the necessity of such a virtue in his present situation, and was determined to attain it. He carefully avoided every appearance of ostentation, and dreaded being suspected of being a mere hunter after adventures.

'By perseverance and discernment,' says Gamba, 'Byron hoped to assist in the liberation of Greece. To know and to be known was consequently, from the outset, his principal object.'

How far he succeeded we shall see later. From the time of Byron's arrival at Argostoli until September 6 he lived on board the *Hercules*. Colonel Napier had frequently begged him to take up his quarters with him, but Byron declined the hospitality; mainly because he feared that he might thereby embroil the British authorities on the island with their own Government, whose dispositions were yet unknown. Early in September Byron removed with Gamba to a village named Metaxata, in a healthy situation and amidst magnificent scenery. A month later letters arrived from Edward Trelawny, saying that things were not so bad as had been reported. It was evident that great apathy and total disorganization prevailed among those who had got the upper hand, but that the mass of the people—well disposed towards the revolution—was beginning to take an interest in the war. A general determination of never again submitting to the Turkish yoke had taken deep root. The existing Greek Government sent pressing letters to Byron inviting him to set out immediately, but Byron still thought it wiser not to move; for the reasons which had governed his conduct hitherto still prevailed. He was determined neither to waste his services nor his money on furthering the greed of some particular chieftain, or at best of some faction. Letters arrived from the Greek Committee in London, informing Byron that arrangements had been made for the floating of a Greek loan. Meanwhile Mavrocordato wrote to Byron from Hydra, whither he had fled, inviting him to that island. Lord Byron replied that so long as the dissensions between the factions continued he would remain a mere spectator, as he was resolved not to be mixed up in quarrels whose effects were so disastrous to the cause. He at the same time begged Mavrocordato to expedite the departure of the fleet, and to send the Greek deputies to London. The Turkish fleet meanwhile had sailed for the Dardanelles, leaving a squadron of fourteen vessels for the blockade of Missolonghi, and for the protection of a fortress in the gulf, which was still in the hands of the Turks.

The gallant Marco Botzari had been killed in action, and Missolonghi was in a state of siege. Its Governor wrote and implored Byron to come there; but as the place was in no danger, either from famine or from assault, he declined the proposal.

DEPARTURE OF THE GREEK DEPUTIES

In the middle of November, 1823, Mr. Hamilton Browne and the deputies arrived at Cephalonia. They brought letters from the Greek Government asking Byron to advance £6,000 (30,000 dollars) for the payment of the Greek fleet. An assurance was offered by the legislative body that, upon payment of this money, a Greek squadron would immediately put to sea. Byron consented to advance £4,000, and gave the deputies letters for London. In allusion to the loan about to be raised in England, he thus addressed them:

'Everyone believes that a loan will be the salvation of Greece, both as to its internal disunion and external enemies. But I shall refrain from insisting much on this point, for fear that I should be suspected of interested views, and of wishing to repay myself the loan of money which I have advanced to your Government.'

On December 17, 1823, while Byron was at Metaxata, awaiting definite information as to the progress of events, he resumed his journal, which had been abruptly discontinued in consequence of news having reached him that his daughter was ill.

'I know not,' he wrote, 'why I resume it even now, except that, standing at the window of my apartment in this beautiful village, the calm though cool serenity of a beautiful and transparent moonlight, showing the islands, the mountains, the sea, with a distant outline of the Morea traced between the double azure of the waves and skies, has quieted me enough to be able to write, which (however difficult it may seem for one who has written so much publicly to refrain) is, and always has been, to me a task, and a painful one. I could summon testimonies were it necessary; but my handwriting is sufficient. It is that of one who thinks much, rapidly, perhaps deeply, but rarely with pleasure.'

The Greeks were still quarrelling among themselves, and Byron almost despaired of being able to unite the factions in one common interest. Mavrocordato and the squadron from Hydra, for whose coming Byron had bargained when he advanced £4,000, had at length arrived after the inglorious capture of a small Turkish vessel with 50,000 dollars on board. This prize having been captured within the bounds of neutrality, on the coast of Ithaca, Byron naturally foresaw that it would bring the Greeks into trouble with the British authorities. Meanwhile, news from London confirmed the accounts of an increasing interest in the Greek cause, and gave good promise of a successful floating of the loan.

In the middle of November Colonel Leicester Stanhope arrived at Cephalonia. He had been deputed by the London Committee to act with Lord Byron. News also came from Greece that the Pasha of Scutari had abandoned Anatolico, and that the Turkish army had been put to flight. But the Greek factions, whose jealous dissensions promised to wreck the cause of Greek independence, had come to blows in the Morea.

As Byron had been recognized as a representative of the English and German Committees interested in the Greek cause, he was advised to write a public remonstrance to the general Government of Greece, pointing out that their dissensions would be fatal to the cause which it was presumed they all had at heart. Byron disliked to take so prominent a step, but he was eventually persuaded that such a letter might do a great deal of good. Gamba cites the following extract from Byron's appeal to the executive and legislative bodies of the Greek nation:

A REMONSTRANCE

'CEPHALONIA,
'*November* 30, 1823.

'The affair of the loan, the expectation so long and vainly indulged of the arrival of the Greek fleet, and the danger to which Missolonghi is still exposed, have detained me here, and will still detain me till some of them are removed. But when the money shall be advanced for the fleet, I will start for the Morea, not knowing, however, of what use my presence can be in the present state of things. We have heard some rumours of new dissensions—nay, of the existence of a civil war. With all my heart, I pray that these reports may be false or exaggerated, for I can imagine no calamity more serious than this; and I must frankly confess, that unless union and order are established, all hopes of a loan will be vain. All the assistance which the Greeks could expect from abroad—an assistance neither trifling nor worthless—will be suspended or destroyed. And, what is worse, the Great Powers of Europe, of whom no one is an enemy to Greece, but seems to favour her establishment of an independent power, will be persuaded that the Greeks are unable to govern themselves, and will, perhaps, themselves undertake to settle your disorders in such a way as to blast the hopes of yourselves and of your friends.

'And allow me to add once for all—I desire the wellbeing of Greece, and nothing else, I will do all I can to secure it. But I cannot consent, I never will consent, that the English public or English individuals should be deceived as to the real state of Greek affairs. The rest, gentlemen, depends on you. You have fought gloriously; act honourably towards your fellow-citizens and towards the world. Then it will no more be said, as it has been said for two thousand years, with the Roman historian, that Philopœmen was the last of the Grecians. Let not calumny itself (and it is difficult, I own, to guard against it in so arduous a struggle) compare the patriot Greek, when resting from his labours, to the Turkish Pacha, whom his victories have exterminated.

'I pray you to accept these my sentiments as a sincere proof of my attachment to your real interests; and to believe that I am, and always shall be,

'Your, etc.,
'NOEL BYRON.'

Byron at the same time wrote to Prince Mavrocordato, and sent the letter by Colonel Leicester Stanhope. He tells the Prince that he is very uneasy at the news about the dissensions among the Greek chieftains, and warns him that Greece must prepare herself for three alternatives. She must either reconquer her liberty by united action, or become a Dependence of the Sovereigns of Europe; or, failing in either direction, she would revert to her position as a mere province of Turkey. There was no other choice open to her Civil war was nothing short of ruin.

'If Greece desires the fate of Walachia and the Crimea,' says Byron, 'she may obtain it to-morrow; if that of Italy, the day after; but if she wishes to become truly Greece, free and independent, she must resolve to-day, or she will never again have the opportunity.'

Byron, in his journal dated December 17, 1823, says:

'The Turks have retired from before Missolonghi—nobody knows why—since they left provisions and ammunition behind them in quantities, and the garrison made no sallies, or none to any purpose. They never invested Missolonghi this year, but bombarded Anatoliko, near the Achelous.'

Finlay, in his 'History of Greece,' states that the Turks made no effort to capture the place, and after a harmless bombardment the siege was raised, and the Turkish forces retired into Epirus.

The following extract from a letter, which Byron wrote to his sister* conveys an unimpeachable record of his feelings and motives in coming to Greece:

You ask me why I came up amongst the Greeks. It was stated to me that my doing so might tend to

* 'Letters and Journals of Lord Byron,' edited by Rowland Prothero, vol. vi., p. 259.

their advantage in some measure, in their present struggle for independence, both as an individual and as a member for the Committee now in England. How far this may be realized I cannot pretend to anticipate, but I am willing to do what I can. They have at length found leisure to quarrel amongst themselves, after repelling their other enemies, and it is no very easy part that I may have to play to avoid appearing partial to one or other of their factions. . . . I have written to their Government at Tripolizza and Salamis, and am waiting for instructions *where* to proceed, for things are in such a state amongst them, that it is difficult to conjecture where one could be useful to them, if at all. However, I have some hopes that they will see their own interest sufficiently not to quarrel till they have received their national independence, and then they can fight it out among them in a domestic manner—and welcome. You may suppose that I have something to *think* of at least, for you can have no idea what an intriguing, cunning, unquiet generation they are; and as emissaries of all parties come to me at present, and I must act impartially, it makes me exclaim, as Julian did at his military exercises, "Oh! Plato, what a task for a Philosopher!"'

CHAPTER VII

IT was during the time that Byron was in the neighbourhood of Cephalonia that Dr. Kennedy, a Scottish medical man, methodistically inclined, undertook the so-called 'conversion' of the poet. Gamba tells us that their disputes on religious matters sometimes lasted five or six hours. 'The Bible was so familiar to Byron that he frequently corrected the citations of the theological doctor.'

Byron, in the letter from which we have quoted, says:

'There is a clever but eccentric man here, a Dr. Kennedy, who is very pious and tries in good earnest to make converts; but his Christianity is a queer one, for he says that the priesthood of the Church of England are no more Christians than "Mahound or Termagant" are. . . . I like what I have seen of him. He says that the dozen shocks of an earthquake we had the other day are a sign of his doctrine, or a judgment on his audience, but this opinion has not acquired proselytes.'

As disputants, Byron and Kennedy stood far as the poles asunder. The former, while believing firmly in the existence and supreme attributes of God, doubted, but never denied, manifestations that could not be tested or demonstrated by positive proof. The latter, through blind unquestioning faith, believed in everything which an inspired Bible had revealed to mankind. Thus both were believers up to a certain point, and both were equally well-meaning and sincere. The intensity of their faith had its limitations. They did not agree, and never could have agreed, in their views of religion. They moved on parallel lines that might have been extended indefinitely, but could never meet. Kennedy discouraged the unlimited use of reason, and preferred an absolute reliance on the traditional teaching of his Church. To Byron the exercise of reason was an absolute necessity. He would not admit that God had given us minds, and had denied us the right to use them intelligently; or that the Almighty desired us to sacrifice reason to faith. 'It is useless,' said Byron, 'to tell me that I am to believe, and not to reason; you might as well say to a man: "Wake not, but sleep."' While Byron profoundly disbelieved in eternal punishments, Kennedy would have mankind kept straight by fear of them. Kennedy, though versed in the Bible, was, as events proved, hardly a match for Byron.

Hodgson, an old friend of Byron's, has left a record that a Bible presented to him 'by that better angel of his life,' his beloved sister, was among the books which Byron always kept near him. The following lines, taken from Scott, were inserted by Byron on the fly-leaf:

> 'Within this awful volume lies
> The Mystery of Mysteries.
> Oh! happiest they of human race
> To whom our God has given grace
> To hear, to read, to fear, to pray,
> To lift the latch, and force the way;
> But better had he ne'er been born
> Who reads to doubt, or reads to scorn!'*

---

* 'Memoir of Rev. F. Hodgson,' vol. ii., p. 150.

During the discussions which took place, Kennedy was forced to admit that Byron was well versed in the Bible; but he maintained that prayer was necessary in order to understand its message. Byron said that, in his opinion, prayer does not consist in the act of kneeling, or of repeating certain words in a solemn manner, as devotion is the affection of the heart.

'When I look at the marvels of the creation,' said he, 'I bow before the Majesty of Heaven; and when I experience the delights of life, health, and happiness, then my heart dilates in gratitude towards God for all His blessings.'

Kennedy maintained that this was not sufficient; it must be an earnest supplication for grace and humility. In Kennedy's opinion Byron had not sufficient humility to understand the truths of the Gospel. At this time, certainly, Byron was not prepared to believe implicitly in the Divinity of Christ. He lacked the necessary faith to do so, but he did not reject the doctrine.

'I have not the slightest desire,' he said, 'to reject a doctrine without having investigated it. Quite the contrary; I wish to believe, because I feel extremely unhappy in a state of uncertainty as to what I am to believe.'

He wanted proofs—as so many others have before and since—and without it conviction was impossible.

'Byron,' said Countess Guiccioli, 'would never have contested absolutely the truth of any mystery, but have merely stated that, so long as the testimony of its truth was hidden in obscurity, such a mystery must be liable to be questioned.'

Byron had been brought up by his mother in very strict religious principles, and in his youth had read many theological works. He told Dr. Kennedy that he was in no sense an unbeliever who denied the Scriptures, or was content to grope in atheism, but, on the contrary, that it was his earnest wish to increase his belief, as half-convictions made him wretched. He declared that, with the best will in the world, he could not understand the Scriptures. Kennedy, on the other hand, took the Bible to be the salvation of mankind, and was strong in his condemnation of the Catholic Church. He objected to the Roman Communion as strongly as he repudiated and despised Deism and Socinianism.

Byron had at this time a decided leaning towards the Roman Communion, and, while deploring hypocrisies and superstitions, deeply respected those who believed conscientiously, whatever that belief might be. He loathed hypocrites of all kinds, and especially hypocrites in religion.

'I do not reject the doctrines of Christianity,' he said; 'I only ask a few more proofs to profess them sincerely. I do not believe myself to be the vile Christian which so many assert that I am.'

Kennedy advised Byron to put aside all difficult subjects—such as the origin of sin, the fall of man, the nature of the Trinity, the doctrine of predestination, and kindred mysteries—and to study Christianity by the light of the Bible alone, which contains the only means of salvation. We give Byron's answer in full on Dr. Kennedy's authority:

'You recommend what is very difficult; for how is it possible for one who is acquainted with ecclesiastical history, as well as with the writings of the most renowned theologians, with all the difficult questions which have agitated the minds of the most learned, and who sees the divisions and sects which abound in Christianity, and the bitter language which is often used by the one against the other; how is it possible, I ask, for such a one not to inquire into the nature of the doctrines which have given rise to so much discussion? One Council has pronounced against another; Popes have belied their predecessors, books have been written against other books, and sects have risen to replace other sects. The Pope has opposed the Protestants, and the Protestants the Pope. We have heard of Arianism, Socinianism, Methodism, Quakerism, and numberless other sects. Why have these existed? It is a puzzle for the brain; and does it not, after all, seem safer to say: "Let us be neutral: let those fight who will, and when they have settled which is the best religion, then shall we also begin to study it." I like your way of thinking, in many respects; you make short work of decrees and Councils, you reject all which is not in harmony with the Scriptures. You do not admit of theological works filled with Latin and Greek, of both High and Low Church; you would even suppress many abuses which have crept into the Church, and you are right; but I question whether the Archbishop of Canterbury or the Scotch Presbyterians would consider you their ally.'

Kennedy, in reply, alluded to the differences which existed in religious opinions, and expressed regret at this, but pleaded indulgence for those sects which do not attack the fundamental doctrines of Christianity. He strongly condemned Arianism, Socinianism, and Swedenborgianism, which were anathema to him.

'You seem to hate the Socinians greatly,' said Byron, 'but is this charitable? Why exclude a Socinian, who believes honestly, from any hope of salvation? Does he not also found his belief upon the Bible? It is a religion which gains ground daily. Lady Byron is much in favour with its followers. We were wont to discuss religious matters together, and many of our misunderstandings have arisen from that. Yet, on the whole, I think her religion and mine were much alike.'

Whether Byron was justified in this opinion or not may be see from a letter which Lady Byron wrote to Mr. Crabb Robinson* in reference to Dr. Kennedy's book:

'Strange as it may seem, Dr. Kennedy is most faithful where you doubt his being so. Not merely from casual expressions, but from the whole tenor of Lord Byron's feelings, I could not but conclude he was a believer in the inspiration of the Bible, and had the gloomiest Calvinistic tenets. To that unhappy view of the relation of the creature to the Creator, I have always ascribed the misery of his life. . . . It is enough for me to remember, that he who thinks his transgressions beyond *forgiveness* (and such was his own deepest feeling) *has* righteousness beyond that of the self-satisfied sinner; or, perhaps, of the half awakened. It was impossible for me to doubt, that, could he have been at once assured of pardon, his living faith in a moral duty and love of virtue ("I love the virtues which I cannot claim") would have conquered every temptation. Judge, then, how I must hate the Creed which made him see God as an Avenger, not a Father. My own impressions were just the reverse, but could have little weight, and it was in vain to seek to turn his thoughts for long from that *idée fixe*, with which he connected his physical peculiarity as a stamp. Instead of being made happier by any apparent good, he felt convinced that every blessing would be "turned into a curse" for him. Who, possessed of such ideas, could lead a life of love and service to God or man? They must in a measure realize themselves. "The worst of it is I *do* believe,' he said. I, like all connected with him, was broken against the rock of Predestination.'

Lady Byron writes from her own personal experience of a time when tender affection or sympathy formed no part of Byron's nature; of a time when he had no regard for the interests or the happiness of others;

---

* 'Diary,' vol. iii., pp. 435, 436.

when he lived according to his own humours, and when his will was his law. Byron's earlier poetry amply supports Lady Byron's view of so miserable a state of mind. But there is reason to hope—nay, we might say to believe—that, in the last years of his life, Byron began to realize that a merciful God would be wholly incapable of such manifest injustice as to condemn His creatures to suffer for crimes which they were powerless to resist and predestined to commit. He believed in God and in the immortality of the soul, and has publicly declared that all punishment which is to revenge, rather than to correct, must be morally wrong. 'Human passions,' wrote Byron, 'have probably disfigured the Divine doctrines here: but the whole thing is inscrutable.'

Countess Guiccioli tells us that, whatever may have been Byron's opinions with regard to certain points of religious doctrine, sects, and modes of worship, in essential matters his mind never seriously doubted. Matthews in his Cambridge days, and Shelley towards the close of life, moved him not at all. Between the commencement of Byron's career and its close, his mind passed successively through different phases before arriving at the last result. Leicester Stanhope, who was at Missolonghi with Byron, and who knew him well latterly, says:

'Most persons assume a virtuous character. Lord Byron's ambition, on the contrary, was to make the world imagine that he was a sort of Satan, though occasionally influenced by lofty sentiments to the performance of great actions. Fortunately for his fame, he possessed another quality, by which he stood completely unmasked. He was the most ingenuous of men, and his nature, in the main good, always triumphed over his acting.'

Parry, who stood at Byron's bedside when he died at Missolonghi, tells us that Byron died fearless and resigned. Could there be a better proof than these words, spoken by Byron a few hours before he passed away?—

'Eternity and space are before me; but on this subject, thank God, I am happy and at ease. The thought of living eternally, of again reviving, is a great pleasure. Christianity is the purest and most liberal religion in the world; but the numerous teachers who are eternally worrying mankind with their denunciations and their doctrines are the greatest enemies of religion. I have read, with more attention than half of them, the Book of Christianity, and I admire the liberal and truly charitable principles which Christ has laid down. There are questions connected with this subject which none but Almighty God can solve. Time and Space, who can conceive? None but God: on Him I rely.'

During the time that Byron lived at Metaxata, in Cephalonia, he seldom saw anyone in the evening except Dr. Stravolemo, one of the most estimable men in the island, who lived in that village. He had been first physician to Ali Pacha. He was an entertaining man, and afforded Byron much amusement by disputing with Dr. Bruno on medical questions.

'Lord Byron,' says Gamba, 'had generally three or four books lying before him, of which he read first one, then the other, and used to contrive to foment those friendly contentions, which, however, never exceeded the proper bounds. Lord Byron's favourite reading consisted of Greek history, of memoirs, and of romances. Never a day passed without his reading some pages of Scott's novels. His admiration of Walter Scott, both as a writer and as a companion, was unbounded. Speaking of him to his English friends, he used to say: " You should know Scott; you would like him so much; he is the most delightful man in a room; no affectation, no nonsense; and, what I like above all things, nothing of the author about him.'

One evening Colonel Napier, the British Resident, arrived at Byron's house at a gallop, and asked for Drs. Bruno and Stravolemo. He said that a party of peasants who were road-making had, in excavating a high bank, fallen under a landslide and were in danger of their lives. There were at least a dozen persons entombed. Colonel Napier happened to be passing at the moment when the catastrophe occurred; help was urgently needed. Byron sent Dr. Bruno to their assistance, while he and Gamba followed as soon as their horses could be saddled.

'When we came to the place,' says Gamba, 'we saw a lamentable spectacle indeed. A crowd of women and children were assembled round the ruins, and filled the air with their cries. Three or four of the peasants who had been extricated were carried before us half dead to the neighbouring cottages; and we found Mr. Hill, a friend of Lord Byron, and the superintendent of the works, in a state of the utmost consternation. Although an immense crowd continued flocking to the place, and it was thought that there were still some other workmen under the fallen mass of earth, no one would make any further efforts. The Greeks stood looking on without moving, as if totally indifferent to the catastrophe, and despaired of doing any good. This enraged Lord Byron; he seized a spade, and began to work as hard as he could; but it was not until the peasants had been threatened with the horsewhip that they followed his example. Some shoes and hats were found, but no human beings. Lord Byron never could be an idle spectator of any calamity. He was peculiarly alive to the distress of others, and was perhaps a little too easily imposed upon by every tale of woe, however clumsily contrived. The slightest appearance of injustice or cruelty, not only to his own species, but to animals, roused

GREEK SQUADRON AT MISSOLONGHI

his indignation and compelled his interference, and personal consequences never for one moment entered into his calculations.'

In the month of December the Greek squadron anchored off Missolonghi, where Prince Mavrocordato was received with enthusiasm. He was given full powers to organize Western Greece. The Turkish squadron was at this time shut up in the Gulf of Lepanto.

Byron sent to inform Mavrocordato that the loan which he had promised to the Government was ready, and that he was prepared either to go on board some vessel belonging to the Greek fleet, or to come to Missolonghi and confer with him. Mavrocordato and Colonel Leicester Stanhope wrote to beg Byron to come as soon as possible to Missolonghi, where his presence would be of great service to the cause. In the first place money to pay the fleet was much wanted; the sailors were on the verge of mutiny. Mavrocordato was in a state of anxiety, the Greek Admiral looked gloomy, and the sailors grumbled aloud.

'It is right and necessary to tell you,' wrote Stanhope, 'that a great deal is expected of you, both in the way of counsel and money. If the money does not arrive soon, I expect that the remaining five ships (the others are off) will soon make sail for Spezia. All are eager to see you. They calculate on your aiding them with resources for their expedition against Lepanto, and hope that you will take about 1,500 Suliotes into your pay for two or three months. Missolonghi is swarming with soldiers, and the Government has neither quarters nor provisions for them. I walked along the street this evening, and the people asked me after Lord Byron. Your further delay in coming will be attended with serious consequences.'

Byron at the same time received a letter from the Legislative Council, begging him to co-operate with

Mavrocordato in the organization of Western Greece. It was now December 26, 1823. Byron chartered a vessel for part of the baggage; a mistico, or light fast-sailing vessel, for himself and his suite; and a larger vessel for the horses, baggage, and munitions of war. The weather was unfavourable and squally, the vessels could not get under-weigh, and the whole party were detained for two days, during which time Byron lodged with his banker, Mr. Charles Hancock, and passed the greater part of the day in the society of the British authorities of the island.

We are able, through the courtesy of General Skey Muir, the son of Byron's friend at Cephalonia, to give extracts from a letter which Mr. Charles Hancock wrote to Dr Muir on June 1, 1824. During Byron's residence at Metaxata, Dr. Muir was the principal medical officer at Cephalonia, and it was in his house that some of the conversations on religion between Dr. Kennedy and Byron were held. Mr. Charles Hancock writes:

'The day before Byron left the island I happened to receive a copy of "Quentin Durward," which I put into his hands, knowing that he had not seen it, and that he wished to obtain the perusal of it. Lord Byron was very fond of Scott's novels — you will have observed they were always scattered about his rooms at Metaxata. He immediately shut himself in his room, and, in his eagerness to indulge in it, refused to dine with the officers of the 8th Regiment at their mess, or even to join us at table, but merely came out once or twice to say how much he was entertained, returning to his chamber with a plate of figs in his hand. He was exceedingly delighted with "Quentin Durward"—said it was excellent, especially the first volume and part of the second, but that it fell off towards the conclusion, like all the more recent of these novels: it might be, he added, owing to the extreme rapidity with which they were written—admirably conceived, and as well executed at the outset, but hastily finished off. . . .

'I will close these remarks with the mention of the period when we took our final leave of him. It was on the 29th December last that, after a slight repast, you and I accompanied him in a boat, gay and animated at finding himself embarked once more on the element he loved; and we put him on board the little vessel that conveyed him to Zante and Missolonghi. He mentioned the poetic feeling with which the sea always inspired him, rallied you on your grave and thoughtful looks, me on my bad steering; quizzed Dr. Bruno, but added in English (which the doctor did not understand), "He is the most sincere Italian I ever met with"; and laughed at Fletcher, who was getting well ducked by the spray that broke over the bows of the boat. The vessel was lying sheltered from the wind in the little creek that is surmounted by the Convent of San Constantino, but it was not till she had stood out and caught the breeze that we parted from him, to see him no more.'

The wind becoming fair, on December 28, at 3 p.m., the vessels got under way, Byron in the mistico, Pietro Gamba in the larger vessel. On the morning of the 29th they were at Zante, and spent the day in transacting business with Mr. Barff and shipping a considerable sum of money. Byron declined the Commandant's invitation to his residence, as his time was fully occupied with the business in hand. At about six in the evening they sailed for Missolonghi, without the slightest suspicion that the Turkish fleet was on the lookout for prizes. They knew that the Greek fleet was lying before Missolonghi, and they expected to sight a convoy sent out to meet them. Gamba says:

'We sailed together till after ten at night, with a fair wind and a clear sky; the air was fresh but not sharp. Our sailors sang patriotic songs, monotonous indeed, but to persons in our situation extremely touching. We were all, Lord Byron particularly, in excellent spirits. His vessel sailed the fastest. Then the waves parted us, and our voices could no longer reach each other. We made signals by firing pistols and carabines, and shouted, "To morrow we meet at Missolonghi—to morrow!"

'Thus, full of confidence and spirit, we sailed along. At midnight we were out of sight.'

At 6.30 a.m. the vessel which bore Gamba along gaily approached the rocks which border the shallows of Missolonghi. They saw a large vessel bearing down upon them, which they at first took for one of the Greek fleet; in appearance it seemed superior to a Turkish man-of-war. But as Gamba's vessel hoisted the Ionian flag, to their dismay the stranger hoisted the Ottoman ensign. The Turkish commander ordered Gamba's captain to come on board, and the poor fellow gave himself up for lost. They could think of no excuse which would have any weight with their captors, and were in some trepidation as to Byron's fate, he having money, arms, and some Greeks, with him.

Writing from Missolonghi on January 5, 1824, Colonel Stanhope says:

'Count Gamba has just arrived here, with all the articles belonging to the Committee. He was taken early in the morning by a Turkish ship. The captain thereof ordered the master on board. The moment he came on deck, the captain drew his dazzling sabre and placed himself in an attitude as if to cut his head off, and at the same time asked him where he was bound. The frightened Greek said, to Missolonghi. They gazed at each other, and all at once the Turk recognized in his prisoner one who, on a former occasion, had saved his life. They embraced. Next came Count Gamba's turn. He declared—swore that he was bound to Calamata, and that the master had

ARRIVAL AT MISSOLONGHI

told a lie through fear, and that his bill of lading would bear him out. They were both taken to the castle of the Morea, were well treated, and after three days released.'

On January 5, 1824, Byron arrived at Missolonghi. He was received with military honours and popular applause.

' He landed,' says Gamba, ' in a Speziot boat, dressed in a red uniform. He was in excellent health, and appeared moved by the scene. I met him as he disembarked, and in a few minutes we entered the house prepared for him—the same in which Colonel Stanhope resided. The Colonel and Prince Mavrocordato, with a long suite of Greek and European officers, received him at the door. I cannot describe the emotions which such a scene excited. Crowds of soldiery and citizens of every rank, sex, and age, were assembled to testify their delight. Hope and content were pictured on every countenance.'

Byron seems to have escaped from perils quite as great, though differing in nature, from those through which Gamba had passed. His vessel passed close to the Turkish frigate, but under favour of the night, and by preserving complete silence, the master ran her close under the rocks of the Scrofes, whither the Turk dared not follow her. Byron saw Gamba's vessel taken and conducted to Patras. Byron, thinking it wiser not to make straight for Missolonghi steered for Petala; but finding that port open and unsafe, his vessel was taken to Dragomestri, a small town on the coast of Acarnania. On his arrival there, Byron was visited by the Primates and officers of the place, who offered him their good offices. From this place Byron sent messengers both to Zante and Missolonghi. On receipt of Byron's letter, Mavrocordato sent five gun-boats and a brig-of-war to escort him to Missolonghi.

On January 4, the flotilla was caught in a violent storm, which threw Byron's vessel in dangerous proximity to the rocks on that inhospitable coast. The sailors at first behaved remarkably well, and got the vessel off the rocks; but a second squall burst upon them with great violence, and drove the Mistico into dangerous waters, causing the sailors to lose all hope of saving her. They abandoned the vessel to her fate, and thought only of their own safety. But Byron persuaded them to remain; and by his firmness, and no small share of nautical skill, not only got the crew out of danger, but also saved the vessel, several lives, and 25,000 dollars, the greater part of which was in hard cash. Byron does not seem to have pulled off his clothes since leaving Cephalonia.

It was an adventurous voyage—appropriately so—for it was his last journey in this world.

CHAPTER VIII

AT the beginning of the war, Missolonghi consisted of about 800 scattered houses, built close to the seaside on a muddy and most unhealthy site, scarcely above the level of the waters, 'which a few centuries ago must have covered the spot, as may be judged from the nature of the soil, consisting of decomposed seaweed and dried mud.' The population was exceedingly poor, and amounted to nearly 3,000 souls. The town had a most uninviting appearance; the streets were narrow and badly paved. But, says Millingen, what most revolted a stranger was the practice of having the buildings so constructed that the most loathsome substances were emptied into the streets. The inhabitants were so accustomed to this abominable state of things that they ridiculed the complaints of strangers, and even swore at people who ventured to suggest reform. Missolonghi must indeed have been a wretched place even for a strong man in his full powers and vitality—for Byron it was nothing short of Death! Trelawny tells us that this place is situated on the verge of a dismal swamp. The marvel to him was that Byron, who was always liable to fevers, should have consented to live three months on this mud-bank, shut in by a circle of stagnant pools 'which might be called the belt of death.' When Trelawny arrived in the early spring, he found most of the strangers suffering from gastric fevers. He waded through the streets, 'between wind and water,' to the house where Byron had lived—a detached building on the margin of the shallow, slimy sea-waters.

Such, then, was the residence which was destined to be the last home of the author of 'Childe Harold!'

Byron had scarcely reached the modest apartment which had been assigned to him, when he was greeted by the tumultuous visits of the Primates and chiefs. All the chieftains of Western Greece—that is to say, the mountainous districts occupied by the Greeks—were now collected at Missolonghi in a general assembly, together with many of the Primates of the same districts. Mavrocordato, at that time Governor-General of the province, was President of the Assembly, with a bodyguard of 5,000 armed men. The first object of this assembly, says Gamba, was to organize the military forces, the assignment of the soldiers' pay, and the establishment of the national constitution and some regular form of government for Western Greece. The chieftains were not all of them well disposed towards Mavrocordato; the soldiers were badly paid—in fact, hardly paid at all; and so great was the fear of disturbances, quarrels, and even of a civil war, that without the influence of Prince Mavrocordato, and the presence of Byron with his money, there could have been no harmony.

After the departure of the Turks, who had blockaded Missolonghi, there was a general feeling of security, and no one expected them to return before the spring. The Peloponnesus, with exception of the castles of

AN ACT OF GRACE

the Morea and of Patras, of Modon and of Covon, was in the hands of the Greeks. The northern shore of the Gulf of Lepanto, with the exception of the two castles, were also in Greek hands. They swayed Bœotia and Attica, together with the whole isthmus of Corinth.

Such was the state of affairs when Byron arrived on that dismal swamp. The position in which he found himself required much skill and tact; for the dissension among the various leaders in other parts of Greece was in its bitterest phase, and public opinion everywhere was dead against the executive body. It would have been fatal to the prestige of Byron if, in a moment of impetuosity, he had cast in his lot with some particular faction. It was his fixed intention, as it was clearly his best policy, to reconcile differences, and to bring the contending factions closer together. His influence amongst all parties was daily increasing, and everyone believed that Byron would eventually be able to bring discordant voices into harmony, and pave the way for the formation of a strong, patriotic Government. He faced the situation bravely, and closed his ears to the unworthy squabbles of ambitious cliques. He made arrangements, with the best assistance at hand, to turn the expected loan from England to the best account, in order to insure the freedom and independence of Greece.

The first day of his arrival at Missolonghi was signalized by an act of grace. A Turk, who had fallen into the hands of some Greek sailors, was released by Byron's orders, and, having been clothed and fed at his own expense, was given quarters at Byron's house until an opportunity occurred of sending him in freedom to Patras. About a fortnight later, hearing that four Turkish prisoners were at Missolonghi in a state of destitution, Byron caused them to be set at liberty, and sent them to Usouff Pacha at Patras, with a letter which, though it has been often printed, deserves a place in this narrative:

'HIGHNESS!
'A vessel, in which a friend and some domestics of mine were embarked, was detained a few days ago, and released by order of your Highness. I have now to thank you, not for liberating the vessel, which as carrying a neutral flag, and being under British protection, no one had a right to detain, but for having treated my friends with so much kindness while they were in your hands.

'In the hope that it may not be altogether displeasing to your Highness, I have requested the Governor of this place to release four Turkish prisoners, and he has humanely consented to do so. I lose no time, therefore, in sending them back, in order to make as early a return as I could, for your courtesy on the late occasion. These prisoners are liberated without any conditions; but should the circumstance find a place in your recollection, I venture to beg that your Highness will treat such Greeks as may henceforth fall into your hands, with humanity; more especially as the horrors of war are sufficiently great in themselves, without being aggravated by wanton cruelties on either side.

'NOEL BYRON.
'MISSOLONGHI,
'*January* 23, 1824.'

This letter was the keynote of Byron's policy during the remainder of his life. The horrors of war were sufficient in themselves without that unnecessary cruelty so often exhibited by Eastern nations in their treatment of prisoners of war.

The following account of an incident connected with Byron's clemency to a prisoner pictures the state of things at Missolonghi.

'This evening,' says Gamba, 'whilst Mavrocordato was with Lord Byron, two sailors belonging to the privateer which had taken the Turk came into the room, demanding in an insolent tone that their prisoner should be delivered up to them. Lord Byron refused; their importunity became more violent, and they refused to leave the room without their Turk (such was their expression) on which Lord Byron, presenting a pistol at the intruders, threatened to proceed to extremities unless they instantly retired. The sailors withdrew, but Byron complained to Mavrocordato of his want of authority, and said to him: "If your Government cannot protect me in my own house, I will find means to protect myself." From that time Lord Byron retained a Suliote guard in his house.'

During the winter preparations were being made for an expedition against Lepanto, a fortress which, if captured by the Greeks, would facilitate the siege of Patras. Its fortifications were constructed on the slope of a hill, forming a triangle, the base of which was close to the sea. Its walls were of Venetian construction, but without ditches. As portions of its walls were commanded by a neighbouring hill, its siege would have proved a very arduous undertaking even with regular troops; but with raw Greek levies its reduction, except by famine, would have been almost impossible. On January 14, 1824, Colonel Stanhope writes to Mr. Bowring in the following terms: 'Lord Byron has taken 500 Suliotes into pay. He burns with military ardour and chivalry, and will proceed with the expedition to Lepanto.' Circumstances were, however, against this expedition from the very beginning. Great hopes had been entertained by Lord Byron and by Colonel Stanhope that the Suliotes would conform to discipline, and that Mr. Parry, who had been sent out by the Greek Committee with stores and ammunition, would on his arrival organize the artillery, and manufacture Congreve rockets—a projectile of which the Turks were said to be in great awe.

Parry arrived at Missolonghi early in February, on board the brig *Anna*, which had been chartered by the London Greek Committee. He brought cannons, ammunition, printing-presses, medicines, and all the apparatus necessary for the establishment of a military laboratory. Several English mechanics came with him, and some English, German, and Swedish gentlemen, who wished to serve the Greek cause.

Mr. (or, as he was afterwards called) Major, Parry was a peculiar person in every way. He had at one time served as a shipwright, then as Firemaster in the King's service, and won favour with Byron through his buffoonery and plain speaking—two very useful qualifications in environments of stress and duplicity. When Byron appointed him Major in the Artillery Brigade, the best officers in the brigade tendered their resignations, stating that, while they would be proud to serve under Lord Byron, neither their honour nor the interests of the service would allow them to serve under a man who had no practical experience of military evolutions. The German officers also, who had previously served in the Prussian army, appealed against Parry's appointment, and offered proofs of his ignorance of artillery. But Byron would not listen to complaints, which he attributed partly to jealousy and partly to German notions of etiquette, which seemed to him to be wholly out of place in a country where merit rather than former titles should regulate such appointments.

In supporting Parry against these officers, Byron was in a measure influenced by the recommendations of both the Greek Committee who sent him out, and of Colonel Leicester Stanhope, who at that time considered Parry to be an exceedingly capable officer. Perhaps, if Parry had not appeared on parade in an apron, brandishing a hammer, and if he had not asserted himself so extravagantly, he might possibly have passed muster. But tact and modesty were not in Parry's line; and having boasted to the London Committee that he was acquainted with almost every branch of military mechanics, he bullied its members into a belief that his pretentions were well founded. As a matter of fact, Parry proved to be unsuited for high command, although it must be admitted that he worked indefatigably. He made plans for the erection of a laboratory, and presided over the works. He paved the yard of the Seraglio, repaired the batteries, instructed the troops in musketry and gunnery; he gave lessons with the broadsword, inspected the fortifications, and directed the operations of Cocchini, the chief engineer. He repaired gun-carriages, and put his hand to anything wanted, so that it appeared as if really nothing could be done without him. In one thing only did Parry seem to fall short of general expectation. He had boasted that he knew the composition of 'Congreve rockets.' With this mighty instrument of mischief he prophesied that the Greeks would be able to paralyze all the efforts of their enemy, both by land and sea. The Turkish cavalry, the only arm against which the Greeks were impotent, would be rendered useless, and the Turkish vessels, by the same means, would be easily destroyed.

Unfortunately, the manufacture of these rockets was impossible without the assistance of the English mechanics whom he had brought with him, and these men were unable to work without materials, which were not obtainable. Thus the principal part of Parry's 'stock-in-trade'—his rockets, incendiary kites, and improved Grecian fires—were not forthcoming.

For a long time the roads in the neighbourhood of Missolonghi were so broken up by incessant rain that Byron could not ride or take any outdoor exercise. This affected his health. His only means of getting a little fresh air was by paddling through the murky waters in a sort of canoe. During these expeditions, says Gamba, who always accompanied him, he spoke often of his anxiety to begin the campaign. He had not much hope of success, but felt that something must be done during these tedious months, if only to employ the troops and keep them from creating disturbances in the town.

'I am not come here in search of adventures,' said Byron, 'but to assist the regeneration of a nation, whose very debasement makes it more honourable to become their friend. Regular troops are certainly necessary, but not in great numbers: regular troops alone would not succeed in a country like Greece; and irregular troops alone are only just better than nothing. Only let the loan be raised; and in the meantime let us try to form a strong national Government, ready to apply our pecuniary resources, when they arrive, to the organization of troops, the establishment of internal civilization, and the preparations for acting defensively now, and on the offensive next winter. Nothing is so insupportable to me as all these minute details and these repeated delays. But patience is indispensable, and that I find the most difficult of all attainments.'

It was Byron's custom to spend his evenings in Colonel Stanhope's room, with his English comrades. Sometimes the Germans would join the party, play on their flutes, and sing their national airs to the accompaniment of a guitar. Byron was fond of music in general, and was especially partial to German music, particularly to their national songs.

Millingen tells us that in the evening all the English who had not, with Colonel Stanhope, turned Odysseans assembled at Byron's house, and enjoyed the charm of his conversation till late at night. Byron's character, says Millingen,

'differed so much from what I had been induced to imagine from the relations of travellers, that either their reports must have been inaccurate, or his character must have totally changed after his departure from Genoa. It would be difficult, indeed impossible, to convey an idea of the pleasure his conversation afforded. Among his works, that which may perhaps be more particularly regarded as exhibiting the mirror of his conversation, and the spirit which animated it, is "Don Juan." He was indeed too open, and too indiscreet in respect to the reminiscences of his early days. Sometimes, when his vein of humour flowed more copiously than usual, he would play tricks on individuals. Fletcher's boundless credulity afforded him an ever-ready fund of amusement, and he one evening planned a farce, which was as well executed and as laughable as any ever exhibited on the stage. Having observed how nervous Parry had been, a few days before, during an earthquake, he felt desirous of renewing the ludicrous sight which the fat, horror-struck figure of the Major had exhibited on that occasion. He placed, therefore, fifty of his Suliotes in the room above that where Parry slept, and towards midnight ordered them to shake the house, so as to imitate that phenomenon. He himself at the same time banged the doors, and rushed downstairs delighted to see the almost distracted Major imploring tremblingly the mercy of heaven.'

Lord Byron was very much taken with Parry, whose drolleries relieved the tedium and constant vexations incidental to the situation at Missolonghi.

The Major appears to have been an excellent mimic, and possessed a fund of quaint expressions that made up for the deficiency of real wit. Millingen says that he could tell, in his coarse language, a good story, and could play Falstaff's, or the part of a clown very naturally. He ranted Richard III.'s or Hamlet's soliloquies in a mock-tragic manner like a player at Bartholomew Fair, which made everyone laugh, and beguiled the length of many a rainy evening.

On January 21, 1824, Missolonghi was blockaded by the Turkish fleet. There were neither guns nor even sailors fit to man the gunboats; the only chance was to make a night attack upon the Turks in boats manned by the European volunteers then residing at Missolonghi. Byron took the matter in hand, and insisted on joining personally in the expedition. He was so determined on this project that Mavrocordato and others, realizing the folly of exposing so valuable a life on so desperate an enterprise, dissuaded Byron from risking it in a business for which there were already sufficient volunteers. As things turned out, it did not much matter, for the Turkish fleet suddenly abandoned the blockade and returned to the gulf.

On January 22, while Colonel Stanhope and some friends were assembled, Byron came from his bedroom and said, with a smile: 'You were complaining the other day that I never write any poetry now: this is my birthday, and I have just finished something, which, I think, is better than what I usually write.' He then produced those affecting verses on his own birthday which were afterwards found written in his journal, with the following introduction: 'January 22: on this day I complete my thirty-sixth year.'

A PRESENTIMENT OF DEATH 97

'We perceived from these lines,' says Gamba, 'as well as from his daily conversations, that his ambition and his hope were irrevocably fixed upon the glorious objects of his expedition to Greece, and that he had made up his mind to "return victorious, or return no more." Indeed, he often said to me, "Others may do as they please—they may go—but I stay here, *that is certain.*"

This resolution was accompanied with the natural presentiment that he should never leave Greece alive. He one day asked his faithful servant Tita whether he thought of returning to Italy. 'Yes,' said Tita; 'if your lordship goes, I go.' Lord Byron smiled, and said: 'No, Tita, I shall never go back from Greece; either the Turks, or the Greeks, or the climate, will prevent that.'

Parry tells us that Byron's mind on this point was irrevocably fixed.

'My future intentions,' he said, 'may be explained in a few words. I will remain here in Greece till she is secure against the Turks, or till she has fallen under her power. All my income shall be spent in her service; but, unless driven by some great necessity, I will not touch a farthing of the sum intended for my sister's children. Whatever I can accomplish with my income, and my personal exertions, shall be cheerfully done. When Greece is secure against external enemies, I will leave the Greeks to settle their government as they like. One service more, and an eminent service it will be, I think I may perform for them. You shall have a schooner built for me, or I will buy a vessel; the Greeks shall invest me with the character of their Ambassador or agent; I will go to the United States, and procure that free and enlightened Government, to set the example of recognizing the Federation of Greece, as an independent State. This done, England must follow the example, and then the fate of Greece will be permanently fixed, and she will enter into all her rights, as a member of the great commonwealth of Christian Europe. . . .

The cause of Greece naturally excites our sympathy. Her people are Christians contending against Turks, and slaves struggling to be free. There never was a cause which had such strong claims on the sympathy of the people of Europe, and particularly of the people of England.'*

The following extract from a letter written by Mr. George Finlay in June, 1824, seems worthy of production in this place:

'I arrived at Missolonghi at the latter end of February. During my stay there, in the forenoon I rode out with Lord Byron; and generally Mr. Fowke and myself spent the evenings in his room.

'In our rides, the state of Greece was the usual subject of our conversation; and at times he expressed a strong wish to revisit Athens. I mentioned the great cheapness of property in Attica, and the possibility of my purchasing some of the villas near the city. He said that, if I could find any eligible property, he would have no objections to purchase likewise, as he wished to have some real property in Greece; and he authorized me to treat for him. I always urged him to make Corinth his headquarters. Sometimes he appeared inclined to do so, and remarked, that it would be a strange coincidence if, after writing an unsuccessful defence of Corinth, he should himself make a successful one. An event so fortunate, I said, would leave him no more to ask from fortune, and reminded him how very much of fame depends on mere accident. Cæsar's conquests and his works would not have raised his fame so high, but for the manner of his death.

'In the evenings Lord Byron was generally extremely communicative, and talked much of his youthful scenes at Cambridge, Brighton, and London; spoke very often of his friends, Mr. Hobhouse and Mr. Scrope B. Davies—told many anecdotes of himself which are well known, and many which were

* Parry, p. 170.

amusing from his narration, but which would lose their interest from another; but what astonished me the most was the ease with which he spoke of all those reports which were spread by his enemies—he gave his denials and explanations with the frankness of an unconcerned person.

'I often spoke to him about Newstead Abbey, which I had visited in 1821, a few months before leaving England. On informing him of the repairs and improvements which were then going on, he said, if he had been rich enough, he should have liked to have kept it as the old abbey; but he enjoyed the excellent bargain he had made at the sale. A solicitor sent him a very long bill, and, on his grumbling at the amount, he said he was silenced by a letter, reminding him that he had received £20,000 forfeit-money from the first purchaser. I mentioned the picture of his bear in the cottage near the lodge—the Newfoundland dog and the verses on its tomb. He said, Newfoundland dogs had twice saved his life, and that he could not live without one.

'He spoke frequently of the time he lived at Aberdeen. Their house was near the college. He described the place, but I have forgotten it. He said his mother's "lassack" used to put him to bed at a very early hour, and then go to converse with her lover; he had heard the house was haunted, and sometimes used to get out of bed and run along the lobby in his shirt, till he saw a light, and there remain standing till he was so cold he was forced to go to bed again. One night the servant returning, he grew frightened and ran towards his room; the maid saw him, and fled more frightened than he; she declared she had seen a ghost. Lord Byron said, he was so frightened at the maid, he kept the secret till she was turned away; and, he added, he never since kept a secret half so long. The first passion he ever felt was for a young lady who was on a visit to his mother while they lived in Scotland; he was at the time about six years old, and the young lady about nine, yet he was almost ill on her leaving his mother's house to return home. He told me, if I should ever meet the lady (giving me her address), to ask her if she remembers him. On some conversation about the

"English Bards and Scotch Reviewers," he gave as a reason for his attacking many of the persons included, that he was informed, some time before the publication of the review, that the next number was to contain an article on his poems which had been read at Holland House. "Judge of my fever; was it not a pleasant situation for a young author?"

'In conversation he used to deliver very different opinions on many authors from those contained in his works; in the one case he might be guided more by his judgment, and in the other submit entirely to his own particular taste. I have quoted his writings in opposition to his words, and he replied, "Never mind what I print; that is not what I think." He certainly did not consider much of the poetry of the present day as "possessing buoyancy enough to float down the stream of time." I remarked, he ought really to alter the passage in the preface of "Marino Faliero," on living dramatic talent; he exclaimed, laughing, "Do you mean me to erase the name of *moral me?*" In this manner he constantly distinguished Milman, alluding to some nonsense in the *Quarterly Review*. He was extremely amused with *Blackwood's Magazine*, and read it whenever he could get a number; he has frequently repeated to me passages of Ensign O'Doherty's poetry, which I had not read, and expressed great astonishment at the ability displayed by the author.

'On a gentleman present once asking his opinion of the works of a female author of some note, he said, "A bad imitation of me—all pause and start."

'On my borrowing Mitford's "History of Greece" from him, and saying I had read it once, and intended commencing it again in Greece, he said, "I hate the book; it makes you too well acquainted with the ancient Greeks, and robs antiquity of all its charms. History in his hands, has no poetry."

'I was in the habit of praising Sir William Gell's Itineraries to Lord B., and he, on the other hand, took every opportunity of attacking his Argolis, though his attacks were chiefly directed against the drawings, and particularly the view of the bay. He told me he was the author of the article on Sir W. Gell's Argolis in the *Monthly Review*, and said he had written two other articles in this work; but I have forgotten them.*

'Whenever the drama was mentioned, he defended the unities most eagerly, and usually attacked Shakspeare. A gentleman present, on hearing his anti-Shakspearean opinions, rushed out of the room, and afterwards entered his protest most anxiously against such doctrines. Lord B. was quite delighted with this, and redoubled the severity of his criticism. I had heard that Shelley once said to Lord B. in his extraordinary way, "B., you are a most wonderful man." "How?" "You are envious of Shakspeare." I, therefore, never expressed the smallest astonishment at hearing Shakspeare abused; but remarked, it was curious that Lord B. was so strangely conversant in an author of such inferior merit, and that he should so continually have the most melodious lines of Shakspeare in his mouth as examples of blank verse. He said once, when we were alone, "I like to astonish Englishmen: they come abroad full of Shakspeare, and contempt for the dramatic literature of other nations; they think it blasphemy to find a fault in his writings, which are full of them. People talk of the tendency of my writings, and yet read the sonnets to Master Hughes." Lord B. certainly did not admire the French tragedians enthusiastically. I said to him, "There is a subject for the Drama which, I believe, has never been touched, and which, I think, affords the greatest possible scope for the representation of all that is sublime in human character—but then it would require an abandonment of the unities—the attack of Maurice of Saxony on Charles V., which saved the Protestant religion; it is a subject of more than national interest." He said it was certainly a fine subject; but he held that the drama could not exist without a strict adherence to the unities; and besides, he knew well he had failed in his dramatic attempts, and that he intended to make no more. He said he thought "Sardaṇapalus" his best tragedy.

'The memory of Lord B. was very extraordinary; it was not the mere mechanical memory which can

* Byron wrote a review of Wordsworth's 'Poems' in *Monthly Literary Recreations* for July, 1807, and a review of Gell's 'Geography of Ithaca' in the *Monthly Review* for August, 1811.

repeat the advertisements of a newspaper and such nonsense; but of all the innumerable novels which he had read, he seemed to recollect perfectly the story and every scene of merit.

'Once I had a bet with Mr. Fowke that Maurice of Orange was not the grandson of Maurice of Saxony, as it ran in my head that Maurice was a son of Count Horn's sister. On applying for a decision of our bet to Lord B., he immediately told me I was wrong, that William of Orange was thrice married, and that he had Maurice by a daughter of Maurice of Saxony: he repeated the names of all the children. I said, "This is the most extraordinary instance of your memory I ever heard." He replied, "It's not very extraordinary —I read it all a few days ago in Watson's "Philip II.," and you will find it in a note at the bottom of the last page but one" (I think he said) "of the second volume." He went to his bedroom and brought the book, in which we found the note he had repeated. It seemed to me wonderful enough that such a man could recollect the names of William of Orange's children and their families even for ten minutes.

'Once, on receiving some newspapers, in reading the advertisements of new publications aloud, I read the name of Sir Aubrey de Vere Hunt; Lord B. instantly said, "Sir Aubrey was at Harrow, I remember, but he was younger than me. He was an excellent swimmer, and once saved a boy's life; nobody would venture in, and the boy was nearly drowned, when Sir Aubrey was called. The boy's name was M'Kinnon, and he went afterwards to India." I think B. said he died there.

'"It is strange," I replied; "I heard this very circumstance from Sir Aubrey de Vere Hunt, who inquired if I knew the boy, who must now be a man, but said, I think, that his name was Mackenzie." "Depend upon it, I am right," said Byron.

'Lord B. said he had kept a very exact journal of every circumstance of his life, and many of his thoughts while young, that he had let Mr. Hobhouse see it in Albania, and that he at last persuaded him to burn it. He said Hobhouse had robbed the world of a treat. He used to say that many of his acquaintances, particularly his female ones, while he was in London, did not like Mr. Hobhouse, "for they thought he kept me within bounds."

'When he was asked for a motto for the *Greek Telegraph*, by Gamba, during the time he felt averse to the publication of a European newspaper in Greece, he gave, "To the Greeks foolishness"—in allusion to the publication in languages which the natives generally do not understand.

'On a discussion in his presence concerning the resemblance of character between the ancient and modern Greeks, he said: "At least we have St. Paul's authority that they had their present character in his time; for he says there is no difference between the Jew and the Greek."

'A few days before I left Missolonghi, riding out together, he told me that he had received a letter from his sister, in which she mentioned that one of the family had displayed some poetical talent, but that she would not tell him who, as she hoped she should hear no more of it. I said "That is a strange wish from the sister of such a poet." He replied that he believed the poetical talent was always a source of pain, and that he certainly would have been happier had he never written a line.

'Those only who were personally acquainted with him can be aware of the influence which every passing event had over his mind, or know the innumerable modifications under which his character was daily presenting itself; even his writings took a shade of colouring from those around him. His passions and feelings were so lively that each occurrence made a strong impression, and his conduct became so entirely governed by impulse that he immediately and vehemently declared his sentiments. It is not wonderful, therefore, that instances of his inconsistency should be found; though in the most important actions of his life he has acted with no common consistency, and his death attests his sincerity. To attempt by scattered facts to illustrate his character is really useless. A hundred could be immediately told to prove him a miser; as many to prove him the most generous of men; an equal number, perhaps, to show he was nervously alive to the distresses of others, or heartlessly unfeeling; at times that he indulged in every desire; at others, that he pursued the most determined system of self-denial; that he ridiculed his friends, or defended them with the greatest anxiety. At one time he was all enthusiasm; at another perfect indifference on the very same subject. All this would be true, and yet our inference most probably incorrect. Such hearts as Lord B.'s must become old at an early age, from the continual excitement to which they are exposed, and those only can judge fairly of him, even from his personal acquaintance, who knew him from his youth, when his feelings were warmer than they could be latterly. From some of those who have seen the whole course of his wonderful existence, we may, indeed, expect information; and it is information, not scandal, that will be sought for.'

CHAPTER IX

MILLINGEN tells us that Byron, even before his arrival in Greece, was a favourite among the people and soldiers. Popular imagination had been kindled by reports of his genius, his wealth, and his rank. Everything that a man could perform was expected of him; and many a hardship and grievance was borne patiently, in hope that on Byron's arrival everything would be set right. The people were not disappointed; his conduct towards them after he had landed soon made him a popular idol. It was perceived that Byron was not a theoretical, but a practical, friend to Greece; and his repeated acts of kindness and charity in relieving the poor and distressed, the heavy expenses he daily incurred for the furtherance of every plan, and every institution which he deemed worthy of support, showed the people of Missolonghi that Byron was not less alive to their private than he was to their public interests. But there were some people, of course, who felt a slight attack of that pernicious malady known euphuistically as 'the green-eyed monster.' Mavrocordato, the Governor-General of Western Greece, was, according to Millingen, slightly afflicted with envy. He had imagined, when using every means during Byron's stay at Cephalonia to induce him to come to Missolonghi, that he was preparing for himself a powerful instrument to execute his own designs, and that, by placing Byron in a prominent position which would require far more knowledge of the state of things than Byron could possibly possess, he would helplessly drift, and eventually fall entirely under his own guidance. But in this Mavrocordato was entirely mistaken, for Byron had long made up his mind as to the course which he meant to steer, and by sheer honesty of purpose and by the glamour of his fame his authority daily increased, while that of Mavrocordato fell in proportion, until his high-sounding title was little better than an empty phrase. The people of Missolonghi were fascinated by the personality of a man who had practically thrown his whole fortune at their feet. They openly spoke of the advantages that would be derived by Western Greece were Byron to be appointed its Governor-General.

'Ambitious and suspicious by nature,' says Millingen, 'Mavrocordato felt his authority aimed at. He began by seconding his supposed rival's measures in a lukewarm manner, whilst he endeavoured in secret to thwart them. He was looked upon as the cause of the rupture between the Suliotes and Lord Byron, fearing that the latter might, with such soldiers, become too powerful.'

Byron perceived the change in Mavrocordato's conduct, and from that moment lost much of the confidence which he had at first felt in him.

'The plain, undisguised manner in which Byron expressed himself on this subject, and the haughty manner in which he received Mavrocordato, tended to confirm the latter's opinion that Byron sought to supplant him.'

Mavrocordato thus laboured under a delusion. Far from having ambitious views, Byron would, in Millingen's opinion, have refused, if the offer had been made to him, ever to take a part in civil administration. He knew too well how little his impetuous character fitted him for the tedious and intricate details of Greek affairs. 'He had come to Greece to assist her sacred cause with his wealth, his talents, his courage; and the only reward he sought was a soldier's grave.'

Had Lord Byron lived, says Millingen, the misunderstanding between these two distinguished individuals would have been merely temporary. Their principles and love of order were the same, as also the ends they proposed to attain. However different were the roads upon which they marched, they would have been sure to meet at last.

'Lord Byron,' wrote Colonel Stanhope, 'possesses all the means of playing a great part in the glorious revolution of Greece. He has talent; he professes liberal principles; he has money; and is inspired with fervent and chivalrous feelings.'

Colonel Leicester Stanhope was himself deserving of the praise which he thus bestows on Byron, the item 'money' being equally discarded. Colonel Stanhope was a chivalrous gentleman, and devoted himself heart and soul to the regeneration of Greece. But his views were not those of Byron. He was all for printing-presses, freedom of the press, and schools. Byron was all for fighting and organization in a military sense. Their aims were the same, but their methods entirely different. Byron recognized the virtues of Stanhope, and never seriously opposed any of his schemes. Stanhope was absolutely boiling over with enthusiasm regarding the advantages of publishing a newspaper. His paramount policy, as he states himself in a letter to Mr. Bowring, was 'to strive to offend no one, but, on the contrary, to make all friendly to the press.' He contended for the absolute liberty of the press, and for publicity in every shape! It would be difficult to match such a contention applied to such a period and such a people. In forwarding the third number of the *Greek Chronicle* to Mr. Bowring, Stanhope writes: 'The last article in the *Chronicle* is on Mr. Bentham. Its object is to dispose the people to read and contemplate his works. Conviction follows.'

Byron had a peculiar antipathy to Mr. Bentham and all his works, but he provided money to support the *Chronicle*. On January 24 Colonel Stanhope wrote to Mr. Bowring a letter which explains the position exactly; and a very peculiar position it was. After asking Byron whether he will subscribe £50 for the support of the *Greek Chronicle*, which Byron cheerfully agreed to do, Colonel Stanhope proceeds to 'heckle' him. The conversation is well worth transcribing:

'Stanhope (*loquitur*): "Your lordship stated yesterday evening that you had said to Prince Mavrocordato that, 'were you in his place (as Governor-General of Western Greece), you would have placed the press under a censor,' and that he replied, 'No; the liberty of the press is guaranteed by the Constitution.' Now, I wish to know whether your lordship was serious when you made the observation, or whether you only said so to provoke me? If your lordship was serious, I shall consider it my duty to communicate this affair to the Committee in England, in order to show them how difficult a task I have to fulfil in promoting the liberties of Greece, if your lordship is to throw the weight of your vast talents into the opposite scale on a question of such vital importance."

'Byron, in reply, said that he was an ardent friend of

publicity and the press; but he feared that it was not applicable to this society in its present combustible state. Stanhope replied that he thought it applicable to all countries, and essential in Greece, in order to put an end to the state of anarchy which then prevailed. Byron said that he was afraid of libels and licentiousness. Stanhope maintained that the object of a free press was to check public licentiousness and to expose libellers to odium.'

In a subsequent letter to Mr. Bowring, Colonel Stanhope repeats a conversation with Byron on the subject of Mr. Bentham. One does not know whether to laugh or cry; there is both humour and pathos in the incident.

'His lordship,' writes Stanhope, 'began, according to custom, to attack Mr. Bentham. I said that it was highly illiberal to make personal attacks on Mr. Bentham before a friend who held him in high estimation. He said that he only attacked his public principles, which were mere theories, but dangerous—injurious to Spain and calculated to do great mischief in Greece. I did not object to his lordship's attacking Mr. Bentham's principles; what I objected to were his personalities. His lordship never reasoned on any of Mr. Bentham's writings, but merely made sport of them. I therefore asked him what it was that he objected to. Lord Byron mentioned his "Panopticon" as visionary. I said that experience in Pennsylvania, at Milbank, etc., had proved it otherwise. I said that Bentham had a truly British heart; but that Lord Byron, after professing liberal principles from his boyhood, had, when called upon to act, proved himself a Turk.

'Lord Byron asked what proofs I had of this.

'I replied : " Your conduct in endeavouring to crush the press, by declaiming against it to Mavrocordato, and your general abuse of Liberal principles." Lord Byron said that if he had held up his finger he could have crushed the press. I replied: " With all this power, which, by the way, you never possessed, you went to the Prince and poisoned his ear."

'Lord Byron declaimed against the Liberals whom he knew.

'"But what Liberals?" I asked. Did he borrow his notions of free men from the Italians? Lord Byron said: "No; from the Hunts, Cartwrights, etc." "And still," said I, "you presented Cartwright's Reform Bill, and aided Hunt by praising his poetry and giving him the sale of your works."

'Lord Byron exclaimed: "You are worse than Wilson,* and should quit the army." I replied that I was a mere soldier, but never would abandon my principles. Our principles,' continues Stanhope, 'are diametrically opposite. If Lord Byron acts up to his professions, he will be the greatest—if not, the meanest —of mankind. He said he hoped his character did not depend on my assertions. "No," said I, "your genius has immortalized you. The worst could not deprive you of fame."

'Lord Byron replied: "Well, you shall see; judge me by my acts."

'When he wished me good-night, I took up the light

---

* General Sir Robert Wilson (1777-1849), commonly known as 'Jaffa Wilson,' entered Parliament in 1818. Having held Napoleon up to horror and execration for his cruelty at Jaffa, Wilson subsequently became one of his strongest eulogists. Being by nature a demagogue, he posed as a champion in the cause of freedom and civil government; he accused England of injustice and tyranny towards other nations, and prophesied her speedy fall. He warmly espoused the cause of Queen Caroline, and was present at the riot in Hyde Park on the occasion of her funeral, when there was a collision between the Horse Guards and the mob. For his conduct on that occasion, despite a long record of gallant service in the field, Wilson was dismissed the Army in 1821, but was reinstated on the accession of William IV. He appears to have been both foolish and vain, and fond of creating effect. He was constantly brooding over services which he conceived to have been overlooked, and merits which he fancied were neglected. He attached himself to the ultra-radicals, and puffed himself into notoriety by swimming against the stream. A writer in the *Quarterly Review* (Vol. xix., July, 1818) says: 'The obliquity of his (Wilson's) perceptions make his talents worse than useless as a politician, and form, even in his own profession, a serious drawback to energy however great, and to bravery however distinguished.'

to conduct him to the passage, but he said : " What ! hold up a light to a Turk !"'

It would be difficult indeed to find anything in the wide range of literature dealing with that period which would throw a stronger light upon both these men. Imagine the agent appointed by the London Committee wasting his precious time in writing such a letter as this for the information of its chairman. Stanhope meant no harm, we feel sure of that; but such a letter was little calculated to advance either his own reputation or Byron's, and it was above all things necessary for the London Committee to have a good opinion of both. But Stanhope was decidedly impetuous, and lacked all sense of humour.

Millingen tells us that it soon became evident that little co-operation could be expected between Byron and Colonel Stanhope. Byron was fully persuaded that, in the degraded state of the Greek nation, a republican form of Government was totally unsuited, as well as incompatible with her situation, in respect to the neighbouring States of Europe. Colonel Stanhope, whose enthusiasm for the cause was extreme, supposed the Greeks to be endowed with the same virtue which their ancestors displayed. We, who live in the twentieth century, are able by the light of subsequent events to decide which of these two men held the sounder view; and we can honestly deplore that a mere matter of opinion should have caused any disagreements between two men who had sacrificed so much in a common cause.

Gamba, who seems to have been present during the altercation above alluded to, says that Colonel Stanhope, in accusing Lord Byron of being an enemy to the press, laid himself open to a rejoinder which is not recorded in the report of these proceedings. Byron's reply was to the point: 'And yet, without my money, where would your Greek newspaper be?' And he concluded the sentence, 'Judge me by my actions,' cited by Stanhope, with, '*not by my words.*'

Colonel Stanhope could not understand Byron's bantering moods. They seemed to him to be entirely out of place. The more Byron laughed and joked, the more serious Stanhope became, and their discussions seldom ended without a strong reproof, which irritated Byron for the moment. But so far from leaving any unfavourable impression on Byron's mind, it increased his regard for an antagonist of such evident sincerity:

'When parting from him one evening, after a discussion of this nature, Lord Byron went up to him, and exclaimed: "Give me that honest right hand." Two such men were worthy of being friends, and it is to be regretted that an injudicious champion of the one should, by a partial detail of their trifling differences, try to raise him at the expense of the other.'

With the money provided by Byron, Colonel Stanhope's pet scheme, the *Greek Chronicle*, printed in Greek type, came into being. Its editor, 'a hot-headed republican' named Jean Jacques Meyer, who had been a Swiss doctor, was particularly unfitted for the post, and soon came to loggerheads with Byron for publishing a violent attack on the Austrian Government. In a letter to Samuel Barff, Byron says:

'From the very first I foretold to Colonel Stanhope and to Prince Mavrocordato that a Greek newspaper (as indeed any other), in *the present state* of Greece, might and probably *would* lead to much mischief and misconstruction, unless under *some* restrictions; nor have I ever had anything to do with it, as a writer or otherwise, except as a pecuniary contributor to its support in the outset, which I could not refuse to the earnest request of the projectors. Colonel Stanhope and myself had considerable differences of opinion on this subject, and (what will appear laughable enough) to such a degree that he charged me with *despotic* principles, and I *him* with *ultra-radicalism*. Dr. Meyer, the Editor, with his unrestrained freedom of the press, and who has the freedom to exercise an unlimited discretion—not allowing any articles but his own and those like them to appear—and in declaiming against restrictions, cuts, carves, and restricts, at his own will and pleasure. He is the author of an article against Monarchy, of which he may have the advantage and fame—but they (the Editors) will get themselves into a scrape, if they do not take care. Of all petty tyrants, he (Meyer) is one of the pettiest, as are most demagogues that ever I knew. He is a Swiss by birth, and a Greek by assumption, having married a wife and changed his religion.'

On the appearance of Meyer's stupid attack on monarchy, Byron immediately suppressed the whole edition.

Early in March the prospectus of a polyglot newspaper, entitled the *Greek Telegraph*, was published at Missolonghi. Millingen says:

'The sentiments imprudently advocated in this prospectus induced the British authorities in the Ionian Islands to entertain so unfavourable an impression of the spirit which would guide its conductors, that its admission into the heptarchy was interdicted under severe penalties. The same took place in the Austrian States, where they began to look upon Greece as "the city of refuge," as it were, for the Carbonari and discontented English reformers. The first number appeared on 20th March; but it was written in a tone so opposite to what had been expected, that it might, in some degree, be considered as a protest against its prospectus. Lord Byron was the cause of this change. More than ever convinced that nothing could be more useless, and even more dangerous, to the interests of Greece, both at home and abroad, than an unlimited freedom of the press, he insisted on Count Gamba becoming Editor. Byron cautioned him to restrict the paper to a simple narrative of events as they occurred, and an unprejudiced statement of opinions in respect to political relations and wants, so as to make them subjects of interest to the friends of Greece in the western parts of Europe.'

Gamba says:

'Lord Byron's view of the politics of Greece was, that this revolution had little or nothing in common with the great struggles with which Europe had been for thirty years distracted, and that it would be most foolish for the friends of Greece to mix up their cause with that of other nations, who had attempted to change their form of government, and by so doing to draw down the hatred and opposition of one of the two great parties that at present divide the civilized world. Lord Byron's wish was to show that the contest was simply one between barbarism and civilization—between Christianity and Islamism—and that the struggle was on behalf of the descendants of those to whom we are indebted for the first principles of science and the most perfect models of literature and art. For such a cause he hoped that all politicians of all parties, in every European State, might fairly be expected to unite.'

Byron believed that the moment had arrived for uniting the Greeks; the approach of danger and the chance of succour seemed favourable to his designs.

'To be in time to defend ourselves,' said Byron, 'we have only to put in action and unite all the means the Greeks possess; with money we have experienced the facility of raising troops. I cannot calculate to what a height Greece may rise.

'Hitherto it has been a subject for the hymns and elegies of fanatics and enthusiasts; but now it will draw the attention of the politician.'

DEATH OF SIR THOMAS MAITLAND

Early in February, 1824, Colonel Stanhope proposed to go into the Morea, in order to co-operate in the great work of appeasing the discords of that country. Prince Mavrocordato wrote privately to Sir Thomas Maitland * in the hope of averting trouble consequent upon the infraction of the neutrality of the Ionian territory at Ithaca. Lord Byron forwarded his letter to Lord Sidney Osborne,† with the following explanation:

'Enclosed is a private communication from Prince Mavrocordato to Sir Thomas Maitland, which you will oblige me much by delivering. Sir Thomas can take as much or as little of it as he pleases; but I hope and believe that it is rather calculated to conciliate than to irritate on the subject of the late event near Ithaca and Sta Mauro, which there is every disposition on the part of the Government here to disavow; and they are also disposed to give every satisfaction in their power. You must all be persuaded how difficult it is, under existing circumstances, for the Greeks to keep up discipline, however they may all be disposed to do so. I am doing all I can to convince them of the necessity of the strictest observance of the regulations of the island, and, I trust, with some effect. I was received here with every possible public and private mark of respect. If you write to any of our friends, you can say that I am in good health and spirits; and that I shall *stick* by the cause as long as a man of honour can, without sparing purse, and (I hope, if need be) *person*.'

This letter is dated from Missolonghi, February 9, 1824. On February 11 Byron heard the news of the death of Sir Thomas Maitland. Parry says:

'The news certainly caused considerable satisfaction among the Greeks, and among some of the English. He was generally looked on by them as the great enemy of their cause; but there is no proof of this. I

---

* High Commissioner of the Ionian Islands.
† Acting as Secretary to High Commissioner.

know that his government has been very much censured in England, and far be it from me to approve of the arbitrary or despotic measures of any man; but those who know anything of the people he had to deal with will find, in their character, an excuse for his conduct. I believe, in general, his government was well calculated for his subjects.'

Parry throws light upon Byron's attitude towards Mavrocordato, to which we alluded in a previous chapter.

'I took an opportunity, one evening, of asking Lord Byron what he thought of Prince Mavrocordato. He replied he considered him an honest man and a man of talent. He had shown his devotion to his country's service by expending his private fortune in its cause, and was probably the most capable and trustworthy of all the Greek chieftains. Lord Byron said that he agreed with Mavrocordato, that Missolonghi and its dependencies were of the greatest importance to Greece; and as long as the Prince acted as he had done, he would give him all the support in his power. Lord Byron seemed, at the same time, to suppose that a little more energy and industry in the Prince, with a disposition to make fewer promises, would tend much to his advantage.'

The following incident, related by Parry, seems to fall naturally into this part of our narrative:

'When the Turkish fleet was blockading Missolonghi, I was one day ordered by Lord Byron to accompany him to the mouth of the harbour to inspect the fortifications, in order to make a report of the state they were in. He and I were in his own punt, a little boat which he had, rowed by a boy; and in a large boat, accompanying us, were Prince Mavrocordato and his attendants. As I was viewing, on one hand, the Turkish fleet attentively, and reflecting on its powers, and our means of defence; and looking, on the other, at Prince Mavrocordato and his attendants, perfectly unconcerned, smoking their pipes and gossiping, as if Greece were liberated and at peace, and Missolonghi in a state of perfect security, I could not help giving vent to a feeling of contempt and indignation.

'"What is the matter?" said Lord Byron, appearing to be very serious; "what makes you so angry, Parry?"

'"I am not angry, my lord," I replied, "but somewhat indignant. The Turks, if they were not the most stupid wretches breathing, might take the fort of Vasaladi, by means of two pinnaces, any night they pleased; they have only to approach it with muffled oars, they would not be heard, I will answer for their not being seen, and they may storm it in a few minutes. With eight gunboats properly armed with 24-pounders, they might batter both Missolonghi and Anatolica to the ground. And there sits the old gentlewoman, Prince Mavrocordato and his troop, to whom I applied an epithet I will not here repeat, as if they were all perfectly safe. They know that their means of defence are inadequate, and they have no means of improving them. If I were in their place, I should be in a fever at the thought of my own incapacity and ignorance, and I should burn with impatience to attempt the destruction of those stupid Turkish rascals. The Greeks and the Turks are opponents, worthy by their imbecility of each other."

'I had scarcely explained myself fully, when Lord Byron ordered our boat to be placed alongside the other, and actually related our whole conversation to the Prince. In doing it, however, he took upon himself the task of pacifying both the Prince and me, and though I was at first very angry, and the Prince, I believe, very much annoyed, he succeeded. It was, in fact, only Lord Byron's manner of reproving us both. It taught me to be prudent and discreet. To the Prince and the Greeks it probably conveyed a lesson, which Lord Byron could have found no better means of giving them.'

Byron was remarkably sincere and frank in all his words and actions. Parry says that he never harboured a thought concerning another man that he did not express to his face; neither could he bear duplicity in others. If one person were to speak against a third party, in Byron's presence, he would be sure to repeat it the first time the two opponents were in presence of one another. This was a habit, says Parry, of which his acquaintance were well aware, and it spared Byron the trouble of listening to many idle and degrading calumnies. He probably expected thereby to teach others a sincerity which he so highly prized; but it must be added that he derived pleasure from witnessing the confusion of the person thus exposed. We recognize Byron in this trait, as none of his biographers have omitted to mention the extraordinary indiscretion of his confidences; but never before was his habit of 'blabbing' turned to a better use.

It is generally admitted that the Greeks were supine to the last degree. Little or nothing had been done to repair the losses resulting from the late campaign, nor had adequate preparations been made for the struggle in prospect. Through their improvidence, the Greeks had neither money nor materials. Neither in the Morea nor in Western Greece had any steps been taken to meet an assault by the enemy. The fortifications, that had suffered in the previous campaign, were left *in statu quo*. The Greek fleet was practically non-existent, owing to the insufficiency of money wherewith to pay the crews. In addition to internal dissensions, which might at any moment give rise to a civil war, the French and English Governments were continually demanding satisfaction for breaches of neutrality, or for acts of piracy committed by vessels of the Greek fleet, under a singular misapprehension of the game of war. In the midst of all these depressing conditions Byron kept his intense enthusiasm for the cause, and whatever may have

MAVROCORDATO AND STANHOPE

been the errors in his policy, everyone acknowledged the purity of his motives and the intensity of his zeal.

Prince Mavrocordato and Colonel Stanhope were not on very good terms. The Colonel had no confidence in the Prince, and, indeed, openly defied and opposed him. His hostility to Mavrocordato became so marked that both Greeks and English were persuaded that he was endeavouring to break up the establishment at Missolonghi, and to remove all the stores, belonging to the Committee, to Athens.

'This report,' says Parry, 'was conveyed to Lord Byron, who had not parted with Colonel Stanhope on very good terms, and caused him much annoyance. He had before attributed both neglect and deceit to the Greek Committee or some of its agents; and this report of the proceedings of their special and chosen messenger made him, in the irritation of the moment, regard them as acting even treacherously towards himself. "By the cant of religious pretenders," he said, "I have already deeply suffered, and now I know what the cant of pretended reformers and philanthropists amounts to."'

Byron was much displeased by the neglect which he had experienced at the hands of the London Committee, who, instead of sending supplies that would have been of some use, sent printing-presses, maps, and bugles. Books and Bibles were sent to a people who wanted guns, and when they asked for a sword they sent the lever of a printing-press. The only wonder was that they did not send out a pack of beagles. Colonel Stanhope, who might perhaps have been of some use in a military capacity, began organizing the whole country in accordance with Mr. Bentham's views of morality and justice. In this he acted entirely on his own responsibility, and rarely consulted Byron or Mavrocordato before carrying his wild schemes into execution. Byron said of him, in a moment of exasperation:

'He is a mere schemer and talker, more of a saint than a soldier; and, with a great deal of pretended plainness, a mere politician, and no patriot. I thought Colonel Stanhope, being a soldier, would have shown himself differently. He ought to know what a nation like Greece needs for its defence; and should have told the Committee that arms, and the materials for carrying on war, were what the Greeks required.'

Byron placed practice before precept, and was content to wait until the Turks had been driven out of Greece before entering upon any scheme for the cultivation of the soil and the development of commerce. He always maintained that Colonel Stanhope began at the wrong end, and was foolish to expect, by introducing some signs of wealth and knowledge, to make the people of Greece both rich and intelligent.

'I hear,' said Byron, in a conversation with Parry, 'that missionaries are to be introduced before the country is cleared of the enemy, and religious disputes are to be added to the other sources of discord. How very improper are such proceedings! nothing could be more impolitic; it will cause ill blood throughout the country, and very possibly be the means of again bringing Greece under the Turkish yoke. Can it be supposed that the Greek Priesthood, who have great influence, and even power, will tamely submit to see interested self-opinionated foreigners interfere with their flocks? I say again, clear the country, teach the people to read and write, and the labouring people will judge for themselves.'

The vexations to which Byron was daily subjected during his stay at Missolonghi, and the insufficiency of the diet which he prescribed for himself against the advice of his medical attendant, so affected his nervous

SIEGE OF LEPANTO ABANDONED

system, which by nature was highly irritable, that at last he broke down. Count Gamba says :

'Lord Byron was exceedingly vexed at the necessary abandonment of his project against Lepanto, at a time when success seemed so probable. He had not been able to ride that day, nor for some days, on account of the rain. He had been extremely annoyed at the vexations caused by the Suliotes, as also with the various other interruptions from petitions, demands, and remonstrances, which never left him a moment's peace at any hour of the day. At seven in the evening I went into his room on some business, and found him lying on the sofa : he was not asleep, and, seeing me enter, called out, "I am not asleep—come in—I am not well." At eight o'clock he went downstairs to visit Colonel Stanhope. The conversation turned upon our newspaper. We agreed that it was not calculated to give foreigners the necessary intelligence of what was passing in Greece; because, being written in Romaic, it was not intelligible, except to a few strangers. We resolved to publish another, in several languages, and Lord Byron promised to furnish some articles himself. When I left the room, he was laughing and joking with Parry and the Colonel; he was drinking some cider.'

As Gamba is no longer a witness of what actually happened, we refer the reader to the statement of Parry himself :

'Lord Byron's quarters were on the second-floor of the house, and Colonel Stanhope lived on the first-floor. In the evening, about eight o'clock, Lord Byron came downstairs into the Colonel's room where I was. He seated himself on a cane settee, and began talking with me on various subjects. Colonel Stanhope, who was employed in a neighbouring apartment, fitting up printing-presses, and Count Gamba, both came into the room for a short time, and some conversation ensued about the newspaper, which was never to Lord Byron a pleasant topic, as he disagreed with his friends about it. After a little time they went their several ways, and more agreeable subjects were introduced. Lord Byron began joking with me about Colonel Stanhope's occupations, and said he thought the author would have his brigade of artillery ready before the soldier got his printing-press fixed. There was then nobody in the room but his lordship, Mr. Hesketh, and myself. There was evidently a constrained manner about Lord Byron, and he complained of thirst. He ordered his servant to bring him some cider, which I entreated him not to drink in that state. There was a flush in his countenance, which seemed to indicate great nervous agitation; and as I thought Lord Byron had been much agitated and harassed for several days past, I recommended him, at least, to qualify his cider with some brandy. He said he had frequently drunk cider, and felt no bad consequences from it, and he accordingly drank it off. He had scarcely drunk the cider, when he complained of a very strange sensation, and I noticed a great change in his countenance. He rose from his seat, but could not walk, staggered a step or two, and fell into my arms.

'I had no other stimulant than brandy at hand, and having before seen it administered in similar cases with considerable benefit, I succeeded in making him swallow a small quantity. In another minute his teeth were closed, his speech and senses gone, and he was in strong convulsions. I laid him down on the settee, and with the assistance of his servant kept him quiet.

'When he fell into my arms, his countenance was very much distorted, his mouth being drawn on one side. After a short time his medical attendant came, and he speedily recovered his senses and his speech. He asked for Colonel Stanhope, as he had something particular to say to him, should there be a probability of his not recovering. Colonel Stanhope came from the next room. On recovering his senses, Lord Byron's countenance assumed its ordinary appearance, except that it was pale and haggard. No other effect remained visible except great weakness.'

According to Gamba:

'Lord Byron was carried upstairs to his own bed, and complained only of weakness. He asked whether his attack was likely to prove fatal. "Let me know," he said. "Do not think I am afraid to die—I am not." He told me that when he lost his speech he did not lose his senses; that he had suffered great pain, and that he believed, if the convulsion had lasted a minute longer, he must have died.'

The attack had been brought on by the vexations which he had long suffered in silence, and borne heroically. But his mode of living was a contributory cause. He ate nothing but fish, cheese, and vegetables—having regulated his table, says Gamba, so as not to cost more than 45 paras. This he did to show that he could live on fare as simple as that of the Greek soldiers.

Byron had scarcely recovered consciousness, when a false alarm was brought to him that the Suliotes had risen, and were about to attack the building where the arms were stored.

'We ran to our arsenal,' says Gamba, 'Parry ordered the artillerymen under arms: our cannon were loaded and pointed on the approaches to the gates; the sentries were doubled. This alarm had originated with two Germans, who, having taken too much wine, and seeing a body of soldiers with their guns in their hands proceeding towards the Seraglio, thought that a revolution had broken out, and spread an alarm over the whole town. As a matter of fact, these troops were merely changing their quarters. These Germans were so inconsiderate, that during our absence at the arsenal they forced their way into Byron's bedroom, swearing that they had come to defend him and his house. Fortunately, we were not present, for, as this was only half an hour after Byron's attack, we should have been tempted to fling the intruders out of the window. On the following day Byron was better, and got up at noon; but he was very pale and weak, and complained of a sensation of weight in his head. The doctor applied eight leeches to his temples, and the blood flowed copiously; it was stopped with difficulty, and he fainted.'

Dr. Millingen says that Dr. Bruno had at first proposed opening a vein; but finding it impossible to obtain Byron's consent, he applied leeches to the temples, which bled so copiously as almost to bring on syncope. Byron, alarmed to see the difficulty Dr. Bruno had in stopping the hæmorrhage, sent for Millingen, who, by the application of lunar caustic, succeeded in stopping the flow of blood.

In Millingen's opinion, Byron was never the same man after this; a change took place in his mental and bodily functions.

'That wonderful elasticity of disposition, that continual flow of wit, that facility of jest by which his conversation had been so distinguished, returned only at distant intervals,' says Millingen: 'from this time Byron fell into a state of melancholy from which none of our arguments could relieve him. He felt certain that his constitution had been ruined; that he was a worn-out man; and that his muscular power was gone. Flashes before his eyes, palpitations and anxieties, hourly afflicted him; and at times such a sense of faintness would overpower him, that, fearing to be attacked by similar convulsions, he would send in great haste for medical assistance. His nervous system was, in fact, in a continual state of erethism, which was certainly augmented by the low, debilitating diet which Dr. Bruno had recommended.'

On one occasion Byron said to Dr. Millingen that he did not wish for life; it had ceased to have any attraction for him.

'But,' said Byron, 'the fear of two things now haunt me. I picture myself slowly expiring on a bed of torture, or ending my days like Swift—a grinning idiot! Would to Heaven the day were arrived in which, rushing, sword in hand, on a body of Turks, and fighting like one weary of existence, I shall meet immediate, painless death—the object of my wishes.'

Two days after this seizure Byron made the following entry in his journal:

'With regard to the presumed causes of this attack, so far as I know, there might be several. The state of the place and the weather permit little exercise at present. I have been violently agitated with more than one passion recently, and amidst conflicting parties, politics, and (as far as regards public matters) circumstances. I have also been in an anxious state with regard to things which may be only interesting to my own private feelings, and, perhaps, not uniformly so temperate as I may generally affirm that I was wont to be. How far any or all of these may have acted on the mind or body of one who had already undergone many previous changes of place and passion during a life of thirty-six years, I cannot tell.'

The following note, which is entered by Mr. Rowland Prothero in the new edition of Lord Byron's 'Letters and Journals,'* was dashed off by Byron in pencil, on the day of his seizure, February 15, 1824:

'Having tried in vain at great expense, considerable trouble, and some danger, to unite the Suliotes for the good of Greece—and their own—I have come to the following resolution:
'I will have nothing more to do with the Suliotes. They may go to the Turks, or the Devil,—they may cut me into more pieces than they have dissensions among themselves,—sooner than change my resolution.
'For the rest, I hold my means and person at the disposal of the Greek nation and Government the same as before.'

No better proof could be given of the perplexities which worried him at that particular time. But the surrounding gloom was lightened now and then by some of Parry's stories. The following anecdote about Jeremy Bentham was an especial favourite with

* Vol. vi., p. 326.

Byron; Parry's sea-terms and drollery doubtless heightened its effect:

'Shortly before I left London for Greece, Mr. Bowring, the honorary secretary to the Greek Committee, informed me that Mr. Jeremy Bentham wished to see the stores and materials, preparing for the Greeks, and that he had done me the honour of asking me to breakfast with him some day, that I might afterwards conduct him to see the guns, etc.

'"Who the devil is Mr. Bentham?" was my rough reply; "I never heard of him before." Many of my readers may still be in the same state of ignorance, and it will be acceptable to them, I hope, to hear of the philosopher.

'"Mr. Bentham," said Mr. Bowring, "is one of the greatest men of the age, and for the honour now offered to you, I waited impatiently many a long day—I believe for more than two years."

'"Great or little, I never heard of him before; but if he wants to see me, why I'll go."

'It was accordingly arranged that I should visit Mr. Bentham, and that Mr. Bowring should see him to fix the time, and then inform me. In a day or two afterwards, I received a note from the honorary secretary to say I was to breakfast with Mr. Bentham on Saturday. It happened that I lived at a distance from town, and having heard something of the primitive manner of living and early hours of philosophers, I arranged with my wife overnight that I would get up very early on the Saturday morning, that I might not keep Mr. Bentham waiting. Accordingly, I rose with the dawn, dressed myself in haste, and brushed off for Queen's Square, Westminster, as hard as my legs could carry me. On reaching the Strand, fearing I might be late, being rather corpulent, and not being willing to go into the presence of so very great a man, as I understood Mr. Jeremy Bentham to be, puffing and blowing, I took a hackney-coach and drove up to his door about eight o'clock. I found a servant girl afoot, and told her I came to breakfast with Mr. Bentham by appointment.

'She ushered me in, and introduced me to two young men, who looked no more like philosophers, however, than my own children. I thought they might be Mr. Bentham's sons, but this, I understood, was a mistake. I showed them the note I had received from Mr. Bowring, and they told me Mr. Bentham did not breakfast till three o'clock. This surprised me much, but they told me I might breakfast with them, which I did, though I was not much flattered by the honour of sitting down with Mr. Bentham's clerks, when I was invited by their master. Poor Mr. Bowring! thought I, he must be a meek-spirited young man if it was for this he waited so impatiently. I supposed the philosopher himself did not get up till noon, as he did not breakfast till so late, but in this I was also mistaken. About ten o'clock I was summoned to his presence, and mustered up all my courage and all my ideas for the meeting. His appearance struck me forcibly. His thin white locks, cut straight in the fashion of the Quakers, and hanging, or rather floating, on his shoulders; his garments something of Quaker colour and cut, and his frame rather square and muscular, with no exuberance of flesh, made up a singular-looking and not an inelegant old man. He welcomed me with a few hurried words, but without any ceremony, and then conducted me into several rooms to show me *his* ammunition and materials of war. One very large room was nearly filled with books, and another with unbound works, which, I understood, were the philosopher's own composition. The former, he said, furnished him his supplies; and there was a great deal of labour required to read so many volumes. I said inadvertently, "I suppose you have quite forgotten what is said in the first before you read the last." Mr. Bentham, however, took this in good part, and, taking hold of my arm, said we would proceed on our journey. Accordingly, off we set, accompanied by one of his young men carrying a portfolio, to keep, I suppose, a log of our proceedings.

'We went through a small garden, and, passing out of a gate, I found we were in St. James's Park. Here I noticed that Mr. Bentham had a very snug dwelling, with many accommodations, and such a garden as belongs in London only to the first nobility. But for his neighbours, I thought—for he has a barrack of soldiers on one side of his premises—I should envy him his garden more than his great reputation. On looking at him, I could but admire his hale, and even venerable, appearance. I understood he was seventy-three years of age, and therefore I concluded we should have a quiet, comfortable walk. Very much to my surprise, however, we had scarcely got into the Park, when he let go my arm, and set off trotting like a Highland messenger. The Park was crowded, and the people one and all seemed to stare at the old man; but, heedless of all this, he trotted on, his white locks floating in the wind, as if he were not seen by a single human being.

As soon as I could recover from my surprise, I asked the young man, "Is Mr. Bentham flighty?" pointing to my head. "Oh no, it's his way," was the hurried answer; "he thinks it good for his health. But I must run after him;" and off set the youth in chase of the philosopher. I must not lose my companions, thought I, and off I set also. Of course the eyes of every human being in the Park were fixed on the running veteran and his pursuers. There was Jerry ahead, then came his clerk and his portfolio, and I, being a heavier sailer than either, was bringing up the rear.

'What the people might think, I don't know; but it seemed to me a very strange scene, and I was not much delighted at being made such an object of attraction. Mr. Bentham's activity surprised me, and I never overtook him or came near him till we reached the Horse Guards, where his speed was checked by the Blues drawn up in array. Here we threaded in amongst horses and men till we escaped at the other gate into Whitehall. I now thought the crowded streets would prevent any more racing; but several times he escaped from us, and trotted off, compelling us to trot after him till we reached Mr. Galloway's manufactory in Smithfield. Here he exulted in his activity, and inquired particularly if I had ever seen a man at his time of life so active. I could not possibly answer no, while I was almost breathless with the exertion of following him through the crowded streets. After seeing at Mr. Galloway's manufactory, not only the things which had been prepared for the Greeks, but his other engines and machines, we proceeded to another manufactory at the foot of Southwark Bridge, where our brigade of guns stood ready mounted. When Mr. Bentham had satisfied his curiosity here also, and I had given him every information in my power, we set off to return to his house, that he might breakfast; I endeavoured to persuade him to take a hackney-coach, but in vain. We got on tolerably well, and without any adventures, tragical or comical, till we arrived at Fleet Street. We crossed from Fleet Market over towards Mr. Waithman's shop, and here, letting go my arm, he quitted the foot pavement, and set off again in one of his vagaries up Fleet Street. His clerk again set off after him, and I again followed. The race here excited universal attention. The perambulating ladies, who are always in great numbers about that part of the town, and ready to laugh at any kind of oddity, and catch hold of every simpleton, stood and stared at or followed the venerable philosopher. One of them, well known to all the neighbourhood by the appellation of the *City Barge*, given to her on account of her extraordinary bulk, was coming with a consort full sail down Fleet Street, but whenever they saw the flight of Mr. Jeremy Bentham they hove to, tacked, and followed to witness the fun or share the prize. I was heartily ashamed of participating in this scene, and supposed that everybody would take me for a mad doctor, the young man for my assistant, and Mr. Bentham for my patient, just broke adrift from his keepers.

'Fortunately the chase did not continue long. Mr. Bentham hove to abreast of Carlisle's shop, and stood for a little time to admire the books and portraits hanging in the window. At length one of them arrested his attention more particularly. "Ah, ah," said he, in a hurried indistinct tone, "there it is, there it is!" pointing to a portrait which I afterwards found was that of the illustrious Jeremy himself.

'Soon after this, I invented an excuse to quit Mr. Bentham and his man, promising to go to Queen's Square to dine. I was not, however, to be again taken in by the philosopher's meal hours; so, laying in a stock of provisions, I went at his dining hour, half-past ten o'clock, and supped with him. We had a great deal of conversation, particularly about mechanical subjects and the art of war. I found the old gentleman as lively with his tongue as with his feet, and passed a very pleasant evening; which ended by my pointing out, at his request, a plan for playing his organ by the steam of his tea-kettle.

'This little story,' says Parry, 'gave Byron a great deal of pleasure. 'He very often laughed as I told it; he laughed much at its conclusion. He declared, when he had fished out every little circumstance, that he would not have lost it for 1,000 guineas. Lord Byron frequently asked me to repeat what he called: *Jerry Bentham's Cruise.*'

Parry tells us that Byron took a great interest in all that concerned the welfare of the working classes, and particularly of the artisans.

'I have lately read,' said Byron on one occasion, 'of an institution lately established in London for the instruction of mechanics. I highly approve of this, and intend to subscribe £50 to it; but I shall at the same time write and give my opinion on the subject. I am always afraid that schemes of this kind are intended to deceive people; and, unless all the offices in such an institution are filled with real practical mechanics, the working classes will soon find themselves deceived. If they permit any but mechanics to have the direction of their affairs, they will only become the tools of others. The real working man will soon be ousted, and his more cunning pretended friends will take possession and reap all the benefits. It gives me pleasure to think what a mass of natural intellect this will call into action. If the plan succeeds, and I hope it may, the ancient aristocracy of England will be secure for ages to come. The most useful and numerous body of people in the nation will then judge for themselves, and, when properly informed, will judge correctly. There is not on earth a more honourable body of men than the English nobility; and there is no system of government under which life and property are better secured than under the British constitution.

'The mechanics and working classes who can maintain their families are, in my opinion, the happiest body of men. Poverty is wretchedness; but it is perhaps to be preferred to the heartless, unmeaning dissipation of the higher orders. I am thankful that I am now entirely clear of this, and my resolution to remain clear of it for the rest of my life is immutable.'

Parry remarks that it would be folly to attribute to Byron any love for democracy, as the term was then understood. Although the bent of his mind was more Liberal than Conservative, he was not a party man in its narrow sense. He was a sworn foe to injustice, cruelty, and oppression; such was the alpha and omega of his political prejudices. He would be an inveterate enemy to any Government which oppressed one class for the benefit of another class, and which did not allow its subjects to be free and happy.

In speaking of America, Byron said:

'I have always thought the mode in which the Americans separated from Great Britain was unfortunate for them. It made them despise or regret everything English. They disinherited themselves of all the historical glory of England; there was nothing left for them to admire or venerate but their own immediate success, and they became egotists, like savages, from wanting a history. The spirit of jealousy and animosity excited by the contests between England and America is now subsiding. Should peace continue, prejudices on both sides will gradually decrease. Already the Americans are beginning, I think, to cultivate the antiquities of England, and, as they extend their inquiries, they will find other objects of admiration besides themselves. It was of some importance, both for them and for us, that they did not reject our language with our government. Time, I should hope, will approximate the institutions of both countries to one another; and the use of the same language will do more to unite the two nations than if they both had only one King.'

CHAPTER X

ACCORDING to Gamba's journal, on the day following the seizure to which we have referred, Byron followed up his former efforts to inculcate the principles and practice of humanity into both the nations engaged in the war. There were twenty-four Turks, including women and children, who had suffered all the rigours of captivity at Missolonghi since the beginning of the revolution. Byron caused them to be released, and sent at his own cost to Prevesa. The following letter, which he addressed to the English Consul at that port, deserves a place in this record:

'SIR,
     Coming to Greece, one of my principal objects was to alleviate as much as possible the miseries incident to a warfare so cruel as the present. When the dictates of humanity are in question, I know no difference between Turks and Greeks. It is enough that those who want assistance are men, in order to claim the pity and protection of the meanest pretender to humane feelings. I have found here twenty-four Turks, including women and children, who have long pined in distress, far from the means of support and the consolations of their home. The Government has consigned them to me: I transmit them to Prevesa, whither they desire to be sent. I hope you will not object to take care that they may be restored to a place of safety, and that the Governor of your town may accept of my present. The best recompense I can hope for would be to find that I had inspired the

THE RELEASE OF PRISONERS

Ottoman commanders with the same sentiments towards those unhappy Greeks who may hereafter fall into their hands.

'I beg you to believe me, etc.,
'NOEL BYRON.'

The details of this incident have hitherto passed almost unnoticed. The whole story is full of pathos, and affords a view of Byron's real character.

In June, 1821, when Missolonghi and Anatolico proclaimed themselves parts of independent Greece, all Turkish residents were arrested. The males were cruelly put to death, and their wives and families were handed over to the Greek householders as slaves. The miseries these defenceless people endured while Death stared them daily in the face are indescribable. Millingen says:

'One day, as I entered the dispensary, I found the wife of one of the Turkish inhabitants of Missolonghi who had fled to Patras. The poor woman came to implore my pity, and begged me to allow her to take shelter under my roof from the brutality and cruelty of the Greeks. They had murdered all her relations, and two of her boys; and the marks remained on the angle of the wall against which, a few weeks previously, they had dashed the brains of the youngest, only five years of age. A little girl, nine years old, remained to be the only companion of her misery. Like a timid lamb, she stood by her mother, naked and shivering, drawing closer and closer to her side. Her little hands were folded like a suppliant's, and her large, beautiful eyes—so accustomed to see acts of horror and cruelty—looked at me now and then, hardly daring to implore pity. "Take us," said the mother; "we will serve you and be your slaves; or you will be responsible before God for whatever may happen to us."

'I could not see so eloquent a picture of distress unmoved, and from that day I treated them as relatives. Some weeks after, I happened to mention before Lord Byron some circumstances relative to these individuals, and spoke with so much admiration of the noble fortitude displayed by the mother in the midst of her calamities; of the courage with which maternal love inspired her on several occasions; of the dignified manner in which she replied to the insults of her persecutors, that he expressed a wish to see the mother and child. On doing so, he became so struck by Hatajè's beauty, the naïveté of her answers, and the spiritedness of her observations on the murderers of her brethren, that he decided on adopting her. "Banish fear for ever from your mind," said he to the mother; "your child shall henceforth be mine. I have a daughter in England. To her I will send the child. They are both of the same age; and as she is alone, she will, no doubt, like a companion who may, at times, talk to her of her father. Do not shudder at the idea of changing your religion, for I insist on your professing none other but the Musulman."

'She seized his hand, kissed it with energy, and raising her eyes to heaven, eyes now filled with tears, she repeated the familiar words: "Allah is great!" Byron ordered costly dresses to be made for them, and sent to Hatajè a necklace of sequins. He desired me to send them twice a week to his house. He would then take the little child on his knees, and caress her with all the fondness of a father.

'From the moment I received the mother and child into my house, the other unfortunate Turkish women, who had miraculously escaped the general slaughter, seeing how different were the feelings and treatment of the English towards their nation and sex from those of the Greeks, began to feel more hopeful of their lot in life. They daily called at my lodgings, and by means of my servant, a Suliote who spoke Turkish fluently, narrated their misfortunes, and the numberless horrors of which they had been spectators. One woman said: "Our fears are not yet over; we are kept as victims for future sacrifices, hourly expecting our doom. An unpleasant piece of news, a drunken party, a fit of ill-humour or of caprice, may decide our fate. We are then hunted down the streets like wild beasts, till some one of us, or of our children, is immolated to

HATAJÈ

their insatiable cruelty. Our only hope centres in you. One word of yours to Lord Byron can save many lives. Can you refuse to speak for us. Let Lord Byron send us to any part of Turkey. We are women and children; can the Greeks fear us?"

'I hastened to give Lord Byron a faithful picture of the position of these wretched people. Knowing and relieving the distressed were, with him, simultaneous actions. A few days later notice was given to every Turkish woman to prepare for departure. All, a few excepted, embarked and were conveyed at Byron's expense to Prevesa. They amounted to twenty-two. A few days previously four Turkish prisoners had been sent by him to Patras. Repeated examples of humanity like these were for the Greeks more useful and appropriate lessons than the finest compositions which all the printing-presses could have spread amongst them.'

Hatajè! and what became of little Hatajè? On February 23 Byron wrote to his sister:

'I have been obtaining the release of about nine-and-twenty Turkish prisoners—men, women, and children—and have sent them home to their friends; but one, a pretty little girl of nine years of age named Hato or Hatagèe, has expressed a strong wish to remain with me, or under my care, and I have nearly determined to adopt her. If I thought that Lady B. would let her come to England as a companion to Ada (they are about the same age), and we could easily provide for her; if not, I can send her to Italy for education. She is very lively and quick, and with great black Oriental eyes and Asiatic features. All her brothers were killed in the Revolution; her mother wishes to return to her husband, but says that she would rather entrust the child to me, in the present state of the country. Her extreme youth and sex have hitherto saved her life, but there is no saying what might occur in the course of the war (and of *such* a war), and I shall probably commit her to the charge of some English lady in the islands for the present. The child herself has the same wish, and seems to have a decided character for her age. You can mention this matter if you think it worth while. I merely wish her to be respectably educated and treated, and, if my years and all things be considered, I presume it would be difficult to conceive me to have any other views.'

Meanwhile, Byron, wishing to remove the child from Missolonghi, seems to have proposed to Dr. Kennedy at Cephalonia that Mrs. Kennedy should take temporary charge of her. Writing to Kennedy on March 4, 1824, Byron says:

'Your future convert Hato, or Hatagèe, appears to me lively, intelligent, and promising; she possesses an interesting countenance. With regard to her disposition I can say little, but Millingen speaks well of both mother and daughter, and he is to be relied on. As far as I know, I have only seen the child a few times with her mother, and what I have seen is favourable, or I should not take so much interest in her behalf. If she turns out well, my idea would be to send her to my daughter in England (if not to respectable persons in Italy), and so to provide for her as to enable her to live with reputation either singly or in marriage, if she arrive at maturity. I will make proper arrangements about her expenses through Messrs. Barff and Hancock, and the rest I leave to your discretion, and to Mrs. K.'s, with a great sense of obligation for your kindness in undertaking her temporary superintendence.'

This arrangement fell through, and was never carried out. The child remained at Missolonghi with her mother until Byron's death. Then, by the irony of fate, they departed in the *Florida*— the vessel that bore the dead body of their protector to the inhospitable lazaretto at Zante. With wonderful prophetic instinct, Byron, long before his voyage to Greece, gave to the world the vision of another Hatajè, rescued from death on the field of battle:

> 'The Moslem orphan went with her protector,
>   For she was homeless, houseless, helpless; all
>   Her friends, like the sad family of Hector,
>   Had perished in the field or by the wall:
>   Her very place of birth was but a spectre
>   Of what it had been; there the Muezzin's call
> To prayer was heard no more—and Juan wept,
>   And made a vow to shield her, which he kept.'

Blaquière, who was at Zante when the *Florida* was placed in quarantine, says:

'The child, whom I have frequently seen in the lazaretto, is extremely interesting, and about eight years of age. She came over with Byron's body, under her mother's care. They had not been here many days, before an application came from Usouff Pacha, to give them up. It being customary, whenever claims of this kind are made, to consult the parties themselves, both the mother and her child were questioned as to their wishes on the subject. The latter, with tears in her eyes, said that, had his lordship lived, she would always have considered him as a father; but as he was no more, she preferred going back to her own country. The mother having expressed the same wish, they were sent to Patras.'

According to Millingen, when Hatajè and her mother arrived at Patras, the child's father received them in a transport of joy. 'I thought you slaves,' said the father in embracing them, 'and, lo! you return to me decked like brides.'

And that is all that we know—all, we suppose, that *can* be known—of little Hatajè! She may still be alive, the last survivor of those who had spoken to Byron! If, in her ninety-third year, she still recalls the events of 1824, she will hold up the torch with modest pride, while the present writer commemorates one, out of many, of the noble actions performed by the poet Byron.

> ' This special honour was conferred, because
> He had behaved with courage and humanity—
> Which *last* men like, when they have time to pause
> From their ferocities produced by vanity.
> His little captive gained him some applause
> For saving her amidst the wild insanity
> Of carnage—and I think he was more glad in her
> Safety, than his new order of St. Vladimir.'
> *Don Juan*, Canto VIII., CXL.

CHAPTER XI

ON February 17 there was great excitement at Missolonghi on account of a Turkish brig-of-war, which had run ashore on a sand-bank about seven miles from the city.

Byron sent for Parry, and accosted him in his liveliest manner:

'Now's the day, Parry, and now's the hour; now for your rockets, your fire-kites, and red-hot shots; now, Parry, for your Grecian fires. Onward, death or victory!'

Byron was still so weak that he could not rise from the sofa; but all the available soldiers manned the Greek boats, and set off in the hope of plunder. Parry and some other European officers went out to reconnoitre the brig, and discovered a broad and long neck of land, which separated the shallows from the sea, upon which it would be easy to plant a couple of guns and make an attack upon the brig. Parry says that he had only two guns fit for immediate service—a long three-pounder and a howitzer. The attack was to be made on the following day, and Byron gave orders that, in the event of any prisoners being taken, their lives were, if possible, to be spared. He offered to pay two dollars a head for each prisoner saved, to pay something more for officers, and have them cared for at Missolonghi at his own expense. He also gave strict orders that the artillery brigade should be kept in reserve, so as to relieve and protect the Turkish prisoners. Early on the following day the guns were shipped, but, unfortunately, the boats ran aground, and much valuable time was lost. Meanwhile three Turkish brigs came to the rescue, and got into position so as to enfilade the beach. They manned their boats and tried to haul the brig into deep water, but without success; and seeing the Greeks preparing to attack, they thought it better to sheer off. But before doing so they managed to remove all the men, and as many of the brig's stores as they could save, and then set the vessel on fire. Although Byron was disappointed in not having captured a prize, he was glad to hear that the brig had been burnt to the water's edge. It was estimated that the loss of that vessel to the enemy would amount to nearly 20,000 dollars, and the little garrison of Missolonghi was highly elated at so important an achievement.

On February 19 a serious event occurred, which caused something like a revolution at Missolonghi, and might have been attended with more serious consequences if Byron had not shown a firm hand. It is thus related by Millingen:

'A sentry had been placed at the gate of the Seraglio to prevent anyone who did not belong to the laboratory from entering. A Suliote named Toti, presented himself, and, without paying the slightest attention to the prohibition, boldly walked in. Lieutenant Sass, a Swede, informed of this, came up to the Suliote, and, pushing him roughly, ordered him to go out. On his refusal the officer drew his sword and struck him with its flat side. Incensed at this, the Suliote, who was of Herculean strength, cut the Swede's left arm almost entirely off with one stroke of his yataghan, and immediately after shot him through the head. The soldiers belonging to the artillery brigade shut the gate, and after inflicting several wounds on Toti, who continued to defend himself, succeeded in securing him. His countrymen, with whom he was a favourite, being informed of the accident, hastened to the Seraglio, and would have proceeded to acts of violence, had not their comrade been delivered into their hands. The next morning Lieutenant Sass was buried with military honours. The Suliotes attended the funeral; and thus terminated the temporary misunderstanding between them and the Franks.'

It appears, from Gamba's account of this unfortunate affair, that Lieutenant Sass was universally esteemed as one of the best and bravest of the foreigners in the service of Greece. The Suliote chiefs laid all the blame of this affray on Sass himself, whose imprudence in striking one of the proud and warlike race cannot be justified.

The Suliotes had already given many proofs of lawless insubordination, and several skirmishes had previously taken place between them and the people of Missolonghi. This last affair brought matters to a head, and Byron agreed, with the Primates and Mavrocordato, that these lawless troops must, at any cost, be got rid of.

Not only did their presence at Missolonghi alarm its inhabitants, but their fighting value had diminished, owing to their determination not to take any part in the projected siege of Lepanto, alleging as a reason that they were not disposed to fight against stone walls. Their dismissal was, however, not an easy matter, for they were practically masters of the city, and claimed 3,000 dollars as arrears of pay. The Primates, being applied to by Byron, declared that they had no money. Under these circumstances it became absolutely necessary for Byron to find the money himself, which he did on the understanding that the Primates bound themselves to clear the town of this turbulent band. Upon payment of this money the Suliotes packed up their effects, and departed for Arta, thus putting an end to all Byron's hopes of capturing the fortress of Lepanto. A report was at this time circulated in Missolonghi that the Turkish authorities had set a price on the lives of all Europeans engaged in the Greek service. This rumour added enormously to the difficulties of the situation; for the artificers, whom Parry had brought out from England to work in the arsenal, struck work, and applied to Byron for permission to return home. They said that they had bargained to be conducted into a place of safety. Byron tried, says Gamba, to persuade them that the affray had been accidental, that, after the departure of the Suliotes, nothing of the kind would happen again, and so long as he himself remained there could not be any serious danger. But all arguments were useless; the men were thoroughly demoralized, and went from Byron's presence unshaken in their resolve to return to their native land.

Byron, writing to Kennedy on March 10, says with his usual good-nature:

'The mechanics were all pretty much of the same mind. Perhaps they are less to blame than is imagined, since Colonel Stanhope is said to have told them *that he could not positively say their lives were safe.* I should like to know *where* our life *is* safe, either here or anywhere else? With regard to a place of safety, at least such hermetically sealed safety as these persons appeared to desiderate, it is not to be found in Greece, at any rate; but Missolonghi was supposed to be the place where they would be useful, and their risk was no greater than that of others.'

In a letter to Barff, some days later, Byron once more alludes to these artificers, whose absence began to be seriously felt at the arsenal:

'Captain Parry will write to you himself on the subject of the artificers' wages, but, with all due allowance for their situation, I cannot see a great deal to pity in their circumstances. They were well paid, housed and fed, expenses granted of every kind, and they marched off at the first alarm. Were *they* more exposed than the rest? or *so much?* Neither are they very much embarrassed, for Captain Parry says that *he knows* all of them have money, and one in particular a considerable sum.'

These are the men in whose interests Byron had written to Barff:

'Six Englishmen will soon be in quarantine at Zante; they are artificers, and have had enough of Greece in fourteen days; if you could recommend them to a passage home, I would thank you; they are good men enough, but do not quite understand the little discrepancies in these countries, and are not used to see shooting and slashing in a domestic quiet way, or (as it forms here) a part of housekeeping. If they should want anything during their quarantine, you can advance them *not more* than a dollar a day (amongst them) for that period, to purchase them some little extras as comforts (as they are quite out of their element). I cannot afford them more at present. The Committee pays their passage.'

Byron was exceedingly vexed by these proceedings, and began to lose all hope of being of any real service to the Greeks. He told Gamba that he had lost time, money, patience, and even health, only to meet with deception, calumny, and ingratitude. Gamba begged

Byron to visit Athens, partly for the benefit of his health, and partly to be quit for a time from the daily annoyances to which he was subjected. But he refused, and determined to remain in that dismal swamp until he saw what turn things would take in the Morea, and until he received news of the success of the loan from London. He resolved meanwhile to fortify Missolonghi and Anatolico, and to drill the Greek troops into something like discipline.

In order to reorganize the artillery brigade, Byron agreed to furnish money which would encourage the Greeks to enlist. Artillery was the only arm that it was possible to form, as there were no muskets with bayonets suitable for infantry regiments, and the artillery was deficient both in officers and men. With great difficulty Parry succeeded in collecting some Greek artificers, and made some slight progress with his laboratory.

The weather improved, and Byron was able to take long rides, which had an excellent effect on his health and spirits. Artillery recruits came in faster than was expected, and were regularly trained for efficient service. It seemed as though the tide had turned. At about this time Byron received a letter from Mr. Barff, strongly urging his return to Zante for the purpose of regaining his usual health, which it was feared he would not attain at Missolonghi. Byron was touched by this mark of friendship, but would not grasp the hand that might have saved his life.

'I am extremely obliged by your offer of your country house (as for all other kindness), in case that my health should require any removal; but I cannot quit Greece while there is a chance of my being of (even *supposed*) utility. There is a stake worth millions such as I am, and while I can stand at all,

I must stand by the cause. While I say this, I am aware of the difficulties, dissensions, and defects of the Greeks themselves; but allowances must be made for them by all reasonable people.'

It may seem strange, but it is nevertheless certain, that Byron found more pleasure in the society of Parry, that 'rough, burly fellow,' than he did in the companionship of anyone else at Missolonghi. He thoroughly trusted the man, and even confided in him without reserve. Parry appreciated the honour of Byron's intimacy, and his evidence of what passed during the last few weeks of Byron's life is, so far as we are able to judge, quite reliable. He tells us that Byron had taken a small body of Suliotes into his own pay, and kept them about his person as a bodyguard. They consisted altogether of fifty-six men, and of these a certain number were always on duty. A large outer room in Byron's house was used by them, and their carbines were hung upon its walls.

'In this room,' says Parry, 'and among these rude soldiers, Lord Byron was accustomed to walk a great deal, especially in wet weather. On these occasions he was almost always accompanied by his favourite dog, Lion, who was perhaps his dearest and most affectionate friend. They were, indeed, very seldom separated. Riding or walking, sitting or standing, Lion was his constant attendant. He can scarcely be said to have forsaken him even in sleep. Every evening Lion went to see that his master was safe before he lay down himself, and then he took his station close to his door, a guard certainly as faithful as Lord Byron's Suliotes.

'With Lion Lord Byron was accustomed, not only to associate, but to commune very much. His most usual phrase was, "Lion, you are no rogue, Lion"; or, "Lion, thou art an honest fellow, Lion." The dog's eyes sparkled, and his tail swept the floor, as he sat with haunches on the ground. "Thou art more faithful than men, Lion; I trust thee more." Lion sprang up, and barked, and bounded round his master, as much as to say, "You may trust me; I will watch actively on every side." Then Byron would fondle the dog, and say, "Lion, I love thee; thou art my faithful dog!" and Lion jumped and kissed his master's hand, by way of acknowledgment. In this manner, when in the dog's company, Byron passed a good deal of time, and seemed more contented and happy than at any other hour during the day. This valuable and affectionate animal was, after Byron's death, brought to England and placed under the care of Mrs. Leigh, his lordship's sister.'

Parry gives a graphic description of the state of Missolonghi during this period, which compelled Byron to take a circuitous route whenever the state of the weather permitted him to ride. The pavements and condition of the streets were so bad that it was impossible to ride through them without the risk of breaking one's neck.

'Lord Byron's horses were therefore generally led to the gate of the town, while his lordship, in a small punt, was rowed along the harbour, and up what is called the Military Canal. This terminates not far from the gate; here he would land, and mount his horse.'

The Suliote guard always attended Byron during his rides; and, though on foot, it was surprising to see their swiftness, says Parry. With carbines carried at the trail in their right hands, these agile mountaineers kept pace with the horses, even when Byron went at a gallop. It was a matter of honour with these Suliotes never to desert their chief; for they considered themselves responsible both to Greece and to England for his safety. Parry says:

'They were tall men, and remarkably well formed. Perhaps, taken all together, no Sovereign in Europe could boast of having a finer set of men for his body-guard.'

Byron while in Greece abandoned his habit of spending the whole morning in bed, as was his custom in Italy. He rose at nine o'clock, and breakfasted at ten. This meal consisted of tea without either milk or sugar, dry toast, and water-cresses.

'During his breakfast,' says Parry, 'I generally waited on him to make the necessary reports, and to take his orders for the work of the day. When this business was settled, I retired to give the orders which I had received, and returned to Lord Byron by eleven o'clock at latest. His lordship would then inspect the accounts, and, with the assistance of his secretary, checked every item in a business-like manner. If the weather permitted, he afterwards rode out; if it did not, he used to amuse himself by shooting at a mark with pistols. Though his hand trembled much, his aim was sure, and he could hit an egg four times out of five at a distance of ten or twelve yards.'

After an early dinner, composed of dried toast, vegetables, and cheese, with a very small quantity of wine or cider (Parry assures us that he never drank any spirituous liquors during any part of the day or night). Byron would attend the drilling of the officers of his corps, in an outer apartment of his own dwelling, and went through all the exercises which it was proper for them to learn. When this was finished he very often played a bout of singlestick, or underwent some other severe muscular exertion. He then retired for the evening, to spin yarns with his friends or to study military tactics. Parry says:

'At eleven o'clock I left him, and I was generally the last person he saw, except his servants. He then retired, not to sleep, but to study. Till nearly four o'clock every morning Byron was continually engaged reading or writing, and rarely slept more than five hours. In this manner did he pass nearly every day of the time I had the pleasure of knowing him.'

It was at the end of February that Mr. George Finlay, who afterwards wrote a 'History of Greece,' arrived at Missolonghi. He brought a message from Odysseus, and also from Edward Trelawny, inviting both Byron and Mavrocordato to a Conference at Salona. Gamba, writing on February 28, 1824, says:

'We had news from the Morea that their discords were almost at an end. The Government was daily acquiring credit. . . . On the whole, Greek affairs appeared to take as favourable an aspect as we could well desire. . . . My Lord and Prince Mavrocordato have settled to go to Salona in a fortnight.'

On the following day Gamba wrote in his journal these ominous words:

'Lord Byron is indisposed. He complained to me that he was often attacked by vertigoes, which made him feel as if intoxicated. He had also very disagreeable nervous sensations, which he said resembled the feeling of fear, although he knew there was no cause for alarm. The weather got worse, and he could not ride on horseback.'

On March 13 all the shops in the town of Missolonghi were shut, owing to a report that there was a case of the plague there. It seems that a Greek merchant who came from Gastuni was attacked with violent sickness and died within a few hours. After death several black pustules appeared on his face, arms, and back. The doctors were undecided as to whether it was a case of poisoning or of plague. It was ascertained

A SCARE OF PLAGUE

that great mortality prevailed at Gastuni, but whether the plague or a fever was not known. Every possible precaution was taken to prevent infection, and the greatest alarm prevailed in the town. Everyone walked with a stick, to keep off the passer-by. It was realized by the doctors that, in a country so devoid o cleanliness, the plague would make alarming strides. Byron sent an express to Zante to communicate the intelligence to the Resident, and began to make plans for going into the mountains if the plague broke out. On the following day news arrived from Gastuni that there were no cases of the plague there. This intelligence restored a general confidence, and business was resumed as usual. Meanwhile, says Gamba,

'the drilling of our company made great progress, and in three or four weeks we should have been ready to take the field. We exercised the brigade in all sorts of movements. Lord Byron joined us, and practised with us at the sabre and foil: notwithstanding his lameness, he was very adroit.'

The following anecdote, which is given on the authority of Parry, will show the respect in which Byron was held by the peasants in Greece:

'Byron one day returned from his ride more than usually pleased. An interesting country-woman, with a fine family, had come out of her cottage and presented him with a curd cheese and some honey, and could not be persuaded to accept payment for it.

'"I have felt," he said, "more pleasure this day, and at this circumstance, than for a long time past." Then, describing to me where he had seen her, he ordered me to find her out, and make her a present in return. "The peasantry," he said, "are by far the most kind, humane, and honest part of the population; they redeem the character of their countrymen. The other classes are so debased by slavery—accustomed, like all slaves, never to speak truth, but only what will please their masters—that they cannot be trusted. Greece would not be worth saving but for the peasantry."

'Lord Byron then sat down to his cheese, and insisted on our partaking of his fare. A bottle of porter was sent for and broached, that we might join Byron in drinking health and happiness to the kind family, which had procured him so great a pleasure.'

CHAPTER XII

It has been suggested by Byron's enemies that he flattered himself with the notion of some day becoming King of Greece, and that his conduct during the latter part of his life was influenced by ambition. The idea is, of course, absurd. No one knew better than Byron that the Greek *leaders* were not disposed to accept a King at that time. He also knew that, in order to attain that position, it would have been necessary to have recourse to measures which were utterly repugnant to his deep sense of humanity and justice. That Byron may have been sounded by some of the intriguing chieftains with some such suggestion is more than probable, but he was far too honest to walk into the snare. One day he said to Parry:

'I have experienced, since my arrival at Missolonghi, offers that would surprise you, were I to tell you of them, and which would turn the head of any man less satiated than I am, and more desirous of possessing power than of contributing to freedom and happiness. To all these offers, and to every application made to me, which had a tendency to provoke disputes or increase discord, I have always replied: " I came here to serve Greece; agree among yourselves for the good of your country, and whatever is your *united* resolve, and whatever the Government commands, I shall be ready to support with my fortune and my sword." We who came here to fight for Greece have no right to meddle with its internal affairs, or dictate to the people or Government.'

That Byron, if he had lived, and if he had chosen to *usurp* power, could have made himself a Dictator admits of no doubt. In the then state of that distracted country, and the well-known mercenary disposition of the Greeks, he might with his dollars have raised an army which would have made him supreme in Greece.

'No single chieftain,' Parry says, '*could* have resisted; and all of them would have been compelled—because they would not trust one another—to join their forces with Byron's. The whole of the Suliotes were at his beck and call. He could have procured the assassination of any man in Greece for a sum too trifling to mention.'

But Byron had no such views; he never wished to possess political power in Greece. He had come to serve the Greeks on their own conditions, and nothing could have made him swerve from that intention.

Byron's talk with Trelawny at Cephalonia on this subject was not serious, and it took place before he had mastered all the perplexing problems connected with Greece.

It is to Byron's lasting credit that, with so many opportunities for self-aggrandizement, he should have proved himself so unselfish and high-minded.

What might have happened if he had been able to attend the Congress at Salona we shall never know. But we feel confident, from a long and close study of Byron's character, that, even if the Government and the chieftains had offered him the throne of Greece, he would have refused it. Not only would such a throne have been, figuratively, poised in air, swayed by every breath which the rival chieftains would have blown upon it, but Byron himself would have been accused, throughout the length and breadth of Europe, of exploiting the sufferings of Greece for his own personal aggrandizement. While we are discussing this question, it is well to understand the position of affairs at the time when the proposal to hold a Congress at Salona was made.

The ostensible object of the Congress was to shake hands all round, to let bygones be bygones, and to unite all available forces in a spirit of amity. It was high time. The Morea was troubled by the hostilities between Colocotroni's men and Government factions. Colocotroni* himself was shut up in Tripolitza, and his son Pano in Napoli di Romagna. Eastern Greece was more or less tranquil. Odysseus† was at Negropont, from whence seven hundred Albanians had lately absconded. The passes of Thermopylæ were insecure. Although Western Greece was for the moment tranquil, life in Missolonghi was not worth an hour's purchase; and there was a serious split between the so-called Odysseans and the party of Mavrocordato, skilfully fostered by both Colonel Stanhope and Odysseus. Though Candia was subdued, the peasantry threatened a rising in the mountains; the Albanians were discontented; and, finally, the Government itself was not sleeping on a bed of roses, for it had most of the great military chiefs dead against it.

There were, in fact, at that time two Governments—one at Argos and one at Tripolitza—and both hostile

---

* One of the turbulent capitani who was playing for his own hand. He was at one time a member of the Executive Body, and was afterwards proclaimed by the Legislative Assembly as an enemy of the State.

† A leader of Greek insurgents—Byron calls him Ulysses—who broke away from Government control to form an independent party in opposition to Mavrocordato, with whose views Byron sympathized. Trelawny and Colonel Stanhope believed in Odysseus, who after having acquired great influence in Eastern Greece was proclaimed by the Government, imprisoned, and murdered while in captivity.

to each other. The Primates were in favour of a Turkish form of government, and they had great influence in the Morea. The chiefs, on the contrary, while professing democratic principles, were really in favour of frank terrorism and plunder. Some of them were personally brave; others were the offspring of heroes, whom the Turks had never been able to subdue, and who held a sort of feudal tenure over lands which they had kept by the sword. The people of the Peloponnesus were under the influence of the civil and military oligarchs; those of Eastern and Western Greece were chiefly under the captains. Of these, Odysseus and Mavrocordato were the most influential. The islands Hydra and Spezzia were under the influence of some rich oligarchs; while Ipsara was purely democratic. The only virtue to be found in Greece was monopolized by the peasantry, who had passed through a long period of Turkish oppression without being tainted by that corruption which was so prevalent in the towns. Indeed, the peasants and some of the islanders were the finest examples of the 'national' party, which had never been subdued by military or civil tyrants. When we consider the mercenary character of the Greeks, their real or assumed poverty, their insatiable demands for Byron's money; when one realizes the hopeless tangle into which greed and ambition had thrown the affairs of Greece (the open hostility of the capitanis to any settled form of government), it is evident that the supreme management of such a circus would have been no sinecure. No one believed that Greece, under the conditions then prevailing, would have found repose under a foreign King. Nothing short of a cruel, unflinching despotism would have quieted the country.

ANDREA LONDOS

It is, of course, possible that the chiefs assembled at Salona would have offered to Byron the general direction of affairs in the western continent. Gamba says that he had heard rumours to the effect that in a short time the general government of Greece would have been placed in Byron's hands. 'Considering,' he says, 'the vast addition to his authority which the arrival of the moneys from England would have insured to Byron, such an idea is by no means chimerical.'

Writing to Barff on March 22, Byron says:

'In a few days Prince Mavrocordato and myself intend to proceed to Salona at the request of Odysseus and the chiefs of Eastern Greece, to concert, if possible, a plan of union between Western and Eastern Greece, and to take measures, offensive and defensive, for the ensuing campaign. Mavrocordato is *almost* recalled by the *new* Government to the Morea (to take the lead, I rather think), and they have written to propose to me to go either to the Morea with him, or to take the general direction of affairs in this quarter with General Londos, and any other I may choose, to form a Council. Andrea Londos is my old friend and acquaintance, since we were lads in Greece together. It would be difficult to give a positive answer till the Salona meeting is over; but I am willing to serve them in any capacity they please, either commanding or commanded—it is much the same to me, as long as I can be of any presumed use to them.'

CHAPTER XIII

ON March 22 news reached Missolonghi that the Greek loan had been successfully raised in London. Byron sent this welcome intelligence to the Greek Government, with a request that no time should be lost in fitting out the fleet at the different islands. The artillery corps at Missolonghi was augmented by one hundred regular troops under the command of Lambro, a brave Suliote chief, for the better protection of the guns stationed in the mountains. Unfortunately, the weather, upon which Byron so much depended for exercise, could not possibly have been worse. Incessant rain and impassable roads confined him to the house until his health was seriously affected. He constantly complained of oppression on his chest, and was altogether in a depressed condition of mind.

On the day fixed for his departure for Salona, the River Phidari was so swollen as not to be fordable, and the roads in every direction were impassable. For many days the rain poured down in torrents, until, to employ Byron's quaint phrase, 'The dykes of Holland, when broken down, would be the deserts of Arabia for dryness, in comparison.'

On March 28 an event occurred to which Byron has alluded in his published correspondence. It was a trifling matter enough, but might have had serious consequences if Byron had not shown great firmness.

A DUEL PREVENTED

One of the artillerymen, an Italian, had robbed a poor peasant in the market-place of 25 piastres. The man was in due course arrested, tried by court-martial, and convicted. There was no doubt as to his guilt, but a serious dispute arose among the officers as to his punishment. The Germans were for the bastinado; but that was contrary to the French military code, under which the man was tried, and Byron strongly opposed its infliction. He declared that, so far as he was concerned, no barbarous usages should be introduced into Greece, especially as such a mode of punishment would disgust rather than reform. He proposed that, instead of corporal punishment, the offender should have his uniform stripped off his back, and be marched through the streets, bearing a label describing the nature of his offence. He was then to be handed over to the regular police and imprisoned for a time. This example of severity, tempered by humanity, produced an excellent effect upon the soldiers and the citizens of Missolonghi. In the course of the evening some high words passed on the subject between three Englishmen, two of them being officers of the brigade, cards were exchanged, and two duels were to be fought the next morning. Byron did not hear of this until late at night. He then ordered Gamba to arrest the whole party. When they were afterwards brought before Byron, he with some difficulty prevailed upon them to shake hands, and thus averted a serious scandal. Gamba, writing on March 30, says that the Primates of Missolonghi on that day presented Byron with the freedom of their town.

'This new honour,' he says, 'did but entail upon Lord Byron the necessity for greater sacrifices. The poverty of the Government and the town became daily more apparent. They could not furnish the soldiers' rations nor pay their arrears; nor was there forthcoming a single piastre of the 1,500 dollars which the Primates had agreed to furnish for the fortifications. Thus the whole charge fell upon Lord Byron.'

On the following night a Greek came with tears rolling down his cheeks, and complained that one of Byron's soldiers had, in a drunken frenzy, broken open his door and with drawn sword alarmed his whole family. He appealed to Byron for protection. Without a moment's hesitation Byron sent an officer with a file of men to arrest the delinquent. He was a Russian who had lately arrived and enlisted in the artillery brigade. The man vowed that the charge was false; that he had lodged in that house for several days, and that he only broke the door open because the Greek would not admit him, and kept him outside in the rain. He moreover complained of the time and manner of his arrest, and sent a letter to Byron accusing the officer who had arrested him. Byron's reply was as follows:

'*April* 1, 1824.

'SIR,

'I have the honour to reply to your letter of this day. In consequence of an urgent and, to all appearances, a well-founded complaint, made to me yesterday evening, I gave orders to Mr. Hesketh to proceed to your quarters with the soldiers of his guard, and to remove you from your house to the Seraglio, because the owner of your house declared himself and his family to be in immediate danger from your conduct; and added that that was not the first time that you had placed them in similar circumstances. Neither Mr. Hesketh nor myself could imagine that you were in bed, as we had been assured to the contrary; and certainly such a situation was not contemplated. But Mr. Hesketh had positive orders to conduct you from your quarters to those of the artillery brigade; at the

CARIASCACHI CREATES DISTURBANCE

same time being desired to use no violence; nor does it appear that any was had recourse to. This measure was adopted because your landlord assured me, when I proposed to put off the inquiry until the next day, that he could not return to his house without a guard for his protection, and that he had left his wife and daughter, and family, in the greatest alarm; on that account putting them under our immediate protection; the case admitted of no delay. As I am not aware that Mr. Hesketh exceeded his orders, I cannot take any measures to punish him; but I have no objection to examine minutely into his conduct. You ought to recollect that entering into the auxiliary Greek Corps, now under my orders, at your own sole request and positive desire, you incurred the obligation of obeying the laws of the country, as well as those of the service.

'I have the honour to be, etc.,
'N. B.'

It is doubtful whether any other commanding officer would, in similar circumstances, have taken the trouble to write such a letter to a private in his regiment. We merely allude to the incident in order to show that even in trivial matters Byron performed his duty towards those under his command, taking especial interest in each case, so that breaches of discipline might not be too harshly treated by his subordinates.

On April 3 the whole town of Missolonghi was thrown into a panic of alarm. A rumour quickly spread that a body of troops had disembarked at Chioneri, a village on the southern shore of the city. At two o'clock in the afternoon about one hundred and fifty men, belonging to the chief Cariascachi, landed, and demanded reparation for an injury which had been inflicted on his nephew by some boatmen belonging to Missolonghi. Meanwhile the man who wounded the young man had absconded; and the soldiers, unable to wreak their vengeance upon them, arrested two of the Primates, and sent them to Cariascachi as hostages.

They then seized the fort at Vasiladi, a small mud island commanding the flats, which on the sea side afford an impenetrable defence to the town. Cariascachi further declared that he would neither give up the Primates nor Vasiladi until the men who had wounded his nephew were delivered into his hands. On the same day seven Turkish vessels anchored off Vasiladi. Cariascachi had long been suspected of a treasonable correspondence with the Turks, and Mavrocordato was quick to perceive that his conduct on this occasion, coinciding as it did with the movements of the enemy, was part of a conspiracy against his authority in Western Greece. He expected every moment to hear that the Turks had taken possession of Vasiladi, and guessed that the soldiers sent by Cariascachi, ostensibly to avenge a private injury, had really come to open the gates to the Turks. It was a critical moment indeed. All the disposable troops were in the provinces; the Suliotes were marching to Arta, and some of them had already accepted service under Cariascachi himself.

Byron, with wonderful self-command, concealed his indignation at such evidence of treason, and urged Mavrocordato to dismiss his fears, and to display all possible energy in order to defeat Cariascachi's designs. He offered his own services, that of the artillery brigade, and of the three hundred Suliotes who formed his guard. Gunboats were sent to Vasiladi with orders to dislodge the rebels, and Byron resolved that the suspected treason of this Greek chieftain should be severely punished. The batteries of Missolonghi were immediately secured by the artillerymen, and several of their guns were pointed towards the town, so as to prevent a surprise.

At the approach of the gunboats the rebels precipitately fled, and, perceiving the resolute bearing assumed by Byron's troops, they immediately surrendered the Primates, and humbly asked permission to retire unmolested. This was of course granted, but Cariascachi was subsequently tried by court-martial, and found guilty of holding treasonable communications with the enemy.

According to Millingen, who was at Missolonghi at that time, it was not proved against Cariascachi that he had ever proposed to deliver up Vasiladi and Missolonghi to the Turks; but appearances were certainly against him, and his subsequent flight to Agraffa seems to have given evidence of a guilty conscience. Byron was deeply mortified by this example of treason on the part of a Greek chieftain. He had not been prepared to meet with black-hearted treachery, or to see Greeks conspiring against their own country, courting the chains of their former masters, and bargaining the liberties and very existence of their own fellow-countrymen.

'Ignorant at first,' says Millingen, 'how far the ramifications of this conspiracy might extend, he trembled to think of the consequences. Personal fear never entered his mind, although most of the Suliotes who composed his guard, as soon as they heard that their compatriots at Anatolico sided with Cariascachi, declared openly that they would not act against their countrymen. The hopes that Byron had formed for the future of Greece were for a moment obscured. He feared lest the news of a civil war in the Peloponnesus, and of a conspiracy to introduce the Turks into Western Greece, would, on reaching England, ruin the Greek credit, and preclude all hope of obtaining a loan, which to him appeared indispensable to the salvation of her liberty.'

While absorbed by the gloomy reflections to which this incident gave rise, a spy was discovered under Byron's own roof. A man named Constantine Volpiotti, it was asserted, had had several conferences with Cariascachi at Anatolico. Letters found upon him confirmed the worst suspicions, and he was handed over by Byron's orders to the tender mercies of the town guard. A military commission subsequently examined minutely into the whole affair. It appears that the incriminating letters found in Volpiotti's clothes were those written by Mavrocordato and other patriots to Cariascachi, reproaching him for his treachery and connivance with the enemy. These Volpiotti was to show to Omer Pacha as certificates to prove how faithful Cariascachi had ever been to his engagements with him.

'It resulted, from the examination which Volpiotti underwent, that he had been charged to ask Omer Pacha for a *Bouyourtè*, appointing Cariascachi Capitano of the province of Agraffa. Cariascachi engaged in return to co-operate with Vernakiotti in the reduction of Western Greece, and to draw over to his party several of the chiefs who had hitherto most faithfully adhered to the Greek Government.'

Under these circumstances it was not wise, even if it were politic, to allow Cariascachi to escape. Byron felt this keenly, and foresaw what actually happened. Cariascachi was no sooner clear of Anatolico than he placed himself at the head of his followers, and, assisted by Andrea Isco, of Macrinoro, he again made Agraffa and its adjoining provinces the scene of his depredations and daily sanguinary encounters.

'At no time in his life,' says Millingen, 'did Lord Byron find himself in circumstances more calculated to render him unhappy. The cup of health had

BYRON NERVOUS AND IRRITABLE

dropped from his lips, and constant anxiety and suffering operated powerfully on his mind, already a prey to melancholy apprehensions, and disappointment, increased by disgust. Continually haunted by a dread of epilepsy or palsy, he fell into the lowest state of hypochondriasis, and vented his sorrows in language which, though sometimes sublime, was at others as peevish and capricious as that of an unruly and quarrelsome child.'

Gamba tells us that Byron, after the events above mentioned, became nervous and irritable. He had not been on horseback for some days on account of the weather, but on April 9, though the weather was threatening, he determined to ride. Three miles from the town he and Gamba were caught in a heavy downpour of rain, and they returned to the town walls wet through and in a violent perspiration. Gamba says:

'I have before mentioned that it was our practice to dismount at the walls, and return to our house in a boat. This day, however, I entreated Byron to return home on horseback the whole way, as it would be dangerous, hot as he was, to remain exposed to the rain in a boat for half an hour. But he would not listen to me, and said: "I should make a pretty soldier indeed, if I were to care for such a trifle." Accordingly we dismounted, and got into the boat as usual. Two hours after his return home, he was seized with a shuddering: he complained of fever and rheumatic pains. At eight in the evening I entered his rooms; he was lying on a sofa, restless and melancholy.'

Byron said that he suffered a great deal of pain, and in consequence Dr. Bruno proposed to bleed him. Bruno seems to have considered the lancet as a sovereign remedy for all the ills of life.

'Have you no other remedy than bleeding? There are many more die of the lancet than the lance,' said Byron, as he declined his doctor's proposal. On the following day he was perpetually shuddering, but he got up at his usual hour and transacted business. He did not, however, leave the house. On April 11 Byron resolved to ride out an hour before his usual time, fearing that, if he waited, he would be prevented by the rain.

'We rode for a long time in the olive woods,' says Gamba. 'Lambro, a Suliote officer, accompanied by a numerous suite, attended Byron, who spoke much and appeared to be in good spirits.

'The next day he kept his bed with an attack of rheumatic fever. It was thought that his saddle was wet; but it is more probable that he was really suffering from his previous exposure to the rain, which perhaps affected him the more readily on account of his over-abstemious mode of life.'

The dates to which Gamba refers in the statement we have quoted were April 11 and 12. It is important to remark that in Fletcher's account, published in the *Westminster Review*, it is stated that the last time Byron rode out was on April 10. According to Parry, who supports Fletcher's opinion, Byron was very unwell on April 11, and did not leave his house. He had shivering fits, and complained of pains, particularly in his bones and head.

'He talked a great deal,' says Parry, 'and I thought in rather a wandering manner. I became alarmed for his safety, and earnestly begged him to try a change of air and scene at Zante.'

Gamba, in his journal, says that Byron rose from his bed on April 13, but did not leave the house. The fever appeared to be diminished, but the pains in his head and bones continued. He was melancholy and irritable. He had not slept since his attack, and could take no other nourishment than a little broth and a spoonful or two of arrowroot. On the 14th he got out of bed at noon; he was calmer. The fever had apparently diminished, but he was very weak, and still complained of pains in his head. It was with the greatest difficulty, says Gamba, that the physicians dissuaded him from going out riding, which, in spite of the threatening weather, he desired to do. There seems at that time to have been no suspicion of danger, and it was even supposed by his doctors that the malady was under control. Byron himself said that he was rather glad of his fever, as it might cure him of his tendency to epilepsy. He attended to his correspondence as usual. Gamba says:

'I think it was on this day that, as I was sitting near him on his sofa, he said to me, "I was afraid I was losing my memory, and, in order to try, I attempted to repeat some Latin verses with the English translation, which I have not tried to recollect since I was at school. I remembered them all except the last word of one of the hexameters."'

On April 15 the fever was still upon him, says Gamba, but all pain had ceased. He was easier, and expressed a wish to ride out, but the weather would not permit. He transacted business, and received, among others, a letter from the Turkish Governor to whom he had sent the prisoners he had liberated. The Turk thanked Byron for his courtesy, and asked for a repetition of this favour. 'The letter pleased him much,' says Gamba.

According to Fletcher, it appears that both on that day and the day previous Byron had a suspicion that his complaint was not understood by his doctors.

Parry says that on April 15 the doctors thought there was no danger, and said so, openly. He paid

Byron a visit, and remained at his bedside from 7 p.m. until 10 o'clock.

'Lord Byron spoke of death with great composure,' says Parry; 'and though he did not think that his end was so very near, there was something about him so serious and so firm, so resigned and composed, so different from anything I had ever before seen in him, that my mind misgave me.'

Byron then spoke of the sadness of being ill in such a place as Missolonghi, and seemed to have imagined the possibility of a reconciliation with his wife.

'When I left Italy,' said Byron, 'I had time on board the brig to give full scope to memory and reflection. I am convinced of the happiness of domestic life. No man on earth respects a virtuous woman more than I do, and the prospect of retirement in England with my wife and daughter gives me an idea of happiness I have never before experienced. Retirement will be everything for me, for heretofore my life has been like the ocean in a storm.'

Byron then spoke of Tita (and Fletcher also, doubtless, though Parry does not mention that honest and faithful servant), and said that Bruno was an excellent young man and very skilful, but too much agitated. He hoped that Parry would come to him as often as possible, as he was jaded to death by the worrying of his doctors, and the evident anxiety of all those who wished him well. On a wretched fever-stricken swamp, in a house barely weather-tight, in a miserable room, far from all those whom he loved on earth, lay the 'pilgrim of eternity,' his life, so full of promise, slowly flickering out. The pestilent sirocco was blowing a hurricane, and the rain was falling with almost tropical violence. Gamba had met with an accident which confined him to his quarters in another part of the town, a circumstance which deprived Byron of a loyal friend in the hour of his direst need. Under these circumstances, Parry was a godsend to Byron, and he seems to have done everything possible to cheer him in his moments of depression.

On April 16 Byron was alarmingly ill, and, according to Parry, almost constantly delirious. He spoke alternately in English and Italian, and his thoughts wandered. The doctors were not alarmed, and told Parry that Byron would certainly recover. According to Millingen's account, Dr. Bruno called him in for a consultation on the 15th, and we shall see what Millingen thought of his patient's condition when we lay his narrative before the reader.

When Parry visited Byron on the morning of the 17th, he was at times delirious. He appeared to be much worse than on the day before. The doctors succeeded in bleeding him twice, and both times he fainted.

'His debility was excessive. He complained bitterly of the want of sleep, as delirious patients do complain, in a wild, rambling manner. He said he had not slept for more than a week, when, in fact, he had repeatedly slept at short intervals, disturbedly indeed, but still it was sleep. He had now ceased to think or talk of death; he had probably no idea that death was so near at hand, for his senses were in such a state that they rarely allowed him to form a correct idea of anything.'

On the 17th Gamba managed to get to Byron's room, and was struck by the change in his appearance.

'He was very calm,' says Gamba, 'and talked to me in the kindest manner about my having sprained my ankle. In a hollow, sepulchral tone, he said: "Take care of your foot. I know by experience how painful it must be." I could not stay near his bed: a flood of tears rushed into my eyes, and I was obliged to withdraw. This was the first day that the medical men seemed to entertain serious apprehensions.'

On this day Gamba heard that Dr. Thomas, of Zante, had been sent for. It is unfortunate that this was not done sooner; but Byron had forbidden Fletcher to send for that excellent medical man, when he proposed it two days previously. During the night of the 17th Byron became delirious, and wandered in his speech; he fancied himself at the head of his Suliotes, assailing the walls of Lepanto—a wish that had lain very close to his heart for many and many a day. It was his dream of a soldier's glory, to die fighting, sword in hand. On the morning of the 18th Drs. Millingen and Bruno were alarmed by symptoms of an inflammation of the brain, and proposed another bleeding, to which Byron consented, but soon ordered the vein to be closed.

'At noon,' says Gamba, 'I came to his bedside. He asked me if there were any letters for him. There was one from the Archbishop Ignatius to him, which told Byron that the Sultan had proclaimed him, in full divan, an enemy of the Porte. I thought it best not to let him know of the arrival of that letter. A few hours afterwards other letters arrived from England from his most intimate friends, full of good news, and most consolatory in every way, particularly one from Mr. Hobhouse, and another from Douglas Kinnaird; but he had then become unconscious—it was too late!'

April 18, 1824, was Easter Day, a holiday throughout the length and breadth of Greece, and a noisy one, too. It is the day on which the Greeks at Missolonghi were accustomed to discharge their firearms and great guns. Prince Mavrocordato gave orders that Parry should march his artillery brigade and Suliotes to some distance from the town, in order

CONSULTATION AMONG PHYSICIANS

to attract the populace from the vicinity of Byron's house. At the same time the town guard patrolled the streets, and informed people of Byron's danger, begging them to make as little noise as possible. The plan succeeded admirably; Byron was not disturbed, and at three o'clock in the afternoon he rose, and, leaning on the arm of Tita, went into the next room. When seated, he told Tita to bring him a book, mentioning it by name. About this time Dr. Bruno entreated him, with tears in his eyes, to be again bled.

'No,' said Byron; 'if my hour is come, I shall die whether I lose my blood or keep it.'

After reading a few minutes he became faint, and, leaning on Tita's arm, he tottered into the next room and returned to bed.

At half-past three, Dr. Bruno and Dr. Millingen, becoming more alarmed, wished to call in two other physicians, a Dr. Freiber, a German, and a Greek named Luca Vaya, the most distinguished of his profession in the town, and physician to Mavrocordato. Lord Byron at first refused to see them; but being told that Mavrocordato advised it, he said: 'Very well, let them come; but let them look at me and say nothing.' They promised this, and were admitted. When about him and feeling his pulse, one of them wished to speak. 'Recollect your promise,' said Byron, 'and go away.'

In order to form some idea of the state of things while Byron's life was slowly ebbing away, we will quote a passage from Parry's book, which was published soon after the poet's death:

'Dr. Bruno I believe to be a very good young man, but he was certainly inadequate to his situation. I do not allude to his medical knowledge, of which I cannot pretend to be a judge; but he lacked firmness, and was so much agitated that he was incapable of bringing whatever knowledge he might possess into use. Tita was kind and attentive, and by far the most teachable and useful of all the persons about Lord Byron. As there was nobody invested with any authority over his household after he fell ill, there was neither method, order, nor quiet, in his apartments. A clever, skilful English surgeon, possessing the confidence of his patient, would have put all this in train; but Dr. Bruno had no idea of doing any such thing. There was also a want of many comforts which, to the sick, may be called necessaries, and there was a dreadful confusion of tongues. In his agitation Dr. Bruno's English, and he spoke but imperfectly, was unintellegible; Fletcher's Italian was equally bad. I speak nothing but English; Tita then spoke nothing but Italian; and the ordinary Greek domestics were incomprehensible to us all. In all the attendants there was the officiousness of zeal; but, owing to their ignorance of each other's language, their zeal only added to the confusion. This circumstance, and the absence of common necessaries, made Lord Byron's apartment such a picture of distress, and even anguish, during the two or three last days of his life, as I never before beheld, and wish never again to witness.'

At four o'clock on April 18, according to Gamba, Byron seemed to be aware of his approaching end. Dr. Millingen, Fletcher, and Tita, were at his bedside. Strange though it may seem to us in these far-off days, with our experience of medical men, Dr. Millingen, unable to restrain his tears, walked out of the room. Tita also wept profusely, and would have retired if Byron had not held his hand. Byron looked at him steadily, and said, half smiling, in Italian: 'Oh, questa è una bella scena.' He then seemed to reflect a moment, and exclaimed, 'Call Parry.'

'Almost immediately afterwards,' says Gamba, 'a fit of delirium ensued, and he began to talk wildly, as if he were mounting a breach in an assault. He called out, half in English, half in Italian: "Forwards—forwards —courage—follow my example—don't be afraid!"'

When he came to himself Fletcher was with him. He then knew that he was dying, and seemed very anxious to make his servant understand his wishes. He was very considerate about his servants, and said that he was afraid they would suffer from sitting up so long in attendance upon him. Byron said, 'I wish to do something for Tita and Luca.' 'My lord,' said Fletcher, 'for God's sake never mind that now, but talk of something of more importance.' But he returned to the same topic, and, taking Fletcher by the hand, continued: 'You will be provided for—and now hear my last wishes.'

Fletcher begged that he might bring pen and paper to take down his words. 'No,' replied Lord Byron, 'there is no time—mind you execute my orders. Go to my sister—tell her—go to Lady Byron—you will see her, and say——' Here his voice faltered, and gradually became indistinct; but still he continued muttering something in a very earnest manner for nearly twenty minutes, though in such a tone that only a few words could be distinguished. These were only names: 'Augusta,' 'Ada,' 'Hobhouse,' 'Kinnaird.' He then said: 'Now I have told you all.'

'My lord,' replied Fletcher, 'I have not understood a word your lordship has been saying.' Byron looked most distressed at this, and said, 'Not understand me? What a pity! Then it is too late—all is over.' 'I hope not,' answered Fletcher; 'but the Lord's will be done.' Byron continued, 'Yes, not mine.' He then tried to utter a few words, of which none were intelligible except, 'My sister—my child.' The doctors began to concur in an opinion which one might have thought sufficiently obvious from the first, namely, that the principal danger to the patient was his extreme weakness, and now agreed to administer restoratives. Dr. Bruno, however, thought otherwise, but agreed to administer a dose of claret, bark, and opium, and to apply blisters to the soles of Byron's feet. He took the draught readily, but for some time refused the blisters. At last they were applied, and Byron fell asleep.

Gamba says: 'He awoke in half an hour. I wished to go to him, but I had not the heart. Parry went; Byron knew him, and squeezed his hand.'

Parry says:

'When Lord Byron took my hand, I found his hands were deadly cold. With Tita's assistance, I endeavoured gently to create a little warmth in them, and I also loosened the bandage which was tied round his head. Till this was done, he seemed in great pain—clenched his hands at times, and gnashed his teeth. He bore the loosening of the band passively; and after it was loosened, he shed tears. I encouraged him to weep, and said: "My lord, I thank God, I hope you will now be better; shed as many tears as you can; you will sleep and find ease." He replied faintly, "Yes, the pain is gone; I shall sleep now." He took my hand, uttered a faint "Good-night," and dropped to sleep. My heart ached, but I thought then his sufferings were over, and that he would wake no more. He did wake again, however, and I went to him; he knew me, though scarcely. He was less distracted than I had seen him for some time before; there was the calmness of resignation, but there was also the stupor of death. He tried to utter his wishes, but he was not able to do so. He said something about rewarding Tita, and uttered several incoherent words. There was either no meaning in what he said, or it was such a meaning as we could not expect at that moment. His eyes continued open only a short time,

THE DEATH OF BYRON

and then, at about six o'clock in the evening of the 18th April, he sank into a slumber, or rather, I should say, a stupor, and woke and knew no more.'

It must be borne in mind that the details given above were written by a man who asserts that he was present during the period of which he gives an account. Gamba, as we have seen, was not present, and the details which he gives are avowedly gathered from those who happened to be in the room.

'From those about him,' says Gamba, 'I collected that, either at this time or in his former interval of reason, Byron could be understood to say, "Poor Greece! Poor town! My poor servants!" Also, 'Why was I not aware of this sooner?" and, "My hour is come! I do not care for death. But why did I not go home before I came here?" At another time he said: "There are things which make the world dear to me."'

He said this in Italian, and Parry may of course not have understood him. 'Io lascio qualche cosa di caro nel mondo.' He also said: 'I am content to die.' In speaking of Greece, he said: 'I have given her my time, my means, my health, and now I give her my life! What could I do more?"

Byron remained insensible, immovable, for twenty-four hours. There were occasional symptoms of suffocation, and a rattling in the throat, which induced his servants occasionally to raise his head. Gamba says:

'Means were taken to rouse him from his lethargy, but in vain. A great many leeches were applied to his temples, and the blood flowed copiously all night. It was exactly a quarter past six on the next day, the 19th April, that he was seen to open his eyes, and immediately close them again. The doctors felt his pulse—he was gone!'

CHAPTER XIV

It matters little what we now think of Byron as a man. After eighty-four years, his personality is of less public interest than his achievements, while our capacity for forming an adequate judgment of his character is necessarily dependent on second-hand evidence, some of which is false, and much tainted by prejudice. But what did those hard men of action who stood at his side in those terrible days in Greece—Stanhope, Parry, Finlay, Blaquière, Millingen, Trelawny—what did they think of Byron?

Stanhope, who was at Salona, wrote to Bowring on April 30:

'A courier has just arrived from the chief Scalza. Alas! all our fears are realized. The soul of Byron has taken its last flight. England has lost her brightest genius—Greece her noblest friend. To console them for the loss, he has left behind the emanations of his splendid mind. If Byron had faults, he had redeeming virtues too—he sacrificed his comfort, fortune, health, and life, to the cause of an oppressed nation. Honoured be his memory! Had I the disposal of his ashes, I would place them in the Temple of Theseus, or in the Parthenon at Athens.'

Three days later Stanhope wrote again to Bowring:

'Byron would not refuse to an entire people the benefit of his virtues; he condescended to display them wherever Humanity beckoned him to her aid. This single object of devotion to the well-being of a people has raised him to a distinguished pitch of glory among characters dignified by their virtues, of which the illustrious British nation can make so ample a display, and of whom Greece hopes to behold many co-operating in her regeneration. Having here paid the tribute of admiration due to the virtues of Lord Byron, eternal may his memory remain with the world!'

Parry says:

'Thus died the truest and greatest poet England has lately given birth to, the warmest-hearted of her philanthropists, the least selfish of her patriots. That the disappointment of his ardent hopes was the primary cause of his illness and death cannot, I think, be doubted. The weight of that disappointment was augmented by the numerous difficulties he met with. He was fretted and annoyed, but he disdained to complain. As soon as it was known that Lord Byron was dead, sorrow and grief were generally felt in Greece. They spread from his own apartments over the town of Missolonghi, through the whole of Greece, and over every part of civilized Europe. No persons, perhaps, after his domestics and personal friends, felt his loss more acutely than the poor citizens of Missolonghi. His residence among them procured them food, and insured their protection. But for him they would have been first plundered by the unpaid Suliotes, and then left a prey to the Turks. Not only were the Primates and Mavrocordato affected on the occasion, but the poorest citizen felt that he had lost a friend. Mavrocordato spoke of Lord Byron as the best friend of Greece, and said that his conduct was admirable. "Nobody knows," he was heard to say, "except perhaps myself, the loss Greece has suffered. Her safety even depended on his life. His presence at Missolonghi has checked intrigues which will now have uncontrolled sway. By his aid alone have I been able to preserve this city; and now I know that every assistance I derived from and through him will be withdrawn."

'At other cities and places of Greece—at Salona, where the Congress had just assembled; at Athens— the grief was equally sincere. Lord Byron was mourned as the best benefactor to Greece. Orations were pronounced by the priests, and the same honours were paid to his memory as to the memory of one of their own revered chiefs.'

After Byron's death Finlay wrote these words:

'Lord Byron's death has shed a lustre on both his writings and his actions; they are in accordance. His life was sacrificed in the cause for which he had early written, and which he constantly supported. His merit would not have been greater had he breathed his last on the isthmus of Corinth at the conclusion of a baffled siege. Yet such a death would certainly have been more fortunate; for it would have recalled his name oftener to the memory, at least, of those who have no souls. Time will put an end to all undue admiration and malicious cant, and the world will ultimately form an estimate of Byron's character from his writings and his public conduct. It will then be possible to form a just estimate of the greatness of his genius and his mind, and the real extent of his faults. The ridiculous calumnies which have found a moment's credit will then be utterly forgotten. Nor will it be from the cursory memoirs or anecdotes of his contemporaries that his character can be drawn.'

Blaquière, who had brought out the first instalment of the Greek loan, arrived at Zante on April 24, and was there informed of Byron's death. He had been among the first to urge Byron to hasten his projected visit to Greece, and had held a long conversation with him at Genoa on the state of affairs in the Morea. The following extract is taken from a letter which he wrote to a friend in England:

'Thus terminated the life of Lord Byron, at a moment the most glorious for his own fame, but the most unfortunate for Greece; since there is no doubt but, had he lived, many calamities would have been avoided, while his personal credit and guarantee would have prevented the ruinous delay which has taken place

CONSTERNATION AT MISSOLONGHI 177

with regard to transferring the loan. In thus devoting his life and fortune to the cause of religion and humanity, when he might have continued to enjoy the enthusiastic praises of his contemporaries, he has raised the best monument to his own fame, and has furnished the most conclusive reply to calumny and detraction. When all he had done, and was about to do for the cause, is considered, no wonder that Lord Byron's death should have produced such an effect. It was, in fact, regarded not only as a national calamity, but as an irreparable loss to every individual in the town of Missolonghi, and the English volunteers state that hundreds of the Greeks were seen to shed tears when the event was announced.

'With respect to Prince Mavrocordato, to whom Lord Byron had rendered the most important services, both as a personal friend and in his capacity of Governor-General of Western Greece, it is unnecessary to say that he could not have received a severer blow. When I saw Lord Byron at Genoa last year, I well remember with what enthusiasm he spoke of his intended visit, and how much he regretted not having joined the standard of freedom long before. When once in Greece, he espoused her most sacred cause with zeal. Up to the time of his fatal illness he had not advanced less than fifty thousand dollars, and there is no doubt but he intended to devote the whole of his private income to the service of the confederation.'

Millingen says:

'The most dreadful public calamity could not have spread more general consternation, or more profound and sincere grief, than the unexpected news of Lord Byron's death. During the few months he had lived among the people of Missolonghi, he had given so many proofs of the sincerity and extent of his zeal for the advancement of their best interests. He had, with so much generosity, sacrificed considerable sums to that purpose; he had relieved the distress of so many unfortunate persons, that everyone looked upon him as a father and public benefactor. These titles were not, as they mostly are, the incense of adulation, but the spontaneous tribute of overflowing gratitude. He had succeeded in inspiring the soldiers with the brightest and most sanguine expectations. Full of confidence in a chief they loved, they would have followed him in the boldest enterprises. To-day they must follow the corpse of him whom they received but yesterday with the liveliest acclamations.'

Trelawny, who arrived at Missolonghi four days after Byron's death, thus writes to Stanhope at Salona:

'Lord Byron is dead. With all his faults, I loved him truly; he is connected with every event of the most interesting years of my wandering life. His everyday companion, we lived in ships, boats, and in houses, together; we had no secrets, no reserve, and though we often differed in opinion, we never quarrelled. It gave me pain witnessing his frailties; he only wanted a little excitement to awaken and put forth virtues that redeemed them all. . . . This is no private grief; the world has lost its greatest man, I my best friend.'

On April 28 Trelawny wrote again to Stanhope:

'I think Byron's name was the great means of getting the loan. A Mr. Marshall with £8,000 per annum was as far as Corfu, and turned back on hearing of Byron's death. . . . The greatest man in the world has resigned his mortality in favour of this sublime cause; for had he remained in Italy he had lived!'

Such was Trelawny's opinion of Byron in April, 1824. From all that the present writer has been able to gather, both from Trelawny's lips and from his 'Recollections,' published thirty-four years after Byron's death, such was his real opinion to the last.

Mrs. Julian Marshall, having called attention* to the fact that, four months after Byron's death, Trelawny, in a letter to Mary Shelley, spoke in contemptuous

* 'Life and Letters of Mary Wollstonecraft Shelley,' edited by Mrs. Julian Marshall.

TRELAWNY AND MAVROCORDATO

terms of Byron, we feel bound to refer to it here. It must be remembered that the letter in question was of a strictly private nature. In making it public, Mrs. Marshall *unintentionally* dealt a severe blow at Trelawny, which, in justice to his memory, we will endeavour to soften.

To anyone acquainted with the character of this remarkable man—the fearless soul of honour—such a *volte-face* seems absurd, except on the hypothesis that something had transpired, since Byron's death, sufficient to destroy a long-tried friendship. The fact is that during those four months the whole situation had changed. Trelawny, no longer a free-lance, was practically a prisoner in a cave on Mount Parnassus. His friend Odysseus went about in daily fear of assassination, and was persecuted by the active hostility of a Government which both Odysseus and Trelawny thought was inspired by Mavrocordato. Trelawny's opinion of the latter, whose cause Byron had espoused, may be gathered from his letter to Mary Shelley:

'A word as to your wooden god Mavrocordato. He is a miserable Jew, and I hope ere long to see his head removed from his worthless and heartless body. He is a mere shuffling soldier, an aristocratic brute—wants Kings and Congresses—a poor, weak, shuffling, intriguing, cowardly fellow; so no more about him.'

It will be seen that Trelawny, when fairly warmed up, did not mince his words. It is indeed a pity that these heated adjectives were served up to the public. It was only because Byron had consistently supported Mavrocordato as the Governor of Western Greece that Trelawny, in his indiscriminative manner, assailed his memory. But his letter was evidently only the peevish outburst of an angry man, and closed with these words:

'I would do much to see and talk to you, but, as I am now too much irritated to disclose the real state of things, I will not mislead you by false statements.'

The state of things at the time may be gathered from a letter addressed to Colonel Stanhope by Captain Humphreys, who was then serving the Greek cause as a volunteer.

'I write, not from a land of liberty and freedom, but from a country at present a prey to anarchy and confusion, with the dismal prospect of future tyranny. . . . Odysseus is at his fortress of Parnassus; bribery, assassination, and every provocation, have been employed against him. An English officer, Captain Fenton, who is with Odysseus, as well as Trelawny, has been twice attempted to be assassinated, after refusing to accept a bribe of 10,000 dollars, to deliver up the fortress. *Mavrocordato's agents principally influence the Government; the executive body remains stationary; and part of the loan has been employed to secure their re-election.*'

There is enough in this letter to account for Trelawny's irritation; but he was entirely wrong in thinking that Byron was in any sense subservient to the man whom he then regarded as the real author of his misfortunes. Trelawny had made the mistake of joining the faction of Odysseus, but Byron was never connected with any faction whatever. Odysseus seems to have persuaded Trelawny that Byron had become a mere tool of Mavrocordato, and it was under that erroneous impression that his letter to Mary Shelley was written.

If, as Mrs. Julian Marshall says, 'Trelawny's mercurial and impulsive temperament—ever in extremes—was liable to the most sudden revulsion of feeling it,'

PRINCE MAVROCORDATO

would surely have been wiser, and certainly fairer, to have withheld the publication of opinions which were not intended for publication, and which he had, in later life, openly disavowed. In his estimate of the character and policy of Mavrocordato, he was also mistaken. It would be quite easy to show that Mavrocordato was perhaps the only man of his nation, then in Greece, who united in an eminent degree unadulterated patriotism with the talents which form a statesman. Millingen, who knew him well, tells us that it was fortunate for Greece that Mavrocordato was so well acquainted with the character of those with whom he had to deal. That knowledge preserved Missolonghi, until the arrival of reinforcements enabled it to hold out against Omer Pacha's assault. Mavrocordato, he tells us, never pursued any other object than the good of his country, and never sacrificed her interests to his own ambition. He alone was capable of organizing a civil administration; in fact, he created a stable form of government from the ashes of chaos. So far from his having been a coward, as Trelawny asserts, Mavrocordato, in his intense desire to serve his country, often placed himself at the head of troops and fought bravely. Having held the position of Governor-General of Western Greece in very trying times, he relinquished his command in 1825, in compliance with the orders of his Government, which recalled him to Anapli, there to fill the post of Secretary of State. He sacrificed the whole of his fortune in the service of Greece. According to Millingen, he was occasionally so distressed for money as to be unable to provide for his daily expenses.

Enough has been said to show that Trelawny's abuse of Byron must not be taken too seriously, and that his opinion of Mavrocordato was not endorsed by those whose opportunities for judging the Prince's conduct were far greater than Trelawny's.

Let us dismiss from our minds the recollection of hasty words written in anger, and let us remember those truer and deeper sentiments which Trelawny expressed in his old age:

'I withdrew the black pall and the white shroud, and beheld the body of the Pilgrim—more beautiful in death than in life. The contraction of the muscles and skin had effaced every line that Time or Passion had ever traced upon it. Few marble busts would have matched its stainless white, the harmony of its proportions, and perfect finish. And yet he had been dissatisfied with that body, and longed to cast its slough! He was jealous of the genius of Shakespeare—that might well be—but where had he seen the face or the form worthy to excite his envy?'

CHAPTER XV

THE news of Byron's death spread like wildfire through the streets and bazaars of Missolonghi. The whole city seemed stunned by the unexpected blow. Byron's illness had been known, but no one dreamed that it would end so fatally. As Gamba has well said: 'He died in a strange land, and amongst strangers; but more loved, more sincerely wept, he could never have been wherever he had breathed his last.'

On the day of Byron's death, Mavrocordato issued the following proclamation, which forms a real and enduring tribute to the memory of one who, in the prime of life, died in a great cause:

PROVISIONAL GOVERNMENT OF WESTERN GREECE.

The present day of festivity and rejoicing is turned into one of sorrow and mourning.

The Lord Noel Byron departed this life at eleven o'clock last night, after an illness of ten days, his death being caused by an inflammatory fever. Such was the effect of his lordship's illness on the public mind, that all classes had forgotten their usual recreations of Easter, even before the afflicting end was apprehended.

The loss of this illustrious individual is undoubtedly to be deplored by all Greece; but it must be more especially a subject of lamentation at Missolonghi, where his generosity has been so conspicuously displayed, and of which he had even become a citizen, with the ulterior determination of participating in all the dangers of the war.

Everybody is acquainted with the beneficent acts of his lordship, and none can cease to hail his name as that of a real benefactor.

Until, therefore, the final determination of the National Government be known, and by virtue of the powers with which it has been pleased to invest me, I hereby decree:

1st. To-morrow morning at daylight, 37 minute-guns shall be fired from the grand battery, being the number which corresponds with the age of the illustrious deceased.

2nd. All the public offices, even to the tribunals, are to remain closed for three successive days.

3rd. All the shops, except those in which provisions or medicines are sold, will also be shut; and it is strictly enjoined, that every species of public amusement and other demonstrations of festivity at Easter may be suspended.

4th. A general mourning will be observed for twenty-one days.

5th. Prayers and a funeral service are to be offered up in all the churches.

(Signed) A. MAVROCORDATO.
GIORGIUS PRAIDIS,
Secretary.

Given at Missolonghi,
  this 19th day of April, 1824.

At sunrise, on the day following Byron's death, thirty-seven minute-guns were fired from the principal battery; and one of the batteries belonging to the corps immediately under his orders fired a gun every half-hour during the day. We take the following from Gamba's journal:

'*April* 21.—For the remainder of this day and the next, a silence, like that of the grave, prevailed over the city. We had intended to perform the funeral ceremony on the 21st, but the continued rain prevented us. On the 22nd, however, we acquitted ourselves of that sad duty, so far as our humble means would permit. In the midst of his own brigade, of the Government troops, and of the whole population, on the shoulders of his own officers, the most precious portion of his honoured remains was carried to the church, where lie the bodies of Marco Bozzari and of General Normann. There we laid them down. The coffin was a rude, ill-constructed chest of wood; a black mantle served for a pall; and over it we placed a helmet and sword, with a crown of laurels. No funeral pomp could have left the impression, nor spoken the feelings, of this simple ceremony. The wretchedness and desolation of the place itself; the wild, half-civilized warriors around us; their deep, unaffected grief; the fond recollections and disappointed hopes; the anxieties and sad presentiments depicted on every countenance, contributed to form a scene more moving, more truly affecting, than perhaps was ever before witnessed round the coffin of a great man.'

Spiridion Tricoupi, a son of one of the Primates of Missolonghi, pronounced the funeral oration in the following words, translated from the modern Greek by an inhabitant of Missolonghi:

'Unlooked-for event! Deplorable misfortune! But a short time has elapsed since the people of this deeply suffering country welcomed, with unfeigned joy and open arms, this celebrated individual to their bosoms. To-day, overwhelmed with grief and despair, they bathe his funeral couch with tears of bitterness, and mourn over it with inconsolable affliction. On Easter Sunday, the happy salutation of the day, "Christ is risen," remained but half spoken on the lips of every Greek; and as they met, before even congratulating one another on the return of that joyous day, the universal question was, "How is Lord Byron?" Thousands assembled in the spacious plain outside the city, to commemorate the sacred day, appeared as if they had assembled for the sole purpose of imploring the Saviour of the world to restore to health him who was a partaker with us in our present struggle for the deliverance of our native land. And how is it possible that any heart should remain unmoved, any lip closed, upon the present occasion? Was ever

Greece in greater want of assistance than when Lord Byron, at the peril of his life, crossed over to Missolonghi? Then, and ever since he has been with us, his liberal hand has been opened to our necessities—necessities which our own poverty would have otherwise rendered irremediable. How many and much greater benefits did we not expect from him! And to-day, alas! to-day, the unrelenting grave closes over him and all our hopes.

'Residing out of Greece, and enjoying all the pleasures and luxuries of Europe, he might have contributed materially to the success of our cause without coming personally amongst us; and this would have been sufficient for us, for the well-proved ability and profound judgment of our Governor, the President of the Senate, would have insured our safety with the means so supplied. But if this was sufficient for us, it was not so for Lord Byron. Destined by Nature to uphold the rights of man whenever he saw them trampled upon; born in a free and enlightened country; early taught, by reading the works of our ancestors, which teach all who can read them, not only what man is, but what he ought to be, and what he may be, he saw the persecuted and enslaved Greek determined to break the heavy chains with which he was bound, and to convert the iron into sharp-edged swords, that he might regain by force what force had torn from him. He came to share our sufferings; assisting us, not only with his wealth, of which he was profuse; not only with his judgment, of which he has given us so many salutary examples; but with his sword, which he was preparing to unsheath against our barbarous and tyrannical oppressors. He came—according to the testimony of those who were intimate with him—with a determination to die in Greece and for Greece. How, therefore, can we do otherwise than lament with deep sorrow the loss of such a man! How can we do otherwise than bewail it as the loss of the whole Greek nation! Thus far, my friends, you have seen him liberal, generous, courageous, a true Philhellenist; and you have seen him as your benefactor. This is indeed a sufficient cause for your tears, but it is not sufficient for his honour. It is not sufficient for the greatness of the undertaking in which he had engaged. He, whose death we are now so deeply deploring, was a man who, in one great branch of literature, gave his name to the age in which we live : the vastness of his genius and the richness of his fancy did not permit him to follow the splendid though beaten track of the literary fame of the ancients; he chose a new road—a road which ancient prejudice had endeavoured, and was still endeavouring, to shut against the learned of Europe : but as long as his writings live, and they must live as long as the world exists, this road will remain always open; for it is, as well as the other, a sure road to true knowledge. I will not detain you at the present time by expressing all the respect and enthusiasm with which the perusal of his writings has always inspired me, and which, indeed, I feel much more powerfully now than at any other period. The learned men of all Europe celebrate him, and have celebrated him; and all ages will celebrate the poet of our age, for he was born for all Europe and for all ages.

'One consideration occurs to me, as striking and true as it is applicable to the present state of our country: listen to it, my friends, with attention, that you may make it your own, and that it may become a generally acknowledged truth. There have been many great and splendid nations in the world, but few have been the epochs of their true glory : one phenomenon, I am inclined to believe, is wanting in the history of these nations, and one the possibility of the appearance of which the all-considering mind of the philosopher has much doubted. Almost all the nations of the world have fallen from the hands of one master into those of another; some have been benefited, others have been injured by the change; but the eye of the historian has not yet seen a nation enslaved by barbarians, and more particularly by barbarians rooted for ages in their soil—has not yet seen, I say, such a people throw off their slavery unassisted and alone. This is the phenomenon; and now, for the first time in the history of the world, we witness it in Greece—yes, in Greece alone! The philosopher beholds it from afar, and his doubts are dissipated; the historian sees it, and prepares his citation of it as a new event in the fortunes of nations; the statesman sees it, and becomes more observant and more on his guard. Such is the extraordinary time in which we live. My friends, the insurrection of Greece is not an epoch of our nation alone; it is an epoch of all nations: for, as I before observed, it is a phenomenon which stands alone in the political history of nations.

'The great mind of the highly gifted and much lamented Byron observed this phenomenon, and he wished to unite his name with our glory. Other revolutions have happened in his time, but he did not enter into any of them—he did not assist any of them; for their character and nature were totally different: the cause of Greece alone was a cause worthy of him whom all the learned men of Europe celebrate. Consider then, my friends, consider the time in which you live—in what a struggle you are engaged; consider that the glory of past ages admits not of comparison with yours: the friends of liberty, the philanthropists, the philosophers of all nations, and especially of the enlightened and generous English nation, congratulate you, and from afar rejoice with you; all animate you; and the poet of our age, already crowned with immortality, emulous of your glory, came personally to your shores, that he might, together with yourselves, wash out with his blood the marks of tyranny from our polluted soil.

'Born in the great capital of England, his descent noble on the side of both his father and his mother, what unfeigned joy did his Philhellenic heart feel when our poor city, in token of our gratitude, inscribed his name among the number of her citizens! In the agonies of death—yes, at the moment when eternity appeared before him; as he was lingering on the brink of mortal and immortal life; when all the material world appeared but as a speck in the great works of the Divine Omnipotence; in that awful hour, but two names dwelt upon the lips of this illustrious individual, leaving all the world besides—the names of his only and much-beloved daughter, and of Greece: these two names, deeply engraven on his heart, even the moment of death could not efface. "My daughter!" he said; "Greece!" he exclaimed; and his spirit passed away. What Grecian heart will not be deeply affected as often as it recalls this moment?

'Our tears, my friends, will be grateful, very grateful, to his shade, for they are the tears of sincere affection; but much more grateful will be our deeds in the cause of our country, which, though removed from us, he will observe from the heavens, of which his virtues have doubtless opened to him the gates. This return alone does he require from us for all his munificence; this reward for his love towards us; this consolation for his sufferings in our cause; and this inheritance for the loss of his invaluable life. When your exertions, my friends, shall have liberated us from the hands which have so long held us down in chains; from the hands which have torn from our arms, our property, our brothers, our children—then will his spirit rejoice, then will his shade be satisfied. Yes, in that blessed hour of our freedom the Archbishop will extend his sacred and free hand, and pronounce a blessing over his venerated tomb; the young warrior sheathing his sword, red with the blood of his tyrannical oppressors, will strew it with laurel; the statesman will consecrate it with his oratory; and the poet, resting upon the marble, will become doubly inspired; the virgins of Greece (whose beauty our illustrious fellow-citizen Byron has celebrated in many of his poems), without any longer fearing contamination from the rapacious hands of our oppressors, crowning their heads with garlands, will dance round it, and sing of the beauty of our land, which the poet of our age has already commemorated with such grace and truth. But what sorrowful thought now presses upon my mind! My fancy has carried me away; I had pictured to myself all that my heart could have desired; I had imagined the blessing of our Bishops, the hymns, and laurel crowns, and the dance of the virgins of Greece round the tomb of the benefactor of Greece;—but this tomb will not contain his precious remains; the tomb will remain void; but a few days more will his body remain on the face of our land—of his new chosen country; it cannot be given over to our arms; it must be borne to his own native land, which is honoured by his birth.

'Oh daughter! most dearly beloved by him, your arms will receive him; your tears will bathe the tomb which shall contain his body; and the tears of the orphans of Greece will be shed over the urn containing his precious heart, and over all the land of Greece, for all the land of Greece is his tomb. As in the last moments of his life you and Greece were alone in his heart and upon his lips, it was but just that she (Greece) should retain a share of the precious remains. Missolonghi, his country, will ever watch over and protect with all her strength the urn containing his venerated heart, as a symbol of his love towards us. All Greece, clothed in mourning and inconsolable, accompanies the procession in which it is borne; all ecclesiastical, civil, and military honours attend it; all his fellow-citizens of Missolonghi and fellow-countrymen of Greece follow it, crowning it with their gratitude and bedewing it with their tears; it is blessed by the pious benedictions and prayers of our Archbishop, Bishop, and all our clergy. Learn, noble lady, learn that chieftains bore it on their shoulders, and carried it to the church; thousands of Greek soldiers lined the way through which it passed, with the muzzles of their muskets, which had destroyed so many tyrants, pointed towards the ground, as though they would war against that earth which was to deprive them for ever of the sight of their benefactor;—all this crowd of soldiers, ready at a moment to march against the implacable enemy of Christ and man, surrounded the funeral couch, and swore never to forget the sacrifices made by your father for us, and never to allow the spot where his heart is placed to be trampled upon by barbarous and tyrannical feet. Thousands of Christian voices were in a moment heard, and the temple of the Almighty resounded with supplications and prayers that his venerated remains might be safely conveyed to his native land, and that his soul might repose where the righteous alone find rest.'

'When the funeral service was over,' says Gamba, 'we left the bier in the middle of the church, where it remained until the evening of the next day, guarded by a detachment of his own brigade. The church was crowded without cessation by those who came to honour and to regret the benefactor of Greece.

'On the evening of the 23rd the bier was privately carried back by Byron's officers to his own house. The coffin was not closed until the 29th April.

'Immediately after death Byron's countenance had an air of calmness, mingled with a severity that seemed gradually to soften. When I took a last look at him, the expression, at least to my eyes, was truly sublime.'

Soon after death, Byron's body was embalmed, and a report of the autopsy will be found in the Appendix.

Millingen says :

'Before we proceeded to embalm the body, we could not refrain from pausing to contemplate the lifeless clay of one who, but a few days before, was the hope of a whole nation, and the admiration of the civilized world. We could not but admire the perfect symmetry of his body. Nothing could surpass the beauty of his forehead ; its height was extraordinary, and the protuberances under which the nobler intellectual faculties are supposed to reside were strongly pronounced. His hair, which curled naturally, was quite grey; the mustachios light-coloured. His physiognomy had suffered little alteration, and still preserved the sarcastic, haughty expression which habitually characterized it. The chest was broad, high-vaulted; the waist very small; the muscular system well pronounced; the skin delicate and white; and the habit of the body plump. The only blemish of his body, which might otherwise have vied with that of Apollo himself, was the congenital malconformation of his *left* foot and leg. The foot was deformed and turned inwards, and the leg was smaller and shorter than the sound one.'*

Trelawny arrived at Missolonghi on April 24, after the body had been embalmed. He states that Byron's right leg was shorter than the other, and the *right* foot was the most distorted, being twisted inwards, so that only the edge could have touched the ground. The discrepancy between Trelawny's statement and that of Millingen is probably due to the fact that nearly

---

* For further evidence on this point, see 'Letters of Lord Byron,' edited by Rowland Prothero, vol. i., pp. 9-11.

thirty-four years had passed before Trelawny's book was written.

Trelawny wrote, from Fletcher's dictation, full particulars of Byron's last illness and death. It is presumably from these notes that Trelawny drafted his letter to Colonel Stanhope, dated April 28, 1814. In reference to that letter, Gamba says:

'The details there given of Lord Byron's last illness and death are not quite correct. But where Mr. Trelawny speaks of the general impression produced by that lamentable event, he pathetically describes what is recognized for truth by all those who were witnesses of the melancholy scene.'

As Trelawny was not present during the illness and death of Byron, he cannot be held responsible for any inaccuracies that may appear in his 'Records.' He merely wrote from Fletcher's dictation, without adding one word of his own.

On Fletcher's return to England, he gave the following evidence:

'My master continued his usual custom of riding daily, when the weather would permit, until the 9th of April. But on that ill-fated day he got very wet, and on his return home his lordship changed the whole of his dress; but he had been too long in his wet clothes, and the cold, of which he had complained more or less ever since we left Cephalonia, made this attack be more severely felt. Though rather feverish during the night, his lordship slept pretty well, but complained in the morning of a pain in his bones and a headache: this did not, however, prevent him from taking a ride in the afternoon, which, I grieve to say, was his last. On his return, my master said that the saddle was not perfectly dry, from being so wet the day before, and observed that he thought it had made him worse. His lordship was again visited by the same slow fever, and I was sorry to perceive, on the next morning, that his illness appeared to be increasing. He was very low, and complained of not having had any sleep during the night. His lordship's appetite was also quite gone. I prepared a little arrowroot, of which he took three or four spoonfuls, saying it was very good, but could take no more. It was not till the third day, the 12th, that I began to be alarmed for my master. In all his former colds he always slept well, and was never affected by this slow fever. I therefore went to Dr. Bruno and Mr. Millingen, the two medical attendants, and inquired minutely into every circumstance connected with my master's present illness: both replied that there was no danger, and I might make myself perfectly easy on the subject, for all would be well in a few days. This was on the 13th. On the following day I found my master in such a state, that I could not feel happy without supplicating that he would send to Zante for Dr. Thomas. After expressing my fears lest his lordship should get worse, he desired me to consult the doctors; which I did, and was told there was no occasion for calling in any person, as they hoped all would be well in a few days. Here I should remark that his lordship repeatedly said, in the course of the day, he was sure the doctors did not understand his disease; to which I answered, "Then, my lord, have other advice, by all means." "They tell me," said his lordship, "that it is only a common cold, which, you know, I have had a thousand times." "I am sure, my lord," said I, "that you never had one of so serious a nature." "I think I never had," was his lordship's answer. I repeated my supplications that Dr. Thomas should be sent for on the 15th, and was again assured that my master would be better in two or three days. After these confident assurances, I did not renew my entreaties until it was too late.

'With respect to the medicines that were given to my master, I could not persuade myself that those of a strong purgative nature were the best adapted for his complaint, concluding that, as he had nothing on his stomach, the only effect would be to create pain: indeed, this must have been the case with a person in perfect health. The whole nourishment taken by my master, for the last eight days, consisted of a small quantity of broth at two or three different times, and two spoonfuls of arrowroot on the 18th, the day before his death. The first time I heard of there being any intention of bleeding his lordship was on the 15th, when it was proposed by Dr. Bruno, but objected to at first by my master, who asked Mr. Millingen if there was any very great reason for taking blood. The latter replied that it might be of service, but added that it could be deferred till the next day; and accordingly my master was bled in the right arm on the evening of the 16th, and a pound of blood was taken. I observed at the time that it had a most inflamed appearance. Dr. Bruno now began to say he had frequently urged my master to be bled, but that he always refused. A long dispute now arose about the time that had been lost, and the necessity of sending for medical assistance to Zante; upon which I was informed, for the first time, that it would be of no use, as my master would be better, or no more, before the arrival of Dr. Thomas. His lordship continued to get worse: but Dr. Bruno said he thought letting blood again would save his life; and I lost no time in telling my master how necessary it was to comply with the doctor's wishes. To this he replied by saying he feared they knew nothing about his disorder; and then, stretching out his arm, said, "Here, take my arm, and do whatever you like." His lordship continued to get weaker; and on the 17th he was bled twice in the morning, and at two o'clock in the afternoon. The bleeding at both times was followed by fainting fits, and he would have fallen down more than once had I not caught him in my arms. In order to prevent such an accident, I took care not to let his lordship stir without supporting him. On this day my master said to me twice, "I cannot sleep, and you well know I have not been able to sleep for more than a week: I know," added his lordship, "that a man can only be a certain time without sleep, and then he must go mad, without anyone being able to save him; and I would ten times sooner shoot myself than be mad, for I am not afraid of dying—I am more fit to die than people think." I do not, however, believe that his lordship had any apprehension of his fate till the day after, the 18th, when he said, "I fear you and Tita will be ill by sitting up constantly night and day." I

THE CLOSING SCENE

answered, "We shall never leave your lordship till you are better." As my master had a slight fit of delirium on the 16th, I took care to remove the pistols and stiletto which had hitherto been kept at his bedside in the night. On the 18th his lordship addressed me frequently, and seemed to be very much dissatisfied with his medical treatment. I then said, "Do allow me to send for Dr. Thomas," to which he answered, "Do so, but be quick. I am sorry I did not let you do so before, as I am sure they have mistaken my disease. Write yourself, for I know they would not like to see other doctors here."

'I did not lose a moment in obeying my master's orders; and on informing Dr. Bruno and Mr. Millingen of it, they said it was very right, as they now began to be afraid themselves. On returning to my master's room, his first words were, "Have you sent?" "I have, my lord," was my answer; upon which he said, "You have done right, for I should like to know what is the matter with me." Although his lordship did not appear to think his dissolution was so near, I could perceive he was getting weaker every hour, and he even began to have occasional fits of delirium. He afterwards said, "I now begin to think I am seriously ill; and, in case I should be taken off suddenly, I wish to give you several directions, which I hope you will be particular in seeing executed." I answered I would, in case such an event came to pass, but expressed a hope that he would live many years to execute them much better himself than I could. To this my master replied, "No, it is now nearly over," and then added, "I must tell you all without losing a moment." I then said, "Shall I go, my lord, and fetch pen, ink, and paper?" "Oh, my God! no, you will lose too much time; and I have it not to spare, for my time is now short," said his Lordship; and immediately after, "Now, pay attention." His lordship commenced by saying, "You will be provided for." I begged him, however, to proceed with things of more consequence. He then continued, "Oh, my poor dear child!—my dear Ada! My God! could I but have seen her! Give her my blessing—and my dear sister Augusta and her children;—and you will go to Lady Byron, and say—tell her everything;—you are friends with her."

His lordship appeared to be greatly affected at this moment. Here my master's voice failed him, so that I could only catch a word at intervals; but he kept muttering something very seriously for some time, and would often raise his voice and say, "Fletcher, now, if you do not execute every order which I have given you, I will torment you hereafter if possible." Here I told his lordship, in a state of the greatest perplexity, that I had not understood a word of what he said; to which he replied, "Oh, my God! then all is lost, for it is now too late! Can it be possible you have not understood me?" "No, my lord," said I, "but I pray you to try and inform me once more." "How can I?" rejoined my master; "it is now too late, and all is over!" I said, "Not our will, but God's be done!" and he answered, "Yes, not mine be done—but I will try." His lordship did indeed make several efforts to speak, but could only repeat two or three words at a time, such as "My wife! my child! my sister! You know all—you must say all—you know my wishes." The rest was quite unintelligible.

'A consultation was now held about noon, when it was determined to administer some Peruvian bark and wine. My master had now been nine days without any sustenance whatever, except what I have already mentioned. With the exception of a few words which can only interest those to whom they were addressed, and which, if required, I shall communicate to themselves, it was impossible to understand anything his lordship said after taking the bark. He expressed a wish to sleep. I at one time asked whether I should call Mr. Parry; to which he replied, "Yes, you may call him." Mr. Parry desired him to compose himself. He shed tears, and apparently sunk into a slumber. Mr. Parry went away, expecting to find him refreshed on his return; but it was the commencement of the lethargy preceding his death. The last words I heard my master utter were at six o'clock on the evening of the 18th, when he said, "I must sleep now"; upon which he laid down never to rise again!—for he did not move hand or foot during the following twenty-four hours. His lordship appeared, however, to be in a state of suffocation at intervals, and had a frequent rattling in the throat. On these occasions I called

Tita to assist me in raising his head, and I thought he seemed to get quite stiff. The rattling and choking in the throat took place every half-hour; and we continued to raise his head whenever the fit came on, till six o'clock in the evening of the 19th, when I saw my master open his eyes and then shut them, but without showing any symptom of pain, or moving hand or foot. "Oh, my God!" I exclaimed, "I fear his lordship is gone." The doctors then felt his pulse, and said, "You are right—he is gone."'

Dr. Bruno's answer to the above statement will be found in the Appendix.

CHAPTER XVI

SEVERAL days passed after the requiem service held in the Church of S. Spiridion. Meanwhile the necessary preparations were made for transporting the body to Zante. On May 2 the coffin was carried down to the seaside on the shoulders of four military chiefs, and attended in the same order as before. The guns of the fortress saluted until the moment of embarkation. The vessel which bore the body reached the island of Zante on the third day after leaving Missolonghi, having, as Gamba says, taken the same course exactly as on the voyage out. The vessel, owing to head-winds, was brought to anchor close to the same rocks where Byron had sought shelter from the Turkish frigate.

'On the evening of the 4th May,' says Gamba, 'we made the port of Zante, and heard that Lord Sidney Osborne had arrived, but, not finding us in that island, had sailed for Missolonghi.'

Blaquière, who was at Zante at the time, says:

'The vessel was recognized at a considerable distance, owing to her flag being at half-mast. She entered the mole towards sunset. The body was accompanied by the whole of his lordship's attendants, who conveyed it to the lazaretto on the following morning.'

During the time that the body of Lord Byron was detained at the lazaretto, a discussion arose as to the

BLAQUIÈRE'S TRIBUTE

final disposal of the remains, Colonel Stanhope and others being of opinion that they should be interred in the Parthenon at Athens. It would seem that such a course would have met with Byron's approval; but, in deference to what were then supposed to have been the wishes of the poet's family, it was finally arranged to charter the brig *Florida*, which had lately arrived at Zante with the first instalment of the Greek loan. In this connection, the last entry in Gamba's journal may be quoted in full:

'A few days after our arrival at Zante, Colonel Stanhope came from the Morea. He had already written to inform us that the Greek chieftains of Athens had expressed their desire that Lord Byron should be buried in the Temple of Theseus. The citizens of Missolonghi had made a similar request for their town; and we thought it advisable to accede to their wishes so far as to leave with them, for interment, one of the vessels containing a portion of the honoured remains. As he had not expressed any wishes on the subject,* we thought the most becoming course was to convey him to his native country. Accordingly, the ship that had brought us the specie was engaged for that purpose. Colonel Stanhope kindly took charge; and on the 25th May the *Florida*, having on board the remains of Lord Byron, set sail for England from the port of Zante.'

The following tribute to Byron from the pen of Blaquière, written on May 24, 1824, must here be given:

'Every letter of Byron's, in which any allusion was made to the Greek cause, proved how judiciously he viewed that great question, while it displayed a thorough knowledge of the people he had come to assist. This latter circumstance, which made him more cautious in avoiding every interference calculated to

* It is difficult to reconcile this with Millingen's statement.

wound the self-love of the Greeks, who, though fallen, are still remarkable for their pride, accounts for the great popularity he had acquired.

'It may be truly said that no foreigner who has hitherto espoused the cause made greater allowance for the errors inseparable from it than did Lord Byron.

'With respect to his opinion as to the best mode of bringing the contest to a triumphant close, and healing those differences which have been created by party spirit or faction, there is reason to believe that the subject occupied his particular attention, and he was even more than once heard to say that "no person had as yet hit upon the right plan for securing the independence of Greece."

'While sedulously employed in reconciling jarring interests and promoting a spirit of union, the grand maxim which he laboured to instil into the Greeks was that of making every other object secondary and subservient to the paramount one of driving out the Turks.'

At six o'clock on the evening of that day, Blaquière added the following words:

'I have this instant returned on shore, after having performed the melancholy duty of towing the remains of Lord Byron alongside the *Florida*.

'I should add that, in consequence of there being no means of procuring lead for the coffin at Zante, it was arranged that the tin case prepared at Missolonghi should be enclosed in wood; so that there is now no fear that the body will not reach England in perfect preservation. The only mark of respect shown to-day was displayed by the merchant vessels in the bay and mole. The whole of these, whether English or foreign, had their flags at half-mast, and many of them fired guns. The *Florida* fired minute-guns from the time of our leaving the lazaretto until we got alongside, when the body was taken on board, and placed in a space prepared for that purpose. The whole is painted black, and, thanks to the foresight of my friend Robinson, an escutcheon very well executed designates the mournful receptacle. Although no honours have been paid to the remains of our immortal poet here, we look forward with melancholy satisfaction to those which await him in the land of his birth.

'However bitterly his pen may have lashed the vices and follies of his day, it is not the least honourable trait in our national character that neither personal dislike nor those prejudices which arise from literary jealousy and political animosity prevent us from duly appreciating departed worth, and even forgetting those aberrations to which all are more or less liable in this state of imperfection and fallibility.'

The following extracts are taken from Lord Broughton's 'Recollections of a Long Life,' a work that was printed, but not published, in 1865. As the opinions of Byron's life-long friend, John Cam Hobhouse, they cannot fail to interest the reader :*

'How much soever the Greeks of that day may have differed on other topics, there was no difference of opinion in regard to the loss they had sustained by the death of Byron. Those who have read Colonel Leicester Stanhope's interesting volume, "Greece in 1823 and 1824," and more particularly Colonel Stanhope's "Sketch" and Mr. Finlay's "Reminiscences" of Byron, will have seen him just as he appeared to me during our long intimacy. I liked him a great deal too well to be an impartial judge of his character; but I can confidently appeal to the impressions he made upon the two above-mentioned witnesses of his conduct, under very trying circumstances, for a justification of my strong affection for him—an affection not weakened by the forty years of a busy and chequered life that have passed over me since I saw him laid in his grave.

'The influence he had acquired in Greece was unbounded, and he had exerted it in a manner most useful to her cause. Lord Sidney Osborne, writing to Mrs. Leigh, said that, if Byron had never written a line in his life, he had done enough, during the last six months in Greece, to immortalize his name. He added

* *Edinburgh Review*, April, 1871, pp. 294-298.

that no one unacquainted with the circumstances of the case could have any idea of the difficulties he had overcome. He had reconciled the contending parties, and had given a character of humanity and civilization to the warfare in which they were engaged, besides contriving to prevent them from offending their powerful neighbours in the Ionian Islands.

'I heard that Sir F. Adam,* in a despatch to Lord Bathurst, bore testimony to his great qualities, and lamented his death as depriving the Ionian Government of the only man with whom they could act with safety. Mavrocordato, in his letter to Dr. Bowring, called him "a great man," and confessed that he was almost ignorant how to act when deprived of such a coadjutor. . . . On Thursday, July 1, I heard that the *Florida*, with the remains of Byron, had arrived in the Downs, and I went the same evening to Rochester. The next morning I went to Standgate Creek, and, taking a boat, went on board the vessel. There I found Colonel Leicester Stanhope, Dr. Bruno, Fletcher, Byron's valet, with three others of his servants. Three dogs that had belonged to my friend were playing about the deck. I could hardly bring myself to look at them. The vessel had got under-weigh, and we beat up the river to Gravesend. I cannot describe what I felt during the five or six hours of our passage. I was the last person who shook hands with Byron when he left England in 1816. I recollected his waving his cap to me as the packet bounded off on a curling wave from the pier-head at Dover, and here I was now coming back to England with his corpse.

'Poor Fletcher burst into tears when he first saw me, and wept bitterly when he told me the particulars of my friend's last illness. These have been frequently made public, and need not be repeated here. I heard, however, on undoubted authority, that until he became delirious he was perfectly calm; and I called to mind how often I had heard him say that he was not apprehensive as to death itself, but as to how, from physical infirmity, he might behave at that inevitable hour. On one occasion he said to me, "Let no one come near me

* He succeeded Sir Thomas Maitland as High Commissioner of the Ionian Islands.

when I am dying, if you can help it, and we happen to be together at the time."

'The *Florida* anchored at Gravesend, and I returned to London; Colonel Stanhope accompanied me. This was on Friday, July 2. On the following Monday I went to Doctors' Commons and proved Byron's will. Mr. Hanson did so likewise. Thence I went to London Bridge, got into a boat, and went to London Docks Buoy, where the *Florida* was anchored. I found Mr. Woodeson, the undertaker, on board, employed in emptying the spirit from the large barrel containing the box that held the corpse. This box was removed, and placed on deck by the side of a leaden coffin. I stayed whilst the iron hoops were knocked off the box; but I could not bear to see the remainder of the operation, and went into the cabin. Whilst there I looked over the sealed packet of papers belonging to Byron, which he had deposited at Cephalonia, and which had not been opened since he left them there. Captain Hodgson of the *Florida*, the captain's father, and Fletcher, were with me; we examined every paper, and did not find any will. Those present signed a document to that effect.

'After the removal of the corpse into the coffin, and the arrival of the order from the Custom-house, I accompanied the undertaker in the barge with the coffin. There were many boats round the ship at the time, and the shore was crowded with spectators. We passed quietly up the river, and landed at Palace Yard stairs. Thence the coffin and the small chest containing the heart were carried to the house in George Street, and deposited in the room prepared for their reception. The room was decently hung with black, but there was no other decoration than an escutcheon of the Byron arms, roughly daubed on a deal board.

'On reaching my rooms at the Albany, I found a note from Mr. Murray, telling me that he had received a letter from Dr. Ireland, politely declining to allow the burial of Byron in Westminster Abbey; but it was not until the next day that, to my great surprise, I learnt, on reading the doctor's note, that Mr. Murray had made the request to the Dean in my name. I thought that it had been settled that Mr. Gifford should sound the Dean of Westminster previously to any formal request being made. I wrote to Mr. Murray, asking him to inform the Dean that I had not made the request. Whether he did so, I never inquired.

'I ascertained from Mrs. Leigh that it was wished the interment should take place at the family vault at Hucknall in Nottinghamshire. The utmost eagerness was shown, both publicly and privately, to get sight of anything connected with Byron. Lafayette was at that time on his way to America, and a young Frenchman came over from the General at Havre, and wrote me a note requesting a sight of the deceased poet. The coffin had been closed, and his wishes could not be complied with. A young man came on board the *Florida*, and in very moving terms besought me to allow him to take one look at him. I was sorry to be obliged to refuse, as I did not know the young man, and there were many round the vessel who would have made the same request. He was bitterly disappointed; and when I gave him a piece of the cotton in which the corpse had been wrapped, he took it with much devotion, and placed it in his pocket-book. Mr. Phillips, the Academician, applied for permission to take a likeness, but I heard from Mrs. Leigh that the features of her brother had been so disfigured by the means used to preserve his remains, that she scarcely recognized them. This was the fact; for I had summoned courage enough to look at my dead friend; so completely was he altered, that the sight did not affect me so much as looking at his handwriting, or anything that I knew had belonged to him.'

The following account by Colonel Leicester Stanhope, probably outlined during his voyage home with Byron's body, is well worth reading. It unveils the personality of Byron as he appeared during those trying times at Missolonghi, when, tortured by illness and worried by dissensions among his coadjutors, he gave his life to Greece. Stanhope's sketch conveys the honest opinion of a man whose political views, differing fundamentally from those of Byron, brought them often in collision. But for this reason, perhaps, this record is the more valuable. It is written without prejudice, with considerable perspicuity, and with unquestionable sincerity. Its peculiar value lies in the approval which, as we have seen, it received from Mr. Hobhouse, who undoubtedly was better acquainted with the character of Byron than any of his contemporaries.

'In much of what certain authors have lately said in praise of Lord Byron I concur. The public are indebted to them for useful information concerning that extraordinary man's biography. I do not, however, think that any of them have given of him a full and masterly description. It would require a person of his own wonderful capacity to draw his character, and even he could not perform this task otherwise than by continuing the history of what passed in his mind; for his character was as versatile as his genius. From his writings, therefore, he must be judged, and from them can he alone be understood. His character was, indeed, poetic, like his works, and he partook of the virtues and vices of the heroes of his imagination. Lord Byron was original and eccentric in all things, and his conduct and his writings were unlike those of other men. He might have said with Rousseau : " Moi seul. Je sens mon cœur et je connois les hommes. Je ne suis fait comme aucun de ceux qui existent. Si je ne vaux pas mieux, au moins, je suis autre. Si la nature a bien ou mal fait de briser le moule dans lequel elle m'a jetté, c'est dont on ne peut juger qu'après m'avoir lu." All that can be hoped is, that, after a number of the ephemeral sketches of Lord Byron have been published, and ample information concerning him obtained, some master-hand will undertake the task of drawing his portrait. If anything like justice be done to Lord Byron, his character will appear far more extraordinary than any his imagination has produced, and not less wonderful than those sublime and inimitable sketches created and painted by the fanciful pen of Shakespeare.

'There were two circumstances which appear to me to have had a powerful influence on Byron's conduct. I allude to his lameness and his marriage. The deformity of his foot constantly preyed on his spirits and soured his temper. It is extraordinary, however, and contrary, I believe, to the conduct of the generality of lame persons, that he pitied, sympathized, and befriended, those who laboured under similar defects.

'With respect to Lady Byron, her image appeared to be rooted in his mind. She had wounded Lord Byron's pride by having refused his first offer of marriage; by having separated herself from him whom others assiduously courted; and by having resisted all the efforts of his genius to compel her again to yield to his dominion. Had Lady Byron been submissive, could she have stooped to become a caressing slave, like other ingenious slaves, she might have governed her lord and master. But no, she had a mind too great, and was too much of an Englishwoman to bow so low. These contrarieties set Lord Byron's heart on fire, roused all his passions, gave birth, no doubt, to many of his sublimest thoughts, and impelled him impetuously forward in his zigzag career. When angry or humorous, she became the subject of his wild sport; at other times she seemed, though he loved her not, to be the mistress of his feelings, and one whom he in vain attempted to cast from his thoughts. Thus, in a frolicsome tone, I have heard him sketch characters, and, speaking of a certain acquaintance, say, " With the exception of Southey and Lady Byron, there is no one I hate so much." This was a noisy shot—a sort of a *feu de joie*, that inflicted no wound, and left no scar behind. Lord Byron was in reality a good-natured man, and it was a violence to his nature, which he seldom practised, either to conceal what he thought or to harbour revenge. In one conversation which I had with Lord Byron, he dwelt much upon the acquirements and virtues of Lady Byron, and even said she had committed no fault but that of having married him. The truth is, that he was not formed for marriage. His riotous genius could not bear restraint. No woman could have lived with him but one devoid of, or of subdued, feelings—an Asiatic slave. Lord Byron, it is well known, was passionately fond of his child; of this he gave me the following proof. He showed me a miniature of Ada, as also a clever description of her character, drawn by her mother, and forwarded to him by the person he most esteemed, his amiable sister. After I had examined the letter, while reflecting on its contents, I gazed intently on the picture; Lord Byron, observing me in deep meditation, impatiently said, "Well, well, what do you think of Ada?" I replied, "If these are true representations of Ada, and are not drawn to flatter your vanity, you have engrafted on her your virtues and your failings. She is in mind and feature the very image of her father." Never did I see man feel more pleasure than Lord Byron felt at this remark; his eyes lightened with ecstasy.

'Lord Byron's mental and personal courage was unlike that of other men. To the superficial observer his conduct seemed to be quite unsettled; this was really the case to a certain extent. His genius was boundless and excursive, and in conversation his tongue went rioting on

'"From grave to gay, from lively to severe."

'Still, upon the whole, no man was more constant, and, I may almost say, more obstinate in the pursuit of some great objects. For example, in religion and politics he seemed firm as a rock, though like a rock he was subjected to occasional rude shocks, the convulsions of agitated nature.

'The assertions I have ventured to make of Lord Byron having fixed opinions on certain material questions are not according to his own judgment. From what fell from his own lips, I could draw no such conclusions, for, in conversing with me on government and religion, and after going wildly over these subjects, sometimes in a grave and philosophical, and sometimes in a laughing and humorous strain, he would say: "The more I think, the more I doubt; I am a perfect sceptic." In contradiction to this assertion, I set Lord Byron's recorded sentiments, and his actions from the period of his boyhood to that of his death; and I contend that although he occasionally veered about, yet he always returned to certain fixed opinions; and that he felt a constant attachment to liberty, according to our notions of liberty, and that, although no Christian, he was a firm believer in the existence of a God. It is, therefore, equally remote from truth to represent him as either an atheist or a Christian: he was, as he has often told me, a confirmed deist.

'Lord Byron was no party politician. Lord Clare was the person whom he liked best, because he was his old school acquaintance. Mr. John Cam Hobhouse was his long-tried, his esteemed, and valued literary and personal friend. Death has severed these, but there is a soul in friendship that can never die. No man ever chose a nobler friend. Mr. Hobhouse has given many proofs of this, and among others, I saw him, from motives of high honour, destroy a beautiful poem of Lord Byron's, and, perhaps, the last he ever composed. The same reason that induced Mr. H. to tear this fine manuscript will, of course, prevent him or me from ever divulging its contents. Mr. Douglas Kinnaird was another for whom Lord Byron entertained the sincerest esteem: no less on account of his high social qualities, than as a clear-sighted man of business, on whose discretion he could implicitly rely. Sir Francis Burdett was the politician whom he most admired. He used to say, "Burdett is an Englishman of the old school." He compared the Baronet to the statesmen of Charles I.'s time, whom he considered the sternest and loftiest spirits that Britain had produced. Lord Byron entertained high aristocratic notions, and had much family pride. He admired, notwithstanding, the American institutions, but did not consider them of so democratic a nature as is generally imagined. He found, he said, many Englishmen and English writers more imbued with liberal notions than those Americans and American authors with whom he was acquainted.

'Lord Byron was chivalrous even to Quixotism. This might have lowered him in the estimation of the wise, had he not given some extraordinary proofs of the noblest courage. For example, the moment he recovered from that alarming fit which took place in my room, he inquired again and again, with the utmost composure, whether he was in danger. If in danger, he desired the physician honestly to apprise him of it, for he feared not death. Soon after this dreadful paroxysm, when Lord Byron, faint with overbleeding, was lying on his sick-bed, with his whole nervous system completely shaken, the mutinous Suliotes,

A SUBLIME SCENE

covered with dirt and splendid attires, broke into his apartment, brandishing their costly arms, and loudly demanding their wild rights. Lord Byron, electrified by this unexpected act, seemed to recover from his sickness; and the more the Suliotes raged, the more his calm courage triumphed. The scene was truly sublime.

'At times Lord Byron would become disgusted with the Greeks, on account of their horrid cruelties, their delays, their importuning him for money, and their not fulfilling their promises. That he should feel thus was very natural, although all this is just what might be anticipated from a people breaking loose from ages of bondage. We are too apt to expect the same conduct from men educated as slaves (and here be it remembered that the Greeks were the Helots of slaves) that we find in those who have, from their infancy, breathed the wholesome atmosphere of liberty.

'Most persons assume a virtuous character. Lord Byron's ambition, on the contrary, was to make the world imagine that he was a sort of "Satan," though occasionally influenced by lofty sentiments to the performance of great actions. Fortunately for his fame, he possessed another quality, by which he stood completely unmasked. He was the most ingenuous of men, and his nature, in the main good, always triumphed over his acting.

'There was nothing that he detested more than to be thought merely a great poet, though he did not wish to be esteemed inferior as a dramatist to Shakspeare. Like Voltaire, he was unconsciously jealous of, and for that reason abused, our immortal bard. His mind was absorbed in detecting Shakspeare's glaring defects, instead of being overpowered by his wonderful creative and redeeming genius. He assured me that he was so far from being a "heaven-born poet" that he was not conscious of possessing any talent in that way when a boy. This gift had burst upon his mind unexpectedly, as if by inspiration, and had excited his wonder. He also declared that he had no love or enthusiasm for poetry. I shook my head doubtingly, and said to him that, although he had displayed a piercing sagacity in reading and developing the characters of others, he knew but little of his own.

He replied: "Often have I told you that I am a perfect sceptic. I have no fixed opinions; that is my character. Like others, I am not in love with what I possess, but with that which I do not possess, and which is difficult to obtain." Lord Byron was for shining as a hero of the first order. He wished to take an active part in the civil and military government of Greece.* On this subject he consulted me; I condemned the direct assumption of command by a foreigner, fearing that it would expose him to envy and danger without promoting the cause. I wished him, by a career of perfect disinterestedness, to preserve a commanding influence over the Greeks, and to act as their great mediator. Lord Byron listened to me with unusual and courteous politeness, for he suspected my motives—he thought me envious—jealous of his increasing power; and though he did not disregard, did not altogether follow my advice. I was not, however, to be disarmed either by politeness or suspicions; they touched me not, for my mind was occupied with loftier thoughts. The attack was renewed the next day in a mild tone. The collision, however, of Lord Byron's arguments, sparkling with jests, and mine, regardless of his brilliancy and satire, all earnestness, ended as usual in a storm. Though most anxious to assume high power, Lord Byron was still modest. He said to me, laughing, that if Napier came, he would *supersede himself*, as Governor and Commander of Western Greece, in favour of that distinguished officer. I laughed at this whimsical expression till I made Lord Byron laugh, too, and repeat over again that he would "supersede himself."

'The mind of Lord Byron was like a volcano, full of fire and wealth, sometimes calm, often dazzling and playful, but ever threatening. It ran swift as the lightning from one subject to another, and occasionally burst forth in passionate throes of intellect, nearly allied to madness. A striking instance of this sort of eruption I shall mention. Lord Byron's apartments were immediately over mine at Missolonghi. In the dead of the night I was frequently startled from my sleep by the thunders of his lordship's voice, either

---

* This must be taken *cum grano salis*.

raging with anger or roaring with laughter, and rousing friends, servants, and, indeed, all the inmates of the dwelling, from their repose. Even when in the utmost danger, Lord Byron contemplated death with calm philosophy. He was, however, superstitious, and dreadfully alarmed at the idea of going mad, which he predicted would be his sad destiny.

'As a companion, no one could be more amusing; he had neither pedantry nor affectation about him, but was natural and playful as a boy. His conversation resembled a stream, sometimes smooth, sometimes rapid, and sometimes rushing down in cataracts; it was a mixture of philosophy and slang—of everything —like his "Don Juan." He was a patient and, in general, a very attentive listener. When, however, he did engage with earnestness in conversation, his ideas succeeded each other with such uncommon rapidity that he could not control them. They burst from him impetuously; and although he both attended to and noticed the remarks of others, yet he did not allow these to check his discourse for an instant.

'Lord Byron professed a deep-rooted antipathy to the English, though he was always surrounded by Englishmen, and, in reality, preferred them (as he did Italian women) to all others. I one day accused him of ingratitude to his countrymen. For many years, I observed, he had been, in spite of his faults, and although he had shocked all her prejudices, the pride, and I might almost say the idol, of Britain. He said they must be a stupid race to worship such an idol, but he had at last cured their superstition, as far as his divinity was concerned, by the publication of his "Cain." It was true, I replied, that he had now lost their favour. This remark stung him to the soul, for he wished not only to occupy the public mind, but to command, by his genius, public esteem.

'This extraordinary person, whom everybody was as anxious to see, and to know, as if he had been a Napoleon, the conqueror of the world, had a notion that he was hated, and avoided like one who had broken quarantine. He used often to mention to me the kindness of this or that insignificant individual, for having given him a good and friendly reception. In this particular Lord Byron was capricious, for at Genoa he would scarcely see anyone but those who lived in his own family; whereas at Cephalonia he was to everyone and at all times accessible. At Genoa he acted the misanthropist; at Cephalonia he appeared in his genuine character, doing good, and rather courting than shunning society.

'Lord Byron conceived that he possessed a profound knowledge of mankind, and of the working of their passions. In this he judged right. He could fathom every mind and heart but his own, the extreme depths of which none ever reached. On my arrival from England at Cephalonia, his lordship asked me what new publications I had brought out. Among others I mentioned "The Springs of Action." "Springs of Action!" said Lord Byron, stamping with rage with his lame foot, and then turning sharply on his heel, "I don't require to be taught on this head. I know well what are the springs of action." Some time afterwards, while speaking on another subject, he desired me to lend him "The Springs of Action." He then suddenly changed the conversation to some humorous remarks for the purpose of diverting my attention. I could not, however, forbear reminding him of his former observations and his furious stamp.

'Avarice and great generosity were among Lord Byron's qualities; these contrarieties are said not unfrequently to be united in the same person. As an instance of Lord Byron's parsimony, he was constantly attacking Count Gamba, sometimes, indeed, playfully, but more often with the bitterest satire, for having purchased for the use of his family, while in Greece, 500 dollars' worth of cloth. This he used to mention as an instance of the Count's imprudence and extravagance. Lord Byron told me one day, with a tone of great gravity, that this 500 dollars would have been most serviceable in promoting the siege of Lepanto; and that he never would, to the last moment of his existence, forgive Gamba for having squandered away his money in the purchase of cloth. No one will suppose that Lord Byron could be serious in such a denunciation; he entertained, in reality, the highest opinion of Count Gamba, who both on account of his talents and devotedness to his friend merited his lordship's esteem.

'Lord Byron's generosity is before the world; he promised to devote his large income to the cause of Greece, and he honestly acted up to his pledge. It was impossible for Lord Byron to have made a more useful, and therefore a more noble, sacrifice of his wealth, than by devoting it, *with discretion*, to the Greek cause. He set a bright example to the millionaires of his own country, who certainly show but little public spirit. Most of them expend their fortunes in acts of ostentation or selfishness. Few there are of this class who will devote, perchance, the hundredth part of their large incomes to acts of benevolence or bettering the condition of their fellow-men. None of our millionaires, with all their pride and their boasting have had the public virtue, like Lord Byron, to sacrifice their incomes or their lives in aid of a people struggling for liberty.

'Lord Byron's reading was desultory, but extensive; his memory was retentive to an extraordinary extent. He was partial to the Italian poets, and is said to have borrowed from them. Their fine thoughts he certainly associated with his own, but with such skill that he could not be accused of plagiarism. Lord Byron possessed, indeed, a genius absolutely boundless, and could create with such facility that it would have been irksome to him to have become a servile imitator. He was original in all things, but especially as a poet.

'The study of voyages and travels was that in which he most delighted; their details he seemed actually to devour. He would sit up all night reading them. His whole soul was absorbed in these adventures, and he appeared to personify the traveller. Lord Byron had a particular aversion to business; his familiar letters were scrawled out at a great rate, and resembled his conversations. Rapid as were his tongue and his pen, neither could keep pace with the quick succession of ideas that flashed across his mind. He hated nothing more than writing formal official letters; this drudgery he would generally put off from day to day, and finish by desiring Count Gamba, or some other friend, to perform the task. No wonder that Lord Byron should dislike this dry antipoetic work, and which he, in reality, performed with so much difficulty. Lord Byron's arduous yet unsuccessful labours in this barren field put me in mind of the difficulty which one of the biographers of Addison describes this politician to have experienced, when attempting to compose an official paragraph for the *Gazette* announcing the death of the Queen. This duty, after a long and ineffectual attempt, the Minister, in despair, handed over to a clerk, who (not being a genius, but a man of business) performed it in an instant.

'Not less was Lord Byron's aversion to reading than to writing official documents; these he used to hand over to me, pretending, spite of all my protestations to the contrary, that I had a passion for documents. When once Lord Byron had taken any whim into his head, he listened not to contradiction, but went on laughing and satirizing till his joke had triumphed over argument and fact. Thus I, for the sake of peace, was sometimes silent, and suffered him to good-naturedly bully me into reading over, or, rather, yawning over, a mass of documents dull and uninteresting.

'Lord Byron once told me, in a humorous tone, but apparently quite in earnest, that he never could acquire a competent knowledge of arithmetic. Addition and subtraction he said he could, though with some difficulty, accomplish. The mechanism of the rule of three pleased him, but then division was a puzzle he could not muster up sufficient courage to unravel. I mention this to show of how low a cast Lord Byron's capacity was in some commonplace matters, where he could not command attention. The reverse was the case on subjects of a higher order, and in those trifling ones, too, that pleased his fancy. Moved by such themes, the impulses of his genius shot forth, by day and night, from his troubled brain, electric sparks or streams of light, like blazing meteors.

'Lord Byron loved Greece. Her climate and her scenery, her history, her struggles, her great men and her antiquities, he admired. He declared that he had no mastery over his own thoughts. In early youth he was no poet, nor was he now, except when the fit was upon him, and he felt his mind agitated and feverish. These attacks, he continued, scarcely ever visited him anywhere but in Greece; there he felt himself exhilarated—metamorphosed into another person, and with another soul—in short, never had he, but in Greece, written one good line of poetry. This is a fact exaggerated, as facts often are, by the impulses of strong feelings. It is not on that account less calculated to convey to others the character of Lord Byron's mind, or to impress it the less upon their recollections.

'Once established at Missolonghi, it required some great impetus to move Lord Byron from that unhealthy swamp. On one occasion, when irritated by the Suliotes and the constant applications for money, he intimated his intention to depart. The citizens of Missolonghi and the soldiers grumbled, and communicated to me, through Dr. Meyer, their discontent. I repeated what I had heard to Lord Byron. He replied, calmly, that he would rather be cut to pieces than imprisoned, for he came to aid the Greeks in their struggle for liberty, and not to be their slave. No wonder that the "Hellenists" endeavoured to impede Lord Byron's departure, for even I, a mere soldier, could not escape from Missolonghi, Athens, Corinth, or Salona, without considerable difficulty. Some time previous to Lord Byron's death, he began to feel a restlessness and a wish to remove to Athens or to Zante.'

On Monday, July 12, at eleven o'clock in the morning, the funeral procession, attended by a great number of carriages and by crowds of people, left No. 20, Great George Street, Westminster, and, passing the Abbey, moved slowly to St. Pancras Gate. Here a halt was made; the carriages returned, and the hearse proceeded by slow stages to Nottingham.

The Mayor and Corporation of Nottingham now joined the funeral procession. Mr. Hobhouse, who attended, tells us that the cortège extended about a quarter of a mile, and, moving very slowly, was five hours on the road to Hucknall-Torkard.

'The view of it as it wound through the villages of Papplewick and Lindlay excited sensations in me which will never be forgotten. As we passed under the Hill of Annesley, "crowned with the peculiar diadem of trees" immortalized by Byron, I called to mind a thousand particulars of my first visit to Newstead. It was dining at Annesley Park that I saw the first interview of Byron, after a long interval, with his early love, Mary Anne Chaworth.

'The churchyard and the little church of Hucknall were so crowded that it was with difficulty we could follow the coffin up the aisle. The contrast between the gorgeous decorations of the coffin and the urn, and the humble village church, was very striking. I was told afterwards that the place was crowded until a late hour in the evening, and that the vault was not closed until the next morning.

'I should mention that I thought Lady Byron ought to be consulted respecting the funeral of her husband; and I advised Mrs. Leigh to write to her, and ask what her wishes might be. Her answer was, if the deceased had left no instructions, she thought the matter might be left to the judgment of Mr. Hobhouse. There was a postscript, saying, "If you like you may show this."'

Hobhouse concludes his account with these words:

'I was present at the marriage of this lady with my friend, and handed her into the carriage which took the bride and bridegroom away. Shaking hands with Lady Byron, I wished her all happiness. Her answer was: "If I am *not* happy, it will be my own fault."'

PART II
WHAT THE POEMS REVEAL

> 'Intesi, che a cosi fatto tormento
> Enno dannati i peccator carnali
> Che la ragion sommettono al talento.'
> *Inferno*, Canto V., 37-39.

WHAT THE POEMS REVEAL

'Every author in some degree portrays himself in his works, even be it against his will.'—GOETHE.

LADY BYRON has expressed her opinion that almost every incident in Byron's poems was drawn from his personal experience. In a letter to Lady Anne Barnard, written two years after the separation, she says:

'In regard to [Byron's] poetry, egotism is the vital principle of his imagination, which it is difficult for him to kindle on any subject with which his own character and interests are not identified; but by the introduction of fictitious incidents, by change of scene or time, he has enveloped his poetical disclosures in a system impenetrable except to a very few.'

Byron himself has told us in 'Don Juan' that his music 'has some mystic diapasons, with much which could not be appreciated in any manner by the *uninitiated.*' In a letter to John Murray (August 23, 1821), he says: 'Almost all "Don Juan" is *real* life, either my own or from people I knew.'

It is no exaggeration to say that in Byron's poems some of the mysterious incidents in his life are plainly revealed. For example, 'Childe Harold,' 'The Giaour,' 'The Bride of Abydos,' 'The Corsair,' 'Lara,' 'The Dream,' 'Manfred,' 'Don Juan,' and several of the smaller pieces, all disclose episodes connected with his own personal experience. In the so-called 'Fugitive Pieces' we get a glimpse of his school life and friendships; his pursuits during the time that he resided with his mother at Southwell; and his introduction to Cambridge. In the 'Hours of Idleness' we are introduced to Mary Chaworth, after her marriage and the ruin of his hopes.

In the verse 'Remembrance' we realize that the dawn of his life is overcast. We see, from some verses written in 1808, how, three years after that marriage, he was still the victim of a fatal infatuation:

> 'I deem'd that Time, I deem'd that Pride,
>   Had quench'd at length my boyish flame;
> Nor knew, till seated by thy side,
>   My heart in all—save hope—the same.'

After lingering for three months in the neighbourhood of the woman whom he so unwisely loved, he finally resolved to break the chain:

> 'In flight I shall be surely wise,
>   Escaping from temptation's snare;
> I cannot view my Paradise
>   Without the wish of dwelling there.'

When about to leave England, in vain pursuit of the happiness he had lost, he addresses passionate verses to Mary Chaworth:

> 'And I must from this land be gone,
>   Because I cannot love but one.'

He tells her that he has had love passages with another woman, in the vain hope of destroying the love of his life:

> 'But some unconquerable spell
>   Forbade my bleeding breast to own
> A kindred care for aught but one.'

He wished to say farewell, but dared not trust himself. In the cantos of 'Childe Harold,' written during

THE 'THYRZA' POEMS

his absence, he recurs to the subject nearest to his heart. He says that before leaving Newstead—

> 'Oft-times in his maddest mirthful mood
> Strange pangs would flash along Childe Harold's brow,
> As if the memory of some *deadly feud*
> Or *disappointed passion* lurked below :
> But this none knew, nor haply cared to know.'

He mentions his mother, from whom he dreaded to part, and his sister Augusta, whom he loved, but had not seen for some time. After his return to England in 1811, he wrote the 'Thyrza' poems, and added some stanzas to 'Childe Harold,' wherein he expresses a hope that the separation between himself and Mary Chaworth may not be eternal. He then pours out the sorrows of his heart to Francis Hodgson. We cannot doubt that the 'Lines written beneath a Picture,' composed at Athens in January, 1811,

> 'Dear object of defeated care !
> Though now of Love and thee bereft,'

referred to Mary Chaworth, for he mentions the death-blow of his hope. In the 'Epistle to a Friend,' Byron mentions the effect which a chance meeting with Mary had upon him, causing him to realize that 'Time had not made him love the less.'

The poems that have puzzled the commentator most were those which Byron addressed to 'Thyrza'— a mysterious personage, whose identity has not hitherto been discovered. The present writer proposes to enter fully, and, he hopes, impartially, into the subject, trusting that the conclusions at which he has arrived may ultimately be endorsed by others who have given their serious attention to the question at issue.

In any attempt to unravel the mystery of the

'Thyrza' poems, it will be necessary to consider, not only the circumstances in which they were written, but also those associations of Byron's youth which inspired a love that endured throughout his life.

Byron's attachment to his distant cousin, Mary Anne Chaworth, is well known. We know that his boyish love was not returned, and that the young heiress of Annesley married, in 1805, Mr. John Musters, of Colwick, in the neighbourhood of Nottingham. In order to account for these love-poems, it has been suggested that, subsequent to this marriage, Byron fell in love with some incognita, whose identity has never been established, and who died soon after his return to England in 1811.

We are unable to concur with so simple a solution of the mystery, for the following reasons: It will be remembered that shortly after Mary Chaworth's marriage Byron entered Trinity College, Cambridge, where he formed a romantic attachment to a young chorister, named Edleston, whose life he had saved from drowning. Writing to Miss Elizabeth Pigot on June 30, 1807, Byron says:

'I quit Cambridge with very little regret, because our *set* are vanished, and my musical *protégé* (Edleston), before mentioned, has left the choir, and is stationed in a mercantile house of considerable eminence in the Metropolis. You may have heard me observe he is, exactly to an hour, two years younger than myself. I found him grown considerably, and, as you may suppose, very glad to see his former *Patron*.* He is nearly my height, very *thin*, very fair complexion, dark eyes, and light locks.

'My opinion of his mind you already know; I hope I shall never have occasion to change it.'

---

* They appear to have met accidentally in Trinity Walks a few days earlier. Edleston did not at first recognize Byron, who had grown so thin.

On July 5, 1807, Byron again wrote to Miss Pigot:

'At this moment I write with a bottle of claret in my *head* and *tears* in my *eyes;* for I have just parted with my "Cornelian,"* who spent the evening with me. As it was our last interview, I postponed my engagement to devote the hours of the *Sabbath* to friendship: Edleston and I have separated for the present, and my mind is a chaos of hope and sorrow. . . . I rejoice to hear you are interested in my *protégé;* he has been my *almost constant* associate since October, 1805, when I entered Trinity College. His *voice* first attracted my attention, his *countenance* fixed it, and his *manner* attached me to him for ever. He departs for a mercantile house in Town in October, and we shall probably not meet till the expiration of my minority, when I shall leave to his decision, either entering as a *partner* through my interest, or residing with me altogether. Of course he would, in his present frame of mind, prefer the latter, but he may alter his opinion previous to that period; however, he shall have his choice. I certainly love him more than any human being, and neither time nor distance have had the least effect on my (in general) changeable disposition. In short, we shall put Lady E. Butler and Miss Ponsonby (the "Ladies of Llangollen," as they were called) to the blush, Pylades and Orestes out of countenance, and want nothing but a catastrophe like Nisus and Euryalus, to give Jonathan and David the "go by." He certainly is perhaps more attached to me than even I am in return. During the whole of my residence at Cambridge we met every day, summer and winter, without passing one tiresome moment, and separated each time with increasing reluctance. I hope you will one day see us together. He is the only being I esteem, though I *like* many.'

This letter shows the depth of the boyish affection that had sprung up between two lads with little experience of life. The attachment on both sides was sincere, but not more so than many similar boy friendships, which,

* Edleston, who some time previously had given Byron a 'Cornelian' as a parting gift on leaving Cambridge for the vacation.

alas! fade away under the chilling influences of time and circumstance. In this case the 'Cornelian Heart' that had sparkled with the tears of Edleston, and which, in the fervour of his feelings, Byron had suspended round his neck, was, not long afterwards, transferred to Miss Elizabeth Pigot.

A vague notion seems to prevail that the inspiration of these 'Thyrza' poems is in some way connected with Edleston. This idea seems to have arisen from Byron's allusion to a pledge of affection given in better days:

'Thou bitter pledge! thou mournful token!'

We cannot accept this theory, being of opinion, not lightly formed, that the 'bitter pledge' referred to had a far deeper and a more lasting significance than ever could have belonged to 'the Cornelian heart that was broken.'

In later years, it will be remembered, Byron told Medwin that, shortly after his arrival at Cambridge, he fell into habits of dissipation, in order to drown the remembrance of a hopeless passion for Mary Chaworth. That Mary Chaworth held his affections at that time is beyond question. She also had given Byron 'a token,' which was still in his possession when the 'Thyrza' poems were written; whereas Edleston's gift had passed to other hands. The following anecdote, related by the Countess Guiccioli, may be accepted on Byron's authority:

'One day (while Byron and Musters were bathing in the Trent—a river that runs through the grounds of Colwick) Mr. Musters perceived a ring among Lord Byron's clothes, left on the bank. To see and take possession of it was the affair of a moment. Musters had recognized it as having belonged to Miss Chaworth. Lord Byron claimed it, but Musters would not restore the ring. High words were exchanged. On returning to the house, Musters jumped on a horse, and galloped off to ask an explanation from Miss Chaworth, who, being forced to confess that Lord Byron wore the ring with her consent, felt obliged to make amends to Musters, by promising to declare immediately her engagement with him.'

It is therefore probable that the 'dear simple gift,' of the first draft, was the ring which Mary Chaworth had given to her boy lover in 1804, and that the words we have quoted had no connection whatever with young Edleston.

Assuming that the 'Thyrza' poems were addressed to a woman—and there is abundant proof of this—it is remarkable that, neither in the whole course of his correspondence with his friends, nor from any source whatever, can any traces be found of any other serious attachment which would account for the poems in question. Between the date of the marriage, in 1805, and the autumn of 1808, Byron and Mary Chaworth had not met. It will be remembered that in the autumn —only eight months before he left England with Hobhouse—Byron met Mary Chaworth at dinner in her own home. The effect of that meeting, which he has himself described, shows the depth of his feelings, and precludes the idea that he could at that time have been deeply interested in anyone else. After that meeting Byron remained three months in the neighbourhood of Annesley; and it may be inferred that an intimacy sprang up between them, which was broken off somewhat abruptly by Mary's husband. There are traces of this in 'Lara.'

At the end of November, 1808, Byron writes from Newstead to his sister:

'I am living here alone, which suits my inclination better than society of any kind. . . . I am a very unlucky fellow, for I think I had naturally not a bad heart; but it has been so bent, twisted, and trampled on, that it has now become as hard as a Highlander's heelpiece.'

A fortnight later he writes to Hanson, his agent, and talks of either marrying for money or blowing his brains out. It was then that he wrote those verses addressed to Mary Chaworth:

> 'When man, expell'd from Eden's bowers,
>   A moment linger'd near the gate,
> Each scene recall'd the vanish'd hours,
>   And bade him curse his future fate.
>
> 'In flight I shall be surely wise,
>   Escaping from temptation's snare;
> I cannot view my Paradise
>   Without the wish of dwelling there.'

On January 25, 1809, Byron returned to London. It is hard to believe that during those three months Byron did not often meet the lady of his love. It is more than probable that the old friendship between them had been renewed, since there is evidence to prove that, after Byron had taken his seat in the House of Lords on March 13, 1809, he confided his Parliamentary robes to Mary Chaworth's safe-keeping, a circumstance which suggests a certain amount of neighbourly friendship.

In May, Byron again visited Newstead, where he entertained Matthews and some of his college friends. That *sérénade indiscrète*,

> ''Tis done—and shivering in the gale,'

which was addressed to Mary Chaworth from Falmouth on, or about, June 22, shows the state of his feelings towards her; but she does not seem to have given him any encouragement, and there was no correspondence between them during Byron's absence from England. Between July 2, 1809, and July 15, 1811, Byron's thoughts were fully occupied in other directions. His distractions, which may be traced in his writings, were, however, not sufficient to crush out the remembrance of that fatal infatuation. When, in 1811, he returned to England, it was without pleasure, and without the faintest hope of any renewal of an intimacy which Mary Chaworth had broken off for both their sakes. He was in no hurry to visit Newstead, where his mother anxiously awaited him, and dawdled about town, under various pretexts, until the first week in August, when he heard of his mother's serious illness. Before Byron reached Newstead his mother had died. He seems to have heard of her illness one day, and of her death on the day following. Although there had long been a certain estrangement between them, all was now forgotten, and Byron felt his mother's death acutely.

It was at this time that he wrote to his friend Scrope Davies:

'Some curse hangs over me and mine. My mother lies a corpse in this house; one of my best friends (Charles Skinner Matthews) is drowned in a ditch. What can I say, or think, or do? I received a letter from him the day before yesterday. . . . Come to me, Scrope; I am almost desolate—left almost alone in the world.'

In that gloomy frame of mind, in the solitude of a ruin—for Newstead at that time was but little better than a ruin—Byron, on August 12, drew up some directions for his will, in which he desired to be buried in the garden at Newstead, by the side of his favourite dog Boatswain.

On the same day he wrote to Dallas, who was

superintending the printing of the first and second cantos of 'Childe Harold':

'Peace be with the dead! ? Regret cannot wake them. With a sigh to the departed, let us resume the dull business of life, in the certainty that we also shall have our repose. Besides her who gave me being, I have lost more than one who made that being tolerable. Matthews, a man of the first talents, and also not the worst of my narrow circle, has perished miserably in the muddy waves of the Cam, always fatal to genius; my poor schoolfellow, Wingfield, at Coimbra—within a month; and whilst I had heard from *all three*, but not seen *one*. . . . But let this pass; we shall all one day pass along with the rest. The world is too full of such things, and our very sorrow is selfish. . . . I am already too familiar with the dead. It is strange that I look on the skulls which stand beside me (I have always had *four* in my study) without emotion, but I cannot strip the features of those I have known of their fleshy covering, even in idea, without a hideous sensation; but the worms are less ceremonious. Surely, the Romans did well when they burned the dead.'

The writer of this letter was in his twenty-fourth year!

Ten days later Byron writes to Hodgson:

'Indeed the blows followed each other so rapidly that I am yet stupid from the shock; and though I do eat, and drink, and talk, and even laugh at times, yet I can hardly persuade myself that I am awake, did not every morning convince me mournfully to the contrary. I shall now waive the subject, the dead are at rest, and none but the dead can be so. . . . I am solitary, and I never felt solitude irksome before.'

At about the same date, in a letter to Dallas, Byron writes:

'At three-and-twenty I am left alone, and what more can we be at seventy? It is true I am young enough to begin again, but with whom can I retrace the laugh-

HAUNTING MEMORIES

ing part of my life? It is odd how few of my friends have died a quiet death—I mean, in their beds!

'I cannot settle to anything, and my days pass, with the exception of bodily exercise to some extent, with uniform indolence and idle insipidity.'

The verses, 'Oh! banish care,' etc., were written at this time.

In the following lines we see that his grief at the losses he had sustained was deepened by the haunting memory of Mary Chaworth:

> 'I've seen my bride another's bride—
> Have seen her seated by his side—
> Have seen the infant which she bore
> Wear the sweet smile the mother wore,
> When she and I in youth have smiled
> As fond and faultless as her child;
> Have seen her eyes, in cold disdain,
> Ask if I felt no secret pain.
> And I have acted well my part,
> And made my cheek belie my heart,
> Returned the freezing glance she gave,
> Yet felt the while *that* woman's slave;
> Have kissed, as if without design,
> The babe which ought to have been mine,
> And showed, alas! in each caress
> Time had not made me love the less.'

Moore, who knew more of the inner workings of Byron's mind in later years than anyone else, has told us that the poems addressed to 'Thyrza' were merely 'the abstract spirit of many griefs,' and that the pseudonym was given to an 'object of affection' to whom he poured out the sorrows of his heart.

'All these recollections,' says Moore, 'of the young and dead now came to mingle themselves in his mind with the image of her who, *though living*, was for him as much lost as they, and diffused that general feeling of sadness and fondness through his soul, which found a vent in these poems. No friendship, however warm, could have inspired sorrow so passionate; as no love, however pure, could have kept passion so chastened.

'It was the blending of the two affections in his memory and imagination that thus gave birth to an ideal object combining the best features of both, and drew from him these saddest and tenderest of love-poems, in which we find all the depth and intensity of real feeling, touched over with such a light as no reality ever wore.'

Moore here expresses himself guardedly. He was one of the very few who knew the whole story of Mary Chaworth's associations with Byron. He could not, of course, betray his full knowledge; but he has made it sufficiently clear that Byron, in writing the 'Thyrza' group of poems, was merely strewing the flowers of poetry on the grave of his love for Mary Chaworth.

The first of these poems was written on the day on which he heard of the death of Edleston. In a letter to Dallas he says:

'I have been again shocked by a *death*, and have lost one very dear to me in happier times. I have become callous, nor have I a tear left for an event which, five years ago, would have bowed down my head to the earth. It seems as though I were to experience in my youth the greatest misery of age. My friends fall around me, and I shall be left a lonely tree before I am withered. Other men can always take refuge in their families; I have no resource but my own reflections, and they present no prospect here or hereafter, except the selfish satisfaction of surviving my betters. I am indeed very wretched, and you will excuse my saying so, as you know I am not apt to cant of sensibility.'*

Shortly after this letter was written Byron visited Cambridge, where, among the many memories which

* Edleston had died five months before Byron heard the sad news.

THE CORNELIAN HEART

that place awakened, a remembrance of the young chorister and their ardent friendship was most vivid. Byron recollected the Cornelian that Edleston gave him as a token of friendship, and, now that the giver had passed away for ever, he regretted that he had parted with it. The following letter to Mrs. Pigot explains itself:

'CAMBRIDGE,
'*October* 28, 1811.

'DEAR MADAM,
    'I am about to write to you on a silly subject, and yet I cannot well do otherwise. You may remember a *cornelian* which some years ago I consigned to Miss Pigot — indeed I *gave* to her — and now I am going to make the most selfish and rude of requests. The person who gave it to me, when I was very young, is *dead*, and though a long time has elapsed since we met, as it was the only memorial I possessed of that person (in whom I was very much interested), it has acquired a value by this event I could have wished it never to have borne in my eyes. If, therefore, Miss Pigot should have preserved it, I must, under these circumstances, beg her to excuse my requesting it to be transmitted to me at No. 8, St. James' Street, London, and I will replace it by something she may remember me by equally well. As she was always so kind as to feel interested in the fate of him that formed the subject of our conversation, you may tell her that the giver of that cornelian died in May last of a consumption at the age of twenty-one, making the sixth, within four months, of friends and relatives that I have lost between May and the end of August.
        'Believe me, dear madam,
            'Yours very sincerely,
                'BYRON.'

The cornelian when found, was returned to Byron, but apparently in a broken condition.

        'Ill-fated Heart! and can it be,
        That thou shouldst thus be rent in twain?'

It was through the depressing influence of solitude that the idea entered Byron's mind to depict his (possibly eternal) separation from Mary Chaworth in terms synonymous with death. With a deep feeling of desolation he recalled every incident of his boyish love. We have seen how the image of his lost Mary, now the wife of his rival, deepened the gloom caused by the sudden death of his mother, and of some of his college friends. It was to Mary, whom he dared not name, that he cried in his agony:

> ' By many a shore and many a sea
> Divided, yet beloved in vain ;
> The Past, the Future fled to thee,
> To bid us meet—no, ne'er again !'

Her absence from Annesley, where he had hoped to find her on his return home, was a great disappointment to him.

> ' Thou too art gone, thou loved and lovely one !
> Whom Youth and Youth's affections bound to me ;
> Who did for me what none beside have done,
> Nor shrank from one albeit unworthy thee.
> What is my Being ! thou hast ceased to be !
> Nor staid to welcome here thy wanderer home,
> Who mourns o'er hours which we no more shall see—
> Would they had never been, or were to come !
> Would he had ne'er returned to find fresh cause to roam !

> ' Oh ! ever loving, lovely, and beloved !
> How selfish Sorrow ponders on the past,
> And clings to thoughts now better far removed !
> But Time shall tear thy shadow from me last.
> All thou couldst have of mine, stern Death ! thou hast ;
> The Parent, Friend, and now the more than Friend :
> Ne'er yet for one thine arrows flew so fast,
> And grief with grief continuing still to blend,
> Hath snatch'd the little joy that Life hath yet to lend.

*   *   *   *   *

What is the worst of woes that wait on Age?
What stamps the wrinkle deeper on the brow?
To view each loved one blotted from Life's page,
And be alone on earth, as I am now.
Before the Chastener humbly let me bow,
O'er Hearts divided and o'er Hopes destroyed:
Roll on, vain days! full reckless may ye flow,
Since Time hath reft whate'er my soul enjoyed,
And with the ills of Eld mine earlier years alloyed.'

These stanzas were attached to the second canto of 'Childe Harold,' after that poem was in the press. Mr. Ernest Hartley Coleridge, who so ably edited the latest edition of the poetry of Byron, states that they were sent to Dallas on the same day that Byron composed the poem 'To Thyrza.' This is significant, as also his attempt to mystify Dallas by telling him that he had again (October 11, 1811) been shocked by a death. This was true enough, for he had on that day heard of the death of Edleston; but it was *not* true that the stanzas we have quoted had any connection with that event. Mr. Coleridge in a note says:

'In connection with this subject, it may be noted that the lines 6 and 7 of Stanza XCV.,

'" Nor staid to welcome here thy wanderer home,
  Who mourns o'er hours which we no more shall see,"

do not bear out Byron's contention to Dallas (Letters, October 14 and 31, 1811) that in these three *in memoriam* stanzas (IX., XCV., XCVI.) he is bewailing an event which took place *after* he returned to Newstead.* The "more than friend" had "ceased to be" before the "wanderer" returned. It is evident that Byron did not take Dallas into his confidence.'

Assuredly he did not. The 'more than friend' was not *dead;* she had merely absented herself, and did not

* 'I think it proper to state to you that this stanza alludes to an event which has taken place since my arrival here, and not to the death of any *male* friend.'—Lord Byron to Mr. Dallas.

stay to welcome the 'wanderer' on his return from his travels. She was, however, *dead to him* in a sense far deeper than mere absence at such a time.

> ' The absent are the dead—for they are cold,
> And ne'er can be what once we did behold.'*

Mary Chaworth's presence would have consoled him at a time when he felt alone in the world. He feared that she was lost to him for ever. He knew her too well to suppose that she could ever be more to him than a friend; and yet it was just that female sympathy and friendship for which he so ardently yearned. In his unreasonableness, he was both hurt and disappointed that this companion of his earlier days should have kept away from her home at that particular time, and of course misconstrued the cause. With the feeling that this parting must be eternal, he wished that they could have met once more.

> ' Could this have been—a word, a look,
> That softly said, "We part in peace,"
> Had taught my bosom how to brook,
> With fainter sighs, thy soul's release."'

In the bitterness of his desolation he recalled the days when they were at Newstead together—probably stolen interviews, which find no place in history—when

> ' many a day
> In these, to me, deserted towers,
> Ere called but for a time away,
> Affection's mingling tears were ours?

---

* That this Thyrza was no passing fancy is proved by Lord Lovelace's statement in 'Astarte' (p. 138): 'He had occasionally spoken of Thyrza to Lady Byron, at Seaham and afterwards in London, *always with strong but contained emotion.* He once showed his wife a beautiful tress of Thyrza's hair, *but never mentioned her real name.*

MRS. GEORGE LAMB

> Ours, too, the glance none saw beside ;
> The smile none else might understand ;
> The whispered thought ; the walks aside ;
> The pressure of the thrilling hand ;
> The kiss so guiltless and refined,
> That Love each warmer wish forbore ;
> Those eyes proclaimed so pure a mind,
> Ev'n Passion blushed to plead for more.
> The tone that taught me to rejoice,
> When prone, unlike thee, to repine ;
> *The song, celestial from thy voice,*
> *But sweet to me from none but thine ;*
> The pledge we wore—*I* wear it still,
> But where is thine ? Ah ! where art thou ?
> Oft have I borne the weight of ill,
> But never bent beneath till now !'

Six days after these lines were written Byron left Newstead. Writing to Hodgson from his lodgings in St. James's Street, he enclosed some stanzas which he had written a day or two before, 'on hearing a song of former days.' The lady, whose singing now so deeply impressed Byron, was the Hon. Mrs. George Lamb, whom he had met at Melbourne House.

In this, the second of the 'Thyrza' poems, the allusions to Mary Chaworth are even more marked. Byron says the songs of Mrs. George Lamb 'speak to him of brighter days,' and that he hopes to hear those strains no more :

> 'For now, alas !
> I must not think, I may not gaze,
>   On what I *am*—on what I *was*.
>
> The voice that made those sounds more sweet
>   Is hush'd, and all their charms are fled.
>
> *   *   *   *   *
>
> 'On my ear
> The well-remembered echoes thrill ;
> I hear a voice I would not hear,
>   A voice that now might well be still.
>
> *   *   *   *   *

> 'Sweet Thyrza ! waking as in sleep,
>   Thou art but now a lovely dream ;
> A *Star* that trembled o'er the deep,
>   Then turned from earth its tender beam.
> But he who through Life's dreary way
>   Must pass, when Heaven is veiled in wrath,
> Will long lament the vanished ray
>   That scattered gladness o'er his path.'

In Byron's imagination Mary Chaworth was always hovering over him like a star. She was the 'starlight of his boyhood,' the 'star of his destiny,' and three years later the poet, in his unpublished fragment 'Harmodia,' speaks of Mary as his

> 'melancholy star
> Whose tearful beam shoots trembling from afar.'

The third and last of the 'Thyrza' poems must have been written at about the same time as the other two. It appeared with 'Childe Harold' in 1812. Byron, weary of the gloom of solitude, and tortured by 'pangs that rent his heart in twain,' now determined to break away and seek inspiration for that mental energy which formed part of his nature. Man, he says, was not made to live alone.

> 'I'll be that light unmeaning thing
>   That smiles with all, and weeps with none.
> It was not thus in days more dear,
>   It never would have been, *but thou
> Hast fled, and left me lonely here.*'

Byron's thoughts went back to the days when he was sailing over the bright waters of the blue Ægean, in the *Salsette* frigate, commanded by 'good old Bathurst'*—those halcyon days when he was weaving his visions into stanzas for 'Childe Harold.'

* Captain (afterwards Commodore) Walter Bathurst was mortally wounded at the Battle of Navarino, on October 20, 1827.—'Battles of the British Navy,' Joseph Allen, vol. ii., p. 518.

> ' On many a lone and lovely night
>   It soothed to gaze upon the sky ;
>   For then I deemed the heavenly light
>   Shone sweetly on thy pensive eye :
>   And oft I thought at Cynthia's noon,
>   When sailing o'er the Ægean wave,
>   "Now Thyrza gazes on that moon"—
>   Alas ! it gleamed upon her grave !
>
> ' When stretched on Fever's sleepless bed,
>   And sickness shrunk my throbbing veins,
>   " 'Tis comfort still," I faintly said,
>   "That Thyrza cannot know my pains."
>   Like freedom to the timeworn slave—
>   A boon 'tis idle then to give—
>   Relenting Nature vainly gave
>   My life, when Thyrza ceased to live !
>
> ' My Thyrza's pledge in better days,
>   *When Love and Life alike were new !*
>   How different now thou meet'st my gaze !
>   How tinged by time with Sorrow's hue !
>   The heart that gave itself with thee
>   Is silent—ah, were mine as still !
>   Though cold as e'en the dead can be,
>   It feels, it sickens with the chill.'

Byron here suggests that the pledge in question was given with the giver's heart. Lovers are apt to interpret such gifts as 'love-tokens,' without suspicion that they may possibly have been due to a feeling far less flattering to their hopes.

> ' Thou bitter pledge ! thou mournful token !
>   Though painful, welcome to my breast !
>   Still, still, preserve that love unbroken,
>   Or break the heart to which thou'rt pressed.
>   Time tempers Love, but not removes,
>   More hallowed when its Hope is fled.'

These three pieces comprise the so-called 'Thyrza' poems, and, in the absence of proof to the contrary, we may reasonably suppose that their subject was Mary Chaworth. This is the more likely because the original manuscripts were the property of Byron's sister, to whom they were probably given by Mary Chaworth, when, in later years, she destroyed or parted with all the letters and documents which she had received from Byron since the days of their childhood.

Byron did not give up the hope of winning Mary Chaworth's love until her marriage in 1805. Two months later he entered Trinity College, Cambridge, and from that time, until his departure with Hobhouse on his first foreign tour, those who were in constant intercourse with him never mentioned any other object of adoration who might fit in with the Thyrza of the poems. If such a person had really existed, Byron would certainly, either in conversation or in writing, have disclosed her identity. Moore makes it clear that the one passion of Byron's life was Mary Chaworth. He tells us that there were many fleeting love-episodes, but only one passion strong enough to have inspired the poems in question. If Byron's heart, during the two years that he passed abroad, had been overflowing with love for some incognita, it was not in his nature to have kept silence. From his well-known effusiveness, reticence under such circumstances is inconceivable.

Finally, as there were no poems, no letters, and no allusion to any such person in the *first* draft of 'Childe Harold,' we may confidently assume that the poet, in the loneliness of his heart, appealed to the only woman whom he ever really loved, and that the legendary Thyrza was a myth.

It will be remembered that the ninth stanza in the second canto of 'Childe Harold' was interpolated long after the manuscript had been given to Dallas. It was forwarded for that purpose, three days after the date

A PERIOD OF DESOLATION

of the poem 'To Thyrza,' and essentially belongs to that period of desolation which inspired those poems:

> 'There, Thou! *whose Love and Life, together fled,*
> *Have left me here to love and live in vain—*
> Twined with my heart, and can I deem thee dead,
> When busy Memory flashes on my brain?
> Well—*I will dream that we may meet again,*
> And woo the vision to my vacant breast:
> If aught of young Remembrance then remain,
> Be as it may Futurity's behest,
> *Or seeing thee no more, to sink to sullen rest.'**

It is difficult to believe that this stanza was inspired by a memory of the dead. Are we not told that 'Love and Life *together* fled'—in other words, when Mary withdrew her love, she was dead to him?

He tells her that in abandoning him she has left him to love and live in vain. And yet he will not give up the hope of meeting her again some day; this is now his sole consolation. Memory of the past (possibly those meetings which took place by stealth, shortly before his departure from England in 1809) feeds the hope that now sustains him. But he will leave everything to chance, and if fate decides that they shall be parted for ever, then will he sink to sullen apathy.

We may remind the reader that at this period (1811) Byron had no belief in any existence after death.

'I will have nothing to do with your immortality,' he writes to Hodgson in September; 'we are miserable enough in this life, without the absurdity of speculating upon another. If men are to live, why die at all? and if they die, why disturb the sweet and sound sleep that "knows no waking"?

'" Post mortem nihil est, ipsaque Mors nihil . . . quæris quo jaceas post obitum loco? Quo *non* Nata jacent."'

* The last line was in the first draft.

Even when, in later years, Byron somewhat modified the views of his youth, he expressed an opinion that

'A material resurrection seems strange, and even absurd, except for purposes of punishment, and all punishment which is to *revenge* rather than *correct* must be *morally wrong*.'

It is therefore tolerably certain that, on the day when he expressed a hope that he might meet his lady-love again, the meeting was to have been in *this* world, and not in that 'land of souls beyond the sable shore.' It must also be remembered that the eighth stanza in the second canto of 'Childe Harold' was substituted for one in which Byron deliberately stated that he did not look for Life, where life may never be. The revise was written to please Dallas, and does not pretend to be a confession of belief in immortality, but merely an admission that, on a subject where 'nothing can be known,' no final decision is possible.

In the summer of 1813 Byron underwent grave vicissitudes, mental, moral, and financial. His letters and journals teem with allusions to some catastrophe. It seemed as though he were threatened with impending ruin. In his depressed state of mind he found relief only, as he tells us, in the composition of poetry. It was at this time that he wrote in swift succession 'The Giaour,' 'The Bride of Abydos,' and 'The Corsair.' It is clear that Byron's dejection was the result of a hopeless attachment. Mr. Hartley Coleridge assumes that Byron's *innamorata* was Lady Frances Wedderburn Webster. But that bright star did not long shine in Byron's orbit—certainly not after October, 1813—and it is doubtful whether they were ever on terms of close intimacy. Her husband had long been Byron's friend. Byron had lent him money, and had given him advice, which he seems to have sorely needed. It is difficult to understand why Lady Frances Webster should have been especially regarded as Byron's Calypso. There is nothing to show that she ever seriously occupied his thoughts. Writing to Moore on September 27, 1813, Byron says:

'I stayed a week with the Websters, and behaved very well, though the lady of the house is young, religious, and pretty, and the master is my particular friend. I felt no wish for anything but a poodle dog, which they kindly gave me.'

So little does Byron seem to have been attracted by Lady Frances, that he only once more visited the Websters, and then only for a few days, on his way to Newstead, between October 3 and 10, 1813.

On June 3 of that year Byron wrote to Mr. John Hanson, his solicitor, a letter which shows the state of his mind at that time He tells Hanson that he is about to visit Salt Hill, near Maidenhead, and that he will be absent for one week. He is determined to go abroad. The prospective lawsuit with Mr. Claughton (about the sale of Newstead) is to be dropped, if it cannot be carried on in Byron's absence. At all hazards, at all losses, he is determined that nothing shall prevent him from leaving the country.

'If utter ruin *were* or *is* before me on the one hand, and wealth at home on the other, I have made my choice, and go I will.'

The pictures, and every movable that could be converted into cash, were, by Byron's orders, to be sold. 'All I want is a few thousand pounds, and then, Adieu. You shan't be troubled with me these ten years, if ever.' Clearly, there must have been something more than a passing fancy which could have induced Byron to sacrifice his chances of selling Newstead, for the sake of a few thousand pounds of ready-money. It *had been* his intention to accompany Lord and Lady Oxford on their travels, but this project was abandoned. After three weeks—spent in running backwards and forwards between Salt Hill and London—Byron confided his troubles to Augusta. She was always his rock of refuge in all his deeper troubles. Augusta Leigh thought that absence might mend matters, and tried hard to keep her brother up to his resolve of going abroad; she even volunteered to accompany him. But Lady Melbourne—who must have had a prurient mind—persuaded Byron that the gossips about town would not consider it 'proper' for him and his sister to travel alone! As Byron was at that time under the influence of an irresistible infatuation, Lady Melbourne's warning turned the scale, and the project fell through. Meanwhile the plot thickened. Something—he told Moore—had ruined all his prospects of matrimony. His financial circumstances, he said, were mending; 'and were not my other prospects blackening, I would take a wife.'

In July he still wishes to get out of England. 'They had better let me go,' he says; 'one can die anywhere.'

On August 22, after another visit to Salt Hill, Byron writes to Moore:

'I have said nothing of the brilliant sex; but the fact is, I am at this moment in a far more serious, and entirely new, scrape, than any of the last twelve months, and that is saying a good deal. It is unlucky we can neither live with nor without these women.'

A week later he wrote again to Moore:

'I would incorporate with any woman of decent demeanour to-morrow—that is, I would a month ago, but at present . . .'

A HOPELESS ATTACHMENT

Moore suggested that Byron's case was similar to that of the youth apostrophized by Horace in his twenty-seventh ode, and invited his confidence:

> 'Come, whisper it—the tender truth—
> To safe and friendly ears!
> What! Her? O miserable youth!
> Oh! doomed to grief and tears!
> In what a whirlpool are you tost,
> Your rudder broke, your pilot lost!'

Recent research has convinced the present writer that the incident which affected Byron so profoundly at this time—about eighteen months before his marriage —indirectly brought about the separation between Lord and Lady Byron in 1816. A careful student of Byron's character could not fail to notice, among all the contradictions and inconsistencies of his life, one point upon which he was resolute—namely, a consistent reticence on the subject of the intimacy which sprang up between himself and Mary Chaworth in the summer of 1813. The strongest impulse of his life— even to the last—was a steadfast, unwavering, hopeless attachment to that lady. Throughout his turbulent youth, in his early as in his later days, the same theme floats through the chords of his melodious verse, a deathless love and a deep remorse. Even at the last, when the shadow of Death was creeping slowly over the flats at Missolonghi, the same wild, despairing note found involuntary expression, and the last words that Byron ever wrote tell the sad story with a distinctness which might well open the eyes even of the blind.

When he first met his fate, he was a schoolboy of sixteen—precocious, pugnacious, probably a prig, and by no means handsome. He must have appeared to Mary much as we see him in his portrait by Sanders. Mary was two years older, and already in love with a fox-hunting squire of good family. 'Love dwells not in our will,' and a nature like Byron's, once under its spell, was sure to feel its force acutely. There was romance, too, in the situation; and the poetic temperament—always precocious—responded to an impulse on the gossamer chance of achieving the impossible Mary was probably half amused and half flattered by the adoration of a boy of whose destiny she divined nothing.

There is no reason to suppose that there was any meeting between Byron and Mary Chaworth after the spring of 1809, until the summer of 1813. Their separation seemed destined to be final. Although Byron, in after-years, wished it to be believed that they had not met since 1808, it is certain that a meeting took place in the summer of 1813. Although Byron took, as we shall see presently, great pains to conceal that fact from the public, he did not attempt to deceive either Moore, Hobhouse, or Hodgson. In his letter to Monsieur Coulmann, written in July, 1823, we have the version which Byron wished the public to believe.

'I had not seen her [Mary Chaworth] for many years. When an occasion offered, I was upon the point, with her consent, of paying her a visit, when my sister, who has always had more influence over me than anyone else, persuaded me not to do it. "For," said she, "if you go, you will fall in love again, and then there will be a scene; one step will lead to another, *et cela fera un éclat*," etc. I was guided by these reasons, and shortly after I married. . . . Mrs. Chaworth some time after, being separated from her husband, became insane; but she has since recovered her reason, and is, I believe, reconciled to her husband.'

At about the same time Byron told Medwin that, *after* Mary's separation from her husband, she proposed an interview with him—a suggestion which

Byron, by the advice of Mrs. Leigh, declined. He also said to Medwin:

'She [Mary Chaworth] was the *beau-idéal* of all that my youthful fancy could paint of beautiful; and I have taken all my fables about the celestial nature of women from the perfection my imagination created in her—I say *created*, for I found her, *like the rest of her sex, anything but angelic.*'

It is difficult to see how Byron could have arrived at so unflattering an estimate of a woman whom he had only *once* seen since her marriage—at a dinner-party, when, as he has told us, he was overcome by shyness and a feeling of awkwardness! But let that pass. Byron wished the world to believe (1) that Mary Chaworth, after the separation from her husband in 1813, proposed a meeting with Byron; (2) that he declined to meet her; (3) that, after his unfortunate marriage, Mary became insane; and (4) that he found her, 'like the rest of her sex, anything but angelic.'

It is quite possible, of course, that Byron may have *at first* refused to meet the only woman on earth whom he sincerely loved, and more than likely that Mrs. Leigh did her utmost to dissuade him from so rash a proceeding. But it is on record that Byron incautiously admitted to Medwin that he *did* meet Mary Chaworth *after his return from Greece.** It will be remembered that he returned from Greece in 1811. Their intimacy had long before been broken off by Mr. John Musters; and, as we have seen, Mary, faithful to a promise which she had made to her husband, kept away from Annesley during the period (1811) when the 'Thyrza' poems were written. It is doubtful whether they would ever again have met if her husband had shown any consideration for her feelings. But he

* Medwin (quarto edition of 1824), p. 63.

showed her none. When, nearly forty years ago, the present writer visited Annesley, there were several people living who remembered both Mary Chaworth and her husband. These people stated that their married life, so full of grief and bitterness, was a constant source of comment both at Annesley and Newstead. The trouble was attributed to the harsh and capricious conduct, and the well-known infidelities, of one to whose kindness and affection Mary had a sacred claim. She seems to have been left for long periods at Annesley with only one companion, Miss Anne Radford, who had been brought up with her from childhood. This state of things eventually broke down, and when, in the early part of 1813, Mary could stand the strain no longer, a separation took place by mutual consent.

In the summer of that year Byron and this unhappy woman were thrown together by the merest accident, and, unfortunately for both, renewed their dangerous friendship.

Byron's friend and biographer, Thomas Moore, took great pains to suppress every allusion to Mary Chaworth in Byron's memoranda and letters. He faithfully kept the secret. There is nothing in Byron's letters or journals, as revised by Moore, to show that they ever met after 1808, and yet they undoubtedly did meet in 1813, *after* Mary's estrangement from her husband. That they were in constant correspondence in November of that year may be gathered from Byron's journal, where Mary's name is veiled by asterisks.

On November 24 he writes:

'I am tremendously in arrear with my letters, except to ****, and to her my thoughts overpower me: my words never compass them.'

'I have been pondering,' he writes on the 26th, 'on the miseries of separation, that—oh! how seldom we see those we love! Yet we live ages in moments *when met.*'

Then follows, on the 27th, a clue:

'I believe, with Clym o' the Clow, or Robin Hood,

' " By our Mary (dear name!) thou art both Mother and May,
I think it never was a man's lot to die before his day." '

It is attested, by all those who were acquainted with Mary Chaworth, that she always bore an exemplary character. It was well known that her marriage was an unhappy one, and that she had been for some time deserted by her husband. In June, 1813, when she fell under the fatal spell of Byron, then the most fascinating man in society,* she was living in deep dejection, parted from her lawful protector, with whom she had a serious disagreement. He had neglected her, and she well knew that she had a rival in his affections at that time.

It was in these distressing circumstances that Byron, with the world at his feet, came to worship her in great humility. As he looked back upon the past, he realized that this neglected woman had always been the light of his life, the lodestar of his destiny. And now that he beheld his 'Morning Star of Annesley' shedding ineffectual rays upon the dead embers of a lost love, the old feeling returned to him with resistless force.

'We met—we gazed—I saw, and sighed;
She did not speak, and yet replied;
There are ten thousand tones and signs
We hear and see, but none defines—

---

* 'A power of fascination rarely, if ever, possessed by any man of his age' ('Recollections of a Long Life,' by Lord Broughton, vol. ii., p. 196).

> Involuntary sparks of thought,
> Which strike from out the heart o'erwrought,
> And form a strange intelligence,
> Alike mysterious and intense,
> Which link the burning chain that binds,
> Without their will, young hearts and minds.
> I saw, and sighed—in silence wept,
> And still reluctant distance kept,
> Until I was made known to her,
> And we might then and there confer
> Without suspicion—then, even then,
>   I longed, and was resolved to speak;
> But on my lips they died again,
>   The accents tremulous and weak,
> Until one hour . . .
>   *   *   *   *   *
>   'I would have given
> My life but to have called her mine
> In the full view of Earth and Heaven;
>   For I did oft and long repine
> That we could only meet by stealth.'

In the remorseful words of Manfred,

> 'Her faults were mine—her virtues were her own—
> I loved her, and destroyed her! . . .
> Not with my hand, but heart—which broke *her* heart—
> It gazed on mine and withered.'

Without attempting to excuse Byron's conduct—indeed, that were useless—it must be remembered that he was only twenty-five years of age, and Mary was very unhappy. After all hope of meeting her again had been abandoned, the force of destiny, so to speak, had unexpectedly restored his lost Thyrza—the *Theresa* of 'Mazeppa.'

> 'I loved her then, I love her still;
> And such as I am, love indeed
> In fierce extremes—in good and ill—
> But still we love. . . .
> Haunted to our very age
> With the vain shadow of the past.'

Byron's punishment was in this world. The remorse which followed endured throughout the remaining portion of his life. It wrecked what might have proved a happy marriage, and drove him, from stone to stone, along life's causeway, to that 'Sea Sodom' where, for many months, he tried to destroy the memory of his crime by reckless profligacy.

Mary Chaworth no sooner realized her awful danger—the madness of an impulse which not even love could excuse—than she recoiled from the precipice which yawned before her. She had been momentarily blinded by the irresistible fascination of one who, after all, really and truly loved her. But she was a good woman in spite of this one episode, and to the last hour of her existence she never swerved from that narrow path which led to an honoured grave.

Although it was too late for happiness, too late to evade the consequences of her weakness, there was still time for repentance. The secret was kept inviolate by the very few to whom it was confided, and the present writer deeply regrets that circumstances have compelled him to break the seal.

If 'Astarte' had not been written, there would have been no need to lift the veil. Lord Lovelace has besmirched the good name of Mrs. Leigh, and it is but an act of simple justice to defend her.

When Mary Chaworth escaped from Byron's fatal influence, he reproached her for leaving him, and tried to shake her resolution with heart-rending appeals. Happily for both, they fell upon deaf ears.

> 'Astarte! my beloved! speak to me;
> Say that thou loath'st me not—that I do bear
> This punishment for both.'

The depth and sincerity of Byron's love for Mary

Chaworth cannot be questioned. Moore, who knew him well, says:

'The all-absorbing and unsuccessful (unsatisfied) love for Mary Chaworth was the agony, without being the death, of an unsated desire which lived on through life, filled his poetry with the very soul of tenderness, lent the colouring of its light to even those unworthy ties which vanity or passion led him afterwards to form, and was the last aspiration of his fervid spirit, in those stanzas written but a few months before his death.'

It was, in fact, a love of such unreasonableness and persistence as might be termed, without exaggeration, a madness of the heart.

Although Mary escaped for ever from that baneful infatuation, which in an unguarded moment had destroyed her peace of mind, her separation from Byron was not complete until he married. Not only did they correspond frequently, but they also met occasionally. In the following January (1814) Byron introduced Mary to Augusta Leigh. From that eventful meeting, *when probable contingencies were provided for*, until Mary's death in 1832, these two women, who had suffered so much through Byron, continued in the closest intimacy; and in November, 1819, Augusta stood sponsor for Mary's youngest daughter.

In a poem which must have been written in 1813, an apostrophe 'To Time,' Byron refers to Mary's resolutions.

> 'In Joy I've sighed to think thy flight
>   Would soon subside from swift to slow;
> Thy cloud could overcast the light,
>   But could not add a night to Woe;
> For then, however drear and dark,
>   My soul was suited to thy sky;
> *One star alone* shot forth a spark
>   To prove thee—not Eternity.
> *That beam hath sunk.*'

MARY CHAWORTH AND MRS. LEIGH

It is of course true that matters were not, and could never again be, on the same footing as in July of that year; but Mary Chaworth was constancy itself, in a higher and a nobler sense than Byron attached to it, when he reproached her for broken vows.

> 'Thy vows are all broken,
> And light is thy fame:
> I hear thy name spoken,
> And share in its shame.'

During the remainder of Byron's life, Mary took a deep interest in everything that affected him. In 1814, believing that marriage would be his salvation, she used her influence in that direction. We know that she did not approve of the choice which Byron so recklessly made, and she certainly had ample cause to deplore its results. Through her close intimacy with Augusta Leigh—an intimacy which has not hitherto been suspected—she became acquainted with every phase in Byron's subsequent career. She could read 'between the lines,' and solve the mysteries to be found in such poems as ' Lara,' ' Mazeppa,' ' Manfred,' and ' Don Juan.'

We believe that Byron's love for Mary was the main cause of the indifference he felt towards his wife. In order to shield Mary from the possible consequences of a public investigation into conduct prior to his marriage, Byron, in 1816, consented to a separation from his wife.

After Byron had left England Mary broke down under the strain she had borne so bravely, and her mind gave way. When at last, in April, 1817, a reconciliation took place between Mary and her husband, it was apparent to everyone that she had, during those four anxious years, become a changed woman. She never entirely regained either health or spirits. Her mind 'had acquired a tinge of religious melancholy, which never afterwards left it.' Sorrow and disappointment had subdued a naturally buoyant nature, and 'melancholy marked her for its own.' Shortly before her death, in 1832, she destroyed every letter she had received from Byron since those distant fateful years when, as boy and girl, they had wandered on the Hills of Annesley. For eight sad years Mary Chaworth survived the lover of her youth. Shortly before her death, in a letter to one of her daughters, she drew her own character, which might fitly form her epitaph: 'Soon led, easily pleased, very hasty, and very relenting, with a heart moulded in a warm and affectionate fashion.'

Such was the woman who, though parted by fate, maintained through sunshine and storm an ascendancy over the heart of Byron which neither time nor absence could impair, and which endured to the end of his earthly existence. We may well believe that those inarticulate words which the dying poet murmured to the bewildered Fletcher—those broken sentences which ended with, 'Tell her everything; you are friends with her'—may have referred, not to Lady Byron, as policy suggested, but to Mary Chaworth, with whom Fletcher had been acquainted since his youth.

We have incontestable proof that, only two months before he died, Byron's thoughts were occupied with one whom he had named 'the starlight of his boyhood.' How deeply Byron thought about Mary Chaworth at the last is proved by the poem which was found among his papers at Missolonghi. In six stanzas the poet revealed the story that he would fain have hidden. A note in his handwriting states that they were addressed 'to no one in particular,' and that they were merely 'a poetical scherzo.' There is, however, no room for doubt that the poem bears a deep significance.

I.

'I watched thee when the foe was at our side,
  Ready to strike at him—or thee and me
  Were safety hopeless—rather than divide
    Aught with one loved, save love and liberty.'

We have here a glimpse of that turbulent scene when Mary's husband, in a fit of jealousy, put an end to their dangerous intimacy.

II.

'I watched thee on the breakers, when the rock
  Received our prow, and all was storm and fear,
  And bade thee cling to me through every shock;
    This arm would be thy bark, or breast thy bier.'

This brings us to that period of suspense and fear, in 1814, which preceded the birth of Medora. In a letter which Byron at that time wrote to Miss Milbanke we find these words:

'I am at present a little feverish—I mean mentally—and, as usual, *on the brink of something or other, which will probably crush me at last, and cut our correspondence short, with everything else.*'

Twelve days later (March 3, 1814), Byron tells Moore that he is 'uncomfortable,' and that he has 'no lack of argument to ponder upon of the most gloomy description.'

'Some day or other,' he writes, 'when we are *veterans*, I may tell you a tale of present and past times; and it is not from want of confidence that I do not now. . . . *All this would be very well if I had no heart;* but, unluckily, I have found that there is such a thing still about me, though in no very good repair, and also that it has a habit of attaching itself to *one*, whether I will or no. *Divide et impera*, I begin to think, will only do for politics.'

When Moore, who was puzzled, asked Byron to explain himself more clearly, he replied: 'Guess darkly, and you will seldom err.'

Thirty-four days later Medora was born, April 15, 1814.

III.

' I watched thee when the fever glazed thine eyes,
   Yielding my couch, and stretched me on the ground,
When overworn with watching, ne'er to rise
   From thence if thou an early grave had found.'

Here we see Byron's agony of remorse. Like Herod, he lamented for Mariamne:

' And mine's the guilt, and mine the hell,
   This bosom's desolation dooming;
And I have earned those tortures well
   Which unconsumed are still consuming!'

In 'Manfred' we find a note of remembrance in the deprecating words:

'Oh! no, no, no!
My injuries came down on those who loved me—
On those whom I best loved: I never quelled
An enemy, save in my just defence—
But my embrace was fatal.'

IV.

' The earthquake came, and rocked the quivering wall,
   And men and Nature reeled as if with wine:
Whom did I seek around the tottering hall?
   For thee. Whose safety first provide for? Thine.'

We now see Byron, at the supreme crisis of his life, standing in solitude on his hearth, with all his household gods shivered around him. We perceive that not least among his troubles at that time was the ever-haunting fear lest the secret of Medora's birth should be disclosed. His greatest anxiety was for Mary's safety, and this could only be secured by keeping his matrimonial squabbles out of a court of law. It was, in fact, by agreeing to sign the deed of separation that the whole situation was saved. The loyalty of Augusta Leigh on this occasion was never forgotten :

> 'There was soft Remembrance and sweet Trust
> In one fond breast.'

> '*That* love was pure—and, far above disguise,
> Had stood the test of mortal enmities
> Still undivided, and cemented more
> By peril, dreaded most in female eyes,
> But this was firm.'

In the fifth stanza we see Byron, eight years later, at Missolonghi, struck down by that attack of epilepsy which preceded his death by only two months :

v.

> 'And when convulsive throes denied my breath
> The faintest utterance to my fading thought,
> To thee—to thee—e'en in the gasp of death
> My spirit turned, oh ! oftener than it ought.'

In the sixth and final stanza, probably the last lines that Byron ever wrote, we find him reiterating, with all a lover's persistency, a belief that Mary could never have loved him, otherwise she would not have left him.

vi.

> 'Thus much and more ; and yet thou lov'st me not,
> And never wilt ! Love dwells not in our will.
> Nor can I blame thee, though it be my lot
> To strongly, wrongly, vainly love thee still.'

The reproaches of lovers are often unjust. Byron either could not, or perhaps *would not*, see that in abandoning him Mary had been actuated by the highest, the purest motives, and that the renunciation must have afforded her deep pain—a sacrifice, not lightly made, for Byron's sake quite as much as for her own. That Byron for a time resented her conduct in this respect is evident from a remark made in a letter to Miss Milbanke, dated November 29, 1813. After saying that he once thought that Mary Chaworth could have made him happy, he added, ' but *subsequent events have proved* that my expectations might not have been fulfilled had I ever proposed to and received my idol.'*

What those 'subsequent events' were may be guessed from reproaches which at this period appear among his poems:

> ' The wholly false the *heart* despises,
>   And spurns deceiver and deceit;
> But she who not a thought disguises,
>   Whose love is as sincere as sweet—
> When *she* can change, who loved so truly,
> It *feels* what mine has *felt* so newly.'

In the letter written five years after their final separation, Byron again reproaches Mary Chaworth, but this time without a tinge of bitterness:

'My own, we may have been very wrong, but I repent of nothing except that cursed marriage, and your refusing to continue to love me as you had loved me. I can neither forget nor *quite forgive* you for that precious piece of reformation. But I can never be other than I have been, and whenever I love anything, it is because it reminds me in some way or other of yourself.'

' The Giaour ' was begun in May and finished in November, 1813. Those parts which relate to Mary Chaworth were added to that poem in July and August:

> ' She was a form of Life and Light,
>   That, seen, became a part of sight;
>   And rose, where'er I turned mine eye,
>   The Morning-Star of Memory!'

---

* ' Letters and Journals of Byron,' vol. iii., p. 406, edited by Rowland E. Prothero.

Byron says that, like the bird that sings within the brake, like the swan that swims upon the waters, he can only have one mate. He despises those who sneer at constancy. He does not envy them their fickleness, and regards such heartless men as lower in the scale of creation than the solitary swan.

> 'Such shame at least was never mine—
> Leila! each thought was only thine!
> My good, *my guilt*, my weal, my woe,
> My hope on high—my all below.
> Earth holds no other like to thee,
> Or, if it doth, in vain for me:
> . . . Thou wert, thou art,
> The cherished madness of my heart!'

> 'Yes, Love indeed is light from heaven;
> A spark of that immortal fire
> With angels shared, by Alla given,
> To lift from earth our low desire.
> I grant *my* love imperfect, all
> That mortals by the name miscall;
> Then deem it evil, what thou wilt;
> But say, oh say, *hers* was not Guilt!
> And she was lost—and yet I breathed,
> But not the breath of human life:
> A serpent round my heart was wreathed,
> And stung my every thought to strife.'

Who can doubt that the friend 'of earlier days,' whose memory the Giaour wishes to bless before he dies, but whom he dares not bless lest Heaven should 'mark the vain attempt' of guilt praying for the guiltless, was Mary Chaworth. He bids the friar tell that friend

> 'What thou didst behold:
> The withered frame—the ruined mind,
> The wreck that Passion leaves behind—
> The shrivelled and discoloured leaf,
> Seared by the Autumn blast of Grief.'

He wonders whether that friend is still his friend, as in those earlier days, when hearts were blended in that sweet land where bloom his native valley's bowers. To that friend he sends a ring, which was the memorial of a youthful vow:

> 'Tell him—unheeding as I was,
>   Through many a busy bitter scene
>   Of all our golden youth hath been,
>   In pain, my faltering tongue had tried
>   To bless his memory—ere I died;
>   I do not ask him not to blame,
>   Too gentle he to wound my name;
>   I do not ask him not to mourn,
>   Such cold request might sound like scorn.
>   But bear this ring, his own of old,*
>   And tell him what thou dost behold!'

The motto chosen by Byron for 'The Giaour' is in itself suggestive:

> 'One fatal remembrance—one sorrow that throws
>   Its bleak shade alike o'er our Joys and our Woes—
>   To which Life nothing darker nor brighter can bring,
>   For which Joy hath no balm—and affliction no sting.'

On October 10, 1813, Byron arrived at Newstead, where he stayed for a month. Mary Chaworth was at Annesley during that time. On his return to town he wrote (November 8) to his sister:

'MY DEAREST AUGUSTA,

'I have only time to say that my long silence has been occasioned by a thousand things (with which *you* are not concerned). It is not Lady Caroline, nor Lady Oxford; *but perhaps you may guess*, and if you do, do not tell. You do not know what mischief your being with me might have prevented. You shall hear from me to-morrow; in the meantime don't be alarmed. I am in *no immediate* peril.

'Believe me, ever yours,
'B.'

On November 30 Byron wrote to Moore:

'We were once very near neighbours this autumn;†

---

* See *ante*, p. 225.

† Moore had rented a cottage in Nottinghamshire, not very remote from Newstead Abbey.

and a good and bad neighbourhood it has proved to me. Suffice it to say that your French quotation (Si je récommençais ma carrière, je ferais tout ce que j'ai fait) was confoundedly to the purpose,—though very *unexpectedly* pertinent, as you may imagine by what I *said* before, and my silence since. However, "Richard's himself again," and, except all night and some part of the morning, I don't think very much about the matter. All convulsions end with me in rhyme; and to solace my midnights I have scribbled another Turkish story ['The Bride of Abydos'] which you will receive soon after this. . . . I have written this, and published it, for the sake of *employment*—to wring my thoughts from reality, and take refuge in "imaginings," however "horrible." . . . This is the work of a week. . . .

In order the more effectually to dispose of the theory that Lady Frances Wedderburn Webster was the cause of Byron's disquietude, we insert an extract from his journal, dated a fortnight earlier (November 14, 1813):

'Last night I finished "Zuleika" [the name was afterwards changed to 'The Bride of Abydos'], my second Turkish tale. I believe the composition of it kept me alive—for it was written to drive my thoughts from the recollection of **** "Dear sacred name, rest ever unrevealed."* At least, even here, my hand would tremble to write it. . . . I have some idea of expectorating a romance, but what romance could equal the events

'". . . quæque ipse . . . vidi,
Et quorum pars magna fui"?'

Surely the name that Byron dared not write, even in his own journal, was not that of Lady Frances Webster, whose name appears often in his correspondence. The 'sacred' name was that of one of whom he afterwards wrote, 'Thou art both Mother and May.'

During October, November, and December, 1813,

* Evidently Mary, the sacred name of the Virgin.

Byron's mind was in a perturbed condition. We gather, from a letter which he wrote to Moore on November 30, that his thoughts were centred on a lady living in Nottinghamshire*, and that the scrape, which he mentions in his letter to Augusta on November 8, referred to that lady and the dreaded prospects of maternity.

Mr. Coleridge believes that the verses, 'Remember him, whom Passion's power,' were addressed to Lady Frances Wedderburn Webster. There is nothing, so far as the present writer knows, to support that opinion. There is no evidence to show the month in which they were written; and, in view of the statement that the lady in question had lived in comparative retirement, 'Thy soul from long seclusion pure,' and that she had, because of his presumption, banished the poet in 1813, it could not well have been Lady Frances Webster, who in September of that year had asked Byron to be godfather to her child, and in October had invited him to her house. It is noteworthy that Byron expressly forbade Murray to publish those verses with 'The Corsair,' where, it must be owned, they would have been sadly out of place. 'Farewell, if ever fondest prayer,' was decidedly more appropriate to the state of things existing at that time.

The motto chosen for his 'Bride of Abydos' is taken from Burns:

> 'Had we never loved sae kindly,
> Had we never loved sae blindly,
> Never met—or never parted,
> We had ne'er been broken-hearted.'

The poem was written early in November, 1813. Byron has told us that it was written to divert his

* See 'Letters and Journals of Lord Byron,' edited by Rowland Prothero, vol. ii., pp. 267, 269, 278, 292.

mind,* 'to wring his thoughts from reality to imagination, from selfish regrets to vivid recollections'; to 'distract his thoughts from the recollection of **** "Dear sacred name, rest ever unrevealed,"' and in a letter to John Galt (December 11, 1813) he says that parts of the poem were drawn 'from existence.' He had been staying at Newstead, in close proximity to Annesley, from October 10 to November 8, during which time, as he says, he regretted the absence of his sister Augusta, 'who might have saved him much trouble.' He says, 'All convulsions end with me in rhyme,' and that 'The Bride of Abydos' was 'the work of a week.' In speaking of a 'dear sacred name, rest ever unrevealed,' he says: 'At least even here my hand would tremble to write it'; and on November 30 he writes to Moore: 'Since I last wrote' (October 2), 'much has happened to me.' On November 27 he writes in his journal: 'Mary—dear name—thou art both Mother and May.'† At the end of November, 1813, after he had returned to town, he writes in his journal:

'**** is distant, and will be at ****, still more distant, till the spring.‡ No one else, except Augusta, cares for me. . . . I am tremendously in arrears with my letters, except to ****, and to her my thoughts overpower me—my words never compass them.'

On November 14 Byron sends a device for the seals of himself and ****; the seal in question is at present in the possession of the Chaworth-Musters family. On

* 'Had I not written "The Bride" (in four nights), I must have gone mad by eating my own heart—bitter diet.'—'Journals and Letters,' vol. ii., p. 321.

† ' Hail be you, Mary, mother and May,
    Mild, and meek, and merciable !'
                            An Ancient Hymn to the Virgin.

‡ In a letter, in Mr. Murray's collection, dated March 26, 1814, to Mr. Hanson, Mary writes: ' We have the prospect of being in London this *Spring*.'

December 10, we find from one of Byron's letters that he had thoughts of committing suicide, and was deterred by the idea that 'it would annoy Augusta, and perhaps ****.'

Byron seems to have put into the mouth of Zuleika words which conveyed his own thoughts:

> 'Think'st thou that I could bear to part
> With thee, and learn to halve my heart?
> Ah! were I severed from thy side,
> Where were thy friend—and who my guide?
> Years have not seen, Time shall not see,
> The hour that tears my soul from thee:
> Ev'n Azrael, from his deadly quiver
>   When flies that shaft, and fly it must,
> That parts all else, shall doom for ever
>   Our hearts to undivided dust!
>   *   *   *   *   *
> What other can she seek to see
> Than thee, companion of her bower,
> The partner of her infancy?
> These cherished thoughts with life begun,
> Say, why must I no more avow?'

Selim suggests that Zuleika should brave the world and fly with him:

> 'But be the Star that guides the wanderer, Thou!
> Thou, my Zuleika, share and bless my bark;
> The Dove of peace and promise to mine ark!
> Or, since that hope denied in worlds of strife,
> Be thou the rainbow to the storms of life!
> The evening beam that smiles the clouds away,
> And tints to-morrow with prophetic ray!
>   *   *   *   *   *
> Not blind to Fate, I see, where'er I rove,
> Unnumbered perils,—but one only love!
> Yet well my toils shall that fond breast repay,
> Though Fortune frown, or falser friends betray.'

Zuleika, we are told, was the 'last of Giaffir's race.'*

---

* Mary was 'the last of a time-honoured race.' The line of the Chaworths ended with her.

Selim tells her that 'life is hazard at the best,' and there is much to fear:

> ' Yes, fear! the doubt, the dread of losing thee.
> That dread shall vanish with the favouring gale;
> Which Love to-night has promised to my sail.
> No danger daunts the pair his smile hath blest,
> Their steps still roving, but their hearts at rest.
> With thee all toils are sweet, each clime hath charms;
> Earth—Sea alike—our world within our arms!'

'The Corsair' was written between December 18, 1813, and January 11, 1814. While it was passing through the press, Byron was at Newstead. He gives a little of his own spirit to Conrad, and all Mary's virtues to Medora—a name which was afterwards given to his child. Conrad

> ' Knew himself a villain—but he deemed
> The rest no better than the thing he seemed;
> And scorned the best as hypocrites who hid
> Those deeds the bolder spirit plainly did.
> Lone, wild, and strange, he stood alike exempt
> From all affection and from all contempt.
> None are all evil—quickening round his heart,
> One softer feeling would not yet depart.
> Yet 'gainst that passion vainly still he strove,
> And even in him it asks the name of Love!
> Yes, it was Love—unchangeable—unchanged,
> Felt but for one from whom he never ranged.
> Yes—it was Love—if thoughts of tenderness,
> Tried in temptation, strengthened by distress,
> Unmoved by absence, firm in every clime,
> And yet—oh! more than all! untired by Time.
> If there be Love in mortals—this was Love!
> He was a villain—aye, reproaches shower
> On him—but not the Passion, nor its power,
> Which only proved—all other virtues gone—
> Not Guilt itself could quench this *earliest* one!'

The following verses are full of meaning for the initiated:

I.

'Deep in my soul that tender secret dwells,
  Lonely and lost to light for evermore,
Save when to thine my heart responsive swells,
  Then trembles into silence as before.

II.

'There, in its centre, a sepulchral lamp
  Burns the slow flame, eternal—but unseen;
Which not the darkness of Despair can damp,
  Though vain its ray as it had never been.

III.

'Remember me—oh! pass not thou my grave
  Without one thought whose relics there recline:
The only pang my bosom dare not brave
  Must be to find forgetfulness in thine.

IV.

'My fondest—faintest—latest accents hear—
  Grief for the dead not Virtue can reprove;
Then give me all I ever asked—a tear,
  The first—last—sole reward of so much love!'

Conrad and Medora part, to meet no more in life

'But she is nothing—wherefore is he here? . . .
By the first glance on that still, marble brow—
It was enough—she died—what recked it how?
The love of youth, the hope of better years,
The source of softest wishes, tenderest fears,
The only living thing he could not hate,
Was reft at once—*and he deserved his fate,*
But did not feel it less.'

The blow he feared the most had fallen at last. The only woman whom he loved had withdrawn her society from him, and his heart,

'Formed for softness—warped to wrong,
  Betrayed too early, and beguiled too long,'

was petrified at last!

A POETIC TRILOGY

> Yet tempests wear, and lightning cleaves the rock;
> If such his heart, so shattered it the shock.
> There grew one flower beneath its rugged brow,
> Though dark the shade—it sheltered—saved till now.
> The thunder came—that bolt hath blasted both,
> The Granite's firmness, and the Lily's growth:
> The gentle plant hath left no leaf to tell
> Its tale, but shrunk and withered where it fell;
> And of its cold protector, blacken round
> But shivered fragments on the barren ground!'

In moments of deep emotion, even the most reticent of men may sometimes reveal themselves. 'The Giaour,' 'The Bride of Abydos,' and 'The Corsair,' formed a trilogy, through which the tragedy of Byron's life swept like a musical theme. Those poems acted like a recording instrument which, by registering his transient moods, was destined ultimately to betray a secret which he had been at so much pains to hide. In 'The Giaour' we see remorse for a crime, which he was at first willing to expiate in sorrow and repentance. In 'The Bride of Abydos' we find him, in an access of madness and passion, proposing to share the fate of his victim, if she will but consent to fly with him. Happily for both, Mary would never have consented to an act of social suicide. In 'The Corsair' we behold his dreams dispelled by the death of his Love and the hope of better years.

> ' He asked no question—all were answered now!'

With the dramatic fate of Medora the curtain falls, and the poet, in whom

> ' I suoi pensieri in lui dormir non ponno,'

crosses the threshold of a new life. He reappears later on the scene of all his woes, a broken, friendless stranger, in the person of Lara—that last phase, in which the poet discloses his identity with characteristic insouciance, brings the tragedy abruptly to a close.*

On January 6, 1814, Byron wrote a remarkable letter to Moore, at that time in Nottinghamshire:

'... I have a confidence for you—a perplexing one to me, and just at present in a state of abeyance in itself.... [Here probably follows the disclosure.] However, we shall see. In the meantime you may amuse yourself with my suspense, and put all the justices of peace in requisition, in case I come into your county [Nottinghamshire] with hackbut bent.† Seriously, whether I am to hear from her or him, it is a pause, which I can fill up with as few thoughts of my own as I can borrow from other people. Anything is better than stagnation; and now, in the interregnum of my autumn and a strange summer adventure, which I don't like to think of.... Of course you will keep my secret, and don't even talk in your sleep of it. Happen what may, your dedication is ensured, being already written; and I shall copy it out fair to-night, in case business or amusement—*Amant alterna Camœnæ.*'

Byron here refers to 'The Corsair,' which he dedicated to Thomas Moore. In order to understand this letter, it may be inferred that one of the letters he had written to his lady-love had remained so long unanswered that Byron feared it might have fallen into her husband's hands. Writing to Moore on the following day, Byron says:

'My last epistle would probably put you in a fidget. But the devil, who *ought* to be civil on such occasions,

---

* It will be remembered that Byron had announced 'The Corsair' as 'the last production with which he should trespass on public patience for some years.' With the loss of Mary's love his inspiration was gone.

† 'With hackbut bent, my secret stand,
    Dark as the purposed deed, I chose,
And mark'd where, mingling in his band,
    Trooped Scottish pikes and English bows.'
               Sir Walter Scott: *Cadyow Castle.*

proved so, and took my letter to the right place. . . .
Is it not odd? the very fate I said she had escaped from
**** she has now undergone from the worthy ****.'

An undated letter from Mary Chaworth, preserved among the Byron letters in Mr. Murray's possession, seems to belong to this period:

'Your kind letter, my dear friend, relieved me much, and came yesterday, when I was by no means well, and was a most agreeable remedy, for I fancied a thousand things. . . . I shall set great value by your *seal*, and, if you come down to Newstead before we leave Annesley, see no reason why you should not call on us and bring it. . . .* I have lately suffered from a pain in my side, which has alarmed me; but I will not, in return for your charming epistle, fill mine with complaints. . . . I am surprised you have not seen Mr. Chaworth, as I hear of him going about a good deal. We [herself and Miss Radford] are now visiting very near Nottingham, but return to Annesley to-morrow, I *trust*, where I have left all my little dears except the eldest, whom *you* saw, and who is with me. We are very anxious to see you, and yet know not how we shall feel on the occasion—*formal*, I dare say, at the *first;* but our meeting must be confined to our trio, and then I think we shall be more at our ease. *Do write* me, and make a *sacrifice* to *friendship*, which I shall consider your visit. You *may* always address your letters to Annesley perfectly safe.

'Your sincere friend,
'MARY ——'

On or about January 7, 1814, Byron writes to his sister Augusta in reference to Mary Chaworth:

'I shall write to-morrow, but did *not* go to Lady M.'s [Melbourne] twelfth cake banquet. M. [Mary] has written again—*all friendship*—and really very simple and pathetic—*bad usage*—*paleness*—*ill-health*—old *friendship*—*once*—*good motive*—virtue—and so forth.'

* Mary's allusion to the seal is explained by an entry in Byron's journal, November 14, 1813. The seal is treasured as a memento of Byron by the Musters family.

Five days later Byron again writes to Augusta Leigh:

'On Sunday or Monday next, with leave of your lord and president, you will be *well* and ready to accompany me to Newstead, which you *should* see, and I will endeavour to render as comfortable as I can, for both our sakes. . . . Claughton is, I believe, inclined to settle. . . . More news from Mrs. [Chaworth], *all friendship;* you shall see her.'

Medora was born on or about April 15, 1814. 'Lara' was written between May 4 and 14. The opening lines, which would have set every tongue wagging, were withheld from publication until January, 1887. They were written in London early in May, and were addressed to the mother of Medora:

> ' When thou art gone—the loved, the lost—the one
> Whose smile hath gladdened, though perchance undone—
> *Whose name too dearly cherished to impart*
> Dies on the lip, but trembles in the heart;
> Whose sudden mention can almost convulse,
> And lightens through the ungovernable pulse—
> Till the heart leaps so keenly to the word
> We fear that throb can hardly beat unheard—*
> Then sinks at once beneath that sickly chill
> That follows when we find her absent still.
> When thou art gone—too far again to bless—
> Oh! God—how slowly comes Forgetfulness!
> Let none complain how faithless and how brief
> The brain's remembrance, or the bosom's grief,
> Or ere they thus forbid us to forget
> Let Mercy strip the memory of regret;
> Yet—selfish still—we would not be forgot,
> What lip dare say—" My Love—remember not "?

---

* No one, we presume, will question the identity of the person mentioned in ' The Dream ':
> ' Upon a tone,
> A touch of hers, his blood would ebb and flow,
> And his cheek change tempestuously—his heart
> Unknowing of its cause of agony.'

'MAGDALEN'

> Oh! best—and dearest! Thou whose thrilling name
> My heart adores too deeply to proclaim—
> My memory, almost ceasing to repine,
> Would mount to Hope if once secure of thine.
> Meantime the tale I weave must mournful be—
> As absence to the heart that lives on thee!'

Lord Lovelace has told us that 'nothing is too stupid for belief.' We are disposed to agree with him, especially as he produces these lines in support of his accusation against Augusta Leigh. The absurdity of supposing that they were addressed to Byron's sister appears to us to be so evident that it seems unnecessary to waste words in disputation. There is abundant proof that during this period Mrs. Leigh and Byron were in constant correspondence, and that he visited her almost daily during her simulated confinement and convalescence. When Murray sent her some books to while away the time, Byron wrote (April 9) on her behalf to thank him. And finally, as Augusta Leigh had no intention whatever of leaving London, she could in no sense have been 'the lost one' whose prospective departure filled Byron with despair. The poet and his sister—whom he was accustomed to address as 'Goose'*—were then, and always, on most familiar terms. The 'mention of her name' (which was often on his lips) would certainly not have convulsed him, nor have caused his heart to beat so loudly that he feared lest others should hear it! The woman to whom those lines were addressed was Mary Chaworth, whose condition induced him, on April 18, to begin a fragment entitled 'Magdalen'—she of whom he wrote on May 4:

> 'I speak not—I trace not—I breathe not thy name—
> There is Love in the sound—there is Guilt in the fame.'

---

* 'Astarte,' p. 134.

Lord Lovelace, in his impetuosity, and with very imperfect knowledge of Byron's life-story, ties every doubtful scrap of his grandfather's poetry into his bundle of proofs against Augusta Leigh, without perceiving any discrepancy in the nature of his evidence. A moment's reflection might have convinced him that the lines we have quoted could not, by any possibility, have applied to one whom he subsequently addressed as:

> 'My sister! my sweet sister! if a name
> Dearer and purer were, it should be thine;
> * * * * *
> Had I but sooner learnt the crowd to shun,
> I had been better than I now can be;
> The passions which have torn me would have slept;
> *I* had not suffered, and *thou* hadst not wept.'

It must be admitted that Byron, through indiscreet confidences and reckless mystifications, was partly the cause of the suspicions which afterwards fell upon his sister. Lady Byron has left it on record that Byron early in 1814—before the birth of Medora—told Lady Caroline Lamb that a woman he passionately loved was with child by him, and that if a daughter was born it should be called Medora.* At about the same time 'he advanced, at Holland House, the most extraordinary theories about the relations of brother and sister, which originated the reports about Mrs. Leigh.'

That, after ninety years, such nonsense should be regarded as evidence against a woman so well known in the society of her day as was Mrs. Leigh, justifies our concurrence with Lord Lovelace's opinion that ' nothing is too stupid for belief.'

---

* Lady Caroline Lamb also asserted that Byron showed her some letters which contained some such expression as this: 'Oh! B——, if we loved one another as we did in childhood—*then* it was innocent.' The reader may judge whether such a remark would be more natural from Augusta, or from Mary Chaworth.

THE MYSTERY IN 'LARA'

It appears that one day Lady Byron was talking to her husband about 'Lara,' which seemed to her to be 'like the darkness in which one fears to behold spectres.' This bait was evidently too tempting for Byron to resist. He replied: '"Lara"—there's more in *that* than in any of them.' As he spoke he shuddered, and turned his eyes to the ground.

Before we examine that poem to see how much it may contain of illuminating matter, we will touch upon a remark Byron made to his wife, which Lord Lovelace quotes without perceiving its depth and meaning. We will quote 'Astarte':

'He told Lady Byron that if she had married him when he first proposed, he should not have written any of the poems which followed [the first and second Cantos] "Childe Harold."'

This is perfectly true. Byron proposed to Miss Milbanke in 1812. If she had married him then, he would not have renewed his intimacy with Mary Chaworth in June, 1813. There would have been no heart-hunger, no misery, no remorse, and, in short, no inspiration for 'The Giaour,' 'The Bride,' 'The Corsair,' and 'Lara.' Miss Milbanke's refusal of his offer of marriage in 1812 rankled long in Byron's mind, and provoked those ungenerous reproaches which have been, with more or less exaggeration, reported by persons in Lady Byron's confidence. The mischief was done between the date of Miss Milbanke's refusal and her acceptance of his offer, which occurred after the fury of his passion for Mary Chaworth had burnt itself out.* No blame attaches to Lady Byron for this misfortune. When Byron first proposed, her affec-

* Writing to a lady on October 5, 1814, Byron, in reference to his engagement, said: 'It might have happened two years ago, and if it had, would have saved me a world of trouble.' ('Letters and Journals,' edited by Rowland Prothero, vol. iii., p. 145.)

tions were elsewhere engaged; she could not, therefore, dispose of her heart to him. When she at last accepted him, it was too late for happiness.

In a letter which Byron wrote to Miss Milbanke previous to his marriage,* he unconsciously prophesied the worst:

'The truth is that could I have foreseen that your life was to be linked to mine—had I even possessed a distinct hope, however distant—I would have been a different and better being. As it is, I have sometimes doubts, even if I should not disappoint the future, nor act hereafter unworthily of you, whether the past ought not to make you still regret me—even that portion of it with which you are not unacquainted. I did not believe such a woman existed—at least for me—*and I sometimes fear I ought to wish that she had not.*'

When Byron said that he had doubts whether the past would not eventually reflect injuriously upon his future wife, he referred, not to Augusta Leigh, but to his fatal intercourse with Mary Chaworth. The following sentences taken from Mrs. Leigh's letters to Francis Hodgson, who knew the truth, prove that the mystery only incidentally affected Augusta. The letters were written February, 1816.

'From what passed [between Captain Byron and Mrs. Clermont] *now,* if *they* choose it, it must come into court! God alone knows the consequences.'

'It strikes me that, if their pecuniary proposals are favourable, Byron will be too happy to escape the exposure. *He must* be anxious. It is impossible he should not in some degree.'

These are the expressions, not of a person connected with a tragedy, but rather of one who was a spectator of it. Every impartial person must see that. When, on another occasion, Byron told his wife

* October 14, 1814.

that he wished he had gone abroad—as he had intended—in June, 1813, he undoubtedly implied that the fatal intimacy with Mary Chaworth would have been avoided. This seems so clear to us that we are surprised that Byron's statement on the subject of his poems should have made no impression on the mind of Lord Lovelace, and should have elicited nothing from him in 'Astarte,' except the *banale* suggestion that Byron's literary activity *must have been accidental!*

Lara, like Conrad, is a portion of Byron himself, and the poem opens with his return to Newstead after some bitter experiences, at which he darkly hints:

> 'Short was the course his restlessness had run,
> But long enough to leave him half undone.'

He tells us that 'Another chief consoled his destined bride.' 'One is absent that most might decorate that gloomy pile.'

> 'Why slept he not when others were at rest?
> Why heard no music, and received no guest?
> All was not well, they deemed—but where the wrong?
> Some knew perchance.'

In stanzas 17, 18, and 19, Byron draws a picture of himself, so like that his sister remarked upon it in a letter to Hodgson. After telling us that 'his heart was not by nature hard,' he says that

> 'His blood in temperate seeming now would flow:
> Ah! happier if it ne'er with guilt had glowed,
> But ever in that icy smoothness flowed!'

The poet tells us that after Lara's death he was mourned by one whose quiet grief endured for long.

> 'Vain was all question asked her of the past,
> And vain e'en menace—silent to the last.'

> 'Why did she love him? Curious fool!—be still—
> Is human love the growth of human will?

> To her he might be gentleness; the stern
> Have deeper thoughts than your dull eyes discern
> And when they love, your smilers guess not how
> Beats the strong heart, though less the lips avow.
> They were not common links, that formed the chain
> That bound to Lara Kaled's heart and brain;
> But that wild tale she brooked not to unfold,
> *And sealed is now each lip that could have told.*

* * * * *

> 'The tempest of his heart in scorn had gazed
> On that the feebler Elements hath raised.
> The Rapture of his Heart had looked on high,
> And asked if greater dwelt beyond the sky:
> Chained to excess, the slave of each extreme,
> How woke he from the wildness of that dream!
> Alas! he told not—*but he did awake
> To curse the withered heart that would not break.*'

On September 8, 1814, four months after Byron had finished 'Lara,' while he was at Newstead with his sister and her children—the little Medora among them—he wrote his fragment 'Harmodia.' The rough draft was given after his marriage to Lady Byron, who had no idea to what it could possibly refer. When the scandal about Augusta was at its height, this fragment was impounded among other incriminating documents, and eventually saw the light in 'Astarte.' Lord Lovelace was firmly convinced that it was addressed to Augusta Leigh!

Between September 7 and 15 Byron and Mary Chaworth were considering the desirability of marriage for Byron, and letters were passing between the distracted poet and two young ladies—Miss Milbanke and another—with that object in view. Although Byron was still in love with Mary Chaworth, he had come to understand that her determination to break the dangerous intimacy was irrevocable, so he resolved to follow her advice and marry. The tone of his letter to Moore, written on September 15, shows that he was not very keen about wedlock. He was making plans for a journey to Italy in the event of his proposal being rejected.

It is possible that, in a conversation between Mary and himself, the former may have spoken of the risks they had incurred in the past, and of her resolve never to transgress again. To which Byron replied:

Harmodia.'

'The things that were—and what and whence are they?
Those clouds and rainbows of thy yesterday?
Their path has vanish'd from th' eternal sky,
And now its hues are of a different dye.
Thus speeds from day to day, and Pole to Pole,
The change of parts, the sameness of the whole;
And all we snatch, amidst the breathing strife,
But gives to Memory what it takes from Life:
Despoils a substance to adorn a shade—
And that frail shadow lengthens but to fade.
Sun of the sleepless! Melancholy Star!
Whose tearful beam shoots trembling from afar—
That chang'st the darkness thou canst not dispel—
How like art thou to Joy, remembered well!
Such is the past—the light of other days
That shines, but warms not with its powerless rays—
A moonbeam *Sorrow* watcheth to behold,
Distinct, but distant—clear, but *death-like* cold.

'Oh! as full thought comes rushing o'er the Mind
Of all we saw before—to leave behind—
Of all!—but words, what are they? Can they give
A trace of truth to thoughts while yet they live?
No—Passion—Feeling speak not—or in vain—
The tear for Grief—the Groan must speak for Pain—
Joy hath its smile—and Love its blush and sigh—
Despair her silence—Hate her lip and eye—
These their interpreters, where deeply lurk—
The Soul's despoilers warring as they work—
The strife once o'er—then words may find their way,
Yet how enfeebled from the forced delay!

> 'But who could paint the progress of the wreck—
> Himself still clinging to the dangerous deck?
> Safe on the shore the artist first must stand,
> And then the pencil trembles in his hand.'

When, four years later, Byron was writing the first canto of 'Don Juan,' with feelings chastened by suffering and time, he recurred to that period—never effaced from his memory—the time when he wrote:

> 'When thou art gone—the loved—the lost—the one
> Whose smile hath gladdened—though, perchance, undone!'

Time could not change the feelings of his youth, nor keep his thoughts for long from the object of his early love.

> 'They tell me 'tis decided you depart:
>   'Tis wise—'tis well, but not the less a pain;
>   I have no further claim on your young heart,
>   Mine is the victim, and would be again:
>   To love too much has been the only art
>   I used.'

> 'I loved, I love you, for this love have lost
>   State, station, Heaven, Mankind's, my own esteem,
>   And yet can not regret what it hath cost,
>   *So dear is still the memory of that dream;*
>   Yet, if I name my guilt, 'tis not to boast,
>   None can deem harshlier of me than I deem.'

> 'All is o'er
>   For me on earth, except some years to hide
>   My shame and sorrow deep in my heart's core:
>   These I could bear, but cannot cast aside
>   The passion which still rages as before—
>   And so farewell—forgive me, love me—No,
>   That word is idle now—but let it go.'

* * * * *

> 'My heart is feminine, nor can forget—
>   To all, except one image, madly blind;
>   So shakes the needle, and so stands the pole,
>   As vibrates my fond heart to my fixed soul.'

It was early in 1814 that Byron also wrote his farewell verses to Mary Chaworth, which appeared in the second edition of 'The Corsair':

I.

'Farewell! if ever fondest prayer
    For other's weal availed on high,
Mine will not all be lost in air,
    But waft thy name beyond the sky.
'Twere vain to speak—to weep—to sigh:
    Oh! more than tears of blood can tell,
When wrung from Guilt's expiring eye,
    Are in that word—Farewell! Farewell!

II.

'These lips are mute, these eyes are dry;
    But in my breast, and in my brain,
Awake the pangs that pass not by,
    The thought that ne'er shall sleep again.
My soul nor deigns nor dares complain,
    Though Grief and Passion there rebel:
I only know we loved in vain—
    I only feel—Farewell! Farewell!'

Even in the 'Hebrew Melodies,' which were probably begun in the autumn of 1814, and finished after Byron's marriage in January, 1815, there are traces of that deathless remorse and love, whose expression could not be altogether repressed. We select some examples at random. In the poem 'Oh, snatched away in Beauty's bloom,' the poet had added two verses which were subsequently suppressed:

'Nor need I write to tell the tale,
    My pen were doubly weak.
Oh! what can idle words avail,
    Unless my heart could speak?

'By day or night, in weal or woe,
    That heart, no longer free,
Must bear the love it cannot show,
    And silent turn for thee.'

In 'Herod's Lament for Mariamne' we find:

> 'She's gone, who shared my diadem;
>   She sunk, with her my joys entombing;
> I swept that flower from Judah's stem,
>   Whose leaves for me alone were blooming;
> And mine's the guilt, and mine the Hell,
>   This bosom's desolation dooming;
> And I have earned those tortures well,
>   Which unconsumed are still consuming!'

While admitting that Byron's avowed object was to portray the remorse of Herod, we suspect that the haunting image of one so dear to him—one who had suffered through guilt which he so frequently deplored in verse—must have been in the poet's mind when these lines were written.

On January 17, 1814, Byron went to Newstead with Augusta Leigh, and stayed there one month.

'A busy month and pleasant, at least three weeks of it. . . . "The Corsair" has been conceived, written, published, etc., since I took up this journal. They tell me it has great success; it was written *con amore*, and much from *existence*.'

On the following day Byron wrote to his friend Wedderburn Webster:

'I am on my way to the country on rather a melancholy expedition. A very old and early connexion [Mary Chaworth], or rather friend of mine, has desired to see me; and, as now we can never be more than friends, I have no objection. She is certainly unhappy and, I fear, ill; and the length and circumstances attending our acquaintance render her request and my visit neither singular nor improper.'

This strange apology for what might have been considered a very natural act of neighbourly friendship, inevitably reminds us of a French proverb, *Qui s'excuse s'accuse*. It is worthy of note that, after Byron had been

DEPRESSED BY ANXIETIES

ten days at Newstead with his sister, he wrote to his lawyer—who must have been surprised at the irrelevant information—to say that Augusta Leigh was 'in the family way.' The significance of this communication has hitherto passed unnoticed. We gather from Byron's letters that he was much depressed by Mary Chaworth's state of health, involving all the risks of discovery.

'My rhyming propensity is quite gone,' he writes, 'and I feel much as I did at Patras on recovering from my fever—weak, but in health, and only afraid of a relapse.'

Soon after his return to London Byron wrote to Moore: 'Seriously, I am in what the learned call a dilemma, and the vulgar, a scrape. . . .'

Moore took care, with his asterisks, that we should not know the nature of that scrape, which certainly had nothing to do with his 'Lines to a Lady Weeping' which appeared in the first edition of 'The Corsair.' If the reader has any doubts on this point, let him refer to Byron's letters to Murray, notably to that one in which the angry poet protests against the suppression of those lines in the second edition of 'The Corsair':

'You have played the devil by that injudicious *suppression*, which you did totally without my consent. . . . Now, I do *not*, and *will* not be supposed to shrink, although myself and everything belonging to me were to perish with my memory.'

Moore's asterisks veiled the record of a deeper scrape, as Byron's letter to him, written three weeks later, plainly show.

On April 10, 1814, Byron wrote in his journal:

'I do not know that I am happiest when alone; but this I am sure of, that I am never long in the society even of *her* I love (God knows too well, and the Devil probably too), without a yearning for the company of my lamp, and my utterly confused and tumbled-over library.'

The latter portion of the journal at this period is much mutilated. There is a gap between April 10 and 19, when, four days after the birth of Medora, he writes in deep dejection:

'There is ice at both poles, north and south—all extremes are the same—misery belongs to the highest and the lowest, only . . . I will keep no further journal . . . and, to prevent me from returning, like a dog, to the vomit of memory, I tear out the remaining leaves of this volume. . . . "O! fool! I shall go mad."'

It was at this time that Byron wrote the following lines, in which he tells Mary Chaworth that all danger of the discovery of their secret is over:

'There is no more for *me* to hope,
  There is no more for thee to fear;
And, if I give my sorrow scope,
  That sorrow *thou* shalt never hear.
Why did I hold thy love so dear?
Why shed for such a heart one tear?
Let deep and dreary silence be
My only memory of thee!
When all are fled who flatter now,
  Save thoughts which will not flatter then;
And thou recall'st the broken vow
  To him who must not love again—
Each hour of now forgotten years
Thou, then, shalt number with thy tears;
And every drop of grief shall be
A vain remembrancer of me!'

On May 4, 1814, Byron sent to Moore the following verses. We quote from Lady Byron's manuscript:

'I speak not—I trace not—I breathe not thy name—
  There is love in the sound—there is Guilt in the fame—

ATTEMPTS TO SUPPRESS HIS POEMS

But the tear which now burns on my cheek may impart
The deep thoughts that dwell in that silence of heart.

'Too brief for our passion—too long for our peace—
Was that hour—can its hope—can its memory cease?
We repent—we abjure—we will break from our chain :
We must part—we must fly to—unite it again !

'Oh ! thine be the gladness—and mine be the Guilt !
Forgive me—adored one—forsake if thou wilt—
But the heart which is thine shall expire undebased,
And Man shall not break it whatever *thou* mayst.

'Oh ! proud to the mighty—but humble to thee
This soul in its bitterest moment shall be,
And our days glide as swift—and our moments more sweet
With thee at my side—than the world at my feet.

'One tear of thy sorrow—one smile of thy love—
Shall turn me or fix—shall reward or reprove—
And the heartless may wonder at all I resign :
Thy lip shall reply—not to them—but to mine.'

These verses were not published until Byron had been five years in his grave. They tell the story plainly, and the manuscript in Mr. Murray's possession speaks plainer still. Before Byron gave the manuscript to his wife, he erased the following lines :

'We have loved—and oh ! still, my adored one, we love !'
'Oh ! the moment is past when that passion might cease.'
'But I cannot repent what we ne'er can recall.'

After Medora's birth Byron became more and more dejected, and on April 29 he wrote a remarkable letter to Murray, enclosing a draft to redeem the copyrights of his poems, and releasing Murray from his engagement to pay £1,000, agreed on for 'The Giaour' and 'The Bride of Abydos.' Byron was evidently afraid that Mr. Chaworth Musters would discover the truth, and that a duel and disgrace would be the inevitable consequence.

'*If any accident occurs to me,* you may do then as you please; but, with the exception of two copies of each for *yourself* only, I expect and request that the advertisements be withdrawn, and the remaining copies of *all* destroyed; and any expense so incurred I will be glad to defray. For all this it may be well to assign some reason. I have none to give except my own caprice, and I do not consider the circumstance of consequence enough to require explanation. Of course, I need hardly assure you that they never shall be published with my consent, directly or indirectly, by any other person whatsoever, and that I am perfectly satisfied, and have every reason so to be, with your conduct in all transactions between us, as publisher and author. It will give me great pleasure to preserve your acquaintance, and to consider you as my friend.'

Two days later Byron seems to have conquered his immediate apprehensions, and, in reply to an appeal from Murray, writes:

'If your present note is serious, and it really would be inconvenient, there is an end of the matter; tear my draft, and go on as usual: in that case we will recur to our former basis. That *I* was perfectly *serious* in wishing to suppress all future publication is true; but certainly not to interfere with the convenience of others, and more particularly your own. *Some day I will tell you the reason of this apparently strange resolution.*'

It had evidently dawned on Byron's mind that a sudden suppression of his poems would have aroused public curiosity, and that a motive for his action would either have been found or invented. This would have been fatal to all concerned. If trouble were to come, it would be wiser not to meet it halfway. Happily, the birth of Medora passed unnoticed.

As time wore on, Byron's hopes that Mary would relent grew apace. But he was doomed to disappointment. Mary Chaworth had the courage and the wisdom

LAST MEETING WITH THYRZA

to crush a love so disastrous to both. Byron in his blindness reproached her:

> 'Thou art not false, but thou art fickle.'

He tells her that he would despise her if she were false; but he knows that her love is sincere:

> 'When *she* can change who loved so truly!'
> 'Ah! sure such grief is *Fancy's* scheming,
> And all the Change can be but dreaming!'

He could not believe that her resolve was serious. Time taught him better. Love died, and friendship took its place. The same love that tempted her to sin was that true love that works out its redemption.

Between April 15 and 21, 1816, before signing the deed of separation, Byron went into the country to take leave of Mary Chaworth. It was their last meeting, and the parting must have been a sad one. The hopes that Mary had formed for his peace and happiness in marriage had suddenly been dashed to the ground. And now he was about to leave England under a cloud, which threatened for a time to overwhelm them both. A terrible anxiety as to the issue of investigations, which were being made into his conduct previous to and during his marriage, oppressed her with the gravest apprehension. Everything seemed to depend upon the silence both of Byron and Augusta. Under this awful strain the mind of Mary Chaworth was flickering towards collapse. By the following verses, which must have been written soon after their final meeting, we find Byron,

> 'Seared in heart—and lone—and blighted,'

reproaching, with a lover's injustice, the woman he

adored, for that act of renunciation which, under happier auspices, might have proved his own salvation:

I.

'When we two parted *
  In silence and tears,
Half broken-hearted
  To sever for years,
Pale grew thy cheek and cold,
  Colder thy kiss;
Truly that hour foretold
  Sorrow to this.

II.

'The dew of the morning
  Sunk chill on my brow—
It felt like the warning
  Of what I feel now.†
Thy vows are all broken,
  And light is thy fame:
I hear thy name spoken,
  And share in its shame.

III.

'They name thee before me,
  A knell to mine ear;
A shudder comes o'er me—
  Why wert thou so dear?
They know not I knew thee,
  Who knew thee too well:
Long, long shall I rue thee,
  Too deeply to tell.

IV.

'In secret we met—
  In silence I grieve,
That thy heart could forget,
  Thy spirit deceive.
If I should meet thee
  After long years,
How should I greet thee?
  With silence and tears.'

---

* Probably in 1809.   † In 1816.

In the first draft Byron had written, after the second verse, the following words :

> '*Our secret lies hidden,
> But never forgot.*'

In 'Fare Thee Well,' written on March 17, 1816, there are only four lines which have any bearing on the point under consideration.

Byron tells his wife that if she really knew the truth, if every inmost thought of his breast were bared before her, she would *not* have forsaken him.

That is true. Lady Byron might, in time, have forgiven everything if the doctors had been able to declare that her husband was not wholly accountable for his actions. But when they pronounced him to be of sound mind, and, as will be seen presently, she subsequently convinced herself that he had committed, and might even then be committing adultery with his sister under her own roof, she resolved never again to place herself in his power. If, in the early stages of disagreement, without betraying Mary Chaworth, it could have been avowed that Mrs. Leigh *was not the mother of Medora*, Lady Byron might not have seen in her husband's strange conduct towards herself 'signs of a deep remorse.' She would certainly have been far more patient under suffering, and the separation might have been avoided. But this avowal was impracticable. Augusta had committed herself too far for that, and the idle gossip of her servants *subsequently* convinced Lady Byron that Byron was the father of Augusta's child. It is clear that neither Augusta nor Byron made any attempts to remove those suspicions ; in fact, they acted in a manner most certain to confirm them. Whether the secret, which they had pledged themselves to keep, could long have been withheld from Lady Byron, if matters had been patched up, is doubtful. Meanwhile, as everything depended on *premat nox alta*, they dared not risk even a partial avowal of the truth.

The separation was inevitable, and in this case it was eternal. It is hard to believe that there had ever been any real love on either side. Under these circumstances we feel sure that any attempts at reconciliation would have ended disastrously for both. Byron's love for Mary Chaworth was strong as death. Many waters could not have quenched it, 'neither could the floods drown it.'

The last verses written by Byron before he left England for ever were addressed to his sister. The deed of separation had been signed, and Augusta Leigh, who had stood at his side in those dark hours when all the world had forsaken him, was about to leave London.

' When all around grew drear and dark,
    And Reason half withheld her ray—
And Hope but shed a dying spark
    Which more misled my lonely way;
When Fortune changed, and Love fled far,
    And Hatred's shafts flew thick and fast,
Thou wert the solitary star
    Which rose, and set not to the last.
And when the cloud upon us came
    Which strove to blacken o'er thy ray—
Then purer spread its gentle flame
    And dashed the darkness all away.
Still may thy Spirit dwell on mine,
    And teach it what to brave or brook—
There's more in one soft word of thine
    Than in the world's defied rebuke.

    *   *   *   *   *

Then let the ties of baffled love
Be broken—thine will never break;
Thy heart can feel.'

These ingenuous words show that Byron's affection for his sister, and his gratitude for her loyalty, were both deep and sincere. If, as Lord Lovelace asserts, Byron had been her lover, we know enough of his character to be certain that he would never have written these lines. He was not a hypocrite—far from it—and it was foreign to his naturally combative nature to attempt to conciliate public opinion. These lines were written *currente calamo,* and are only interesting to us on account of the light they cast upon the situation at the time of the separation. Evidently Byron had heard a rumour of the baseless charge that was afterwards openly made.* He reminds Augusta that a cloud threatened to darken her existence, but the bright rays of her purity dispelled it. He hopes that even in absence she will guide and direct him as in the past; and he compliments her by saying that one word from her had more influence over him than the whole world's censure. Although his love-episode with Mary was over, yet so long as Augusta loves him he will still have something to live for, as she alone can feel for him and understand his position.

In speaking of his sister, in the third canto of 'Childe Harold,' he says:

> 'For there was soft Remembrance, *and sweet Trust*
> In one fond breast, to which his own would melt.'

> '*And he had learned to love*—I know not why,
> For this in such as him seems strange of mood—
> *The helpless looks of blooming Infancy,*
> Even in its earliest nurture; what subdued,
> To change like this, a mind so far imbued
> With scorn of man, it little boots to know;
> But thus it was; and though in solitude
> Small power the nipped affections have to grow,
> In him this glowed when all beside had ceased to glow.'

---

* 'Astarte,' p. 141.

If these words bear any significance, Byron must mean that, since the preceding canto of 'Childe Harold' was written, he had formed (learned to love) a strong attachment to some child, and, in spite of absence, this affection still glowed. That child may possibly have been Ada, as the opening lines seem to suggest. But this is not quite certain. According to Lord Lovelace, Byron never saw his child after January 3, 1816, when the babe was only twenty-four days old. Byron himself states that it was not granted to him 'to watch her dawn of little joys, or hold her lightly on his knee, and print on her soft cheek a parent's kiss.' All this, he tells us, 'was in his nature,' but was denied to him. His sole consolation was the hope that some day Ada would learn to love him. On the other hand, the child mentioned in 'Childe Harold' had won his love by means which 'it little boots to know.' If Byron had alluded to his daughter Ada, there need have been no ambiguity. Possibly the child here indicated may have been little Medora, then nearly three years old, with whom he had often played, and who was living with that sister of 'Soft Remembrance and sweet Trust.'

If that conjecture be correct, this is the only allusion to Medora in Byron's poetry. But she is indicated in prose. In reference to the death of one of Moore's children, Byron wrote (February 2, 1818):

'I know how to feel with you, because I am quite wrapped up in my own children. Besides my little legitimate, I have made unto myself an illegitimate since, *to say nothing of one before;* and I look forward to one of them as the pillar of my old age, supposing that I ever reach, as I hope I never shall, that desolating period.'

In the *one before* Moore will have recognized Medora. In spite of the 'scarlet cloak and double figure,' Moore had no belief in the story that Byron became a father while at Harrow School!

'The Dream,' which was written in July, 1816, is perhaps more widely known than any of Byron's poems. Its theme is the remembrance of a hopeless passion, which neither Time nor Reason could extinguish. Similar notes of lamentation permeate most of his poems, but in 'The Dream' Byron, for the first time, takes the world into his confidence, and tells his tale of woe with such distinctness that we realize its truth, its passion, and its calamity. The publication of that poem was an indiscretion which must have been very disconcerting to his sister. Fortunately, it had no disastrous consequences. It apparently awakened no suspicions, and its sole effect was to incense Mary Chaworth's husband, who, in order to stop all prattle, caused the 'peculiar diadem of trees' to be cut down. In Byron's early poems we see how deeply Mary Chaworth's marriage affected him; but this was known only to a small circle of Southwell friends. In 'The Dream' we realize that she was in fact a portion of his life, and that his own marriage had not in the least affected his feelings towards her. He had tried hard to forget her, but in vain; she was his destiny. Whether Byron, when he wrote this poem, had any idea of publishing it to the world is not known. It may possibly have been written to relieve his overburdened mind, and would not have seen the light but for Lady Byron's treatment of Mrs. Leigh on the memorable occasion when she extracted, under promise of secrecy, the so-called 'Confession,' to which we shall allude presently. In any case, Byron became aware of what had happened in September, 1816. In some lines addressed to his wife, he tells her that she bought others' grief at any price, adding:

> 'The means were worthy, and the end is won;
> I would not do by thee as *thou* hast done.'

Possibly, Byron may have thought that the publication of this poem would act as a barb, and would wound Lady Byron's stubborn pride. Its appearance in the circumstances was certainly *contra bonos mores*, but we must remember that 'men in rage often strike those who wish them best.' Whatever may have been Byron's intention, 'The Dream' affords a proof that Mary Chaworth was never long absent from his thoughts. At this time, when he felt a deep remorse for his conduct towards Mary Chaworth, he asks himself:

> 'What is this Death? a quiet of the heart?
> The whole of that of which we are a part?
> For Life is but a vision—what I see
> Of all which lives alone is Life to me,
> And being so—the absent are the dead
> Who haunt us from tranquillity, and spread
> A dreary shroud around us, and invest
> With sad remembrancers our hours of rest.
> The absent are the dead—for they are cold,
> And ne'er can be what once we did behold;
> And they are changed, and cheerless,—or if yet
> *The unforgotten do not all forget,*
> *Since thus divided*—equal must it be
> *If the deep barrier be of earth, or sea;*
> *It may be both*—but one day end it must
> In the dark union of insensate dust.'

It was at this time also that Byron wrote his 'Stanzas to Augusta,' which show his complete confidence in her loyalty:

> 'Though human, thou didst not deceive me,
>   Though woman, thou didst not forsake,
> Though loved, thou forborest to grieve me,
>   Though tempted, thou never couldst shake;

> *Though trusted, thou didst not betray me,*
> *Though parted, it was not to fly,*
> *Though watchful, 'twas not to defame me,*
> *Nor, mute, that the world might belie.'*

Byron's remorse also found expression in 'Manfred,' where contrition is but slightly veiled by words of mysterious import, breathed in an atmosphere of mountains, magic, and ghost-lore. People in society, whose ears had been poisoned by insinuations against Mrs. Leigh, and who knew nothing of Byron's intercourse with Mary Chaworth, came to the conclusion that 'Manfred' revealed a criminal attachment between Byron and his sister.* Byron was aware of this, and, conscious of his innocence, held his head in proud defiance, and laughed his enemies to scorn. He did not deign to defend himself; and the public—forgetful of the maxim that where there is a sense of guilt there is a jealousy of drawing attention to it—believed the worst. When a critique of 'Manfred,' giving an account of the supposed origin of the story, was sent to Byron, he wrote to Murray:

'The conjecturer is out, and knows nothing of the matter. I had a better origin than he can devise or divine for the soul of him.'

That was the simple truth. The cruel allegation against Mrs. Leigh seemed to be beneath contempt. As Sir Egerton Brydges pointed out at the time, Byron, being of a strong temperament, did not reply to the injuries heaped upon him by whining complaints and cowardly protestations of innocence; he became desperate, and broke out into indignation, sarcasm, and exposure of his opponents, in a manner so severe as to seem inexcusably cruel to those who did not realize the provocation. It was 'war to the knife,' and Byron had the best of it.

---

* 'Astarte,' p. 244.

We propose to examine 'Manfred' closely, to see whether Astarte in any degree resembles the description which Lord Lovelace has given of Augusta Leigh.

Manfred tells us that his slumbers are 'a continuance of enduring thought,' since that 'all-nameless hour' when he committed the crime for which he suffers. He asks 'Forgetfulness of that which is within him—a crime which he cannot utter.' When told by the Seven Spirits that he cannot have self-oblivion, Manfred asks if Death would give it to him; and receives the sad reply that, being immortal, the spirit after death cannot forget the past.

Eventually the Seventh Spirit—typifying, possibly, a Magdalen—appears before Manfred, in the shape of a beautiful woman.

> 'MANFRED. Oh God! if it be thus, and *thou*
> Art not a madness and a mockery,
> I yet might be most happy.'

When the figure vanishes, Manfred falls senseless. In the second act, Manfred, in reply to the chamois-hunter, who offers him a cup of wine, says:

> 'Away, away! there's blood upon the brim!
> Will it then never—never sink in the earth?
> 'Tis blood—my blood! the pure warm stream
> Which ran in the veins of my fathers, and in ours
> When we were in our youth, and had one heart,
> And loved each other as we should not love,
> And *this* was shed: but still it rises up,
> Colouring the clouds that shut me out from Heaven.'

One may well wonder what all this has to do with Augusta. The blood that ran in Byron's veins also ran in the veins of Mary Chaworth, and that blood, shed by Byron's kinsman, had caused a feud, which was not broken until Byron came upon the scene, and fell hopelessly in love with 'the last of a time-honoured race.' Byron from his boyhood always believed that there was a blood-curse upon him.

When, two years later, he wrote 'The Duel' (December, 1818), he again alludes to the subject:

> 'I loved thee—I will not say *how*,
>   Since things like these are best forgot:
> Perhaps thou mayst imagine now
>   Who loved thee and who loved thee not.
> And thou wert wedded to another,
>   And I at last another wedded:
> I am a father, thou a mother,
>   To strangers vowed, with strangers bedded.
>   *   *   *   *   *
>   'Many a bar, and many a feud,
> Though never told, well understood,
> Rolled like a river wide between—
> *And then there was the curse of blood,*
> Which even my Heart's can not remove.
>   *   *   *   *   *
> 'I've seen the sword that slew him; he,
>   The slain, stood in a like degree
> To thee, as he, the Slayer stood
>   (Oh, had it been but other blood!)
> In Kin and Chieftainship to me.
>   Thus came the Heritage to thee.'

Clearly, then, the Spirit, which appeared to Manfred in the form of a beautiful female figure, was Mary Chaworth; the crime for which he suffered was his conduct towards her; and the blood, which his fancy beheld on the cup's brim, was the blood of William Chaworth, which his predecessor, Lord Byron, had shed. When asked by the chamois-hunter whether he had wreaked revenge upon his enemies, Manfred replies:

> 'No, no, no!
> My injuries came down on those who loved me—
> On those whom I best loved: I never quelled
> An enemy, save in my just defence—
> But my embrace was fatal.'

In speaking of the 'core of his heart's grief,' Manfred says:

> 'Yet there was One—
> She was like me in lineaments—her eyes—
> Her hair—her features—all, to the very tone
> Even of her voice, they said were like to mine;
> But softened all, and tempered into beauty:
> She had the same lone thoughts and wanderings,*
> The quest of hidden knowledge, and a mind
> To comprehend the Universe: nor these
> Alone, but with them gentler powers than mine,
> Pity, and smiles, and tears—which I had not;
> And tenderness—but that I had for her;
> Humility—and that I never had.
> Her faults were mine—her virtues were her own—
> I loved her, and destroyed her!
> Not with my hand, but heart, *which broke her heart;
> It gazed on mine, and withered.*'

In order to appreciate the absurdity of connecting this description with Augusta, we will quote her noble accuser, Lord Lovelace:

> 'The character of Augusta is seen in her letters and actions. She was a woman of that great family which is vague about facts, unconscious of duties, impulsive in conduct. The course of her life could not be otherwise explained, by those who had looked into it with close intimacy, than by a kind of moral idiotcy from birth. She was of a sanguine and buoyant disposition, childishly fond and playful, ready to laugh at anything, loving to talk nonsense.'

In fact,

> '*She had the same lone thoughts and wanderings,*
> *The quest of hidden knowledge, and a mind*
> *To comprehend the Universe.*'

Lord Lovelace further tells us that Augusta Leigh 'had a refined species of comic talent'; that she was

---

* See the poem 'Remember Him': 'Thy soul from long seclusion pure.'

'strangely insensible to the nature and magnitude of the offence in question [incest] even as an imputation;' and that 'there was apparently an absence of all deep feeling in her mind, of everything on which a strong impression could be made.' We are also told that 'Byron, after his marriage, generally spoke of Augusta as "a fool," with equal contempt of her understanding and principles.'

In short, Byron's description of the woman, whom he had 'destroyed,' resembles Augusta Leigh about as much as a mountain resembles a haystack. How closely Manfred's description resembles Mary Chaworth will be seen presently. Augusta Leigh had told Byron that, in consequence of his conduct, Mary Chaworth was out of her mind.

Manfred says that if he had never lived, that which he loved had still been living:

> '... Had I never loved,
> That which I love would still be beautiful,
> Happy, and giving happiness. What is she?
> What is she now? *A sufferer for my sins—*
> *A thing I dare not think upon*—or nothing.'

When Nemesis asks Manfred whom he would 'uncharnel,' he replies:

> 'One without a tomb—
> Call up Astarte.'

The name, of course, suggests a star. As we have seen, Byron often employed that metaphor in allusion to Mary Chaworth.

When the phantom of Astarte rises, Manfred exclaims:

> 'Can this be death? there's bloom upon her cheek;
> But now I see it is no living hue,
> But a strange hectic.'

He is afraid to look upon her; he cannot speak to her, and implores Nemesis to intercede:

> 'Bid her speak—
> Forgive me, or condemn me.'

Nemesis tells him that she has no authority over Astarte:

> 'She is not of our order, but belongs
> To the other powers.'*

The fine appeal of Manfred cannot have been addressed by Byron to his sister:

> 'Hear me, hear me—
> Astarte! my belovéd! speak to me:
> I have so much endured—so much endure—
> Look on me! the grave hath not changed thee more
> Than I am changed for thee. Thou lovedst me
> Too much, as I loved thee: we were not made
> To torture thus each other—though it were
> The deadliest sin to love as we have loved.
> Say that thou loath'st me not—that I do bear
> This punishment for both—that thou wilt be
> One of the blesséd—and that I shall die.
> *   *   *   *   *
> 'I cannot rest.
> I know not what I ask, nor what I seek:
> *I feel but what thou art,* and what I am;
> And I would hear yet once before I perish
> The voice which was my music†—speak to me!
> *   *   *   *   *
> Speak to me! I have wandered o'er the earth,
> And never found thy likeness.'

When Manfred implores Astarte to forgive him, she is silent. It is not a matter for forgiveness. He entreats her to speak to him, so that he may once more hear that sweet voice, even though it be for

---

* 'OPHELIA. O heavenly powers, restore him!'
Hamlet, Act III., Scene i.

† 'The song, celestial from thy voice,
But sweet to me from none but thine.'
Poetry of Byron, vol. iv.: 'To Thyrza.'

the last time. The silence is broken by the word 'Farewell!' Manfred, whose doom is sealed, cries in agony:

> 'What I have done is done; I bear within
> A torture which could nothing gain (from others).
> The Mind, which is immortal, makes itself
> Requital for its good or evil thoughts,—
> Is its own origin of ill and end—
> And its own place and time:
> I was my own destroyer, and will be
> My own hereafter. . . .
> The hand of Death is on me. . . .
> All things swim around me, and the Earth
> Heaves, as it were, beneath me.   Fare thee well!'

So far as we know, there is nothing in the whole length of this poem to suggest anything abnormal; and it is hard to understand what resemblance Byron's contemporaries could have discovered between the Astarte of 'Manfred' and Augusta Leigh! Enough has been quoted to show that Byron was not thinking of his sister when he wrote 'Manfred,' but of her whose life he had blasted, and whose 'sacred' name he trembled to reveal.

In April, 1817, Byron was informed by Mrs. Leigh that Mary Chaworth and her husband had made up their differences. The 'Lament of Tasso' was written in that month, and Byron's thoughts were occupied, as usual, with the theme of all his misery.

> 'That thou wert beautiful, and I not blind,
> Hath been the sin that shuts me from mankind;
> But let them go, or torture as they will,
> My heart can multiply thine image still;
> Successful Love may sate itself away;
>   The wretched are the faithful; 'tis their fate
> To have all feeling, save the one, decay,
>   And every passion into one dilate,
> As rapid rivers into Ocean pour;
> But ours is fathomless, and hath no shore.'

In 'Mazeppa' Byron tells how he met 'Theresa' in that month of June, and how 'through his brain the thought did pass that there was something in her air which would not doom him to despair.' This incident is again referred to in 'Don Juan.' The Count Palatine is, probably, intended as a sketch of Mary's husband.

'The Duel,' which was written in December, 1818, is addressed to Mary Chaworth :

> 'I loved thee—I will not say *how*,
> Since things like these are best forgot.'

Byron alludes to 'the curse of blood,' with, 'many a bar and many a feud,' which 'rolled like a wide river between them' :

> 'Alas! how many things have been
> Since we were friends; for I alone
> Feel more for thee than can be shown.'

In the so-called 'Stanzas to the Po,' we find the same prolonged note of suffering. Writing to Murray (May 8, 1820), Byron says :

'I sent a copy of verses to Mr. Kinnaird (they were written last year on crossing the Po) which must *not* be published. Pray recollect this, as they were mere verses of society, and written from private feelings and passions.'

In view of the secrecy which Byron consistently observed, respecting his later intimacy with Mary Chaworth, the publication of these verses would have been highly indiscreet. They were written in June, 1819, after Mary had for some time been reconciled to her husband. She was then living with him at Colwick Hall, near Nottingham.

Ostensibly these stanzas form an apostrophe to the River Po, and the 'lady of the land' was, of course, the Guiccioli. Medwin, to whom Byron gave the poem, believed that the river apostrophized by the poet was the River Po, whose 'deep and ample stream' was 'the mirror of his heart.' But it seems perfectly clear that, if this poem referred only to the Countess Guiccioli, there could have been no objection to its publication in England. The reading public in those days knew nothing of Byron's liaisons abroad, and his mystic allusion to foreign rivers and foreign ladies would have left the British public cold.

A scrutiny of these perplexing stanzas suggests that they were adapted, from a fragment written in early life, to meet the conditions of 1819. Evidently Mary Chaworth was once more 'the ocean to the river of his thoughts,' and the stream indicated in the opening stanza was not the Po, but the River Trent, which flows close to the ancient walls of Colwick, where 'the lady of his love' was then residing. To assist the reader, we insert the poem, having merely transposed three stanzas to make its purport clearer:

I.

'River, that rollest by the ancient walls,
  Where dwells the Lady of my love, when she
Walks by thy brink, *and there perchance recalls
A faint and fleeting memory of me*:

II.

'She will look on thee—I have looked on thee,
  Full of that thought: and from that moment ne'er
Thy waters could I dream of, name, or see
  Without the inseparable sigh for her!

III.

'But that which keepeth us apart is not
  Distance, nor depth of wave, nor space of earth,
But the distraction of a various lot,
  As various as the climates of our birth.

IV.

'What if thy deep and ample stream should be
    A mirror of my heart, where she may read
The thousand thoughts *I now betray to thee*,
    Wild as thy wave, and headlong as thy speed!

V.

'What do I say—a mirror of my heart?
    Are not thy waters sweeping, dark, and strong?
Such as my feelings were and are, thou art;
    And such as thou art were my passions long.

VI.

'Time may have somewhat tamed them—not for ever;
    Thou overflowest thy banks, and not for aye
Thy bosom overboils, congenial river!
    Thy floods subside, and mine have sunk away:

VII.

'But left long wrecks behind, and now again,
    Borne on our old unchanged career, we move:
Thou tendest wildly onwards to the main,
    And I,—to loving *one* I should not love.

VIII.

'My blood is all meridian; were it not,
    I had not left my clime, nor should I be,
In spite of tortures, ne'er to be forgot,
    A slave again to Love—at least of thee.

IX.

'The current I behold will sweep beneath
    Her native walls,* and murmur at her feet;
Her eyes will look on thee, when she shall breathe
    The twilight air, unharmed by summer's heat.

X.

'Her bright eyes will be imaged in thy stream.
    Yes, they will meet the wave I gaze on now:
Mine cannot witness, even in a dream,
    That happy wave repass me in its flow!

---

    * 'Siede la terra, dove nata fui,
      Su la marina dove il Po discende.'
              Inferno, Canto V., 97, 98.

'STANZAS TO THE PO'

XI.

'The wave that bears my tears returns no more:
  Will she return by whom that wave shall sweep?
Both tread thy banks, both wander on thy shore,
  I near thy source, she by the dark-blue deep.*

XII.

'A stranger loves the Lady of the land,
  Born far beyond the mountains, but his blood
Is all meridian, as if never fanned
  By the bleak wind that chills the polar flood.

XIII.

''Tis vain to struggle—let me perish young—
  Live as I lived, and love as I have loved;
To dust if I return, from dust I sprung,
  And then, at least, my heart can ne'er be moved.'

In the first stanza, Byron says that when his lady-love walks by the river's brink 'she may perchance recall a faint and fleeting memory' of him. Those words, which might have been applicable to Mary Chaworth, whom he had not seen for at least three years, could not possibly refer to a woman from whom he had been parted but two short months, and with whom he had since been in constant correspondence. Only a few days before these verses were written, Countess Guiccioli had told him by letter that she had prepared all her relatives and friends to expect him at Ravenna. There must surely have been something more than 'a faint and fleeting' memory of Byron in the mind of the ardent Guiccioli. In the second

---

* Although not near the source of the Po itself, Byron, at Ferrara, was not very far from the point where the Po di Primaro breaks away from the Po, and, becoming an independent river, flows into the dark blue Adriatic, about midway between Comachio and Ravenna.

stanza, Byron, in allusion to the river he had in his thoughts, says:

'She will look on thee—*I have looked on thee*, full of that thought: *and from that moment* ne'er thy waters could I dream of, *name, or see*, without the inseparable sigh for her.'

Now, while there was nothing whatever to connect the River Po with tender recollections, there was Byron's association in childhood with the River Trent, a memory inseparable from his boyish love for Mary Chaworth.

> 'But in his native stream, the Guadalquivir,
>   Juan to lave his youthful limbs was wont;
> And having learnt to swim in that sweet river
>   Had often turned the art to some account.'

In the fourth stanza we perceive that the poet, while thinking of the Trent, 'betrays his thoughts' to the Po, a river as wild and as swift as his native stream.

The ninth stanza has puzzled commentators exceedingly. It has been pointed out that the River Po does not sweep beneath the walls of Ravenna. That is, of course, indisputable. But Byron, in all probability, did not then know the exact course of that river, and blindly followed Dante's geographical description, and almost used his very words:

> 'Siede la terra, *dove nata fui,*
>   *Su la marina dove il Po discende,*
>   *Per aver pace co' seguaci sui.*'

It is, of course, well known that the Po branches off into two streams to the north-west of Ferrara, and flows both northward and southward of that city. The southern portion—the Po di Primaro—is fed by four affluents—the Rheno, the Savena, the Santerno, and the Lamone—and flows into the Adriatic south of Comachio, about midway between that place and Ravenna. It was obviously to the *Po di Primaro* that Dante referred when he wrote *seguaci sui.*

Unless Francesca was born close to the mouth of the Po, which is not impossible, Byron erred in good company. In any case, we may fairly plead poetic licence. That Byron crossed the Po di Primaro as well as the main river admits of no doubt.

In the eleventh stanza Byron is wondering what will be the result of his journey? Will the Guiccioli return to him? Will all be well with the lovers, or will he return to Venice alone? In his fancy they are both wandering on the banks of that river. He is near its source, where the Po di Primaro branches off near Pontelagascuro, while she was on the shore of the Adriatic.

The twelfth stanza would perhaps have been clearer if the first and second lines had been,

> ' A stranger, born far beyond the mountains,
> Loves the Lady of the land,'

which was Byron's meaning. The poet excuses himself for his fickleness on the plea that 'his blood is all meridian'—in short, that he cannot help loving someone. But we plainly see that his love for Mary Chaworth was still paramount. 'In spite of tortures ne'er to be forgot'—tortures of which we had a glimpse in 'Manfred'—he was still her slave. Finally, Byron tells us that it was useless to struggle against the misery his heart endured, and that all his hopes were centred on an early death.

The episode of Francesca and Paolo had made a deep impression on Byron. He likened it to his unfortunate adventure with Mary Chaworth in June and July, 1813. In 'The Corsair'—written after their intimacy had been broken off—Byron prefixes to each canto a motto from 'The Inferno' which seemed to be appropriate to his own case. In the first canto we find:

> 'Nessun maggior dolore,
> Che ricordarsi del tempo felice
> Nella miseria.'

In the second canto:

> 'Conoscesti i dubbiosi desire ?'

In the third canto:

> 'Come vedi—ancor non m' abbandona.'

That Byron had Francesca in his mind when he wrote the stanzas to the Po seems likely; and in the letter which he wrote to Mary from Venice, in the previous month, he compares their misfortunes with those of Paolo and Francesca in plain words.*

'Don Juan' was begun in the autumn of 1818. That poem, Byron tells us, was inspired almost entirely by his own personal experience. Perhaps he drew a portrait of Mary Chaworth when he described Julia:

> 'And she
> Was married, charming, chaste, and twenty-three.'

When they parted in 1809, that was exactly Mary's age.

'Her eye was large and dark, suppressing half its fire until she spoke. Her glossy hair was clustered over a brow bright with intelligence. Her cheek was purple with the beam of youth, mounting at times to a transparent glow; and she had an uncommon grace of manner. She was tall of stature. Her husband was a good-looking man, neither much loved nor disliked. He was of a jealous nature, though he did not show it.

---

* Shortly afterwards he translated 'The Episode of Francesca,' line for line, into English verse.

They lived together, as most people do, suffering each other's foibles.'

On a summer's eve in the month of June, Juan and Julia met:

> 'How beautiful she looked! her conscious heart
> Glowed in her cheek, and yet she felt no wrong.'

For her husband she had honour, virtue, truth, and love. The sun had set, and the yellow moon arose high in the heavens:

> 'There is a dangerous silence in that hour,
> A stillness which leaves room for the full soul.'

Several weeks had passed away:

> 'Julia, in fact, had tolerable grounds,—
> Alfonso's loves with Inez were well known.'

Then came the parting note:

> 'They tell me 'tis decided you depart:
> 'Tis wise—'tis well, but not the less a pain;
> I have no further claim on your young heart,
> Mine is the victim, and would be again:
> To love too much has been the only art
> I used.'

Julia tells Juan that she loved him, and still loves him tenderly:

> 'I loved, I love you, for this love have lost
> State, station, Heaven, mankind's, my own esteem,
> And yet cannot regret what it hath cost,
> So dear is still the memory of that dream.'

> 'All is o'er
> For me on earth, except some years to hide
> My shame and sorrow deep in my heart's core.'

The seal to this letter was a sunflower—*Elle vous suit partout.* It may be mentioned here that Byron had a seal bearing this motto.

When Juan realized that the parting was final, he exclaims:

> 'No more—no more—oh! never more, my heart,
>   Canst thou be my sole world, my universe!
> Once all in all, but now a thing apart,
>   Thou canst not be my blessing or my curse:
> The illusion's gone for ever.'

In the third canto we have a hint of Byron's feelings after his wife had left him:

> 'He entered in the house no more his home,
>   A thing to human feelings the most trying,
> And harder for the heart to overcome,
>   Perhaps, than even the mental pangs of dying;
> To find our hearthstone turned into a tomb,
>   And round its once warm precincts palely lying
> The ashes of our hopes.'

> 'But whatsoe'er he had of love reposed
>   On that belovéd daughter; she had been
> The only thing which kept his heart unclosed
>   Amidst the savage deeds he had done and seen,
> A lonely pure affection unopposed:
>   There wanted but the loss of this to wean
> His feelings from all milk of human kindness,
> And turn him like the Cyclops mad with blindness.'

In the fourth canto we are introduced to Haidée, who resembled Lambro in features and stature, even to the delicacy of their hands.* We are told that owing to the violence of emotion and the agitation of her mind she broke a bloodvessel, and lay unconscious on her couch for days. Like Astarte in 'Manfred,' 'her blood was shed: I saw, but could not stanch it':

> 'She looked on many a face with vacant eye,
>   On many a token without knowing what:
> She saw them watch her without asking why,
>   And recked not who around her pillow sat.

* * * * *

---

* See *ante*, p. 294.

DON JUAN

'Anon her thin wan fingers beat the wall
  In time to the harper's tune: he changed the theme
And sang of Love; the fierce name struck through all
  Her recollection; on her flashed the dream
Of what she was, and is, if ye could call
  To be so being; in a gushing stream
The tears rushed forth from her o'erclouded brain,
Like mountain mists at length dissolved in rain.'

'Short solace, vain relief! Thought came too quick,
  And whirled her brain to madness.'

'She died, but not alone; she held within,
  A second principle of Life, which might
Have dawned a fair and sinless child of sin;
  But closed its little being without light.'

'Thus lived—thus died she; never more on her
  Shall Sorrow light, or Shame.'

In the fifth canto, written in 1820, after the 'Stanzas to the Po,' we find Byron once more in a confidential mood:

I have a passion for the name of "Mary,"
  For once it was a magic sound to me;
And still it half calls up the realms of Fairy,
  Where I beheld what never was to be;
All feelings changed, but this was last to vary
  A spell from which even yet I am not quite free.'

And there is a sigh for Mary Chaworth in the following lines:

'To pay my court, I
Gave what I had—a heart; as the world went, I
Gave what was worth a world; for worlds could never
Restore me those pure feelings, gone for ever.
'Twas the boy's mite, and like the widow's may
  Perhaps be weighed hereafter, if not now;
But whether such things do or do not weigh,
  All who have loved, or love, will still allow
Life has naught like it.'

Early in 1823, little more than a year before his death, Byron refers to 'the fair most fatal Juan ever met.' Under the name of the Lady Adeline, this most fatal fair one is introduced to the reader:

> 'Although she was not evil nor meant ill,
> Both Destiny and Passion spread the net
> And caught them.'

> 'Chaste she was, to Detraction's desperation,
> And wedded unto one she had loved well.'

> 'The World could tell
> Nought against either, and both seemed secure—
> She in her virtue, he in his hauteur.'

Here we have a minute description of Newstead Abbey, the home of the 'noble pair,' where Juan came as a visitor:

> 'What I throw off is ideal—
> Lowered, leavened, like a history of Freemasons,
> Which bears the same relation to the real
> As Captain Parry's Voyage may do to Jason's.
> The grand *Arcanum's* not for men to see all;
> My music has some mystic diapasons;
> And there is much which could not be appreciated
> In any manner by the uninitiated.'

Adeline, we are told, came out at sixteen:

> At eighteen, though below her feet still panted
> A Hecatomb of suitors with devotion,
> She had consented to create again
> That Adam called " The happiest of Men." '

It will be remembered that when Mary Chaworth married she was exactly eighteen. Her husband was:

> ' Tall, stately, formed to lead the courtly van
> On birthdays. The model of a chamberlain.'

> ' But there was something wanting on the whole—
> I don't know what, and therefore cannot tell—
> Which pretty women—the sweet souls !—call *Soul*.
> *Certes* it was not body; he was well
> Proportioned, as a poplar or a pole,
> A handsome man.'

This description would answer equally well for 'handsome Jack Musters,' who married Mary Chaworth. Adeline, we are told, took Juan in hand when she was about seven-and-twenty. That was Mary's age in 1813. But this may have been a mere coincidence.

'She had one defect,' says Byron, in speaking of Adeline: 'her heart was vacant. Her conduct had been perfectly correct. She loved her lord, or thought so; but *that* love cost her an effort. She had nothing to complain of—no bickerings, no connubial turmoil. Their union was a model to behold—serene and noble, conjugal, but cold. There was no great disparity in years, though much in temper. But they never clashed. They moved, so to speak, apart.'

Now, when once Adeline had taken an interest in anything, her impressions grew, and gathered as they ran, like growing water, upon her mind. The more so, perhaps, because she was not at first too readily impressed. She did not know her own heart:

> 'I think not she was *then* in love with Juan:
> If so, she would have had the strength to fly
> The wild sensation, unto her a new one:
> She merely felt a common sympathy
> In him.'

> 'She was, or thought she was, his friend—and this
> Without the farce of Friendship, or romance
> Of Platonism.'

'Few of the soft sex,' says Byron, 'are very stable in their resolves.' She had heard some parts of Juan's history; 'but women hear with more good humour such aberrations than we men of rigour':

> 'Adeline, in all her growing sense
> Of Juan's merits and his situation,
> Felt on the whole an interest intense—
> Partly perhaps because a fresh sensation,

> Or that he had an air of innocence,
>   Which is for Innocence a sad temptation—
> As Women hate half-measures, on the whole,
> She 'gan to ponder how to save his soul.'

After a deal of thought, 'she seriously advised him to get married.'

> 'There was Miss Millpond, smooth as summer's sea,
>   That usual paragon, an only daughter,
> Who seemed the cream of Equanimity,
>   Till skimmed—and then there was some milk and water,
> With a slight shade of blue too, it might be
>   Beneath the surface.'

The mention of Aurora Raby, to whom Juan in the first instance proposed, and by whom he was refused, suggests an incident in his life which is well known. Aurora was very young, and knew but little of the world's ways. In her indifference she confounded him with the crowd of flatterers by whom she was surrounded. Her mind appears to have been of a serious caste; with poetic vision she 'saw worlds beyond this world's perplexing waste,' and

> 'those worlds
> Had more of her existence; for in her
> There was a depth of feeling to embrace
> Thoughts, boundless, deep, but silent too as Space.'

She had 'a pure and placid mien'; her colour was 'never high,'

> 'Though sometimes faintly flushed—and always clear
> As deep seas in a sunny atmosphere.'

We cannot be positive, but perhaps Byron had Aurora Raby in his mind when he wrote:

> 'I've seen some balls and revels in my time,
>   And stayed them over for some silly reason,
> And then I looked (I hope it was no crime)
>   To see what lady best stood out the season;

MISS MERCER ELPHINSTONE

> And though I've seen some thousands in their prime
>   Lovely and pleasing, and who still may please on,
> I never saw but one (the stars withdrawn)
>   Whose bloom could after dancing dare the Dawn.' *

Perhaps Aurora Raby may have been drawn from his recollection of Miss Mercer Elphinstone, who afterwards married Auguste Charles Joseph, Comte de Flahaut de la Billarderie, one of Napoleon's Aides-de-Camp, then an exile in England. This young lady was particularly gracious to Byron at Lady Jersey's party, when others gave him a cold reception. We wonder how matters would have shaped themselves if she had accepted the proposal of marriage which Byron made to her in 1814! But it was not to be. That charming woman passed out of his orbit, and as he waited upon the shore, gazing at the dim outline of the coast of France, the curtain fell upon the first phase of Byron's existence. The Pilgrim of Eternity stood on the threshold of a new life:

> ' Between two worlds life hovers like a star,
>   'Twixt Night and Morn, upon the horizon's verge.
> How little do we know that which we are!
>   How less what we may be! The eternal surge
> Of Time and Tide rolls on and bears afar
>   Our bubbles; as the old burst, new emerge,
> Lashed from the foam of Ages.'

And after eight years of exile, in his 'Last Words on Greece,' written in those closing days at Missolonghi, with the shadow of Death upon him, his mind reverts to one whom, in 1816, he had called 'Soul of my thought':

> ' What are to me those honours or renown
>   Past or to come, a new-born people's cry?
> Albeit for such I could despise a crown
>   Of aught save laurel, or for such could die.

---

* 'Beppo,' stanza 83.

I am a fool of passion, and a frown
   Of thine to me is as an adder's eye—
To the poor bird whose pinion fluttering down
   Wafts unto death the breast it bore so high—
Such is this maddening fascination grown,
   So strong thy magic or so weak am I.'

'The flowers and fruits of Love are gone; the worm,
The canker, and the grief, are mine alone!'

PART III
'ASTARTE'

'The evil that men do lives after them;
The good is oft interred with their bones.'
SHAKESPEARE: *Julius Cæsar.*

CHAPTER I

From the moment when Lord Byron left England until the hour of his death, the question of his separation from his wife was never long out of his thoughts. He was remarkably communicative on the subject, and spoke of it constantly, not only to Madame de Staël, Hobhouse, Lady Blessington, and Trelawny, but, as we have seen, even in casual conversation with comparative strangers. There is no doubt that he felt himself aggrieved, and bitterly resented a verdict which he knew to be unjust. In a pamphlet which was subsequently suppressed, written while he was at Ravenna, Byron sums up his own case. In justice to one who can no longer plead his own cause, we feel bound to transcribe a portion of his reply to strictures on his matrimonial conduct, which appeared in *Blackwood's Magazine*:

'The man who is exiled by a faction has the consolation of thinking that he is a martyr; he is upheld by hope and the dignity of his cause, real or imaginary: he who withdraws from the pressure of debt may indulge in the thought that time and prudence will retrieve his circumstances: he who is condemned by the law has a term to his banishment, or a dream of its abbreviation; or, it may be, the knowledge or the belief of some injustice of the law, or of its administration in his own particular: but he who is outlawed by general opinion, without the intervention of hostile politics, illegal judgment, or embarrassed circumstances, whether he be innocent or guilty, must undergo all the bitterness of exile, without hope, without pride, without alleviation. This case was mine. Upon what grounds the public founded their opinion, I am not aware; but it was general, and it was decisive. Of me or of mine they knew little, except that I had written what is called poetry, was a nobleman, had married, become a father, and was involved in differences with my wife and her relatives, no one knew why, because the persons complaining refused to state their grievances. The fashionable world was divided into parties, mine consisting of a very small minority: the reasonable world was naturally on the stronger side, which happened to be the lady's, as was most proper and polite. The press was active and scurrilous; and such was the rage of the day, that the unfortunate publication of two copies of verses, rather complimentary than otherwise to the subjects of both, was tortured into a species of crime, or constructive petty treason. I was accused of every monstrous vice by public rumour and private rancour; my name, which had been a knightly or a noble one since my fathers helped to conquer the kingdom for William the Norman, was tainted. I felt that, if what was whispered, and muttered, and murmured, was true, I was unfit for England; if false, England was unfit for me. I withdrew; but this was not enough. In other countries, in Switzerland, in the shadow of the Alps, and by the blue depths of the lakes, I was pursued and breathed upon by the same blight. I crossed the mountains, but it was the same: so I went a little farther, and settled myself by the waves of the Adriatic, like the stag at bay, who betakes him to the waters. . . . I have heard of, and believe, that there are human beings so constituted as to be insensible to injuries; but I believe that the best mode to avoid taking vengeance is to get out of the way of temptation. I do not in this allude to the party, who might be right or wrong; but to many who made her cause the pretext of their own bitterness. She, indeed, must have long avenged me in her own feelings, for whatever her reasons may have been (and she never adduced them, to me at least), she probably neither contemplated nor conceived to what she became the means of conducting the father of her child, and the husband of her choice.'

Byron knew of the charge that had been whispered against his sister and himself, and, knowing it to be false, it stung him to the heart. And yet he dared not speak, because a solution of the mystery that surrounded the separation from his wife would have involved the betrayal of one whom he designated as the soul of his thought :

> 'Invisible but gazing, as I glow
> Mixed with thy spirit, blended with thy birth,
> And feeling still with thee in my crush'd feelings dearth.'

Augusta Leigh, the selfless martyr, the most loyal friend that Byron ever possessed, his 'tower of strength in the hour of need,' assisted her brother, so to speak, to place the pack on a false scent, and the whole field blindly followed. There never was a nobler example of self-immolation than that of the sister who bravely endured the odium of a scandal in which she had no part. For Byron's sake she was content to suffer intensely during her lifetime ; and after she had ceased to feel, her name was branded by Lady Byron and her descendants with the mark of infamy.

A curious feature in the case is that, with few exceptions, those who knew Byron and Mrs. Leigh intimately came gradually to accept the story which Lady Caroline Lamb had insidiously whispered, a libel which flourished exceedingly in the noxious vapours of a scandal-loving age. As Nature is said to abhor a vacuum, so falsehood rushed in to fill the void which silence caused.

It is with a deep searching of heart and with great reluctance that we re-open this painful subject.

The entire responsibility must rest with the late Lord Lovelace, whose loud accusation against Byron's devoted sister deprives us of any choice in the matter.

In order to understand the full absurdity of the accusation brought against Augusta Leigh, we have but to contrast the evidence brought against her in 'Astarte' with allusions to her in Byron's poems, and with the esteem in which she was held by men and women well known in society at the time of the separation.

Lord Stanhope, the historian, in a private letter written at the time of the Beecher Stowe scandals, says:

'I was very well acquainted with Mrs. Leigh about forty years ago, and used to call upon her at St. James's Palace to hear her speak about Lord Byron, as she was very fond of doing. That fact itself is a presumption against what is alleged, since, on such a supposition, the subject would surely be felt as painful and avoided. She was extremely unprepossessing in her person and appearance—more like a nun than anything—and never can have had the least pretension to beauty. I thought her shy and sensitive to a fault in her mind and character, and, from what I saw and knew of her, I hold her to have been utterly incapable of such a crime as Mrs. Beecher Stowe is so unwarrantably seeking to cast upon her memory.'

Frances, Lady Shelley, a woman of large experience, penetration, and sagacity, whose husband was a personal friend of the Prince Regent, stated in a letter to the *Times* that Mrs. Leigh was like a mother to Byron, and when she knew her intimately—at the time of the separation—was 'not at all an attractive person.' Her husband was very fond of her, and had a high opinion of her.

These impressions are confirmed by all those friends

and acquaintances of Mrs. Leigh who were still living in 1869.

In 1816 Augusta Leigh was a married woman of thirty-two years of age, and the mother of four children. She had long been attached to the Court, moved in good society, and was much liked by those who knew her intimately. Since her marriage in 1807 she had been more of a mother than a sister to Byron, and her affection for him was deep and sincere. She made allowances for his frailties, bore his uncertain temper with patience, and was never afraid of giving him good advice. In June, 1813, she tried to save him from the catastrophe which she foresaw; and having failed, she made the supreme sacrifice of her life, by adopting his natural child, thus saving the reputation of a woman whom her brother sincerely loved. Henceforward, under suspicions which must have been galling to her pride, she faced Society's 'speechless obloquy,' heedless of consequences. In the after-years, when great trouble fell upon her through the misconduct of that adopted child, she bore her sorrows in silence. Among those who were connected with Byron's life, Hobhouse, Hodgson, and Harness—three men of unimpeachable character—respected and admired her to the last.

Such, then, was the woman who was persecuted during her lifetime and slandered in her grave. Her traducers at first whispered, and afterwards openly stated, not only that she had committed incest with her brother, but that she had employed her influence over him to make a reconciliation with his wife impossible.

If that were so, it is simply inconceivable that Hobhouse should have remained her lifelong friend.

His character is well known. Not only his public but much of his private life is an open book. As a gentleman and a man of honour he was above suspicion. From his long and close intimacy with Byron, there were but few secrets between them; and Hobhouse undoubtedly knew the whole truth of the matter between Byron and his sister. He was Byron's most trusted friend during life, and executor at his death.

It has never been disputed that, at the time of the separation, Hobhouse demanded from Lady Byron's representative a formal disavowal of that monstrous charge; otherwise the whole matter would be taken into a court of law. He would allow no equivocation. The charge must either be withdrawn, then and there, or substantiated in open court. When Lady Byron, through her representative, *unreservedly* disavowed the imputation, Byron was satisfied, and consented to sign the deed of separation.

Six months after Byron left England, Hobhouse visited him in Switzerland; and on September 9, 1816, he wrote as follows to Augusta Leigh:

'It would be a great injustice to suppose that [Byron] has dismissed the subject from his thoughts, or indeed from his conversation, *upon any other motive than that which the most bitter of his enemies would commend.* The uniformly tranquil and guarded manner shows the effect which it is meant to hide. . . . I trust the news from your Lowestoft correspondent [Lady Byron] will not be so bad as it was when I last saw you. Pardon me, dear Mrs. Leigh, if I venture to advise the strictest confinement to very *common* topics in all you say in that quarter. *Repay kindness in any other way than by confidence.* I say this, not in reference to the lady's character, but as a maxim to serve for all cases.

'Ever most faithfully yours,
'J. C. HOBHOUSE.'

This letter shows, not only that the writer was firmly convinced of Mrs. Leigh's innocence, but that he was afraid lest Lady Byron would worm the real secret out of Byron's sister, by appealing, through acts of kindness, to her sense of gratitude. He knew that Mrs. Leigh had a very difficult part to perform. Her loyalty to Byron and Mary Chaworth had already borne a severe test, and he wished her to realize how much depended on her discretion.

The task of keeping in touch with Lady Byron, without dispelling her illusions, was so trying to Augusta Leigh's naturally frank nature as almost to drive her to despair. Lady Byron, knowing that Byron was in constant correspondence with his sister, asked permission to read his letters, and it was difficult, without plausible excuse, to withhold them. Byron's correspondence was never characterized by reticence. He invariably unburdened his mind, heedless of the effect which his words might have upon those to whom his letters were shown. In these circumstances Mrs. Leigh was kept in a fever of apprehension as to what Lady Byron might glean, even from the winnowed portions which, from time to time, were submitted for her perusal.

It has since transpired that, without Augusta's knowledge, Lady Byron kept a copy of everything that was shown to her.

It appears from 'Astarte' that, in the early part of September, 1816, Augusta Leigh underwent a rigorous cross-examination—not only from Lady Byron, but from inquisitive acquaintances, who were determined to extract from her replies proofs of her guilt.

Lord Lovelace, on Lady Byron's authority, states

that between August 31 and September 14 (the precise date is not given) Augusta confessed to Lady Byron that she had committed incest with her brother *previous to his marriage.** This strange admission, which we are told had been long expected, seems to have completely satisfied Lady Byron. *After having promised to keep her secret inviolate*, she wrote to several of her friends, and told them that Augusta had made 'a full confession of her guilt.' There had been no witnesses at the meeting between these two ladies, and the incriminating letters, which Lord Lovelace says Mrs. Leigh wrote to Lady Byron, are not given in 'Astarte'! But in 1817 Lady Byron, referring to these meetings, says: 'She acknowledged that the verses, "I speak not, I trace not, I breathe not thy name," were addressed to her.'

Augusta was certainly in an awkward predicament. By adopting Medora she had, at considerable personal risk, saved the reputation of Mary Chaworth. If she had now told the whole truth—namely, that Medora was merely her daughter by adoption—she would have been pressed to prove it by divulging the identity of that child's mother. This was of course impossible. Not only would she have mortally offended Byron, and have betrayed his trust in her, but the fortune which by his will would devolve upon her children would not have reached Medora at all. For those reasons it was indispensable that the truth should be veiled. As to Mrs. Leigh's alleged statement that the lines, 'I speak not, I trace not, I breathe not thy name,'—

* There is no evidence that Byron knew more than that Augusta, *under the seal of secrecy*, had admitted that he was the father of Medora. Lady Byron was not aware that this admission had been revealed to Byron by his sister.

were addressed to her, we say nothing. By that portion of her so-called 'confession' we may gauge the value of the rest. That Lady Byron should have been thus deceived affords a strong proof of her gullibility. There is nothing to show exactly what passed at these remarkable interviews. We know that Augusta's statements, made orally, were subsequently written down from memory; because Lady Byron told one of her friends that she had sent the said 'confession' to the Lord Chancellor (Eldon), 'as a bar to any future proceedings that might be taken by Lord Byron to obtain the custody of Ada.'

It is clear that Mrs. Leigh's communication would never have been made except under a promise of secrecy. She did not suspect the treachery which Lady Byron contemplated, and thought that she might safely encourage her delusions. Perhaps she divined that Lady Byron had already convinced herself that Medora was Byron's child. At any rate, she knew enough of Lady Byron to be certain that there would be no peace until that lady had satisfied herself that her suspicions were well founded. Unhappily for Mrs. Leigh, Hobhouse's warning arrived too late; her ruse failed, and her reputation suffered during life. Although she was destined to bear the stigma of a crime of which she was innocent,* she never wavered, and died with her secret unrevealed. Lady Byron, with all her ingenuity, never divined the truth. Towards the close of her life she became uneasy in her

* It must here be understood that the scandal was merely whispered among a certain number of their acquaintance, and was in no sense an open accusation.

mind, and died under the impression that 'Augusta had made a fool of her.'

The Rev. Francis Hodgson was entirely in Mrs. Leigh's confidence; he always spoke of her as 'that better angel of Byron's life.' In a letter, which must have been written shortly after Byron's marriage, Augusta says:

'We generally hope as we wish; but I assure you I don't conclude hastily on this subject, and will own to you, what I would not scarcely to any other person, that I *had many fears* and much anxiety founded upon many causes and circumstances of which I cannot *write.* Thank God that they do not appear likely to be realized. . . . My babes are all well; Medora more beautiful than ever.'

Writing to him again on November 14, 1816—after the so-called 'confession'—she says:

'I am afraid to open my lips, though all I say to *you* I know is secure from misinterpretation. On the opinions expressed by Mr. M. [Murray] I am *not surprised.* I have seen letters *to him* which could not but give rise to such, or confirm them. If I may give you mine, it is that *in his own mind there were and are recollections fatal to his peace, and which would have prevented his being happy with any woman whose excellence equalled or approached that of Lady Byron, from the consciousness of being unworthy of it.* Nothing could or can remedy this fatal cause but the consolations to be derived from religion, of which, alas! our beloved Byron is, I fear, destitute. My anxious prayer for him is for that first and *only certain good,* and I should be wretched indeed if bereaved of *hope* on that subject. . . . It is indeed a heartbreaking thought! and, worse than all, not all my affection or anxiety can be either of use or comfort to him. It is a relief to talk of him to one who loves him and feels so rationally all there is to *hope* and *fear* for him. I am sure that it is very useless to try to express my feelings towards him —I *never* could.'

The terms of that letter would, we think, convince any unprejudiced person that the recollections—so fatal to Byron's peace of mind—had nothing to do with Augusta. On March 4, 1817, Mrs. Leigh writes again to Hodgson :

'Of course *you* know to whom "The Dream" alludes, Mrs. Chaworth.'

On December 30, 1818, she writes again :

'I am vexed at your hint from the Midland county, and, do you know, I never allow myself to believe such things except from you, or one as candid *and well acquainted with both sides of the question.*'

Immediately after Mrs. Leigh's interviews with Lady Byron she wrote to Byron, and revealed the state of affairs. That, at the same time, she reproached him for the troubles he had brought upon her is evident from Byron's journal of September 29 :

'I am past reproaches, and there is a time for all things. I am past the wish of vengeance, and I know of none like what I have suffered; but the hour will come when what I feel must be felt, and the [truth will out ?]—but enough.'

It was at this time, also, that Byron thought that the 'Epistle to Augusta'—sent to Murray on August 28—had better not be published. It did not, in fact, see the light until 1830. Lady Byron's conduct in this business affected him profoundly, and his feelings towards her changed completely. He was also angry with Augusta for a time, and told her that it was 'on her account principally that he had given way at all and signed the separation, for he thought they would endeavour to drag her into it, although they had no business with anything previous to his marriage with that infernal fiend, whose destruction he should yet see.'*

In spite of Lady Byron's prejudice against Mrs. Leigh, as time went on she gradually realized that her sister-in-law's so-called 'confession' was not consistent either with her known disposition, her reputation in society, or with her general conduct. In order to satisfy her conscience, Lady Byron, in April, 1851, arranged a meeting with Mrs. Leigh at Reigate. Clearly, it was Lady Byron's purpose to obtain a full confession from Mrs. Leigh of the crime which she had long suspected. Lady Byron came to Reigate accompanied by the Rev. Frederick Robertson of Brighton, who happened then to be her spiritual adviser. This time Augusta Leigh's 'confession' was to be made before an unimpeachable witness, who would keep a record of what passed. It deeply mortified Lady Byron to find that Mrs. Leigh—far from making any 'confession'—appeared before her in 'all the pride of innocence,' and, after saying that she had always been loyal to Byron and his wife, and had never tried to keep them apart, told Lady Byron that Hobhouse—who was still living—had expressed his opinion that Lady Byron had every reason to be grateful to Mrs. Leigh; for she not only risked the loss of property, but what was much dearer to her, Byron's affection.†

* 'Astarte,' p. 166.
† Lady Byron and Rev. F. Robertson drew up a memorandum of this conversation, April 8, 1851.

AN AVOWAL OF INNOCENCE

Alas, the bubble had burst! The *confession*, upon which the peace of Lady Byron's conscience depended, was transformed into an avowal of innocence, which no threats could shake, no arguments could weaken, and no reproaches divert.

CHAPTER II

It is because 'Astarte' is a pretentious and plausible record of fallacies that the present writer feels bound to take note of its arguments.

In order to avoid circumlocution and tedious excursions over debatable ground, we will assume that the reader is tolerably well acquainted with literature relating to the separation of Lord and Lady Byron.

It would certainly have been better if the details of Byron's quarrel with his wife had been ignored. Prior to the publication of Mrs. Beecher Stowe's articles, in 1869, the greatest tenderness had been shown towards Lady Byron by all writers upon Byron's career and poetry, and by all those who alluded to his unhappy marriage. Everyone respected Lady Byron's excellent qualities, and no one accused her of any breach of faith in her conduct towards either her husband or his sister. Lady Byron was generally regarded as a virtuous and high-minded woman, with a hard and cold disposition, but nothing worse was said or thought of her, and the world really sympathized with her sorrows.

But when her self-imposed silence was broken by Mrs. Beecher Stowe, and Byron stood publicly accused on Lady Byron's authority of an odious crime which she had never attempted to prove during the poet's lifetime, there arose a revulsion of feeling against her

THE FALLACIES IN 'ASTARTE'

memory. It was generally felt, after the suffering and the patience of a lifetime, that Lady Byron might well have evinced a deeper Christian spirit at its close.

As time went on, the memory of this untoward incident gradually faded away, and the present generation thought little of the rights or wrongs of a controversy which had moved their forefathers so deeply. The dead, so to speak, had buried their dead, and all would soon have been forgotten. Unfortunately, the late Lord Lovelace, a grandson of Lady Byron, goaded by perusal of the attacks made upon Lady Byron's memory, after Mrs. Beecher Stowe's revelations in 1869, was induced in 1905 to circulate among 'those who, for special reasons, ought to have the means of acquainting themselves with the true position of Lord and Lady Byron,' a work entitled 'Astarte,' which is mainly a compilation of letters and data, skilfully selected for the purpose of defaming his grandfather.

After informing the reader that 'the public of this age would do well to pay no attention to voluminous complications and caricatures of Lord Byron,' Lord Lovelace gaily proceeds, on the flimsiest of evidence, to blast, not only Byron's name, but also the reputation of the poet's half-sister, Augusta Leigh.

After telling the world that Byron 'after his death was less honoured than an outcast,' Lord Lovelace endeavours to justify the public neglect to honour the remains of a great national poet by accusing Byron of incest. Lord Lovelace's claim to have been the sole depositary of so damning a secret is really comical, because, as a matter of fact, he never knew the truth at all. He thought that he had only, like Pandora, to open his box for all the evil to fly out, forgetting that Truth has an awkward habit of lying at the bottom.

He seems, however, to have had some inkling of this, for he is careful to remind us that 'Truth comes in the last, and very late, limping along on the arm of Time.'

In support of a theory which is supposed to be revealed by his papers, Lord Lovelace declares that a solution of Byron's mystery may be found in his poems, and he fixes on 'Manfred' for the key. The haunting remorse of Manfred is once more trotted out to prove that Byron committed incest. There is nothing new in this 'nightmare of folly,' for Byron himself was well aware of the interpretation placed upon that poem by his contemporaries.

Manfred is certainly the revelation of deep remorse, but the crime for which he suffers had no connection with Augusta Leigh. Lord Lovelace says that 'the germ of this nightmare in blank verse *was in the actual letters of the living Astarte.*' The statement may be true; but he was certainly not in a position to prove it, for he knew not, to the last hour of his life, who the living Astarte was.

It is a sad story that should never have been told, and the present writer regrets that circumstances should have compelled him to save the reputation of one good woman by revealing matters affecting the misfortunes of another. But the blame must lie with those inconsiderate, ignorant, and prejudiced persons who, in an attempt to justify Lady Byron's conduct, cruelly assailed the memory of one who

> 'When fortune changed—and love fled far,
> And hatred's shafts flew thick and fast,'

was the solitary star which rose, and set not to the last.

On January 2, 1815, Lord and Lady Byron were married at Seaham. The little that is known of their married life may be found in letters and memoranda of people who were in actual correspondence with them, and the details which we now give from various sources are necessary to a better understanding of the causes which led to a separation between husband and wife in January, 1816.

According to a statement made by Lady Byron to her friend Lady Anne Barnard, shortly after a rumour of the separation spread in London, there never was any real love on either side. The following passages are taken from some private family memoirs written by Lady Anne herself:

'I heard of Lady Byron's distress, and entreated her to come and let me see and hear her, if she conceived my sympathy or counsel could be any comfort to her. She came, but what a tale was unfolded by this interesting young creature, who had so fondly hoped to have made [Byron] happy! They had not been an hour in the carriage . . . when Byron, breaking into a malignant sneer, said: "Oh, what a dupe you have been to your imagination! How is it possible a woman of your sense could form the wild hope of reforming *me*? Many are the tears you will have to shed ere that plan is accomplished. It is enough for me that you are my wife for me to hate you; if you were the wife of any other man, I own you might have charms," etc.

'I listened in astonishment,' writes Lady Anne. '"How could you go on after this, my dear!" said I. "Why did you not return to your father's?"

'"Because I had not a conception he was in earnest; because I reckoned it a bad jest, and told him so—that my opinion of him was very different from his of himself, otherwise he would not find me by his side. He laughed it over when he saw me appear hurt, and I forgot what had passed till forced to remember it. I believe he was pleased with me, too, for a little while. I suppose it had escaped his memory that I was his wife."

'But,' says Lady Anne, 'she described the happiness they enjoyed to have been unequal and perturbed. Her situation in a short time might have entitled her to some tenderness, but she made no claim on him for any. He sometimes reproached her for the motives that had induced her to marry him—"all was vanity, the vanity of Miss Milbanke carrying the point of reforming Lord Byron! He always knew *her* inducements; her pride shut her eyes to *his; he* wished to build up his character and his fortunes; both were somewhat deranged; she had a high name, and would have a fortune worth his attention—let her look to that for *his* motives!"

'"Oh, Byron, Byron," she said, "how you desolate me!" He would then accuse himself of being mad, and throw himself on the ground in a frenzy, which Lady Byron believed was affected to conceal the coldness and malignity of his heart—an affectation which at that time never failed to meet with the tenderest commiseration. . . . Lady Byron saw the precipice on which she stood, and kept his sister with her as much as possible. He returned in the evenings from the haunts of vice, where he made her understand he had been, with manners so profligate.

'"Oh, wretch!" said I. "And had he no moments of remorse?" "Sometimes he appeared to have them," replied Lady Byron. "One night, coming home from one of his lawless parties, he saw me so indignantly collected, bearing all with such determined calmness, that a rush of remorse seemed to come over him; he called himself a monster, though his sister was present, and threw himself in agony at my feet. He said that I could not—no, I could not forgive him such injuries. He was sure that he had lost me for ever! Astonished at the return of virtue, my tears, I believe, flowed over his face, and I said: 'Byron, all is forgotten; never, never shall you hear of it more!' He started up, and, folding his arms while he looked at me, burst into laughter. 'What do you mean?' said I. 'Only a philosophical experiment, that's all,' said he. 'I wished to ascertain the value of your resolutions.'"

'I need not say more of this prince of duplicity,' continues Lady Anne Barnard, 'except that varied were his methods of rendering her wretched, even to the last.'*

There is enough evidence in the above statement to show that a separation between Lord and Lady Byron was inevitable. Byron's temper, always capricious, became ungovernable under the vexatious exigencies of his financial affairs. Several executions had taken place in their house during the year, and it is said that even the beds upon which they slept were in the possession of the bailiffs.

It has been shown by those who knew Byron well that he was never suited to the married state. His temperament was an obstacle to happiness in marriage. He lacked the power of self-command, and the irritation produced by the shattered state of his fortune drove him at times to explosions, which were very like madness. We have an example of this in his conduct one night in Ithaca, when his companions were afraid to enter his room. Lady Byron could not meet these explosions in any effectual manner. The more fiercely he vented his exasperation, the colder she became. Lady Byron, like her husband, was a spoilt child who set her own self-will against his. If she had possessed more tact and deeper affections, she might possibly have managed him. We frankly admit that Byron's conduct during this period was not calculated to win the love and respect of any woman. During his mad moods he did his utmost to blacken his own character, and it is not surprising that Lady Byron, who had heard much of his conduct

* The responsibility for this story rests entirely with Lady Byron. Byron himself has denied it. But, when we remember the description of his feelings as portrayed in 'The Dream,' we perceive that there must have been something akin to a revulsion of feeling against the woman to whom he had bound himself for life.

before marriage, implicitly believed him. His so-called 'mystifications' were all taken seriously. She was, moreover, of a jealous nature, and Byron delighted to torment her by suggestions of immorality which had no foundation in fact. In such a character as Lady Byron's, a hint was enough to awaken the darkest suspicions, and when an impression had been stamped on her mind it was impossible to remove it. Byron, of course, fanned the flame, for he was bored to death in the bonds of wedlock, and we are inclined to believe that he did many outrageous things in order to drive his wife on the road to a separation. When the moment came he was sorry, but he certainly brought matters designedly to a crisis. His sister Augusta was much in favour of his marriage, and had strong hopes that happiness was in store for them, as the following letter will show:

'SIX MILE BOTTOM,
'*February* 15, 1815.

'MY DEAR MR. HODGSON,
   'You could not have gratified me more than by giving me an opportunity of writing on my favourite subject to one so truly worthy of it as you are; indeed, I have repeatedly wished of late that I could communicate with you. Most thankful do I feel that I have so much to say that will delight you. I have every reason to think that my beloved B. is very happy and comfortable. I hear constantly from him and *his Rib*. They are now at Seaham, and not inclined to return to Halnaby, *because* all the world were preparing to visit them there, and at Seaham they are free from this torment, no trifling one in B.'s estimation, as you know. From my own observations on their epistles, and knowledge of B.'s disposition and ways, I really hope *most* confidently that all will turn out very happily. It appears to me that Lady Byron *sets about* making him happy quite in the right way. It is true I judge at a distance, and we generally *hope* as we *wish;* but I assure you I don't conclude hastily

on this subject, and will own to you, what I would not scarcely to any other person, that I had *many fears* and much anxiety *founded upon many causes and circumstances* of which I cannot *write*. Thank God! that they do not appear likely to be realized. In short, there seems to me to be but one drawback to *all our* felicity, and that, alas! is the disposal of dear Newstead, which I am afraid is irrevocably decreed. I received the fatal communication from Lady Byron ten days ago, and will own to you that it was not only grief, but disappointment; for I flattered myself such a sacrifice would not be made. From my representations she had said and urged all she could in favour of keeping it. Mr. Hobhouse the same, and I *believe* that he was deputed to make inquiries and researches, and I knew that he wrote to B. suggesting the propriety and expediency of at least *delaying* the sale. This most excellent advice created so much disturbance in Byron's mind that Lady B. wrote me word, " He had such a fit of vexation he could not appear at dinner, or leave his room. . . ." B.'s spirits had improved at the prospect of a release from the embarrassments which interfered so much with his comfort, and I suppose I *ought* to be satisfied with this. . . . May the future bring peace and comfort to my dearest B.! that is always one of my first wishes; and I am convinced it is my duty to *endeavour* to be resigned to the loss of this dear Abbey from our family, as well as all other griefs which are sent by Him who knows what is good for us. . . . I do not know what are B.'s plans. Lady Byron says nothing can be decided upon till their affairs are in some degree arranged. They have been anxious to procure a temporary habitation in my neighbourhood, which would be convenient to him and delightful to me, if his presence is required in Town upon this sad Newstead business. But I am sorry to say I cannot hear of any likely to suit them; and our house is so *very* small, I could scarcely contrive to take them in. Lady B. is extremely kind to me, for which I am most grateful, and to my dearest B., for I am well aware how much I am indebted to his partiality and affection for her good opinion. I will not give up the hope of seeing them on their way to Town, whenever they do go, as for a few nights they would, perhaps, tolerate the innumerable inconveniences attending the best arrangements I could make for them. . . . My babes are all quite well; Medora more beautiful than ever. . . .* Lady B. writes me word she never saw her father and mother so happy: that she believes the latter would go to the bottom of the sea herself to find fish for B.'s dinner, and that Byron owns at last that he is very happy and comfortable at Seaham, though he had *predetermined* to be very miserable. In some of her letters she mentions his health not being very good, though he seldom complains, but says that his spirits have been improved by some daily walks she had prevailed on him to take; and attributes much of his languor in the morning and *feverish feels* at night to his *long fasts*, succeeded by *too* hearty meals for any weak and empty stomach to bear at one time, waking by night and sleeping by day. I flatter myself her influence will prevail over these bad habits.'

On March 18, 1815, Augusta Leigh again writes to Byron's friend, the Rev. Francis Hodgson, from Six Mile Bottom:

'B. and Lady Byron arrived here last Sunday on their way from the North to London, where they have taken a very good house of the Duke of Devonshire in Piccadilly. I hope they will stay some days longer with me, and I shall regret their departure, whenever it takes place, as much as I now delight in their society. Byron is looking remarkably well, and of Lady B. I scarcely know how to write, for I have a sad trick of being struck dumb when I am most happy and pleased. The expectations I had formed could not be *exceeded*, but at least they are fully answered.

'I think I never saw or heard or read of a more perfect being in mortal mould than she appears to be, and scarcely dared flatter myself such a one would fall to the lot of my dear B. He seems quite sensible of her value, and as happy as the present alarming state of *public* and the tormenting uncertainties of his own private affairs will admit of. Colonel Leigh is in the North.'

* The hiatus is significant. The intervening words were designedly erased by Hodgson. Medora's resemblance to Byron is mentioned in one of Augusta's letters published in 'Astarte.'

On March 31, 1815, Mrs. Leigh again writes to Hodgson:

'Byron and Lady B. left me on Tuesday for London. B. will probably write to you immediately. He talked of it while here after I received your last letter, which was the cause of *my* being silent. . . . I am sorry to say his nerves and spirits are very far from what I wish them, but don't speak of this to him on any account.

'I think the uncomfortable state of his affairs is the cause; at least, I can discern no other. He has every outward blessing this world can bestow. I trust that the Almighty will be graciously pleased to grant him those *inward* feelings of peace and calm which are now unfortunately wanting. This is a subject which I cannot dwell upon, but in which I feel and have felt all you express. I think Lady Byron very judiciously abstains from pressing the consideration of it upon him at the present moment. In short, the more I see of her the more I love and esteem her, and feel how grateful I am, and ought to be, for the blessing of such a wife for my dear, darling Byron.'

Augusta's next letter is written from 13, Piccadilly Terrace, on April 29, 1815, about three weeks after her arrival there on a visit to the Byrons. It also is addressed to Hodgson, and conveys the following message from Byron:

'I am desired to add: Lady B. is ——, and that Lord Wentworth has left all to her mother, and then to Lady Byron and children; but Byron is, *he says*, "a very miserable dog for all that."'

At the end of June, 1815, Augusta Leigh ended her visit, and returned to Six Mile Bottom. There seems to have been some unpleasantness between Augusta and Lady Byron during those ten weeks.

Two months later, on September 4, 1815, Augusta Leigh writes again to Hodgson:

'Your letter reached me at a time of much hurry and confusion, which has been succeeded by many events of an afflicting nature, and compelled me often to neglect those to whom I feel most pleasure in writing. . . . My brother has just left me, having been here since last Wednesday, when he arrived very unexpectedly. I never saw him *so* well, and he is in the best spirits, and desired me to add his congratulations to mine upon your marriage.'

On November 15, 1815, Augusta Leigh arrived at 13, Piccadilly Terrace, on a long visit.

It cannot have been a pleasant experience for Augusta Leigh, this wretched period which culminated in a dire catastrophe for all concerned. Lord Lovelace tells us that, when Mrs. Leigh came to stay with them in November, Byron 'seemed much alienated from his sister, and was entirely occupied with women at the theatre.' And yet

'*the impressions of Mrs. Leigh's guilt had been forced into Lady Byron's mind chiefly by incidents and conversations which occurred while they were all under one roof.*'

What may have given rise to these suspicions is not recorded—probably Byron's mystifications, which were all taken seriously. But there is no attempt to deny the fact that, during this painful time, Lady Byron owed deep gratitude to Mrs. Leigh, who had faithfully striven to protect her when ill and in need of sympathy. It was during this period that Lady Byron wrote the following cryptic note to Byron's sister:

'You will think me very foolish, but I have tried two or three times, and cannot *talk* to you of your departure with a decent visage; so let me say one word in this way to spare my philosophy. With the expectations which I have, I never will nor can ask you to stay one moment longer than you are inclined to do. It would be the worst return for all I ever received from you. But, in this at least, I *am* "truth itself" when I say that, whatever the situation may be,

THE BIRTH OF ADA

there is no one whose society is dearer to me, or can contribute more to my happiness. These feelings will not change under any circumstances, and I should be grieved if you did not understand them.

'Should you hereafter condemn me, I shall not love you less. I will say no more. Judge for yourself about going or staying. I wish you to consider *yourself*, if you could be wise enough to do that for the first time in your life.'

On December 10, 1815, Lady Byron gave birth to a daughter. Lord Lovelace says:

'About three weeks after Lady Byron's confinement, the aversion Byron had already at times displayed towards her struck everyone in the house as more formidable than ever. Augusta, George Byron, and Mrs. Clermont, were then all staying in the house, and were very uneasy at his unaccountable manner and talk. He assumed a more threatening aspect towards Lady Byron. There were paroxysms of frenzy, but a still stronger impression was created by the frequent hints he gave of some suppressed and bitter determination. He often spoke of his conduct and intentions about women of the theatre, particularly on January 3, 1816, when he came to Lady Byron's room and talked on that subject with considerable violence. After that he did not go any more to see her or the child, but three days later sent her the following note:

'"*January* 6, 1816.

'"When you are disposed to leave London, it would be convenient that a day should be fixed—and (if possible) not a very remote one for that purpose. Of my opinion upon that subject you are sufficiently in possession, and of the circumstances which have led to it, as also to my plans—or, rather, intentions—for the future. When in the country I will write to you more fully—as Lady Noel has asked you to Kirkby; there you can be for the present, unless you prefer Seaham.

'"As the dismissal of the present establishment is of importance to me, the sooner you can fix on the day the better—though, of course, your convenience and inclination shall be first consulted.

'" The child will, of course, accompany you : there is a more easy and safer carriage than the chariot (unless you prefer it) which I mentioned before—on that you can do as you please."'

The next day Lady Byron replied in writing as follows : 'I shall obey your wishes, and fix the earliest day that circumstances will admit for leaving London.'

Consequently she quitted London on January 15, 1816. Soon after Lady Byron's arrival at Kirkby, her mother drew from her some of the circumstances of her misery. Lady Byron then told her mother that she believed her life would be endangered by a return to her husband. She expressed an opinion that Byron was out of his mind, although he seemed competent to transact matters connected with his business affairs. Lady Noel, naturally, took her daughter's part entirely, and went to London to seek legal advice. During her stay in London, Lady Noel saw Augusta Leigh and George Byron, who agreed with her that every endeavour should be made to induce Byron to agree to a separation. She also consulted Sir Samuel Romilly, Sergeant Heywood, Dr. Lushington, and Colonel Francis Doyle, an old friend of the Milbanke family. They all agreed that a separation was necessary. It was perhaps a very natural view to take of a marriage which had run its short course so tempestuously, but there were no grounds other than incompatibility of temperament upon which to base that conclusion.

'Nothing had been said at this time,' says Lord Lovelace, 'by Lady Byron of her suspicions about Augusta, except, apparently, a few incoherent words to Lady Noel, when telling her that Lord Byron had threatened to take the child away from her and commit it to Augusta's charge.'

BYRON WISHES TO MAKE PEACE 341

Byron, says Lord Lovelace,* 'was very changeable at this time, sometimes speaking kindly of his wife—though never appearing to wish her to return—and the next hour he would say that the sooner Lady Byron's friends arranged a separation, the better.'

This statement is a fair example of the manner in which Lord Lovelace handles his facts and documents. Mr. Hobhouse, who was in a position to know the truth, has recently shown that Byron was very anxious for his wife's return, was indeed prepared to make great sacrifices to attain that object, and resolutely opposed the wishes of those persons who tried to arrange a legal separation. It was not until Lady Byron herself reminded him of a promise which he had once made to her that, 'when convinced her conduct had not been influenced by others, he should not oppose her wishes,' that he consented to sign the deed of separation. He had done enough to show that he was not afraid of any exposure which might have affected his honour, and was willing, if necessary, to go into a court of law, but he could not resist the petition of his wife.† It is also extremely improbable that Byron should, 'towards the end of January, have spoken of proposing a separation himself,' in view of the letters which he wrote to his wife on February 5, and February 8 following.‡

On February 2 Sir Ralph Noel, under legal advice, wrote a stiff letter requiring a separation. Byron at that time positively refused to accept these terms. The whole affair then became publicly known. Every kind of report was spread about him, and especially

* 'Astarte,' p. 137.
† 'Recollections of a Long Life,' by Lord Broughton, vol. ii., p. 297.
‡ *Ibid.*, vol. ii., pp. 219, 239.

the scandal about Augusta was noised abroad by Lady Caroline Lamb and Mr. Brougham. There can be no doubt whatever that Byron heard of this report, and paid very little attention to it. He found out then, or soon afterwards, how the scandal arose.

Lady Byron's relations were bent on arranging an amicable separation. Should Byron persist in his refusal, it was intended to institute a suit in the Ecclesiastical Court to obtain a divorce on the plea of adultery and cruelty. There is reason to believe that a charge of adultery could *not* have been substantiated at that time.

Meanwhile, Lady Byron, who had lately acquired some documents, which were unknown to her when she left her husband on January 15,* came to London on February 22, and had a long private conversation with Dr. Lushington. She then showed him two packets of letters which Mrs. Clermont had abstracted from Byron's writing-desk. Lady Byron received those letters some time between February 14 and 22, 1816. One packet contained missives from a married lady, with whom Byron had been intimate previous to his marriage. It appears that Lady Byron — whose notions of the ordinary code of honour were peculiar—sent those letters to that lady's husband, who, like a sensible man, threw them into the fire. Of the other packet we cannot speak so positively. It probably comprised letters from Augusta Leigh, referring to the child Medora.† Such expres-

---

* 'Lady Byron said that she founded her determination [to part from her husband] on some communication from London.'—' Recollections of a Long Life,' vol. ii., p. 255.

† There is reason to believe that Lord Chief Justice Cockburn, in 1869, privately saw letters, written by Augusta in 1813 and 1814, which did not convince him that incest had been committed.

sions as 'our child' or 'your child' would have fallen quite naturally from her pen under the circumstances. It is easy to imagine the effect of some such words upon the suspicious mind of Lady Byron. By Mrs. Clermont's masterful stroke of treachery, strong presumptive evidence was thus brought against Augusta Leigh. The letters undoubtedly convinced Dr. Lushington that incest had taken place, and he warned Lady Byron against any personal intercourse with Mrs. Leigh. He at the same time advised her to keep her lips closed until Augusta had of her own free will confessed; and pointed out to Lady Byron that, 'while proofs and impressions were such as left no doubt on *her* mind, *they were decidedly not such as could have been brought forward to establish a charge of incest, in the event of Lady Byron being challenged to bring forward the grounds of her imputation.*'*

From that moment all Lady Byron's wiles were employed to extract a confession from Augusta Leigh, which would have gone far to justify Lady Byron's conduct in leaving her husband. Soon after this momentous interview with Dr. Lushington, an ugly rumour was spread about town affecting Mrs. Leigh's character.

Lord Lovelace says:

'When Augusta's friends vehemently and indignantly resented such a calumny, they were met with the argument that *Lady Byron's refusal to assign a reason for her separation confirmed the report*, and that no one but Augusta could deny it with any effect.'

This, by the nature of her agreement with Byron, was impossible, and Mrs. Clermont's treachery held her in a vice.

* 'Astarte,' p. 77.

During January and February, 1816, Lady Byron, who strongly suspected Mrs. Leigh's conduct to have been disloyal to herself, wrote the most affectionate letters to that lady.

'KIRKBY MALLORY.

'MY DEAREST A.,
 'It is my great comfort that you are in Piccadilly.'

'KIRKBY MALLORY,
'*January* 23, 1816.

'DEAREST A.,
 'I know you feel for me as I do for you, and perhaps I am better understood than I think. You have been, ever since I knew you, my best comforter, and will so remain, unless you grow tired of the office, which may well be.'

'*January* 25, 1816.

'MY DEAREST AUGUSTA,
 'Shall I still be your sister? I must resign my rights to be so considered; but I don't think that will make any difference in the kindness I have so uniformly experienced from you.'

'KIRKBY MALLORY,
'*February* 3, 1816.

'MY DEAREST AUGUSTA,
 'You are desired by your brother to ask if my father has acted with my concurrence in proposing a separation. He has. It cannot be supposed that, in my present distressing situation, I am capable of stating, in a detailed manner, the reasons which will not only justify this measure, but compel me to take it; and it never can be my wish to remember unnecessarily those injuries for which, however deep, I feel no resentment. I will now only recall to Lord Byron's mind his avowed and insurmountable aversion to the married state, and the desire and determination he has expressed ever since its commencement to free himself from that bondage, as finding it quite insupportable, though candidly acknowledging that no effort of duty or affection has been wanting on my part. He has too painfully convinced me that all

these attempts to contribute towards his happiness were wholly useless, and most unwelcome to him. I enclose this letter to my father, wishing it to receive his sanction.
'Ever yours most affectionately,
'A. I. BYRON.'

'*February* 4, 1816.

'I hope, my dear A., that you would on no account withhold from your brother the letter which I sent yesterday, in answer to yours written by his desire; particularly as one which I have received from himself to-day renders it still more important that he should know the contents of that addressed to you. I am, in haste and not very well,
'Yours most affectionately,
'A. I. BYRON.'

'KIRKBY MALLORY,
'*February* 14, 1816.

'The present sufferings of all may yet be repaid in blessings. Do not despair absolutely, dearest; and leave me but enough of your interest to afford you any consolation, by partaking of that sorrow which I am most unhappy to cause thus unintentionally.

'*You will* be of my opinion hereafter, and at present your bitterest reproach would be forgiven; though Heaven knows you have considered me more than a thousand would have done—more than anything but my affection for B., one most dear to you, could deserve. I must not remember these feelings. Farewell! God bless you, from the bottom of my heart.
'A. I. B.'

It is only fair to remind the reader that, when these letters were written, Lady Byron had not consulted Dr. Lushington. We are inclined to think that the last letter was written on the day when she received Mrs. Clermont's 'proofs.' Meanwhile, Augusta, unconscious that an avalanche of scandal threatened to sweep her reputation into an abyss, was catching at every straw that might avert a catastrophe. Her thoughts turned to Hodgson, whose noble character, sound common-sense, and affection for Byron, were undoubted. It was possible, she thought, that the ruin and destruction which she dreaded for her brother might be averted through the advice and assistance of an honourable man of the world. In that wild hope the following letters were written:

'13, PICCADILLY TERRACE,
'*Wednesday, February* 7, 1816.

'DEAR MR. HODGSON,

'Can you by *any means* contrive to come up to Town? Were it only for *a day*, it might be of the most essential service to a friend I know you love and value. There is too much fear of a separation between him and his wife. No time is to be lost, but even if you are *too late* to prevent that happening *decidedly*, yet it would be the greatest comfort and relief to me to confide other circumstances to you, and consult you; and so if *possible* oblige me, if only for *twenty-four* hours. Say not *a word* of my summons, but attribute your coming, if you come, to business of your own or chance. Excuse brevity; I am so perfectly wretched I can only say,

'Ever yours most truly,
'AUGUSTA LEIGH.

'It is probable I may be obliged to go home next week. If my scheme appears wild, pray attribute it to the state of mind I am in. Alas! I see only *ruin* and *destruction* in *every* shape to one most dear to me.'

Hodgson at once responded to this appeal by taking the first stage-coach to London, where the next letter was addressed to him at his lodgings near Piccadilly:

'How very good of you, dear Mr. Hodgson! I intend showing the letter to B., as I *think* he will jump at seeing you just now, but I *must* see you first;

and how? I am now going to Mr. Hanson's from B. I'm afraid of your meeting people here who *do no good*, and would counteract yours; but will you call about two, or after that, and ask for *me* first? I shall be home, I hope, and *must* see you. If I'm out ask for Capt. B.

'Yours sincerely,
'A. L.'

'*Friday evening,* 9 *o'clock.*

'DEAR MR. HODGSON,
    'I've been unable to write to you till this moment. Mr. H.* stayed till a late hour, and is now here again. B. dined with me, and after I left the room I sent your note in, thinking him in better spirits and more free from irritations. He has only just mentioned it to me: "Oh, by-the-by, I've had a note from H., Augusta, whom you must write to, and say I'm so full of domestic calamities that I can't see anybody." Still, I think he *will* see you if he hears you are here, or that even it would be better, if the worst came to the worst, to let the servant announce you and walk in. Can you call here about eleven to-morrow morning, when he will not be up, or scarcely awake, and Capt. B., you, and I, can hold a council on what is best to be done? The fact is, he is now *afraid* of everybody who would tell him the truth. It is a most dreadful situation, dear Mr. H.! The worst is, that *if* you said you have done so-and-so, etc., he would deny it; and I see he is afraid of *your despair*, as he terms it, when you hear of his situation, and, in short, of your telling him the truth. He can only bear to see those who flatter him and encourage him to all that is wrong. I've not mentioned having seen you, because I wish him to suppose your opinions unprejudiced. You *must* see him; and pray see me and George B. to-morrow morning, when we will consult upon the best means. You are the only comfort I've had this long time. I'm quite of your opinion on all that is to be feared.

'Ever yours truly,
'A. L.'

* Hanson.

'PICCADILLY TERRACE.

'DEAR MR. H.,

'About three you will be sure of finding me, if not sooner. I've sent in your letter; he said in return I was to do what I pleased about it. I *think* and *hope* he will find comfort in seeing you.

'Yours truly,
'A. L.'

'*Saturday.*

'DEAR MR. H.,

'B. will see you. I saw him open your note, and said I had given his message this morning, when I had seen you and talked generally on the subject of his present situation, of which you had before heard. He replied, "Oh, then, tell him I will see him, certainly; my reason for *not* was the fear of distressing him." You had better call towards three, and wait if he is not yet out of his room. Mr. Hanson has sent for me in consequence (probably) of your interview. I'm going to him about three with Capt. B., but have said nothing to B. of this.

'Ever yours,
'A. L.'

Immediately after the interview, which took place on the day after the last note was written, Hodgson, feeling that nothing could be lost and that much might be gained by judicious remonstrance, resolved to hazard an appeal to Lady Byron's feelings—with what success will be seen from her ladyship's reply. It is impossible to over-estimate the combined tact and zeal displayed by Hodgson in this most delicate and difficult matter.

'Whether I am outstepping the bounds of prudence in this address to your ladyship I cannot feel assured; and yet there is so much at stake in a quarter so loved and valuable that I cannot forbear running the risk, and making one effort more to plead a cause which your ladyship's own heart must plead with a power so superior to all other voices. If, then, a word that is here said only adds to the pain of this unhappy conflict between affection and views of duty, without lending any weight of reason to the object it seeks, I would earnestly implore that it may be forgiven; and, above all, the interference itself, which nothing but its obvious motive and the present awful circumstance could in any way justify.

'After a long and most confidential conversation with my friend (whom I have known thoroughly, I believe, for many trying years), I am convinced that the deep and rooted feeling in his heart is regret and sorrow for the occurrences which have so deeply wounded you; and the most unmixed admiration of your conduct in all its particulars, and the warmest affection. But may I be allowed to state to Lady Byron that Lord B., after his general acknowledgment of having frequently been very wrong, and, from various causes, in a painful state of irritation, yet declares himself ignorant of the specific things which have given the principal offence, and that he wishes to hear of them; that he may, if extenuation or atonement be possible, endeavour to make some reply; or, at all events, may understand the fulness of those reasons which have now, and as unexpectedly as afflictingly, driven your ladyship to the step you have taken?

'It would be waste of words and idle presumption for me, however your ladyship's goodness might be led to excuse it, to observe how very extreme, how decidedly irreconcilable, such a case should be, before the last measure is resorted to. But it may not be quite so improper to urge, from my deep conviction of their truth and importance, the following reflections. I entreat your ladyship's indulgence to them. What can be the consequence, to a man so peculiarly constituted, of such an event? If I may give vent to my fear, my thorough certainty, nothing short of absolute and utter destruction. I turn from the idea; but *no* being except your ladyship can prevent this. *None*, I am thoroughly convinced, ever could have done so, notwithstanding the unhappy appearances to the contrary. Whatever, then, may be against it, whatever restraining remembrances or anticipations, to a person who was not already qualified by sad experience to teach this very truth, I would say that there *is* a claim paramount to all others—that of attempting to save the human beings nearest and dearest to us from the most comprehensive ruin that can be suffered by them, at the expense of any suffering to ourselves.

'If I have not gone too far, I would add that so suddenly and at once to shut every avenue to returning comfort must, when looked back upon, appear a strong measure; and, if it proceeds (pray pardon the suggestion) from the unfortunate notion of the very person to whom my friend now looks for consolation being unable to administer it, that notion I would combat with all the energy of conviction; and assert, that whatever unguarded and unjustifiable words, and even actions, may have inculcated this idea, it is the very rock on which the peace of both would, as unnecessarily as wretchedly, be sacrificed. But God Almighty forbid that there should be any sacrifice. Be all that is right called out into action, all that is wrong suppressed (and by your only instrumentality, Lady Byron, as by yours only it can be) in my dear friend. May you both yet be what God intended you for: the support, the watchful correction, and improvement, of each other! Of yourself, Lord B. from his heart declares that he would wish nothing altered—nothing but that sudden, surely sudden, determination which must *for ever* destroy one of you, and perhaps even both. God bless both!

'I am, with deep regard,
'Your ladyship's faithful servant,
'Francis Hodgson.'

Lady Byron's answer was as follows:

'Kirkby,
'*February* 15, 1816.

'Dear Sir,
'I feel most sensibly the kindness of a remonstrance which equally proves your friendship for Lord Byron and consideration for me. I have declined all discussion of this subject with others, but my knowledge of your principles induces me to justify my own;

and yet I would forbear to accuse as much as possible.

'I married Lord B. determined to endure everything whilst there was *any* chance of my contributing to his welfare. I remained with him under trials of the severest nature. In leaving him, which, however, I can scarcely call a *voluntary* measure, I probably saved him from the bitterest remorse. I may give you a general idea of what I have experienced by saying that he married me with the deepest determination of Revenge, avowed on the day of my marriage, and executed ever since with systematic and increasing cruelty, which no affection could change. . . . My security depended on the total abandonment of every moral and religious principle, against which (though I trust they were never obtruded) his hatred and endeavours were uniformly directed. . . . The circumstances, which are of too convincing a nature, shall not be generally known whilst Lord B. allows me to spare him. It is not unkindness that can always change affection.

'With you I may consider this subject in a less worldly point of view. Is the present injury to his reputation to be put in competition with the danger of unchecked success to this wicked pride? and may not his actual sufferings (in which, be assured, that affection for me has very little share) expiate a future account? I know him too well to dread the fatal event which he so often mysteriously threatens. I have acquired my knowledge of him bitterly indeed, and it was long before I learned to mistrust the apparent candour by which he deceives all but himself. He *does* know—too well—what he affects to inquire. You reason with me as I have reasoned with myself, and I therefore derive from your letter an additional and melancholy confidence in the rectitude of this determination, which has been deliberated on the grounds that you would approve. It was not suggested, and has not been enforced, by others; though it is sanctioned by my parents.

'You will continue Lord Byron's friend, and the time may yet come when he will receive from that friendship such benefits as he now rejects. I will even indulge the consolatory thought that the remembrance of me, when time has softened the irritation created by my presence, may contribute to the same end. May I hope that you will still retain any value for the regard with which I am,

'Your most obliged and faithful servant,
'A. I. BYRON.'

'I must add that Lord Byron had been fully, earnestly, and affectionately warned of the unhappy consequences of his conduct.'

It is most unfortunate that the second letter which Hodgson wrote on this most distressing occasion is lost, but some clue to its contents may be gathered from Lady Byron's reply:

'*February* 24, 1816.

'DEAR SIR,
'I have received your second letter. First let me thank you for the charity with which you consider my motives; and now of the principal subject.
'I eagerly adopted the belief on insanity as a consolation; and though such malady has been found insufficient to prevent his responsibility with man, I will still trust that it may latently exist, so as to acquit him towards God. This no human being can judge. It certainly does not destroy the powers of self-control, or impair the knowledge of moral good and evil. Considering the case upon the supposition of derangement, you may have heard, what every medical adviser would confirm, that it is in the nature of such malady to reverse the affections, and to make those who would naturally be dearest, the greatest objects of aversion, the most exposed to acts of violence, and the least capable of alleviating the malady. Upon such grounds my absence from Lord B. was medically advised before I left Town. But the advisers had not then seen him, and since Mr. Le Mann has had opportunities of personal observation, it has been found that the supposed physical causes do not exist so as to render him not an accountable agent.
'I believe the nature of Lord B.'s mind to be most benevolent. But there may have been circumstances

A FRAIL SECURITY

(I would hope the *consequences*, not the *causes*, of mental disorder) which would render an original tenderness of conscience the motive of desperation—even of guilt—when self-esteem had been forfeited *too far*. No *external* motive can be so strong. Goodness of heart—when there are impetuous passions and no principles—is a frail security.

'Every possible means have been employed to effect a private and amicable arrangement; and I would sacrifice such advantages in terms as, I believe, the law would insure to me, to avoid this dreadful necessity. Yet I must have some *security*, and Lord B. refuses to afford any. If you could persuade him to the agreement, you would save me from what I most deprecate. I have now applied to Lord Holland for that end.

'If you wish to answer—and I shall always be happy to hear from you—I must request you to enclose your letter to my father, Sir Ralph Noel, Mivart's Hotel, Lower Brook Street, London, as I am not sure where I may be at that time. My considerations of duty are of a very complicated nature; for my duty as a mother seems to point out the same conduct as I pursue upon other principles that I have partly explained.

'I must observe upon one passage of your letter that I *had* (*sic*) expectations of personal violence, though I was too miserable to have *feelings* of fear, and those expectations would now be still stronger.

'In regard to any change which the future state of Lord B.'s mind might justify in my intentions, an amicable arrangement would not destroy the opening for reconciliation. Pray endeavour to promote the dispositions to such an arrangement; there is every reason to desire it.

'Yours very truly,
'A. I. BYRON.'

It is worthy of note that Lady Byron, *two days after her interview with Lushington,* here states that, in the event of 'an amicable arrangement' (an amicable separation) being arrived at, it would not destroy the opening for reconciliation. This is an extraordinary statement, because, as we have seen, Dr. Lushington absolutely declined to be a party to any such step. On March 14 Lady Byron signed a declaration, giving her reasons for the separation, as will be seen presently.

On March 16 Augusta Leigh returned to her apartments in St. James's Palace, and on the following day Byron consented to a separation from his wife. On April 8 Lady Jersey gave a party in honour of Byron, and to show her sympathy for him in his matrimonial troubles. Both Byron and Augusta were present, but it was a cold and spiritless affair, and nothing came of this attempt to stem the tide of prejudice.

On April 14 Augusta parted for ever from her brother, and retired into the country, her health broken down by the worry and anxiety of the past three months. On April 21 and 22, 1816, the deed of separation was signed by both Lord and Lady Byron. On April 23 Byron left London, and travelled to Dover accompanied by his friends Hobhouse and Scrope-Davies. On the 25th he embarked for Ostend, unable to face the consequences of his quarrel with his wife.

'To his susceptible temperament and generous feelings,' says his schoolfellow Harness, 'the reproach of having ill-used a woman must have been poignant in the extreme. It was repulsive to his chivalrous character as a gentleman; it belied all he had written of the devoted fervour of his attachments; and rather than meet the frowns and sneers which awaited him in the world, as many a less sensitive man might have done, he turned his back on them and fled.'

CHAPTER III

THE publication of 'Astarte' has had one good result; it has placed beyond question the precise nature of Lady Byron's complaints against her husband. On March 14, 1816, Lady Byron was induced by Dr. Lushington to draw up and sign a statement which would be useful if her conduct should at any future time be criticized.

We place the entire document before the reader, just as it appears in Lord Lovelace's book:

'STATEMENT.—A. L.

'In case of my death to be given to Colonel Doyle.
A. I. BYRON,
Thursday, March 14, 1816.'

'During the year that Lady Byron lived under the same roof with Lord B. certain circumstances occurred, and some intimations were made, which excited a suspicion in Lady B.'s mind that an improper connection had at one time, and might even still, subsist between Lord B. and Mrs. L——.* The causes, however, of this suspicion did not amount to proof, and Lady Byron did not consider herself justified in acting upon these suspicions by immediately quitting Lord B.'s house, for the following reasons:

'First and principally, because the causes of suspicion, though they made a strong impression upon her mind,

* Leigh.

did not amount to positive proof, and Lady B. considered, that whilst a possibility of innocence existed, every principle of duty and humanity forbad her to act as if Mrs. Leigh was actually guilty, more especially as any intimation of so heinous a crime, even if not distinctly proved, must have seriously affected Mrs. L.'s character and happiness.

'Secondly, Lady B. had it not in her power to pursue a middle course; it was utterly impossible for her to remove Mrs. L. from the society and roof of Lord B. except by a direct accusation.

'Thirdly, because Mrs. L. had from her first acquaintance with Lady B. always manifested towards her the utmost kindness and attention, endeavouring as far as laid in her power to mitigate the violence and cruelty of Lord B.

'Fourthly, because Mrs. L. at times exhibited signs of a deep remorse; at least so Lady B. interpreted them to be, though she does not mean to aver that the feelings Mrs. L. then showed were signs of remorse for the commission of the crime alluded to, or any other of so dark a description.

'And, lastly, because Lady B. conceived it possible that the crime, if committed, might not only be deeply repented of, but never have been perpetrated since her marriage with Lord B.

'It was from these motives, and strongly inclining to a charitable interpretation of all that passed, that Lady B. never during her living with Lord B. intimated a suspicion of this nature. Since Lady B.'s separation from Lord B. the report has become current in the world of such a connection having subsisted. This report was not spread nor sanctioned by Lady B. Mrs. L.'s character has, however, been to some extent affected thereby. Lady B. cannot divest her mind of the impressions before stated; but anxious to avoid all possibility of doing injury to Mrs. L., and not by any conduct of her own to throw any suspicion upon Mrs. L., and it being intimated that Mrs. L.'s character can never be so effectually preserved as by a renewal of intercourse with Lady B., she does for the motives and reasons before mentioned consent to renew that intercourse.

'Now, this statement is made in order to justify

Lady B. in the line of conduct she has now determined to adopt, and in order to prevent all misconstruction of her motives in case Mrs. L. should be proved hereafter to be guilty; and, if any circumstances should compel or render it necessary for Lady B. to prefer the charge, in order that Lady B. may be at full liberty so to do without being prejudiced by her present conduct.

'It is to be observed that this paper does not contain nor pretends to contain any of the grounds which gave rise to the suspicion which has existed and still continues to exist in Lady B.'s mind.

'We whose names are hereunto subscribed are of opinion, that under all the circumstances above stated, and also from our knowledge of what has passed respecting the conduct of all parties mentioned, that the line now adopted by Lady B. is strictly right and honourable, as well as just towards Mrs. L., and Lady B. ought not, whatever may hereafter occur, to be prejudiced thereby.

'ROBT. JOHN WILMOT.
F. H. DOYLE.
STEPHEN LUSHINGTON.
(*Signed by each.*)

'LONDON,
    March 14, 1816.'

One month later, on April 14, Byron writes a letter to his wife, who was staying at an hotel in London, in which he says that he has just parted from Augusta:

'Almost the last being you had left me to part with, and the only unshattered tie of my existence. . . . If any accident occurs to me—be kind to *her*,—if she is then nothing—to her children. Some time ago I informed you that, with the knowledge that any child of ours was already provided for by other and better means, I had made my will in favour of her and her children—as prior to my marriage; this was not done in prejudice to you, for we had not then differed—and even this is useless during your life by the settlements. I say, therefore, be kind to her and hers, for never has she acted or spoken otherwise towards you. She has ever been your friend; this may seem valueless to one who has now so many. Be kind to her, however, and recollect that, though it may be an advantage to you to have lost your husband, it is sorrow to her to have the waters now, or the earth hereafter, between her and her brother. She is gone. I need hardly add that of this request she knows nothing.'

There are two points in this letter which deserve notice. In the first place Byron intimates that he has made a will in favour of Augusta and *her children, as prior to his marriage*. This would insure that Medora would be amply provided for. In addition to this, Byron had already given his sister £3,000 in May, 1814, within one month of Medora's birth. In reply to her scruples, Byron writes: 'Consider the children, and my Georgina in particular—in short, I need say no more.'

In the second place, we appeal to any unprejudiced person whether it is likely that Byron would have made to his wife an especial appeal on behalf of Augusta, if he had not had a clear conscience as to his relations with her? That he had a clear conscience cannot be doubted, and Augusta never hesitated in private intercourse with Lady Byron to speak on that painful subject. To quote Lord Lovelace:

'On all these occasions, one subject, uppermost in the thoughts of both, had been virtually ignored, except that Augusta had had the audacity to name the reports about herself "with the pride of innocence," as it is called.'

Augusta tried to make Lady Byron speak out, and say that she did not believe the reports against her, but in vain. Lady Byron, having once conceived a notion of Augusta's guilt, would not change her opinion, and was far too honest to dissemble. She found refuge in flight, not daring to show to Augusta the letters which had been abstracted from Byron's desk by Mrs. Clermont. In vain Mrs. Villiers and Wilmot urged Lady Byron to avow to Augusta the information of which they were in possession. Lady Byron would not produce her so-called 'proofs,' and said that 'she would experience pain in throwing off a person she had loved, and from whom she had received kindness.'

But eventually Lady Byron, conscious of her false position, had recourse to her pen, and wrote a letter to Augusta telling her all that she knew. We are told that Augusta did not attempt to deny the accusation, and admitted everything in her letters of June, July, and August, 1816.

Lord Lovelace coolly says:

'It is unnecessary to produce these letters here, as their contents are confirmed and made sufficiently clear by the correspondence of 1819, given in another chapter.'

We are further told in a footnote (p. 155) that the late Sir Leslie Stephen said it made him quite uncomfortable to read Mrs. Leigh's letters of humiliation dated 1816. One would have supposed, after such a flourish of trumpets, that Lord Lovelace would have produced those letters! He does nothing of the kind, and expects posterity to accept his *ex-parte* statements without reserve. Lord Lovelace bids us to believe that it was 'from the best and kindest motives, and long habit of silence, that Dr. Lushington's influence was exerted in 1869, to prevent, or at least postpone, revelation.' The fact is, of course, he kept silence because he well knew that there was nothing in those letters* (1813 and 1814) to fix guilt upon Mrs. Leigh.

* See *ante*, p. 342.

Lady Byron herself has told us that 'the causes of her suspicion *did not amount to proof*, and Lady Byron did not consider herself justified in acting upon these suspicions.' She further states that '*the possibility of innocence existed*,' but that

'Mrs. Leigh, at times, exhibited signs of deep remorse; *at least so Lady Byron interpreted them to be*, though she does not mean to aver that the feelings Mrs. Leigh then showed were signs of remorse for the commission of the crime alluded to, or any other of so dark a description.'

But Lady Byron, under Lushington's skilful hand, protects herself against the possibility of legal proceedings for defamation of character by these words:

'This paper does not contain, nor pretend to contain, any of the grounds which give rise *to the suspicion* which has existed, and still continues to exist, in Lady Byron's mind. Her statement is made in order to justify Lady Byron . . . *in case Mrs. Leigh should be proved hereafter to be guilty.*'

As this statement was made after Lady Byron's interview with Dr. Lushington (when he decided to take no part in any attempt at reconciliation), it is perfectly clear that the alleged incriminating letters were not considered as conclusive evidence against Mrs. Leigh. Although they were sufficient to detach Lushington from the party of reconciliation, it was not considered wise to produce them as evidence in 1869, at a time when a strong revulsion of feeling had set in against Lady Byron.

The clear legal brain of Sir Alexander Cockburn, trained to appraise evidence, saw through the flimsy pretext which had deceived an equally great lawyer. Time instructs us, and much has come to light in this so-called 'Byron mystery,' since Lady Byron beguiled Lushington. Among other things, we now know, on Lord Lovelace's authority, that Lady Byron was afraid that her child would be taken from her by Byron, and placed under the care of Mrs. Leigh. We also know, on the authority of Hobhouse,* that Lady Byron's representatives distinctly disavowed, on Lady Byron's behalf, having spread any rumours injurious to Lord Byron's character in that respect, and also stated that a charge of incest would not have been made part of her allegations if she had come into court. This disavowal was signed by Lady Byron herself, and was witnessed by Mr. Wilmot. It is certain that Lord Byron would have gone into a court of law to meet that charge, and that he refused to agree to a separation until that assurance had been given. This grave charge was still in abeyance in 1816; it was not safe to speak of it until after Byron's death, and then only under the seal of secrecy.

'Upon one contingency only,' wrote Sir Francis Doyle in 1830—'namely, the taking from Lady Byron of her child, and placing her under the care of Mrs. Leigh—would the disclosure have been made of Lady Byron's grounds for *suspecting* Mrs. Leigh's guilt.'†

It was evident that Lady Byron was clutching at straws to save her child from Mrs. Leigh, and to prevent this it was essential to prove Mrs. Leigh's unworthiness. In her maternal anxiety she stuck at nothing, and for a time she triumphed. Her private correspondence was drenched with the theme that had impressed Lushington so strongly.

A fortnight after signing her 'statement,' Lady

* 'Recollections of a Long Life,' vol. ii., p. 303.
† 'Astarte,' p. 145.

Byron writes to Mrs. George Lamb, in reference to Mrs. Leigh:

'I am glad that you think of *her* with the feelings of pity which prevail in my mind, and surely if in *mine* there must be some cause for them. I never was, nor ever can be, so *mercilessly* virtuous as to admit *no* excuse for even the worst of errors.'

Such letters go perilously near that charge which Lady Byron's representatives had repudiated in the presence of Hobhouse. But Lady Byron was desperate, and her whole case depended on a general belief in that foul accusation. What could not be done openly could be done secretly, and she poisoned the air to save her child.

Colonel Doyle, who seems to have been one of the few on Lady Byron's side who kept his head, wrote to her on July 9, 1816:*

'I see the possibility of a contingency under which the fullest explanation of the motives and grounds of your conduct may be necessary; I therefore implore of you to suffer no delicacy to interfere with your endeavouring to obtain the fullest *admission* of the fact. If you obtain an acknowledgment of the facts and that your motives be, as you seem to think, properly appreciated, I think on the whole we shall have reason to rejoice that you have acted as you have done, but I shall be very anxious to have a more detailed knowledge of what has passed, and particularly of the state in which you leave it. The step you have taken was attended with great risk, and I could not, contemplating the danger to which it might have exposed you, have originally advised it.

'If, however, your correspondence has produced an acknowledgment of the fact even previous to your marriage, I shall be most happy that it has taken place.'

Colonel Doyle, by no means easy in his own mind, again writes to Lady Byron on July 18, 1816:†

* 'Astarte,' p. 156. † *Ibid.*

ATTEMPT TO INVEIGLE AUGUSTA

'I must recommend you to act as if a time might possibly arise when it would be necessary for you to justify yourself, though nothing short of an absolute necessity so imperative as to be irresistible could ever authorize your advertence to your present communications. Still, I cannot dismiss from my mind the experience we have had, nor so far forget the very serious embarrassment we were under from the effects of your too confiding disposition, as not to implore you to bear in mind the importance of securing yourself from eventual danger.

'This is my first object, and if that be attained, I shall approve and applaud all the kindness you can show [to Mrs. Leigh].'

Here, then, we have a picture of the state of affairs limned by a man who was an accomplice of Lady Byron's, and who was fully awake to the danger of their position in the event of Byron turning round upon them. The husband might insist upon Lady Byron explaining the grounds of her conduct. In order to make their position secure, it would be, above all things, necessary to obtain a full confession from Mrs. Leigh of her criminal intercourse with Byron. With this end in view, Lady Byron opened a correspondence with Augusta Leigh, and tried to inveigle her into making an admission of her guilt. It was not an easy matter to open the subject, but Lady Byron was not abashed, and, under cover of sundry acts of kindness, tried hard to gain her point. In this game of foils Augusta showed remarkable skill, and seems to have eventually fooled Lady Byron to the top of her bent. No wonder, then, that Mrs. Leigh, accused of an abominable crime by her sister-in-law, should have written to a friend:

'None can know *how much* I have suffered from this unhappy business—and, indeed, I have never known a moment's peace, and begin to despair for the future.'

Lady Byron and her friends plied Mrs. Leigh with questions, hoping to gain a confession which would justify their conduct. Lady Noel strongly and repeatedly warned Lady Byron against Mrs. Leigh, who, like a wounded animal, was dangerous. 'Take care of Augusta,' she wrote September 7, 1816. 'If I know anything of human nature, she *does* and must *hate you.*'

As a matter of fact, Augusta, while pretending contrition for imaginary sins,* revenged herself upon Lady Byron by heightening her jealousy, and encouraging her in the belief that Byron had not only been her lover, but was still appealing to her from abroad. She even went so far as to pretend that she was going to join him, which nearly frightened Mrs. Villiers out of her wits. They lied to Augusta profusely, these immaculate people, and had the meanness to tell her that Byron had betrayed her in writing to two or three women. They probably wished to cause a breach between brother and sister, but Augusta, who pretended to be alarmed by this intelligence, laughed in her sleeve. She knew the truth, and saw through these manœuvres; it was part of her plan to keep Lady Byron on a false scent. 'I cannot believe my brother to have been so dishonourable,' was her meek rejoinder, meaning, of course, that it would have been dishonourable for Byron to have defamed one who, having taken his child under her protection, had saved the honour of the woman whom he loved. But Lady Byron regarded Mrs. Leigh's answer as an admission of guilt, and trumpeted the news to all her friends. Lord Lovelace tells us that Augusta, on August 5, 1816, wrote to Lady Byron a letter, in which she asserted most solemnly that Byron had not been her

---

* 'Astarte,' p. 164.

'A MOST WRETCHED BUSINESS'

friend, and that, though there were difficulties in writing to him, she was determined never to see him again in the way she had done. It is remarkable that the letter to which Lord Lovelace refers is not given in 'Astarte,' where one would naturally expect to find it. In order to gauge the impression made upon Augusta's mind, the reader will do well to consult the letters which she wrote a little later to the Rev. Francis Hodgson, in which she speaks of Byron with the greatest affection.

'And now for our old subject, dear B. I wonder whether you have heard from him? The last to me was from Geneva, sending me a short but most interesting journal of an excursion to the Bernese Alps. He speaks of his health as *very* good, but, alas! his spirits appear wofully the contrary. I believe, however, that he does not write in that strain to others. Sometimes I venture to indulge a hope that what I wish most earnestly for him may be working its way in his mind. Heaven grant it!'

In another letter to Hodgson she speaks of Ada, and says:

'The bulletins of the poor child's health, by Byron's desire, pass through me, and I'm very sorry for it, and that I ever had any concern in this most wretched business. I can't, however, explain all my reasons at this distance, and must console myself by the consciousness of having done my duty, and, to the best of my judgment, all I could for the happiness of *both*.'

At a time when Byron was accused of having 'betrayed his sister in writing to two or three women, he was writing that well-known stanza in 'Childe Harold':

> 'But there was one soft breast, as hath been said,
> Which unto his was bound by stronger ties
> Than the Church links withal; and though unwed,
> Yet it was pure—and, far above disguise,

> Had stood the test of mortal enmities
> Still undivided, and cemented more
> By peril, dreaded most in female eyes;
> But this was firm, and from a foreign shore
> Well to that heart might his these absent greetings pour.'

And it was in July, 1816, that Augusta's loyalty to him and to Mary Chaworth moved Byron to write his celebrated 'Stanzas to Augusta':

> '*Though thy soul with my grief was acquainted,*
> It shrunk not to share it with me,
> And the Love which my spirit hath painted
> It never hath found but in *Thee*.'

> 'Though human, thou didst not *betray* me;
> Though tempted, thou never couldst shake.'

Lord Lovelace claims to have found the key of the Byron mystery in 'Manfred,' and employs it as a damning proof against Augusta, with what justice we have seen.

At the time when 'Manfred' was begun Mary Chaworth was temporarily insane. The anxiety which she had undergone at the time of Byron's matrimonial quarrels, when she feared that a public inquiry might disclose her own secret, affected her health. She bore up bravely until after Byron's departure from England; then, the strain relieved, her mind gave way, and she lived for some time in London, under the care of a doctor. Her illness was kept as secret as possible, but Augusta, who was constantly at her side, informed Byron of her condition.

CHAPTER IV

THERE has of late years been a disposition on the part of Byron's biographers unduly to disparage Moore's 'Life of Byron.' Tastes have changed, and Moore's patronizing style of reference to 'his noble friend the noble poet' does not appeal to the democratic sentiment now prevailing. But, after allowance has been made for Moore's manner, it cannot be denied that, in consequence of his personal intimacy with Byron, his work must always have a peculiar value and authority. There are, for instance, portions of Moore's 'Life' which are indispensable to those who seek to fathom the depths of Byron's mind. Moore says that Byron was born with strong affections and ardent passions, and that his life was

'one continued struggle between that instinct of genius, which was for ever drawing him back into the lonely laboratory of self, and those impulses of passion, ambition, and vanity, which again hurried him off into the crowd, and entangled him in its interests.'

Moore assures us that most of Byron's so-called love-affairs were as transitory as the imaginings that gave them birth.

'It may be questioned,' says Moore, 'whether his heart had ever much share in such passions. Actual objects there were, in but too great number, who, as long as the illusion continued, kindled up his thoughts and were the themes of his song. But they were little more than mere dreams of the hour. *There was but one love that lived unquenched through all'*—Byron's love for Mary Chaworth.

Every other attachment faded away, but that endured to the end of his stormy life.

In speaking of Byron's affection for his sister, Moore, who knew all that had been said against Augusta Leigh and Byron, and had read the 'Memoirs,' remarked :

'In a mind sensitive and versatile as [Byron's], long habits of family intercourse might have estranged, or at least dulled, his natural affection for his sister ; but their separation during youth left this feeling fresh and untired. That he was himself fully aware of this appears from a passage in one of his letters : " My sister is in Town, which is a great comfort ; for, never having been much together, we are naturally more attached to each other." His very inexperience in such ties made the smile of a sister no less a novelty than a charm to him ; and before the first gloss of this newly awakened sentiment had time to wear off, they were again separated, and for ever.'

When the parting came it was bitter indeed, for she was, says Moore,

'almost the only person from whom he then parted with regret. Those beautiful and tender verses, " Though the day of my destiny's over," were now his parting tribute to her who, through all this bitter trial, had been his sole consolation.'

Enough has been said to show what kind of woman Augusta was, and it is difficult to understand by what process of reasoning Lord Lovelace persuaded himself that she could have been guilty of the atrocious crime

AUGUSTA THE VICTIM OF A PLOT

which he lays to her charge. We entirely concur with Mrs. Villiers, when she wrote to Augusta Leigh (in September, 1816): 'I consider you the victim to the most infernal plot that has ever entered the heart of man to conceive.'

We must at the same time frankly admit that Augusta, in order to screen Mary Chaworth, did all she could do to keep Lady Byron under a false impression. She seems to have felt so secure in the knowledge of her own innocence that she might afford to allow Lady Byron to think as ill of her as she pleased.

Unfortunately, Augusta, having once entered upon a course of duplicity, was obliged to keep it up by equivocations of all kinds. She went so far as even to show portions of letters addressed to her care, and pretended that they had been written to herself. She seems to have felt no compunction for the sufferings of Lady Byron, having herself suffered intensely through the false suspicions, and the studied insults heaped upon her by many of Lady Byron's adherents.

Byron, who was informed of what had been said against his sister by Lady Byron and others, told the world in ' Marino Faliero ' that he 'had only one fount of quiet left, and *that* they poisoned.' But he was powerless to interfere.

Writing to Moore (September 19, 1818) he said :

'I could have forgiven the dagger or the bowl—anything but the deliberate desolation piled upon me, when I stood alone upon my hearth, with my household gods shivered around me. Do you suppose I have forgotten it ? It has, comparatively, swallowed up in me every other feeling, and I am only a spectator upon earth till a tenfold opportunity offers.'

It may be that Augusta avenged her brother tenfold without his knowledge. But she suffered in the process. Lord Lovelace lays great stress upon what he calls 'the correspondence of 1819,' in order to show us that Augusta had confessed to the crime of incest. That correspondence is very interesting, not as showing the guilt of Augusta Leigh, but as an example of feminine duplicity in which she was an adept. Augusta was hard pressed indeed for some weapon of offence when she pretended, on June 25, 1819, that she had received the following letter from her brother. She must have been some time in making up her mind to send it, as the letter in question had been in her hands three weeks, having arrived in London on June 4. It may be as well to state that all letters written by Byron to Mary Chaworth passed through Mrs. Leigh's hands, and were delivered with circumspection.

'VENICE,
'May 17, 1819.*

'MY DEAREST LOVE,

'I have been negligent in not writing, but what can I say? Three years' absence—and the total change of scene and habit make such a difference that we have never nothing in common but our affections and our relationship. But I have never ceased nor can cease to feel for a moment that perfect and boundless attachment which bound and binds me to you—which renders me utterly incapable of *real* love for any other human being—for what could they be to me after *you*? My own . . .† we may have been very wrong—but I repent of nothing except that cursed marriage—and your refusing to continue to love me as you had loved me. I can neither forget nor *quite forgive* you for that precious piece of reformation, but I can never be other than I have been—and whenever I love anything it is

---

* A fortnight before writing 'Stanzas to the Po.'

† Short name of three or four letters obliterated.'—'Astarte,' p. 180

A LETTER TO 'THYRZA'

because it reminds me in some way or other of yourself. For instance, I not long ago attached myself to a Venetian for no earthly reason* (although a pretty woman) but because she was called . . .† and she often remarked (without knowing the reason) how fond I was of the name.‡ It is heart-breaking to think of our long separation—and I am sure more than punishment enough for all our sins. Dante is more humane in his "Hell," for he places his unfortunate lovers—Francesca of Rimini and Paolo—whose case fell a good deal short of *ours*, though sufficiently naughty) in company; and though they suffer, it is at least together. If ever I return to England it will be to see you; and recollect that in all time, and place, and feelings, I have never ceased to be the same to you in heart. Circumstances may have ruffled my manner and hardened my spirit; you may have seen me harsh and exasperated with all things around me; grieved and tortured with *your new resolution*, and the soon after persecution of that infamous fiend§ who drove me from my country, and conspired against my life—by endeavouring to deprive me of all that could render it precious‖—but remember that even then *you* were the sole object that cost me a tear; and *what tears!* Do you remember our parting? I have not spirits now to write to you upon other subjects. I am well in health, and have no cause of grief but the reflection that we are not together. When you write to me speak to me of yourself, and say that you love me; never mind common-place people and topics which can be in no degree interesting to me who see nothing in England but the country which holds *you*, or around it but the sea which divides us. They say absence destroys weak passions, and confirms strong ones. Alas! *mine* for you is the union of all passions and of all affections—has strengthened itself, but will destroy me; I do not speak of physical destruction, for I have endured, and can endure, much; but the annihilation of all thoughts, feelings, or hopes, which have not

---

* See *ante*, p. 250.
† Short name of three or four letters obliterated.
‡ Marianna (Anglice: Mary Anne).
§ **Lady** Byron (see 'Astarte,' p. 166). ‖ His sister's society.

more or less a reference, to you and to *our recollections*.

'Ever, dearest,'
[Signature erased].

The terms of this letter, which Lord Lovelace produces as conclusive evidence against Augusta Leigh, deserve attention. At first sight they seem to confirm Lady Byron's belief that a criminal intercourse had existed between her husband and his sister. But close examination shows that the letter was not written to Mrs. Leigh at all, but to Mary Chaworth.

On the day it was written Byron was at Venice, where he had recently made the acquaintance of the Countess Guiccioli, whom, as 'Lady of the land,' he followed to Ravenna a fortnight later. It will be noticed that the date synchronizes with the period when the 'Stanzas to the Po' were written. Both letter and poem dwell upon the memory of an unsatisfied passion. The letter bears neither superscription nor signature, both having been erased by Mrs. Leigh before the document reached Lady Byron's hands. The writer excuses himself for not having written to his correspondent (*a*) because three years' absence, (*b*) total change of scene, and (*c*) *because there is nothing in common between them*, except mutual affections and their relationship. Byron could not have excused himself in that manner to a sister, who had much in common with him, and to whom he had written, on an average, twice in every month since he left England. His letters to Augusta entered minutely into all his feelings and actions, and the common bond between them was Ada, whose disposition, appearance, and health, occupied a considerable space in their correspondence.

MARIANNA

Nor would Byron have written in that amatory strain to his dear 'Goose.' In the letter which preceded the one we have quoted, Byron begins, 'Dearest Augusta,' and ends, 'I am in health, and yours, B.' In that which followed it there is nothing in the least effusive. It begins, 'Dearest Augusta,' and ends, 'Yours ever, and very truly, B.' There are not many of Byron's letters to Augusta extant. All those which mentioned Medora were either mutilated or suppressed.

For Byron to have given 'three years' absence, and a total change of scene,' as reasons for not having written to his sister for a month or so would have been absurd. But when he said that he had nothing in common with Mary Chaworth, except 'our affections and our relationship,' his meaning was—their mutual affections, their kinship, and their common relationship to Medora.

We invite any unprejudiced person to say whether Byron would have been likely to write to a sister, who knew his mind thoroughly, 'I have never ceased—nor can cease to feel for a moment that perfect and boundless attachment which bound and binds me to you.' Did not Augusta know very well that he loved and admired her, and that Byron was under the strongest obligations to her for her loyalty at a trying time?

Then, there was the erasure of 'a short name of three or four letters,' which might have opened Lady Byron's eyes to the trick that was being played upon her. Those four letters spelt the name of Mary, and the 'pretty woman' to whom Byron had 'not long ago' attached himself was the Venetian Marianna (Anglice: Mary Anne) Segati, with whom he formed a liaison from November, 1816, to February, 1818.

Augusta would certainly not have understood the allusion.

In this illuminating letter Byron reproaches Mary Chaworth for breaking off her fatal intimacy with him, and for having persuaded him to marry—'that infamous fiend who drove me from my country, and conspired against my life—by *endeavouring to deprive me of all that could render it precious.*' As the person here referred to was, obviously, Augusta herself, this remark could not have been made to her. In speaking of their long separation as a punishment for their sins, he tells Mary Chaworth that, if he ever returns to England, it will be to see *her*, and that his feelings have undergone no change. It will be observed that Byron begs his correspondent *to speak to him only of herself, and to say that she loves him!* It is scarcely necessary to remind the reader that Augusta was the intermediary between Byron and his wife—his confidential agent in purely private affairs. It was to her that he wrote on all matters relating to business transactions with his wife, and from whom he received intelligence of the health and happiness of his daughter. Under those circumstances how could Byron ask Augusta to speak to him of nothing but her love for him?

To show the absurdity of Lord Lovelace's contention, we insert the letter which Byron wrote to his sister seven months later. Many letters had passed between them during the interval, but we have not been allowed to see them:

'BOLOGNA,
'*December* 23, 1819.

'DEAREST AUGUSTA,
'The health of my daughter Allegra, the cold season, and the length of the journey, induce me to

postpone for some time a purpose (never very willing on my part) to revisit Great Britain.

'You can address to me at Venice as usual. Wherever I may be in Italy, the letter will be forwarded. I enclose to you all that long hair on account of which you would not go to see my picture. You will see that it was not so very long. I curtailed it yesterday, my head and hair being weakly after my tertian.

'I wrote to you not very long ago, and, as I do not know that I could add anything satisfactory to that letter, I may as well finish this. In a letter to Murray I requested him to apprise you that my journey was postponed; but here, there, and everywhere, know me

'Yours ever and very truly,
'B.'

It is ridiculous to suppose that these two letters were addressed to the same person. In the one we find the expression of an imperishable attachment, in the other merely commonplace statements. In the first letter Byron says, if ever he returns to England, it will be to see the person to whom he is writing, and that absence has the more deeply confirmed his passion. In the second he tells the lady that he has had his hair cut, and that he was never very willing to revisit Great Britain! And yet, in spite of these inconsistencies, Lady Byron walked into the snare which Augusta had so artfully prepared. In forwarding the amatory epistle to Lady Byron, Augusta tells her to burn it, and says that her brother 'must surely be considered a maniac' for having written it, adding, with adroit mystification:

'*I* do not believe any feelings expressed are by any means permanent—only occasioned by the passing and present reflection and occupation of writing *to the unfortunate Being to whom they are addressed.*'

Augusta did not tell Lady Byron that 'the unfortunate Being' was Mary Chaworth, now reconciled to her husband, and that she had withheld Byron's letter from her, lest her mind should be unsettled by its perusal.

Mrs. Leigh had two excellent reasons for this betrayal of trust. In the first place, she wished Lady Byron to believe that her brother was still making love to her, and that she was keeping her promise in not encouraging his advances. In the second place, she knew that the terms of Byron's letter would deeply wound Lady Byron's pride—and revenge is sometimes sweet!

Lady Byron, who was no match for her sister-in-law, had failed to realize the wisdom of her mother's warning: 'Beware of Augusta, for she *must* hate you.' She received this proof of Augusta's return to virtue with gratitude, thanked her sincerely, and acknowledged that the terms of Byron's letter 'afforded ample testimony that she had not encouraged his tenderness.' Poor Lady Byron! She deserves the pity of posterity. But she was possessed of common sense, and knew how to play her own hand fairly well. She wrote to Augusta in the following terms:

'This letter is a proof of the prior "reformation," which was sufficiently evidenced to *me* by your own assertion, and the agreement of circumstances with it. *But, in case of a more unequivocal disclosure on his part than has yet been made*, this letter would confute those false accusations to which you would undoubtedly be subjected from others.'

In suggesting a more open disclosure on Byron's part, Lady Byron angled for further confidences, so that her evidence against her husband might be over-

LADY BYRON ADVISES AUGUSTA

whelming. She hoped that his repentant sister might be able to show incriminating letters, which would support the clue found in those missives which Mrs. Clermont had 'conveyed.' How little did she understand Augusta Leigh! Never would she have assisted Lady Byron to prejudice the world against her brother, nor would she have furnished Lady Byron with a weapon which might at any moment have been turned against herself.

With the object of proving Augusta's guilt, the whole correspondence between her and Lady Byron from June 27, 1819, to the end of the following January has been printed in 'Astarte.'

We have carefully examined it without finding anything that could convict Augusta and Byron. It seems clear that Mrs. Leigh began this correspondence with an ulterior object in view. She wished to win back Lady Byron's confidence, and to induce her to make some arrangement by which the Leigh children would benefit at Lady Byron's death, in the event of Byron altering the will he had already made in their favour. She began by asking Lady Byron's advice as to how she was to answer the 'Dearest Love' letter. Lady Byron gave her two alternatives. Either she must tell her brother that, so long as his idea of her was associated with the most guilty feelings, it was her duty to break off all communication; or, if Augusta did not approve of that plan, then it was her duty to treat Byron's letter with the silence of contempt. To this excellent advice Augusta humbly replied that, if she were to reprove her brother for the warmth of his letter, he might be mortally offended, in which case her children, otherwise unprovided for, would fare badly. But Mrs. Leigh was too diplomatic to convey that meaning in plain language. Writing June 28, 1819, she says:

'I will tell you what *now* passes in my mind. As to the *gentler* expedient you propose, I certainly lean to it, as the least offensive; but, supposing he suspects the motive, and is piqued to answer: "I wrote you such a letter of such a date: did you receive it?" What then is to be done? I could not reply falsely—and might not that line of conduct, acknowledged, irritate? This consideration would lead me, perhaps preferably, to adopt the other, as most open and honest (certainly to any other character but his), but query whether it might not be most judicious as to its effects; *and* at the same time acknowledging that his victim was wholly in his power, as to temporal good,* and leaving it to his generosity whether to use that power or not. There seem so many reasons why he should for his own sake abstain *for the present* from *gratifying* his revenge, that one can scarcely think he would do so—unless *insane*. It would surely be ruin to all his prospects, and those of a pecuniary nature are not indifferent if others are become so.

'If really and truly he feels, or fancies he feels, that passion he professes, I have constantly imagined he might suppose, from his experience of the *weakness* of disposition of the unfortunate object, that, driven from every other hope or earthly prospect, she might fly to *him!* and that as long as he was impressed with that idea he would persevere in his projects. But, if he considered *that* hopeless, he might desist, for otherwise he must lose everything *but his revenge*, and what good would *that* do him?

'After all, my dearest A., if you cannot calculate the probable consequences, how should I presume to do so! To be sure, the gentler expedient might be the safest, with so violent and irritable a disposition, and at least *for a time* act as a *palliative*—and who knows what changes a little time might produce or how Providence might graciously interpose! With so many reasons to wish to avoid extremities (I mean for the

---

* In case Byron altered his will.

sake of others), one leans to what appears the *safest* and one is a coward.

'But the other at the same time has something gratifying to one's feelings—and I think might be said and done—so that, if he showed the letters, it would be no evidence against *the* person; and worded with that kindness, and appearance of real affectionate concern for *him* as well as the other person concerned, that it *might* possibly touch him. Pray think of what I have *thought*, and write me a line, not to decide, for that I cannot expect, but to tell me if I deceived myself in the ideas I have expressed to you. I shall not, *cannot* answer till the *latest* post-day this week.

'I know you will forgive me for this infliction, and may God bless you for that, and every other kindness.'

We do not remember ever to have read a letter more frankly disingenuous than this. The duplicity lurking in every line shows why the cause of the separation between Lord and Lady Byron has been for so long a mystery. Lady Byron herself was mystified by Augusta Leigh. It certainly was not easy for Lady Byron to gauge the deep deception practised upon her by both her husband and Mrs. Leigh; and yet it is surprising that Lady Byron should not have suspected, in Augusta's self-depreciation, an element of fraud. Was it likely that Augusta, who had good reason to hate Lady Byron, would have provided her with such damning proofs against her brother and herself, if she had not possessed a clear conscience in the matter? She relied implicitly upon Byron's letter being destroyed, and so worded her own that it would be extremely difficult for anyone but Lady Byron to understand what she was writing about. It will be noticed that no names are mentioned in any of her missives. People are referred to either as 'maniacs,' 'victims,' 'unfortunate objects,' or as 'that most detestable woman, your relation by marriage,' which, in a confidential communication to a sister-in-law, would be superfluous caution were she really sincere. But, after the separation period, Mrs. Leigh was never sincere in her intercourse with Lady Byron. Through that lady's unflattering suspicions, Augusta had suffered 'too much to be forgiven.' Lady Byron, on the other hand, with very imperfect understanding of her sister-in-law's character, was entirely at her mercy. To employ a colloquialism, the whole thing was a 'blind,' devised to support Augusta's rôle as a repentant Magdalen; to attract compassion, perhaps even pecuniary assistance; and, above all, to shield the mother of Medora. The *ruse* was successful. Lady Byron saw a chance of eventually procuring, in the handwriting of her husband, conclusive evidence of his crime. In her letter of June 27, 1819, to Mrs. Leigh, she conveyed a hint that Byron might be lured to make 'a more unequivocal disclosure than has yet been made.'

Lady Byron, it must be remembered, craved incessantly for documentary proofs, which might be produced, if necessary, to justify her conduct. It is significant that at the time of writing she possessed no evidence, except the letters which Mrs. Clermont had purloined from Byron's writing-desk, and these were pronounced by Lushington to be far from conclusive.

Mrs. Leigh seems to have been peculiarly trying. 'Decision was never my forte,' she writes to Lady Byron: 'one ought to act *right*, and leave the issue to Providence.'

The whole episode would be intensely comical were it not so pathetic. As might have been expected, Lady Byron eventually suffered far more than the woman she had so cruelly wounded. Augusta seems coolly to suggest that her brother might 'out of revenge' (because his sister acted virtuously?) publish to the world his incestuous intercourse with her! Could anyone in his senses believe such nonsense? Augusta hints that then Lady Byron would be able to procure a divorce; and, as Lady Noel was still alive, Byron would not be able to participate in that lady's fortune at her death.

The words, 'There seem so many reasons why he should for his own sake abstain *for the present* from gratifying his revenge ... it would surely be ruin to all his prospects,' are plain enough. Even if there had been anything to disclose, Byron would never have wounded that sister who stood at his side at the darkest hour of his life, who had sacrificed herself in order to screen his love for Mary Chaworth, and who was his sole rock of refuge in this stormy world. But it was necessary to show Lady Byron that she was standing on the brink ' of a precipice.'

'On the subject of the mortgage,' writes Augusta, 'I mean to decline that wholly; and pray do me the justice to believe that one thought of the interests of my children, as far as *that* channel is concerned, never crosses my mind. I have entreated—I believe more than once—that the will might be altered. [Oh, Augusta!] But if it is not—as far as I understand the matter—there is not the slightest probability of their ever deriving any benefit. Whatever my feelings, dear A., I assure you, never in my life have I looked to advantage of *that* sort. I do not mean that I have any merit in not doing it—but that I have no inclination, therefore nothing to struggle with. I trust my babes to Providence, and, provided they are *good*, I think, perhaps, *too little* of the rest.'

It is plain that Augusta was getting nervous about her brother's attachment to the Guiccioli, a liaison which might end in trouble; and if that lady was avaricious (which she was not) Byron might be induced to alter his will (made in 1815), by which he left all *his* share in the property to Augusta's children. With a mother's keen eye to their ultimate advantage, she tried hard to make their position secure, so that, in the event of Byron changing his mind, Lady Byron might make suitable provision for them. It was a prize worth playing for, and she played the game for all it was worth. 'Leaving her babes to Providence' was just the kind of sentiment most likely to appeal to Lady Byron who did, in a measure, respond to Augusta's hints. In a letter (December 23, 1819) Lady Byron writes:

'With regard to your pecuniary interests . . . I am aware that the interests of your children may *rightly* influence your conduct when guilt is not incurred by consulting them. However, your children cannot, I trust, under any circumstances, be left destitute, for reasons which I will hereafter communicate.'

There was at this time a strong probability of Byron's return to England. Lady Byron tried to extract from Augusta a promise that she would not see him. Augusta fenced with the question, until, when driven into a corner, she was compelled to admit that it would be unnatural to close the door against her brother. Lady Byron was furious:

'I do not consider you bound to me in any way,' she writes. 'I told you what I knew, because I thought that measure would enable me to befriend you—and chiefly by representing the objections to a renewal of personal communication between you and him. . . . We must, *according to your present intentions*, act independently of each other. On my part it will still be with every possible consideration for you and your children, and should I, by your reception of him, be obliged to relinquish my intercourse with you, I will do so in such manner as shall be least prejudicial to your interests. I shall most earnestly wish that the results of your conduct may tend to establish your peace, instead of aggravating your remorse. But, entertaining these views of your duty and my own, could I in honesty, or in friendship, suppress them?'

It might have been supposed that Lady Byron, in 1816, after Augusta's so-called 'confession,' would have kept her secret inviolate. That had been a condition precedent; without it Augusta would not have ventured to deceive even Lady Byron. It appears from the following note, written by Lady Byron to Mrs. Villiers, that Augusta's secret had been confided to the tender mercies of that lady. On January 26, 1820, Lady Byron writes:

'I am reluctant to give you *my* impression of what has passed between Augusta and me, respecting her conduct in case of his return; but I should like to know whether your unbiassed opinion, *formed from the statement of facts*, coincided with it.'

Verily, Augusta had been playing with fire!

CHAPTER V

On December 31, 1819, Byron wrote a letter to his wife. The following is an extract:

'Augusta can tell you all about me and mine, if you think either worth the inquiry. The object of my writing is to come. It is this: I saw Moore three months ago, and gave to his care a long Memoir, written up to the summer of 1816, of my life, which I had been writing since I left England. It will not be published till after my death; and, in fact, it is a Memoir, and not "Confessions." I have omitted the most important and decisive events and passions of my existence, not to compromise others. But it is not so with the part you occupy, which is long and minute; and I could wish you to see, read, and mark any part or parts that do not appear to coincide with the truth. The truth I have always stated—but there are two ways of looking at it, and your way may be not mine. I have never revised the papers since they were written. You may read them and mark what you please. I wish you to know what I think and say of you and yours. You will find nothing to flatter you; nothing to lead you to the most remote supposition that we could ever have been—or be happy together. But I do not choose to give to another generation statements which we cannot arise from the dust to prove or disprove, without letting you see fairly and fully what I look upon you to have been, and what I depict you as being. If, seeing this, you can detect what is false, or answer what is charged, do so; *your mark* shall not be erased. You will perhaps say, *Why* write my life ? Alas ! I say so too. But they who have traduced it, and blasted it, and branded me, should know that it is they, and not I, are the cause. It is no great pleasure to have lived, and less to live over again the details of existence ; but the last becomes sometimes a necessity, and even a duty. If you choose to see this, you may ; if you do not, you have at least had the option.'

The receipt of this letter gave Lady Byron the deepest concern, and, in the impulse of a moment, she drafted a reply full of bitterness and defiance. But Dr. Lushington persuaded her—not without a deal of trouble—to send an answer the terms of which, after considerable delay, were arranged between them. The letter in question has already appeared in Mr. Prothero's 'Letters and Journals of Lord Byron,'* together with Byron's spirited rejoinder of April 3, 1820.

Lord Lovelace throws much light upon the inner workings of Lady Byron's mind at this period. That she should have objected to the publication of Byron's memoirs was natural ; but, instead of saying this in a few dignified sentences, Lady Byron parades her wrongs, and utters dark hints as to the possible complicity of Augusta Leigh in Byron's mysterious scheme of revenge. Dr. Lushington at first thought that it would be wiser and more diplomatic to beg Byron's sister to dissuade him from publishing his memoirs, but Lady Byron scented danger in that course.

'I foresee,' she wrote to Colonel Doyle, 'from the transmission of such a letter . . . this consequence: that an unreserved disclosure from Mrs. Leigh to him being necessitated, they would combine together against me, he being actuated by revenge, she by fear ;

* Vol. v., p. 1.

whereas, from her never having dared to inform him that she has already admitted his guilt to me with her own, they have hitherto been prevented from acting in concert.'

Byron was, of course, well acquainted with what had passed between his wife and Augusta Leigh. It could not have been kept from him, even if there had been any reason for secrecy. He knew that his sister had been driven to admit that Medora was his child, thus *implying* the crime of which she had been suspected. There was nothing, therefore, for Augusta to fear from *him*. She dreaded a public scandal, not so much on her own account as 'for the sake of others.' For that reason she tried to dissuade her brother from inviting a public discussion on family matters. There was no reason why Augusta should 'combine' with Byron against his hapless wife!

The weakness of Lady Byron's position is admitted by herself in a letter dated January 29, 1820:

'My information previous to my separation was derived either directly from Lord Byron, or from my observations on that part of his conduct which he exposed to my view. The infatuation of pride may have blinded him to the conclusions which must inevitably be established by a long series of circumstantial evidences.'

Oh, the pity of it all! There was something demoniacal in Byron's treatment of this excellent woman. Perhaps it was all very natural under the circumstances. Lady Byron seemed to invite attack at every conceivable moment, and did not realize that a wounded tiger is always dangerous. This is the way in which she spoke of Augusta to Colonel Doyle:

'Reluctant as I have ever been to bring my domestic concerns before the public, and anxious as I have felt *to save from ruin a near connection of his*, I shall feel myself compelled by duties of primary importance, if he perseveres in accumulating injuries upon me, to make a disclosure of the past in the *most* authentic form.'

Lady Byron's grandiloquent phrase had no deeper meaning than this: that she was willing to accuse Augusta Leigh on the strength of 'a long series of circumstantial evidences.' We leave it for lawyers to say whether that charge could have been substantiated in the event of Mrs. Leigh's absolute denial, and her disclosure of all the circumstances relating to the birth of Medora.

In the course of the same year (1820) Augusta, having failed to induce Lady Byron to make a definite statement as to her intentions with regard to the Leigh children, urged Byron to intercede with his wife in their interests. He accordingly wrote several times to Lady Byron, asking her to be kind to Augusta—in other words, to make some provision for her children. It seemed, under all circumstances, a strange request to make, but Byron's reasons were sound. In accordance with the restrictions imposed by his marriage settlement, the available portion of the funds would revert to Lady Byron in the event of his predeceasing her. Lady Byron at first made no promise to befriend Augusta's children; but later she wrote to say that the past would not prevent her from befriending Augusta Leigh and her children 'in any future circumstances which may call for my assistance.'

In thanking Lady Byron for this promise, Byron writes:

'As to Augusta ****, whatever she is, or may have been, *you* have never had reason to complain of her;

on the contrary, you are not aware of the obligations under which you have been to her. Her life and mine—and yours and mine—were two things perfectly distinct from each other; when one ceased the other began, and now both are closed.'

Lord Lovelace seeks to make much out of that statement, and says in 'Astarte':

'It is evident, from the allusion in this letter, that Byron had become thoroughly aware of the extent of Lady Byron's information, and did not wish that she should be misled. He probably may have heard from Augusta herself that she had admitted her own guilt, together with his, to Lady Byron.'

What *naïveté!* Byron's meaning is perfectly clear. Whatever she was, or may have been—whatever her virtues or her sins—she had never wronged Lady Byron. On the contrary, she had, at considerable risk to herself, interceded for her with her brother, when the crisis came into their married life. Byron's intercourse with his sister had never borne any connection with his relations towards his wife—it was a thing apart—and at the time of writing was closed perhaps for ever. He plainly repudiates Lady Byron's cruel suspicions of a criminal intercourse having taken place during the brief period of their married existence. He could not have spoken in plainer language without indelicacy, and yet, so persistent was Lady Byron in her evil opinion of both, these simple straightforward words were wholly misconstrued. Malignant casuistry could of course find a dark hint in the sentence, 'When one ceased, the other began'; but the mind must indeed be prurient that could place the worst construction upon the expression of so palpable a fact. It was not Lady Byron's intention to complain of things that had taken place *previous* to her marriage;

her contention had always been that she separated from her husband in consequence of his conduct while under her own roof. When, in 1869, all the documentary evidence upon which she relied was shown to Lord Chief Justice Cockburn, that great lawyer thus expressed his opinion of their value:

'Lady Byron had an ill-conditioned mind, preying upon itself, till morbid delusion was the result. If not, she was an accomplished hypocrite, regardless of truth, and to whose statements no credit whatever ought to be attached.'

Lord Lovelace tells us that all the charges made against Lady Byron in 1869 (when the Beecher Stowe 'Revelations' were published) would have collapsed 'if all her papers had then been accessible and available'; and that Dr. Lushington, who was then alive, 'from the best and kindest motives, and long habit of silence,' exerted his influence over the other trustees to suppress them! Why, we may ask, was this? The answer suggests itself. It was because he well knew that there was nothing in those papers to fix guilt upon Mrs. Leigh. It must not be forgotten that Dr. Lushington, in 1816, expressed his deliberate opinion that the proofs were wholly insufficient to sustain a charge of incest. In this connection Lady Byron's written statement, dated March 14, 1816, is most valuable.

'The causes of this suspicion,' she writes, 'did not amount to proof ... and I considered that, whilst a possibility of innocence existed, every principle of duty and humanity forbade me to act as if Mrs. Leigh was actually guilty, more especially as any intimation of so heinous a crime, even if not distinctly proved, must have seriously affected Mrs. Leigh's character and happiness.'

Exactly one month after Lady Byron had written those words, her husband addressed her in the following terms :

'I have just parted from Augusta—almost the last being you had left me to part with, and the only unshattered tie of my existence. Wherever I may go, and I am going far, you and I can never meet again in this world, nor in the next. Let this content or atone. If any accident occurs to me, be kind to *her;* if she is then nothing, to her children.'

It was, as we have seen, five years before Lady Byron could bring herself to make any reply to this appeal. How far she fulfilled the promise then made, 'to befriend Augusta Leigh and her children in any future circumstances which might call for her assistance,' may be left to the imagination of the reader. We can find no evidence of it in 'Astarte' or in the 'Revelations' of Mrs. Beecher Stowe.

CHAPTER VI

IN order to meet the charges which the late Lord Lovelace brought against Mrs. Leigh in 'Astarte,' we have been compelled to quote rather extensively from its pages. In the chapter entitled 'Manfred' will be found selections from a mass of correspondence which, without qualification or comment, might go far to convince the reader. Lord Lovelace was evidently 'a good hater,' and he detested the very name of Augusta Leigh with all his heart and soul. There was some reason for this. She had, in Lord Lovelace's opinion, '*substituted herself for Lord Byron's right heirs*' ('Astarte,' p. 125). It was evidently a sore point that Augusta should have benefited by Lord Byron's will. Lord Lovelace forgot that Lady Byron had approved of the terms of her husband's will, and that Lady Byron's conduct had not been such as to deserve any pecuniary consideration at Lord Byron's death. But impartiality does not seem to have been Lord Lovelace's forte. Having made up his mind that Mrs. Leigh was guilty, he selected from his papers whatever might appear most likely to convict her. But the violence of his antagonism has impaired the value of his contention; and the effect of his arguments is very different from that which he intended. Having satisfied himself that Mrs. Leigh (though liked and respected by her contemporaries) was an abandoned woman, Lord Lovelace says :

'A real reformation, according to Christian ideals, would not merely have driven Byron and Augusta apart from each other, but expelled them from the world of wickedness, consigned them for the rest of their lives to strict expiation and holiness. But this could never be; and in the long-run her flight to an outcast life would have been a lesser evil than the consequences of preventing it. The fall of Mrs. Leigh would have been a definite catastrophe, affecting a small number of people for a time in a startling manner. The disaster would have been obvious, but partial, immediately over and ended. . . . She would have lived in open revolt against the Christian standard, not in secret disobedience and unrepentant hypocrisy.'

Poor Mrs. Leigh! and was it so bad as all that? Had she committed incest with her brother after the separation of 1816? Did she follow Byron abroad 'in the dress of a page,' as stated by some lying chronicler from the banks of the Lake of Geneva? Did Byron come to England in secret at some period between 1816 and 1824? If not, what on earth is the meaning of this mysterious homily? Does Lord Lovelace, in the book that survives him, wish the world to believe that Lady Byron prevented Augusta from deserting her husband and children, and flying into Byron's arms in a 'far countree'? If that was the author's intention, he has signally failed. There never was a moment, since the trip abroad was abandoned in 1813, when Augusta had the mind to join her brother in his travels. There is not a hint of any such wish in any document published up to the present time. Augusta, who was undoubtedly innocent, had suffered enough from the lying reports that had been spread about town by Lady Caroline Lamb, ever to wish for another dose of scandal. If the Lovelace papers contain any hint of that nature, the author of 'Astarte' would most assuredly have set it forth in Double Pica. It is a baseless calumny.

In Lord Lovelace's opinion,

'judged by the light of nature, a heroism and sincerity of united fates and doom would have seemed, beyond all comparison, purer and nobler than what they actually drifted into. By the social code, sin between man and woman can never be blotted out, as assuredly it is the most irreversible of facts. Nevertheless, societies secretly respect, though they excommunicate, those rebel lovers who sacrifice everything else, but observe a law of their own, and make a religion out of sin itself, by living it through with constancy.'

These be perilous doctrines, surely! But how do those reflections apply to the case of Byron and his sister? The hypothesis may be something like this: Byron and his sister commit a deadly sin. They are found out, but their secret is kept by a select circle of their friends. They part, and never meet again in this world. The sin might have been forgiven, or at least condoned, if they had 'observed a law of their own'—in other words, 'gone on sinning.' Why? because 'societies secretly respect rebel lovers.' But these wretches had not the courage of their profligacy; they parted and sinned no more, therefore they were 'unrepentant hypocrites.' The 'heroism and sincerity of united fates and doom' was denied to them, and no one would ever have suspected them of such a crime, if Lady Byron and Lord Lovelace had not betrayed them. What pestilential rubbish! One wonders how a man of Lord Lovelace's undoubted ability could have sunk to bathos of that kind.

'Byron,' he tells us, 'was ready to sacrifice everything for Augusta, and to defy the world with her. If this *had not been prevented* [the italics are ours], *he would have been a more poetical figure in history* than as the author of "Manfred."'

It is clear, then, that in Lord Lovelace's opinion Byron and Augusta were prevented by someone from becoming poetical figures. Who was that guardian angel? Lady Byron, of course!

Now, what are the facts? Byron parted from his sister on April 14, 1816, *nine days prior to his own departure from London.* They never met again. There was nothing to 'prevent' them from being together up to the last moment if they had felt so disposed. Byron never disguised his deep and lasting affection for Augusta, whom in private he called his 'Dear Goose,' and in public his 'Sweet Sister.' There was no hypocrisy on either side—nothing, in short, except the prurient imagination of a distracted wife, aided and abetted by a circle of fawning gossips.

It is a lamentable example of how public opinion may be misdirected by evidence, which Horace would have called *Parthis mendacior.*

Lord Lovelace comforts himself by the reflection that Augusta

'was not spared misery or degradation by being preserved from flagrant acts; for nothing could be more wretched than her subsequent existence; and far from growing virtuous, she went farther down without end temporally and spiritually.'

Now, that is very strange! How could Augusta have gone farther down spiritually after Byron's departure? According to Lord Lovelace, 'Character regained was the consummation of Mrs. Leigh's ruin!'

A CRYPTIC UTTERANCE

Mrs. Leigh must have been totally unlike anyone else, if character regained proved her ruin. There must be some mistake. No, there it is in black and white. 'Her return to outward respectability was an unmixed misfortune to the third person through whose protection it was possible.'

This cryptic utterance implies that Mrs. Leigh's respectability was injurious to Lady Byron. Why?

'If Augusta had fled to Byron in exile, and was seen with him as *et soror et conjux*, the victory remained with Lady Byron, solid and final. *This was the solution hoped for by Lady Byron's friends*, Lushington and Doyle, as well as Lady Noel.'

So the cat is out of the bag at last! It having been impossible for Lady Byron to bring any proof against Byron and his sister which would have held water in a law-court, her friends and her legal adviser hoped that Augusta would desert her husband and children, and thus furnish them with evidence which would justify their conduct before the world. But Augusta was sorry not to be able to oblige them. This was a pity, because, according to Lord Lovelace, who was the most ingenuous of men: 'Their triumph and Lady Byron's justification would have been complete, and great would have been their rejoicing.'

Well, they made up for it afterwards, when Byron and Augusta were dead; after those memoirs had been destroyed which, in Byron's words, 'will be a kind of guide-post in case of death, and prevent some of the lies which would otherwise be told, and destroy some which have been told already.'

In allusion to the meetings between Lady Byron

and Augusta immediately after the separation, we are told in 'Astarte' that

> 'on all these occasions, one subject—uppermost in the thoughts of both—had been virtually ignored, except that Augusta *had had the audacity* to name the reports about herself with all the pride of innocence. *Intercourse could not continue on that footing*, for Augusta probably aimed at a positive guarantee of her innocence, and at committing Lady Byron irretrievably to that.'

This was great presumption on Mrs. Leigh's part, after all the pains they had taken to make her uncomfortable. Lady Byron, we are told by Lord Lovelace, could no longer bear the false position, and 'before leaving London she went to the Hon. Mrs. Villiers—a most intimate friend of Augusta's'—and deliberately poisoned her mind. That which she told Mrs. Villiers is not stated; but we infer that Lady Byron retailed some of the gossip that had reached her through one of Mrs. Leigh's servants who had overheard part of a a conversation between Augusta and Byron shortly after Medora's birth. After the child had been taken to St. James's Palace, Byron often went there. It is likely that Augusta had been overheard jesting with Byron about his child. We cannot be sure of this; but, at any rate, some such expression, if whispered in Lady Byron's ears, would be sufficient to confirm her erroneous belief.

Mrs. Villiers, we are told, began from this time to be slightly prejudiced against Augusta. Although she believed her to be absolutely pure, the wilful misrepresentation of Lady Byron and her coterie were not without effect, and Lord Lovelace tells us that Augusta's best friend was gradually lured from her allegiance. Mrs. Villiers was also informed of something else by Wilmot-Horton, another friend of Lady Byron's. The plot thickened, and, without any attempt being made to arrive at the truth, Augusta's life became almost unbearable. No wonder the poor woman said in her agony: 'None can know *how much* I have suffered from this unhappy business, and, indeed, I have never known a moment's peace, and begin to despair for the future.'

The 'unhappy business' was, of course, her unwise adoption of Medora. Through that error of judgment she was doomed to plod her way to the grave, suspected by even her dearest friend, and persecuted by the Byron family. Mrs. Villiers was a good woman and abhorred treason. She boldly urged Lady Byron to avow to Augusta the information of which she was in possession. But Lady Byron was at first afraid to run the risk. She knew very well the value of servants' gossip, and feared the open hostility of Augusta if she made common cause with Byron. This much, as we have seen, she ingenuously avowed in a letter to Dr. Lushington. But, upon being further pressed, she consented to *write* to Augusta and announce what she had been told. We have no doubt that the letter was written with great care, after consultation with Colonel Doyle and Lushington, and that the gossip was retailed with every outward consideration for Augusta's feelings. Whatever was said, and there is no evidence of it in 'Astarte,' we are there told that 'Augusta did not attempt to deny it, and, in fact, admitted everything in subsequent letters to Lady Byron during the summer of 1816.' Lord Lovelace ingenuously adds: 'It is unnecessary to produce them here, as their contents are confirmed and made sufficiently clear by the correspondence of 1819, in another chapter.'

It is very strange that Lord Lovelace, who is not thrifty in his selections, should have withheld the only positive proof of Augusta's confession known to be in existence. His reference to the letters of 1819, which he publishes, is a poor substitute for the letters themselves. The only letter which affords any clue to the mystery is the 'Dearest Love' letter, dated May 17, 1819, which we have quoted in a previous chapter. The value of that letter, as evidence against Augusta, we have already shown. When compared with the letter which Byron wrote to his sister on June 3, 1817 —a year after he had parted from her—the conclusion that the incriminating letter is not addressed to Augusta at all, forces itself irresistibly upon the mind. As an example of varying moods, it is worth quoting :

'For the life of me I can't make out whether your disorder is a broken heart or ear-ache—or whether it is you that have been ill or the children—or what your melancholy and mysterious apprehensions tend to—or refer to—whether to Caroline Lamb's novels—Mrs. Clermont's evidence—Lady Byron's magnanimity, or any other piece of imposture.'

It is really laughable to suppose that the writer of the above extract could have written to the same lady two years later in the following strain:

'My dearest love, I have never ceased, nor can cease, to feel for a moment that perfect and boundless attachment which bound and binds me to you—which renders me utterly incapable of *real* love for any other human being—for what could they be to me after *you?* My own **** we may have been very wrong,' etc.

But Lord Lovelace found no difficulty in believing that the letter in question sealed the fate of Augusta

NO EVIDENCE TO BRING INTO COURT

Leigh. In the face of such a document, Lord Lovelace thought that a direct confession in Augusta's handwriting would be superfluous, and Sir Leslie Stephen had warned him against superfluity!

Colonel Doyle, an intimate friend of Lady Byron, seems to have been the only man on her side of the question — not even excepting Lushington — who showed anything approaching to common sense. He perceived that Lady Byron, by avowing the grounds of her suspicions to Mrs. Leigh, had placed herself in an awkward position. He foresaw that this avowal would turn Mrs. Leigh into an enemy, who must sooner or later avenge the insults heaped upon her. On July 9, 1816, Colonel Doyle wrote to Lady Byron:

'Your feelings I perfectly understand; I will even *whisper* to you I approve. But you must remember that your position is very extraordinary, and though, when we have sufficiently deliberated and *decided*, we should pursue our course without embarrassing ourselves with the consequences; yet we should *not neglect the means of fully justifying ourselves* if the necessity be ever imposed upon us.'

We have quoted enough to show that, *five months after the separation was formally proposed to Lord Byron*, they had not sufficient evidence to bring into a court of law. Under those depressing circumstances Lady Byron was urged to induce Augusta to 'confess'; the conspirators would have been grateful even for an admission of guilt as *prior to Lord Byron's marriage !*

Colonel Doyle, as a man of honour, did not wish Lady Byron to rely upon 'confessions' made under the seal of secrecy. They had, apparently, been duped on a previous occasion; and, in case Mrs. Leigh were to bring an action against Lady Byron for defamation of character, it would not be advisable to rely, for her defence, upon letters which were strictly private and confidential. As to Augusta's 'admissions,' made orally and without witnesses, they were absolutely valueless—especially as the conditions under which they were made could not in honour be broken.

Augusta through all this worry fell into a state of deep dejection. She had been accused of a crime which (though innocent) she had tacitly admitted. Her friends were beginning to look coldly upon her, and consequently her position became tenfold more difficult and 'extraordinary' than that of her accuser. Perhaps she came to realize the truth of Dryden's lines :

> ' Smooth the descent and easy is the way ;
> But to return, and view the cheerful skies,
> In this the task and mighty labour lies.'

Equivocation is a dangerous game.

Lord Lovelace tells us that all the papers concerning the marriage of Lord and Lady Byron have been carefully preserved. 'They are a complete record of all the causes of separation, and contain full information on every part of the subject.'

We can only say that it is a pity Lord Lovelace should have withheld those which were most likely to prove his case—for example, the letters which Mrs. Leigh wrote to Lady Byron in the summer of 1816. The public have a right to demand from an accuser the grounds of his accusation. Lord Lovelace gives us none. That his case is built upon Lady Byron's surmises, and upon no more solid foundation, is shown by the following illuminating extract from 'Astarte':

'When a woman is placed as Lady Byron was, her mind works involuntarily, almost unconsciously, and conclusions force their way into it. She has not meant to think so and so, and she has thought it; the dreadful idea is repelled then, and to the last, with the whole force of her will, but when once conceived it cannot be banished. The distinctive features of a true hypothesis, when once in the mind, are a precise conformity to facts already known, and an adaptability to fresh developments, which allow us not to throw it aside at pleasure. Lady Byron's agony of doubt could only end in the still greater agony of certainty; but this was no result of ingenuity or inquiry, as she sought not for information.'

If Lady Byron did not seek for information when she plied Augusta with questions, and encouraged her friends to do the same, she must have derived pleasure from torturing her supposed rival. But that is absurd.

'Women,' says Lord Lovelace, 'are said to excel in piecing together scattered insignificant fragments of conversations and circumstances, and fitting them all into their right places amongst what they know already, and thus reconstruct a whole that is very close to the complete truth. But Lady Byron's whole effort was to resist the light, or rather the darkness, that would flow into her mind.'

In her effort to resist the light, Lady Byron seems to have admirably succeeded. But, in spite of her grandson's statement, that she employed any great effort to resist the darkness that flowed into her mind we entirely disbelieve. We are rather inclined to think that, in her search for evidence to convict Mrs. Leigh, she would have been very grateful for a farthing rushlight.

We now leave 'Astarte' to the judgment of posterity, for whom, in a peculiarly cruel sense, it was originally intended. If in a court of law counsel for the prosecution were to declaim loudly and frequently about evidence which he does not—perhaps dares not—produce, his harangues would make an unfavourable impression on a British jury. We have no wish to speak ill of the dead, but, in justice to Mrs. Leigh, we feel bound to say that the author of 'Astarte,' with all his talk about evidence against Byron and Augusta Leigh, has not produced a scrap of evidence which would have any weight with an impartial jury of their countrymen.

But we will not end upon a jarring note. Let us remember that Lord Lovelace, as Ada's son, felt an affectionate regard for the memory of Lady Byron. It was his misfortune to imbibe a false tradition, and, while groping his way through the darkness, his sole guide was a packet of collected papers by which his grandmother hoped to justify her conduct in leaving her husband. If Lady Byron had deigned to read Byron's 'Memoirs,' she might have been spared those painful delusions by which her mind was obsessed in later years. That she had ample grounds, in Byron's extraordinary conduct during the brief period of their intercourse, to separate herself from him is not disputed; but her premises were wrong, and her vain attempt to justify herself by unsupported accusations against Mrs. Leigh has failed.

Her daughter Ada, the mother of Lord Lovelace, had learnt enough of the family history to come to the conclusion (which she decidedly expressed to Mr. Fonblanque) that the sole cause of the separation was incompatibility. There let it rest. The Byron of the last phase was a very different man from the poet of 'The Dream.'

On the day that Byron was buried at Hucknall-Torkard the great Goethe, in allusion to a letter which

Byron, on the eve of his departure for Greece, had written to him, says:

'What emotions of joy and hope did not that paper once excite! But now it has become, by the premature death of its noble writer, an inestimable relic and a source of unspeakable regret; for it aggravates, to a peculiar degree in me, the mourning and melancholy that pervade the moral and poetic world. In me, who looked forward (after the success of his great efforts) to the prospect of being blessed with the sight of this master-spirit of the age, this friend so fortunately acquired; and of having to welcome on his return the most humane of conquerors.

'But I am consoled by the conviction that his country will at once *awake*, and shake off, like a troubled dream, the partialities, the prejudices, the injuries, and the calumnies, with which he has been assailed; and that these will subside and sink into oblivion; and that she will at length acknowledge that his frailties, whether the effect of temperament, or the defect of the times in which he lived (against which even the best of mortals wrestle painfully), were only momentary, fleeting, and transitory; whilst the imperishable greatness to which he has raised her, now and for ever remains, and will remain, illimitable in its glory and incalculable in its consequences. Certain it is that a nation, who may well pride herself on so many great sons, will place Byron, all radiant as he is, by the side of those who have done most honour to her name.'

With these just words it is fitting to draw our subject to a close. The poetic fame of Byron has passed through several phases, and will probably pass through another before his exact position in the poetical hierarchy is determined. But the world's interest in the man who cheerfully gave his life to the cause of Greek Independence has not declined. Eighty-five years have passed, and Time has gradually fulfilled the prophecy which inspiration wrung from the anguish of his heart:

> ' But I have lived, and have not lived in vain :
> My mind may lose its force, my blood its fire,
> And my frame perish even in conquering pain ;
> But there is that within me which shall tire
> Torture and Time, and breathe when I expire ;
> Something unearthly, which they deem not of,
> Like the remembered tone of a mute lyre,
> Shall on their softened spirits sink, and move
> In hearts all rocky now the late remorse of Love.'

APPENDIX

DR. BRUNO'S REPLY TO FLETCHER'S STATEMENT

THE following remarks appeared in the *Westminster Review*, and gave great annoyance to Dr. Millingen, who thought that he had been accused of having caused the death of Byron by putting off, during four successive days, the operation of bleeding:

Mr. Fletcher has omitted to state that on the second day of Lord Byron's illness his physician, Dr. Bruno, seeing the sudorific medicines had no effect, proposed blood-letting, and that his lordship refused to allow it, and caused Mr. Millingen to be sent for in order to consult with his physician, and see if the rheumatic fever could not be cured without the loss of blood.

Mr. Millingen approved of the medicines previously prescribed by Dr. Bruno, and was not opposed to the opinion that bleeding was necessary; but he said to his lordship that it might be deferred till the next day. He held this language for three successive days, while the other physician (Dr. Bruno) every day threatened Lord Byron that he would die by his obstinacy in not allowing himself to be bled. His lordship always answered: 'You wish to get the reputation of curing my disease, that is why you tell me it is so serious; but I will not permit you to bleed me.'

After the first consultation with Mr. Millingen, the domestic Fletcher asked Dr. Bruno how his lordship's complaint was go ng on. The physician replied that, if he would allow the bleeding, he would be cured in a few days. But the surgeon, Mr. Millingen, assured Lord Byron from day to day that it could wait till to-morrow; and thus four days slipped away, during which the disease, for want of blood-letting, grew much worse. At length Mr. Millingen, seeing that the prognostications which Dr. Bruno had made respecting Lord Byron's malady were more and more confirmed, urged the necessity of bleeding, and of no longer delaying it a moment. This caused Lord Byron, disgusted at finding that he could not be cured without loss of blood, to say that it seemed to him that the doctors did not understand his malady. He then had a man sent to Zante to fetch Dr. Thomas. Mr. Fletcher having mentioned this to Dr. Bruno, the latter observed that, if his lordship would consent to lose as much blood as was necessary, he would answer for his cure; but that if he delayed any longer, or did not entirely follow his advice, Dr. Thomas would not arrive in time: in fact, when Dr. Thomas was ready to set out from Zante, Lord Byron was dead.

The pistols and stiletto were removed from his lordship's bed—not by Fletcher, but by the servant Tita, who was the only person that constantly waited on Lord Byron in his illness, and who had been advised to take this precaution by Dr. Bruno, the latter having perceived that my lord had moments of delirium.

Two days before the death a consultation was held with three other doctors, who appeared to think that his lordship's disease was changing from inflammatory diathesis to languid, and they ordered china,* opium, and ammonia.

Dr. Bruno opposed this with the greatest warmth, and pointed out to them that the symptoms were those, not of an alteration in the disease, but of a fever flying to the brain, which was violently attacked by it; and that the wine, the china, and the stimulants, would kill Lord Byron more speedily than the complaint itself could; while, on the other hand, by copious bleedings and the medicines that had been taken before he might yet be saved. The other physicians, however, were of a different opinion; and it was then that Dr. Bruno declared to his colleagues that he would have no further responsibility for the loss of Lord Byron, which he pronounced inevitable if the china were given him. In effect, after my lord had taken the tincture, with some grains of carbonate of ammonia, he was

* Tinct. chinæ corticis; tinct. cinchonæ.

seized by convulsions. Soon afterwards they gave him a cup of very strong decoction of china, with some drops of laudanum. He instantly fell into a deep lethargic sleep, from which he never rose.

The opening of the body discovered the brain in a state of the highest inflammation; and all the six physicians who were present at that opening were convinced that my lord would have been saved by the bleeding, which his physician, Dr. Bruno, had advised from the beginning with the most pressing urgency and the greatest firmness.

F. B.

DR. MILLINGEN'S ACCOUNT

Mr. Finlay and myself called upon him in the evening, when we found him lying on a sofa, complaining of a slight fever and of pains in the articulations. He was at first more gay than usual; but on a sudden he became pensive, and, after remaining some few minutes in silence, he said that during the whole day he had reflected a great deal on a prediction which had been made to him, when a boy, by a famed fortune-teller in Scotland. His mother, who firmly believed in cheiromancy and astrology, had sent for this person, and desired him to inform her what would be the future destiny of her son. Having examined attentively the palm of his hand, the man looked at him for a while steadfastly, and then with a solemn voice exclaimed: 'Beware of your thirty-seventh year, my young lord—beware!'

He had entered on his thirty-seventh year on the 22nd of January; and it was evident, from the emotion with which he related this circumstance, that the caution of the palmist had produced a deep impression on his mind, which in many respects was so superstitious that we thought proper to accuse him of superstition. 'To say the truth,' answered his lordship, 'I find it equally difficult to know what to believe in this world and what not to believe. There are as many plausible reasons for inducing me to die a bigot as there have been to make me hitherto live a freethinker. You will, I know, ridicule my belief in lucky and unlucky days; but no consideration can now induce me to undertake anything either on a Friday or a Sunday. I am positive it would terminate unfortunately.

Every one of my misfortunes—and God knows I have had my share—have happened to me on one of those days.'

Considering myself on this occasion, not a medical man, but a visitor, and being questioned neither by his physician nor himself, I did not even feel Lord Byron's pulse. I was informed next morning that during the night he had taken diaphoretic infusions, and that he felt himself better. The next day Dr. Bruno administered a purgative, and kept up its effects by a solution of cream of tartar, which the Italians call 'imperial lemonade.' In the evening the fever augmented, and as on the 14th, although the pains in the articulations had diminished, the feverish symptons were equally strong, Dr. Bruno strongly recommended him to be blooded; but as the patient entertained a deep-rooted prejudice against bleeding, his physician could obtain no influence whatever over him, and his lordship obstinately persevered in refusing to submit to the operation.

On the 15th, towards noon, Fletcher called upon me and informed me that his master desired to see me, in order to consult with Dr. Bruno on the state of his health. Dr. Bruno informed me that his patient laboured under a rheumatic fever —that, as at first the symptoms had been of a mild character, he had trusted chiefly to sudorifics; but during the last two days the fever had so much increased that he had repeatedly proposed bleeding, but that he could not overcome his lordship's antipathy to that mode of treatment. Convinced, by an examination of the patient, that bleeding was absolutely necessary, I endeavoured, as mildly and as gently as possible, to persuade him; but, in spite of all my caution, his temper was so morbidly irritable that he refused in a manner excessively peevish. He observed that, of all his prejudices, the strongest was against phlebotomy. 'Besides,' said his lordship, 'does not Dr. Reid observe in his Essays that less slaughter has been effected by the warrior's lance than by the physician's lancet? It is, in fact, a minute instrument of mighty mischief.' On my observing that this remark related to the treatment of nervous disorders, not of inflammatory ones, he angrily replied: 'Who is nervous, if I am not? Do not these words, besides, apply to my case? Drawing blood from a nervous patient is like loosening the chords of a musical instrument, the tones of which are already defective for want of sufficient tension. Before I became ill, you know yourself how weak and irritable I had become. Bleeding, by increasing this state, will inevitably kill me. Do with me whatever else you please, but bleed me you shall not. I have had several inflammatory fevers during my life, and at an age when I was much more robust and plethoric than I am now; yet I got through them without bleeding. This time also I will take my chance.'

After much reasoning and entreaty, however, I at length succeeded in obtaining a promise that, should his fever increase at night, he would allow Bruno to bleed him. Happy to inform the doctor of this partial victory, I left the room, and, with a view of lowering the impetus of the circulatory system, and determining to the skin, I recommended the administration of an ounce of a solution of half a grain of tartarized antimony and two drachms of nitre in twelve ounces of water.

Early the next morning I called on the patient, who told me that, having passed a better night than he had expected, he had not requested Dr. Bruno to bleed him. Chagrined at this, I laid aside all consideration for his feelings, and solemnly assured him how deeply I lamented to see him trifle with his life in this manner. I told him that his pertinacious refusal to be bled had caused a precious opportunity to be lost; that a few hours of hope yet remained; but that, unless he would submit immediately to be bled, neither Dr. Bruno nor myself could answer for the consequences. He might not care for life, it was true; but who could assure him, unless he changed his resolution, the disease might not operate such disorganization in his cerebral and nervous system as entirely to deprive him of his reason? I had now touched the sensible chord, for, partly annoyed by our unceasing importunities, and partly convinced, casting at us both the fiercest glance of vexation, he threw out his arm, and said in the most angry tone: 'Come; you are, I see, a d——d set of butchers. Take away as much blood as you will, but have done with it.'

We seized the moment, and drew about twenty ounces. On coagulating, the blood presented a strong buffy coat. Yet the relief obtained did not correspond to the hopes we had anticipated, and during the night the fever became stronger than it had been hitherto. The restlessness and agitation increased, and the patient spoke several times in an incoherent manner. The next morning (17th) the bleeding was repeated; for, although the rheumatic symptoms had completely disappeared, the cerebral ones were hourly increasing, and this continuing all day, we opened the vein for the third time in the afternoon. Cold applications were from the beginning constantly kept on the head; blisters were also proposed. When on the point of applying them, Lord Byron asked me whether it would answer the same purpose to apply both on the same leg. Guessing the motive that led him to ask this question, I told him I would place them above the knees, on the inside of the thighs. 'Do so,' said he; 'for as long as I live I will not allow anyone to see my lame foot.'

In spite of our endeavours, the danger hourly increased; the different signs of strong nervous affection succeeded each other with surprising rapidity; twitchings and involuntary motions of the tendons began to manifest themselves in the night; and, more frequently than before, the patient muttered to himself and talked incoherently.

In the morning (18th) a consultation was proposed, to which Dr. Lucca Vaga and Dr. Freiber, my assistant, were invited. Our opinions were divided. Bruno and Lucca proposed having recourse to antispasmodics and other remedies employed in the last stage of typhus. Freiber and I maintained that such remedies could only hasten the fatal termination; that nothing could be more empirical than flying from one extreme to the other; that if, as we all thought, the complaint was owing to the metastasis of rheumatic inflammation, the existing symptoms only depended on the rapid and extensive progress it had made in an organ previously so weakened and irritable. Antiphlogistic means could never prove hurtful in this case; they would become useless only if disorganization were already operated; but then, when all hopes were fled, what means would not prove superfluous?

We recommended the application of numerous leeches to the temples, behind the ears, and along the course of the jugular vein, a large blister between the shoulders, and sinapisms to the feet. These we considered to be the only means likely to succeed. Dr. Bruno, however, being the patient's physician, had, of course, the casting vote, and he prepared, in consequence, the antispasmodic potion which he and Dr. Lucca had agreed upon. It was a strong infusion of valerian with ether, etc. After its administration the convulsive movements and the delirium increased; yet, notwithstanding my earnest representations, a second dose was administered half an hour after; when, after articulating confusedly a few broken phrases, our patient sank into a comatose sleep, which the next day terminated in death.

Lord Byron expired on the 19th of April, at six o'clock in the afternoon. Interesting as every circumstance relative to the death of so celebrated a person may prove to some, I should, nevertheless, have hesitated in obtruding so much medical detail on the patience of the reader, had not the accounts published by Dr. Bruno in the *Westminster Review*, and many of the newspapers, rendered it necessary that I should disabuse the friends of the deceased; and at the same time vindicate my own professional character, on which the imputation has been laid of my having been the cause of Lord Byron's death by putting off, during four successive days, the operation of bleeding.

I must first observe that, not knowing a syllable of English, although present at the conversation I had with Lord Byron, Dr. Bruno could neither understand the force of the language I employed to surmount his lordship's deep-rooted prejudice and aversion for bleeding, nor the positive refusals he repeatedly made before I could obtain his promise to consent to the operation. Yet he boldly states that I spoke to Lord Byron in a very undecided manner of the benefits of such an operation, and that I even ventured to recommend procrastination; and these, he says, are the reasons that induced him to consent to the delay—as if he were himself indifferent to such treatment, or as if a few words from me were sufficient to determine him! Conduct like this it is not difficult to appreciate: I shall therefore forbear abandoning myself to the indignation such a falsehood might naturally excite; nor shall I repel his unwarrantable accusation by relating the causes of that deep-rooted jealousy which Dr. Bruno entertained against me from the day he perceived the preference which Lord Byron indicated in favour of English physicians. This narrow-minded, envious feeling, as I could prove, prevented him from insisting on immediately calling me, or other medical men at Missolonghi, to a consultation. Had he done so, he would have exonerated himself from every responsibility; but his vanity made him forget the duty he owed to his patient, and even to himself. For I did not see Lord Byron (medically) till I was sent for by his lordship himself, without any participation on the part of Dr. Bruno. I can refute Dr. Bruno's calumnies, not only from the testimony of others, but even from his own. For the following extract from the article published in the *Telegrapho Greco*, announcing the death of Lord Byron, was at the request of Count Gamba (himself a witness of whatever took place during the fatal illness of his friend) composed by the doctor:

'Notwithstanding the most urgent entreaties and representations of the imminent danger attending his complaint made to him from the onset of his illness, both by his private physician and the medical man sent by the Greek Committee, it was impossible to surmount the great aversion and prejudice he entertained against bleeding, although he lay under imperious want of it' (Vide *Telegrapho Greco*, il di 24 Aprile, 1824).

As to the assertion confidently made by Dr. Bruno, that, had his patient submitted at the onset of his malady to phlebotomy, he would have infallibly recovered, I believe every medical man who maturely considers the subject will be led to esteem this assertion as being founded rather on presumption than on reason. Positive language, which is in general so misplaced in medical science, becomes in the present case even ridiculous; for, if different authors be consulted, it will appear that the very remedy which is proclaimed by some as the anchor of salvation, is by others condemned as the instrument of ruin. Bleeding (as many will be found to assert) favours metastasis in rheumatic fevers; and, in confirmation of this opinion, they will remark that in this case, as soon as the lancet was employed, the cerebral symptoms manifested themselves on the disappearance of the rheumatic; while those who incline to Dr. Reid's and Dr. Heberden's opinion will observe that, after each successive phlebotomy, the cerebral symptoms not only did not remain at the same degree, but that they hourly went on increasing. In this dilemmatic position it is evident that, whatever treatment might have been adopted, detractors could not fail to have some grounds for laying the blame on the medical attendants. The more I consider this difficult question, however, the more I feel convinced that, whatsoever method of cure had been adopted, there is every reason to believe that a fatal termination was inevitable; and here I may be permitted to observe, that it must have been the lot of every medical man to observe how frequently the fear of death produces it, and how seldom a patient, who persuades himself that he must die, is mistaken. The prediction of the Scotch fortune-teller was ever present to Lord Byron, and, like an insidious poison, destroyed that moral energy which is so useful to keep up the patient in dangerous complaints. 'Did I not tell you,' said he repeatedly to me, 'that I should die at thirty-seven?'

There is an entry in Millingen's 'Memoirs of Greece' which has not received the attention it deserves—namely, a request made by Byron on the day before his death. It is given by Millingen in the following words:

'One request let me make to you. Let not my body be hacked, or be sent to England. Here let my bones moulder. Lay me in the first corner without pomp or nonsense.'

After Byron's death Millingen informed Gamba of this request, but it was thought that it would be a sacrilege to leave his remains in a place 'where they might some day become the sport of insulting barbarians.'

INDEX

ADAM, Sir F., High Commissioner of the Ionian islands: his tribute to Byron's character, 202
Agraffa, the scene of Cariaschi's depredations, 162
Allegra, Byron's natural daughter: her life and death, 22; Byron's feelings for, 35
Americans, Byron on, 131
Anatoliko, Turkish abandonment of, 68
Argostoli, Byron arrives at, 63
Astarte, by Earl of Lovelace. See Lovelace
Augusta, Stanzas and Epistle to, 290, 325, 366

Barnard, Lady Anne, on Byron's married life, 331 *et seq.*
Beecher Stowe scandals, 318, 328
Bentham, Jeremy, and Byron, 108 *et seq.*, 119; amusing anecdote about, 126 *et seq.*
Berry, Messrs., Byron's wine merchants: register of Byron's weight, 19
Bible, The, Scott's lines on, 73
Blackwood's Magazine on Byron, 50, 100, 315, 316
Blaquière, Captain, 48; sails for England, 64; describes the return of Hatajè to her parents, 137; eulogy on Byron, 176, 177, 199 *et seq.*
Blessington, Lady, *Conversations of Lord Byron*: describes Byron, 5, 6; character and reminiscences of Byron, 34 *et seq.*, 40, 41
Bolivar, The, Byron's yacht, sold to Lord Blessington, 32; her end, 33

Botzari, Marco, 48; his death, 66
Bowring, Mr., hon. secretary to the Greek Committee, 126
Bride of Abydos, The: what the poem reveals, 240, 259, 260, 262, 265
Brougham, Mr., spreads the scandal, 342
Broughton, Lord (see Hobhouse, John Cam), *Recollections of a Long Life*, 201, 247 n., 341 n., 342 n., 361 n.
Browne, Hamilton, goes with Byron to Greece, 47, 48; Byron's illness, 62; arrives at Cephalonia, 67
Bruno, Dr., travels with Byron to Greece, 47, 48; Byron's illness, 59, 62; medical discussions with Dr. Stravolemo, 79; his medical treatment of Byron, 124, 163, 166, 168, 169, 193 *et seq.*; accompanies Byron's body to England, 202; reply to Fletcher's statement, 405 *et seq.*; Dr. Millingen on, 407 *et seq.*
Brydges, Sir Egerton, 291
Burdett, Sir Francis, 11, 208
Byron, George Gordon (sixth Lord): arrival and habits of life at Pisa, 3, 11, 20-22; personal appearance, 4-7; evidence as to his lameness, 7, 8, 191; portraits of, 9, 10; inherits the Noel property on death of Lady Noel, 10, 11; the society and influence of the Shelleys, 11 *et seq.*; discussion on the most perfect ode produced, 11, 12, 58; religion, 13 *et seq.*;

414

INDEX 415

habit of vaunting his vices, 17, 18, 78; abstinence, 18; weight register, 19; fracas at Pisa and Montenero, 21, 22; his natural daughter Allegra, 22 *et seq.*; effect of Allegra's death on, 24; dealings with Leigh Hunt, 26 *et seq.*; death of Shelley and Williams, 29, 30; refuses Shelley's legacy of £2,000, 32; leaves Pisa with Countess Guiccioli and goes to Albaro, 32; sells his yacht *The Bolivar*, 33; feelings on his own position, and desire for reconciliation with his wife, 33 *et seq.*; admiration for Sir Walter Scott and Shelley, 35; liaison with Countess Guiccioli, 37, 379, 380; conduct after separation from his wife, 39 *et seq.*; Lady Blessington on, 40; anomalies, 41; opinion of his wife, 42; admiration for his sister, 42; affection for his child Ada, 43; craving for celebrity, 45; takes up the Greek cause, 46; travels to Greece with money, arms, and retinue, 47; arrives at Argostoli, 47, 65; practical sympathy, 48, 67; an interesting interview with, 48 *et seq.*; visits the *Fountain of Arethusa*, 51-53; attacks of illness, 51, 52, 59, 62, 63; excursion to the *School of Homer*, 54-57; on the *Waverley Novels*, 57; at Vathi, 58; admiration for Southey, Gifford, and others, 59, 60; reception at Santa Eufemia, 60; on actors, 61; journey over the Black Mountain to Argostoli, 63; action with regard to dissensions in Greece, 64 *et seq.*; resides at Metaxata, 67; advances £4,000 to the Greeks, 67 *et seq.*; appeal to the Greek nation, 69; motives in coming to Greece, 70, 71, 94; discussions with Dr. Kennedy on religion, 72 *et seq.*; favourite books, 79, 82, 100; helps to rescue workmen, 80; sails with money from Zante for Missolonghi to join and help the Greek fleet, 81, 82; adventurous voyage, 83-86; reception at Missolonghi, 88; releases Turkish prisoners, 89, 90, 132; preparations against Lepanto, 91; takes 500 Suliotes into his pay, 91; and Major Parry, 92 *et seq.*, 143; Turks blockade Missolonghi, 96; verses on his birthday, 96; presentiment that he would never leave Greece, and his intentions, 97; some reminiscences of, 98 *et seq.*; wonderful memory, 102; a popular idol in Greece, 105; relations with Mavrocordato, 106, 116; and Colonel Stanhope, 107 *et seq.*, 120, 121, 122; Jeremy Bentham, 108; dealings with the press, 112, 113; views of the politics of Greece, 114; effective mode of reproof, 117; on the useless supplies sent by the London Committee, 119; abandonment of the Lepanto project, 121; illness and feelings as to death, 122-125; dismisses the Suliotes, 125, 142; anecdote of *Jerry Bentham's Cruise*, 126 *et seq.*; interest in the working classes, 130; his politics, 131; on America, 131; the story of Hatajè, 133 *et seq.*; Turkish brig ashore, 139; firmness and tact in difficulties, 140, 156 *et seq.*; desertion of the English artificers, 142, 143; improvement in his health, 144; favourite dogs, 145, 227; daily life, 145, 147; the unhealthy state of Missolonghi, 146; bodyguard, 146; indisposition of, 148; peasants' respect for, 149; no desire for self-aggrandizement in Greece, 151 *et seq.*; Greek loan raised in London, 156; receives the freedom of Missolonghi, 157; Cariascachi's treachery, 159 *et seq.*; detailed accounts of his last illness, and death, 163 *et seq.*, 192 *et seq.*, 405 *et seq.*; eulogies on, 174 *et seq.*, 201, 205; Trelawny's opinion of,

416   INDEX

178 et seq.; effect of his death on Greece, 183 et seq., 201; the funeral oration, 185; body conveyed to Zante, and thence to England, 198 et seq.; arrival of the body in England, 202-204; character sketch by Colonel Stanhope, 205 et seq.; funeral procession and burial at Hucknall-Torkard, 215, 216; what the poems reveal, 219 et seq.; infatuation for Mary Chaworth, 220 et seq.; mystery of the *Thyrza* poems, 221 et seq.; romantic attachment to Edleston, 222, 223, 230, 231; anecdote of Mary Chaworth's gift, 224; his mother's death, 227; on death of his friends, 227, 228; *Childe Harold*, 233, 236, 238, 287, 363; and the Hon. Mrs. George Lamb, 235; disbelief in existence after death, 239, 240; in great dejection writes *The Giaour, The Bride of Abydos,* and *The Corsair*, 240, 256 et seq., 277, 278, 281, 303; and Lady Webster, 240, 241, 259; persuaded to give up going abroad, 241, 242; what he wishes the world to believe about Mary Chaworth, 244, 245; their meetings after her separation from her husband, 246, 258 et seq.; remorse and parting, 249; suspense and fear preceding the birth of Medora, 253, 260; reason of separation from his wife, 255; reproaches Mary Chaworth, 256, 257; device for a seal, 261, 267; remarkable letter to Moore, 266; birth of Medora, 268; *Lara*, 268, 271, 273; partly the cause of the scandal about Mrs. Leigh, 270; effect of Miss Milbanke's first refusal, 271 et seq.; *Harmodia*, 274, 275; *Don Juan*, 276, 304 et seq.; *Hebrew Melodies*, 277; *Herod's Lament for Mariamne*, 278; his significant communication to his lawyer, 279; verses to Mary Chaworth, 280, 281; fear of disgrace, 281; important correspondence with Murray, 282, 283; last meeting with Mary Chaworth, 283; how the secret was kept, 285; verses to his sister, 286, 287; *The Dream*, 289, 290; *Stanzas to Augusta*, 290, 364; *Manfred*, 291 et seq., 328, 364; his treatment of the scandal, 291, 317, 320; *The Duel*, 293, 298; *The Lament of Tasso*, 297; *Stanzas to the Po*, 298 et seq., 372; *Last Words on Greece*, 311; on his separation from his wife, 315 et seq.; Mrs. Leigh's so-called confession, 319 et seq., 358 et seq., 370; *Epistle to Augusta*, 325; story of his married life, 331 et seq.; Sir Ralph Noel requires a separation, 341; Lady Jersey's party, 354; parts for the last time from his sister, 354, 368, 394; consents to separation from his wife, 354; Lady Byron's written statement of complaints, 355; letter to Lady Byron as to his will, 357; Moore's life of, 367 et seq.; writes to Moore about the scandal, 369; letter supposed to be written to Mary Chaworth, 370 et seq.; letter compared with one to his sister, 374; writes to Lady Byron as to the memoir of his life, 384; asks Lady Byron to make provision for Mrs. Leigh's children, 387, 389; Goethe on, 402, 403

Byron, Lord: *Letters and Journals of*, by Rowland Prothero, 70 n., 256 n., 260 n.; *Life of*, by Tom Moore, 367; *Reminiscences of*, by G. Finlay, 201; *Sketch of*, by Colonel Stanhope, 201

Byron, Captain George (afterwards seventh Lord), 339, 340

Byron, Hon. Augusta. See Leigh, Hon. Mrs. Augusta

Byron, Hon. Augusta Ada (afterwards Lady King and Countess of Lovelace), Byron's daughter: separation from her father, 43,

INDEX

44, 288; Hobhouse's opinion of, 206, 207; her health, 365

Byron, Lady (formerly Miss Milbanke): property and settlements on marriage, 10; married life, 36, 331 *et seq.*; her husband's desire for reconciliation, 36, 46, 206; on Byron's religion, 77, 78; the result of first refusal of Byron, 206, 272; *If I am not happy, it will be my own fault*, 216; on Byron's poetry, 219; on his indiscreet confidences, 270; her conduct after the birth of Medora, 285, 289, 322 *et seq.*; interview with Mrs. Leigh at Reigate, 326; Mrs. Leigh's long visit to, 338; birth of a daughter, and her husband's treatment, 339; steps for a separation taken, 340, 343, 353, 354, 359, 360; her treatment of the abstracted letters, 342, 359; attempts to extract a confession from Mrs. Leigh, 323, 326, 343, 359, 363 *et seq.*; letters to Mrs. Leigh, 344, 345, 359; Hodgson's appeal to, 348 *et seq.*; text of the signed statement of her conduct, 355 *et seq.*; Colonel Doyle's advice, 362j; her husband's letter to Mary Chaworth, 370 *et seq.*; and the prospects of Mrs. Leigh's children, 382, 387; confides in Mrs. Villiers, 383; letter from Byron, 384; the weakness of her position, 385, 386; Cockburn's opinion of, 389; Lord Lovelace on, 391 *et seq.*

Campbell, Dr., Presbyterian divine, 55
Campbell, Thomas, *Battle of the Baltic*, 60
Cariascachi, a Greek chieftain, his treachery, 159 *et seq.*
Chaworth, Mary (afterwards Mrs. John Musters): Byron's infatuation for, and references in his poems to, 220 *et seq.*; unhappy married life and separation, 243 *et seq.*; weakness and repentance, 245 *et seq.*; breakdown of health, and reconciliation with her husband, 251; describes her own character, 252; birth of Medora, 254, 268; how the secret was kept by Mrs. Leigh, 255, 285, 287, 317, 322, 364 *et seq.*; letters to Byron, 267, 370 *et seq.*; last parting with Byron, 283

Childe Harold, what the poem reveals, 228, 229, 232 *et seq.*, 287, 365

Clairmont, Claire: her anxiety about her daughter Allegra, 22, 23; her conduct to Byron, 24, 25

Clare, Lord, and Byron, 208

Clermont, Mrs., 339; her abstraction of Byron's letters, 342 *et seq.*, 380

Cockburn, Sir Alexander, Lord Chief Justice, and the Byron mystery, 360; his opinion of Lady Byron, 389

Coleridge, Ernest Hartley, on identity of Byron's infatuation, 233, 240, 260

Colocotroni, one of the turbulent capitani, 153

Congreve rockets, 92, 93

Corsair, The, what the poem reveals, 240, 262 *et seq.*, 277, 279

Dacre, Lord, 11
Davies, Scrope B., 98, 354; Byron's letter to, 227
Don Juan, what the poem reveals, 219, 276, 304 *et seq.*
Dowden, Professor, *Life of Shelley*: on Byron, 13; the death of Allegra, 23
Doyle, Colonel Francis: consulted by Lady Byron as to a separation, 340; signs Lady Byron's statement of her conduct, 357; advises Lady Byron to obtain a confession from Mrs. Leigh, 362, 363, 399
Dragomestri, Byron's visit to, 85
Dream, The, what the poem reveals, 289, 290
Duel, The, the poem's application to Mary Chaworth, 298

27

INDEX

Edleston, a chorister at Cambridge: Byron saves his life and forms a romantic attachment to, 222; his death, 230, 231

Elphinstone, Miss Mercer, and Byron, 311

Fenton, Captain, 180
Finlay, George, *History of Greece*: the siege of Missolonghi, 70; Byron's mode of life at Missolonghi, 98 *et seq.*, 148; on Byron, 176; *Reminiscences of Byron*, 201; Byron's last illness, 407
Fletcher, Byron's valet: Byron's last ride, 164; ignorance of the doctors, 165, 166; Byron's last illness and death, 170, 171, 252; his statement, 192 *et seq.*; accompanies Byron's body to England, 202; Dr. Bruno's reply to the statement, 405 *et seq.*; Dr. Millingen's account of Byron's last illness, 407 *et seq.*
Florida, the brig, brings the loan to Greece, and conveys back Byron's body, 199 *et seq.*
Freiber, Dr., German physician, attends Byron, 169

Gamba, Count Pietro: on Byron's religious opinions, 16, 17; fracas at Pisa, 20; goes to Albaro, 32; travels with Byron to Greece, 47, 48; on Byron's perseverance and discernment, 65; on Byron's favourite reading, 79; Byron's practical sympathy, 80; accompanies Byron to Missolonghi, 83; taken prisoner by the Turks, 84; release and arrival at Missolonghi, 85; the General Assembly at Missolonghi, 88; Byron's interview with the two privateer sailors, 91; becomes editor of the *Greek Telegraph*, 114; Byron's illness, 121, 143, 148, 163 *et seq.*; arrest of English officers, 157; Byron's funeral, 184; conveys Byron's body to Zante, 198

Gamba, Count Ruggiero, Byron's neighbour at Pisa, 3; leaves Pisa and goes to Montenero, 21; ordered to leave Montenero, 22; goes to Albaro, 32; and Byron, 212
Gamba, Teresa. See Guiccioli, Countess
Gell, Sir William, his writings, 100, 101 n.
George IV. makes 'equivocation' the fashion, 17, 18; and Sir Walter Scott, 53
Giaour, The, what the poem reveals, 240, 256, 257, 265
Gifford, William, Byron's opinion of, 51, 60
Greece: Byron sails for, 47; state of the country and army, 64, 87 *et seq.*, 118, 180; Byron advances £4,000, 67; Byron's appeal to the nation, 69, 70; preparations against Lepanto, 91; honours offered to Byron, 151, 152; Congress at Salona, 153; Greek loan raised in London, 156; effect of Byron's death on, 175 *et seq.*
Greece, History of, by G. Finlay, 70; by Mitford, 100
Greek Chronicle: Byron's support, 108; suppression of, 112, 113
Greek Telegraph, 103, 113
Guiccioli, Countess, daughter of Count Ruggiero Gamba: Byron's neighbour at Pisa, 3, 4, 20; describes Byron, 7 *et seq.*; on the characters of Shelley and Byron, 14, 15; on Byron's conduct towards Allegra, 23; on Byron's religion, 74, 78; anecdote about Mary Chaworth's ring, 224; *Lady of the Land*, 298, 301, 372; and Mrs. Leigh, 381

Hancock, Charles, Byron's banker, 82
Hanson, John, Byron's solicitor, 241, 347, 348
Harmodia, 274, 275
Hatajè, Byron's kindness to, 133 *et seq.*
Hay, Captain, fracas at Pisa, 20, 21

INDEX

Hebrew Melodies, 277
Hercules, the, an English brig : Byron and his suite sail to Greece in it, 47 ; Byron lives on board, 64, 65
Herod's Lament for Mariamne, 278
Hesketh, Mr., 158, 159
Heywood, Sergeant, consulted by Lady Byron, 340
Hobhouse, John Cam (afterwards Lord Broughton) : and Byron, 35 ; persuades Byron to burn his journal, 102 ; destroys one of Byron's poems, 208 ; Byron's funeral, 215, 216 ; and Lady Byron, 216, 320 ; life-long friend of Mrs. Leigh, 319. See also Broughton, Lord
Hodgson, captain of the *Florida*, 203
Hodgson, Rev. Francis : consulted by Mrs. Leigh, 344 *et seq.*; appeals to Lady Byron, 348 *et seq.*
Hodgson, Rev. F., *Memoir of*, 73 n.
Holmes, Mr. James, his portrait of Byron, 9
Hours of Idleness, what the poem reveals, 220
Hucknall-Torkard, Byron's burial place, 44
Humphreys, Captain, on state of Greece, 180
Hunt, Sir Aubrey de Vere, 102
Hunt, Leigh : the story of his literary and money relations with Byron, 26 *et seq.*; Byron's opinion of, 31

Ireland, Dr., Dean of Westminster, refuses burial of Byron in Westminster Abbey, 203

Jersey, Countess of, her party in honour of Byron, 354

Kean, Edmund, actor, Byron's opinion of, 61
Kemble, John, actor, Byron's opinion of, 61
Kennedy, Dr., Scottish medical man : tries to 'convert' Byron, 72 *et seq.*; and Hatajè, 136 ; Lady Byron on, 77

King, Lady. See Byron, Hon. Augusta Ada
Kinnaird, the Hon. Douglas, Byron's opinion of, 208
Knox, Captain, 51
Knox, Mrs., 50, 54

Lamb, Hon. Mrs. George, and Byron, 235
Lamb, Lady Caroline, spreads the Byron scandal, 270, 317, 342, 392
Lambro, a Suliote chief, 156, 164
Lara, what the poem reveals, 268, 271, 273
Leigh, Hon. Mrs. Augusta, half-sister of Lord Byron : influence over her brother, 42, 73, 245, 261 ; and his poetry, 103 ; wishes him to go abroad, 242 ; first introduction to, and close intimacy with, Mary Chaworth, 250 ; loyalty to her brother and Mary Chaworth, 255, 287, 317, 321 ; letters from her brother about Mary Chaworth, 258, 267, 268 ; simulated confinement and convalescence, 269 ; her brother's conduct gives colour to the scandal, 270, 279, 285 ; letters to Hodgson on the secret, 272, 346 *et seq.*; spends a month at Newstead with her brother, 279 ; the difficulties of keeping the secret, 285, 317, 364 *et seq.*; lines in *Childe Harold* referring to, 287 ; the so-called confession, 289, 323, 326, 327, 343, 359, 363 *et seq.*; *Stanzas to Augusta*, 290, 368 ; Lord Lovelace's opinion of her character, 294, 295 ; the accusation dealt with in detail, 318 *et seq.*; Lord Stanhope and Frances, Lady Shelley on, 318 ; the story of her life, 319 ; Hobhouse's advice to, 320 ; difficult position with Lady Byron, 321, 343, 364, 369 ; her predicament owing to the adoption of Medora, 322 ; *Epistle to Augusta*, 325 ; letters to Hodgson on her brother's marriage, 334 *et seq.*; a long

visit to her brother and Lady Byron, 338; Lady Byron's feelings towards her, 338, 339, 344, 345, 362; Lady Byron's confinement, 339; Mrs. Clermont's treachery, 343; Lady Jersey's party, 354; parts for ever from her brother, 354; Lady Byron's written statement, 355 *et seq.;* letters to Hodgson on her brother, 364; her line of conduct to Lady Byron, 364 *et seq.;* Moore on Byron's feelings towards her, 368; pretends that her brother's letter to Mary Chaworth was written to herself, 370 *et seq.;* a genuine letter, 374; reply to Lady Byron's advice, 377 *et seq.;* her children's prospects discussed with Lady Byron, 382, 387; Lady Byron's request, 382; Lord Lovelace on, 391 *et seq.*

Lepanto, preparations against, 91

Liberal, The, its unsuccessful career, 31, 32

Lion, Byron's favourite dog, 145, 146

Londos, General Andrea, and Byron, 155

Lovelace, Earl of, *Astarte:* Byron's *Thyrza,* 234 n.; accusations against Mrs. Leigh, 249, 269 *et seq.,* 287, 288, 318, 321, 322, 338, 341, 364, 368 *et seq.,* 370 *et seq.,* 387 *et seq.,* 392; describes Mrs. Leigh's character, 294; *Manfred,* the key of the mystery, 330 *et seq.,* 368; Byron's mutability, 341; Lady Byron's written statement, 355 *et seq.;* important letters from Byron, 370 *et seq.,* 387, 388; and Lady Byron, 389

Lushington, Dr.: advises Lady Byron, 340, 353, 359, 360, 385, 389; his opinion on Byron's letters abstracted by Mrs. Clermont, 342; signs Lady Byron's statement, 355 *et seq.*

Magdalen, a fragment, 269

Maitland, Sir Thomas, High Commissioner of the Ionian Islands, 52, 61; character and death, 115, 116

anfred, the supposed key to the mystery, 291 *et seq.,* 330, 336

Marino Faliero, 100

Marshall, Mrs. Julian, *Life and Letters of Mary Wollstonecraft Shelley,* 178, 180

Masi, Sergeant-Major, fracas at Pisa, 20, 21

Matthews, Charles Skinner, one of Byron's best friends, his death, 227

Mavrocordato, Prince, Governor-General of Western Greece: and Byron, 66, 68, 70, 202; brings the Greek fleet to Missolonghi, 81; Byron's arrival at Missolonghi, 85; Byron's interview with two privateer sailors, 91; his jealousy, 105, 106; infraction of neutrality in Ithaca, 115; Byron's opinion of, 116; opposition by Colonel Stanhope, 119, 153; and Odysseus, 153 *et seq.;* Byron's last illness and death, 164 *et seq.;* effect of Byron's death on, 177, 202; Trelawny's opinion of, 179, 180; his efforts for Greece, 181; issues a proclamation on Byron's death, 183, 184

Medora, birth of, 254, 268; *Childe Harold,* 288; adoption by Mrs. Leigh, 322

Medwin, Captain Thomas: his description of Byron, 4, 6, 11; on Byron's life at Pisa, 20; *The Angler in Wales,* 33 n.

Melbourne, Lady, persuades Byron not to go abroad, 242

Metaxata, Byron's residence at, 65, 79

Meyer, Jean Jacques, editor of the *Greek Chronicle,* 112

Milbanke, Miss. See Byron, Lady

Milbanke, Sir Ralph, his property, 10

Millingen, Dr.: on Byron's character, 95; on Parry, 96; Byron a favourite in Greece, 105, 177; on the Greek press, 113;

INDEX

Byron's illness, 124; Byron's kind treatment of Hataje, 133 et seq.; on Cariascachi's treachery, 161; on Byron's unhappiness and anxieties, 162; attends Byron in his last illness and death, 167 et seq., 190, 193 et seq., 405 et seq.; on Mavrocordato, 181

Missolonghi: blockade of, 66, 96; Turks retire from, 70; Greek squadron at, 81; description of, 87; Byron's arrival and life at, 88, 99; release of Turkish prisoners, 133; Turkish brig-of-war runs ashore off, 139; effect of Byron's death, 175, 183 et seq.

Mitford, William, *History of Greece*, 100

Monthly Literary Recreations, 101 n.

Monthly Review, Byron's reviews in, 100, 101 n.

Moore, Thomas: letters from Shelley and Byron, 13, 14, 266; and Byron, 36; on the *Thyrza* poems, 229; Byron's love for Mary Chaworth, 238, 246, 266, 279; criticism on his *Life of Byron*, 367

Moore, Sir John, ode on the death of, 58

Muir, Dr., principal medical officer at Cephalonia, 82

Muir, General Skey, 82

Murray, John, Byron's publisher: Byron's letters to, 30, 31; *Childe Harold*, 50; asks for Byron to be buried in Westminster Abbey, 203; and Mrs. Leigh, 269; Byron's copyrights, 281; *Epistle to Augusta*, 324

Musters, John, husband of Mary Chaworth: the ring incident and engagement, 224, 225; separation from his wife, 245; behaviour to his wife, 246; reconciliation, 251; cuts down the *peculiar diadem of trees*, 289

Napier, Colonel, British Resident Governor of Argostoli, 48, 80

Newstead Abbey: sale of, 99; Byron's visits, 226, 227

Noel, Lady, Byron's mother-in-law: Byron inherits the Noel property on her death, 10; her bequest of Byron's portrait, 43 n.; advice as to her daughter's separation from Byron, 340; and Mrs. Leigh, 364

Noel, Sir Ralph, writes to Byron requiring a separation, 341

O'Doherty, Ensign, Byron's opinion of his poetry, 100

Odysseus, Greek insurgent leader: his opposition to Mavrocordato, 153; and Trelawny, 179, 180

Osborne, Lord Sidney, and Sir Thomas Maitland, 115; goes to Missolonghi, 198; eulogy of Byron's conduct in Greece, 201

Parry, Major: his arrival at Missolonghi, 91, 92; his peculiarities, 92 et seq.; practical joke on, 95; on Byron's intentions in Greece, 97, 98; on the relationship between Mavrocordato and Byron, 116; on Byron's mode of reproof, 117; account of Byron's illness, 121; anecdote of *Jerry Bentham's Cruise*, 126; Turkish brig-of-war ashore, 139; artillery at Missolonghi, 144; on Byron's mode of life, 145; on Byron's power in Greece, 151, 152; Byron's last illness and death, 164 et seq., 196; his opinion of Byron, 175

Phillips, Thomas, his portrait of Byron, 9

Pigot, Elizabeth, Byron's letters to, 222, 223

Pisa: Shelley's description of, 3; Byron's life at, 20

Po, Stanzas to the, what they reveal, 298 et seq., 372

Pope, Alexander, *Homer*, 51

Prothero, Rowland E.: *Letters and Journals of Lord Byron*, 70 n., 125, 256 n., 260 n., 385

INDEX

Quarterly Review, the, 50, 100

Recollections of a Long Life. See Broughton, Lord
Roberts, Captain, describes the wreck of *The Bolivar*, 33
Robertson, Rev. Frederick, Lady Byron's spiritual adviser, 326
Robinson, Crabb, 77
Romilly, Sir Samuel, consulted by Lady Byron, 340

Salona, Congress at, 152, 153
Sanders, Mr. George, painter, his portrait of Byron, 9
Sardanapalus, a tragedy, 101
Sass, Lieutenant, death of, 141
Schilitzy, a Greek, accompanies Byron to Greece, 47
Scott, Captain, commands the *Hercules*, in which Byron travels to Greece, 47
Scott, Dr., surgeon, and Byron, 54, 58
Scott, Sir Walter: Byron's opinion of, 35, 51, 55, 79; his denial of the authorship of the *Waverley Novels*, 53
Segati, Marianna, Byron's liaison with, 373
Shakespeare, William, Byron's opinion of, 101
Shelley, Percy Bysshe: describes Pisa, 3; and Byron, 11 *et seq.*; fracas at Pisa, 20, 21; and Allegra, 22; leaves Pisa for Lerici, 26; and Leigh Hunt, 26 *et seq.*; his death, 30; Byron's opinion of, 30, 35; his legacy to Byron, 32
Shelley, Life and Letters of Mary Wollstonecraft, by Mrs. Julian Marshall, 178
Stanhope, Col. the Hon. Leicester: arrives in Cephalonia to co-operate with Byron, 68; on Byron's character, 78, 174; begs Byron to come to Missolonghi, 81; on Byron's conduct in Greece, 91, 107; interviews and misunderstandings with Byron, 108 *et seq.*; his conduct in Greece, 119, 153; accompanies Byron's body to England, 199, 202; *Greece in 1823 and 1824*, and *Sketch of Byron*, 201; character sketch of Byron, 205 *et seq.*
Stanhope, Earl, historian, opinion of Mrs. Leigh, 318
Stephen, Sir Leslie, and Mrs. Leigh's letters, 359
Stowe. See Beecher Stowe
Stravolemo, Dr., physician, and Dr. Bruno, 79
Suliotes: Byron takes 500 into his pay, 91; false alarm, 123; serious fracas, 140; their dismissal, 142
Swift, William, bootmaker at Southwell, his evidence of Byron's lameness, 8

Taaffe, Mr., fracas at Pisa, 20, 21
Thomas, Dr., invited to attend Byron in his last illness, 168, 193 *et seq.*
Thorwaldsen, his marble bust of Byron, 10
Thyrza poems, what they reveal, 221, 232, 235
Tita, Giovanni Battista Falcieri, Byron's faithful servant, 97, 166, 169 *et seq.*
Toole, Mr., receives Byron at Santa Eufemia, 60
Trelawny, Edward John: arrives at Pisa, 4; describes Byron and his peculiarities, 5, 17, 18; on Leigh Hunt and Byron, 28; effect of Shelley's death, 32; lays up *The Bolivar*, 32; travels with Byron to Greece, 47, 48; and Byron's seizure, 62; mistaken views of Byron's motives, 64, 65; unhealthiness of Missolonghi, 87; his opinion of Byron, 178 *et seq.*; and Mavrocordato, 179; on Byron's deformity, 191, 192
Tricoupi, Spiridion, pronounces funeral oration over Byron, 185

Vaga, Dr. Lucca, Greek physician, attends Byron in his last illness, 169, 410
Vathi, Byron at, 58

INDEX

Villiers, Hon. Mrs., and Mrs. Leigh, 359, 364, 369; Lady Byron confides the secret to, 383, 396
Vivian, Charles, his death, 30
Volpiotti, Constantine, spy under Byron's roof, 162

Watson's *Philip II.*, 102
Webster, Lady Frances Wedderburn, and Byron, 240, 241, 259
Wentworth, Lord, Byron inherits his property, 10
West, William Edward, American painter, his portrait of Byron, 9
Wildman, Colonel Thomas, 44
Wildman, Mrs., owner of Byron's boot-trees and the bootmaker's statement as to Byron's deformity, 7, 8
Williams, Edward, and Leigh Hunt, 29; on Byron's treatment of Mrs. Hunt, 29; his death, 30
Wilmot, Robert John, signs Lady Byron's statement, 357, 359, 361
Wilson, John, 60
Wilson, General Sir Robert, known as 'Jaffa Wilson,' 110
Wordsworth, William, 60; Byron reviews his poems, 101 n.

York, Duke of, and Sir Walter Scott, 53
Young, Charles, actor, Byron's opinion of, 61

Zante, Byron at, 83, 198

THE END

www.ingramcontent.com/pod-product-compliance
Lightning Source LLC
Chambersburg PA
CBHW020539300426
44111CB00008B/727